TO THE EHLERT ?

GOOD READING!

Mark Usher

The Rape of the House of Usher

Stuart Usher

Exposé Publishing
KELSO

First Published 2020
Exposé Publishing
Kelso
Roxburghshire

isbn 978-0-9574092-0-0

The Rape of the House of Usher
Stuart Usher

Printed in the UK by
The Bedrule Press
Hawick
Scottish Borders

Dedicated to All Victims of Crooked Lawyers

Contents

Shortened Family Tree - The Ushers of Norton and Wells

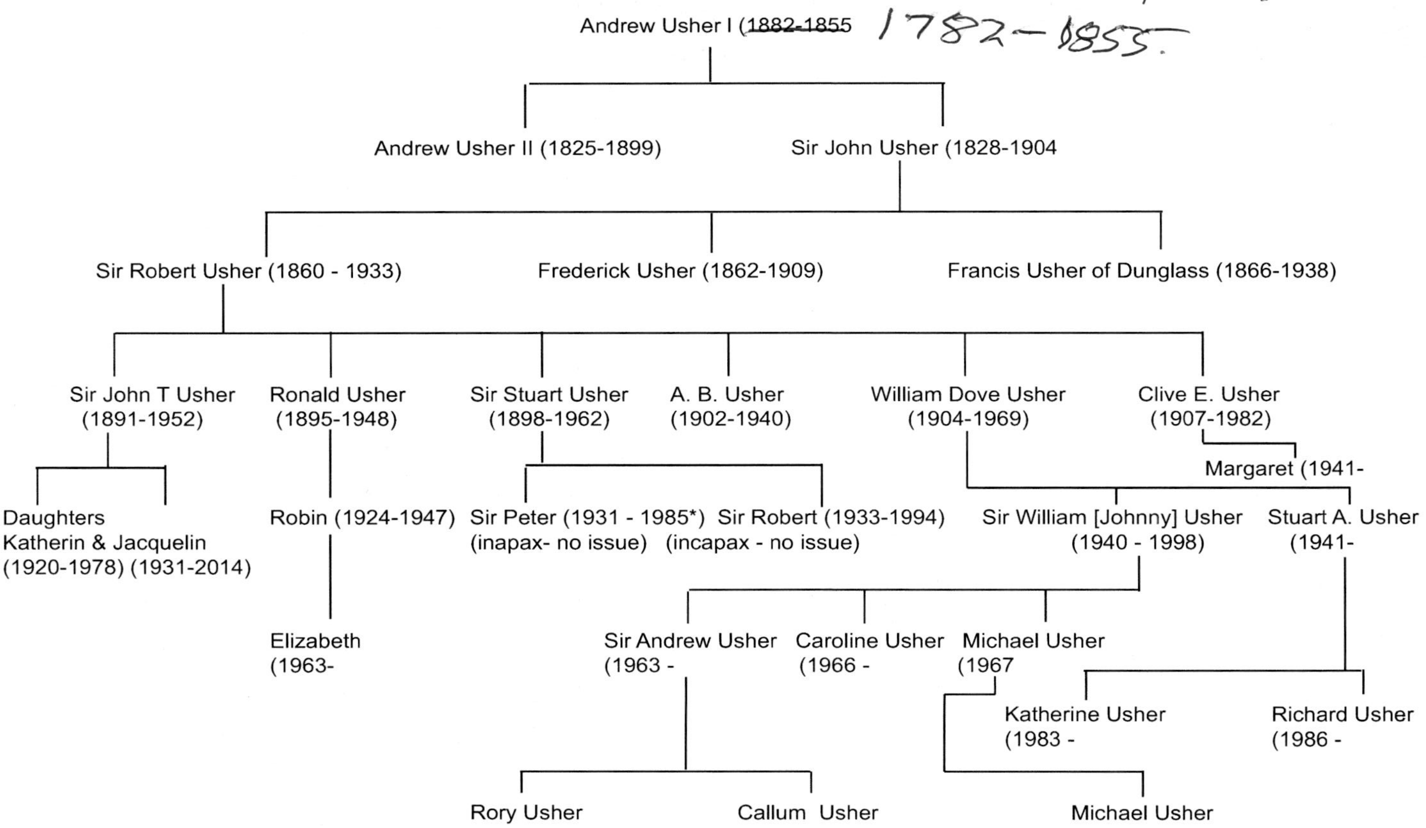

Sir John Usher 1st Baronet of Norton and Wells, by Sir George Reid.

'Look with me at this sad old city [Edinburgh] – you see her pinioned by her judges and preyed upon by her wig-lice, that countless vermin of lawyerlings, swollen and small.'

Sir Patrick Geddes (1854 – 1932).

INTRODUCTION

This book is about a monumental fraud executed upon my family by the law firm of Brodies of Edinburgh and before them, the law firm of Mackenzie & Black of Edinburgh over most of the 20th Century and into the 21st. It also relates to my decades-long struggle to have the Scottish Legal establishment, the Police, the Scottish Devolved Administration, and the Scottish Parliament to do something about it.

My struggle resulted in much-printed Media as well as Radio and Television broadcasts. Newspapers such as *The Sunday Times*, *The Guardian* and *The Scotsman* published lengthy reports, articles and magazine features on my fight against Brodies and the wider Scottish Legal system. These newspaper articles and features ultimately resulted in a Channel Four Television Documentary under the title of 'The Fall of the House of Usher' first broadcast in September 2002

In the following pages I describe the history and rise of the Usher family, becoming the founders of blended Scotch Whisky, arguably the most spectacularly successful Distillers and Blenders of whisky in history and its fall at the hands of immoral law firms and lawyers who took ruthless advantage at a time when my family, through illness, had become vulnerable.

The main lawyer criminals involved in the Rape of the House of Usher are *et al*:

Brodies WS (now LLP) of Atholl Crescent, Edinburgh, one of the largest Law firms in Scotland. Their lawyers most involved in the fraud were: Logan McLure, Thomas Greig Dempster, David Henry Houldsworth, Hugh John Stevens, Hugh Drummond, and Alastair Campbell, a recent Chairman of Brodies.

Tods Murray of Queen Street, Edinburgh another large Edinburgh Law firm and their Michael Simpson.

Shepherd & Wedderburn of Castle Terrace, Edinburgh and their Robin Fulton.

HBJ Gateley Wareing and Company, Canning Street, Edinburgh and their Alastair Shepherd (an ex Brodies lawyer).

Gillespie & MacAndrew (Brodies' near neighbour in Edinburgh) and their Scott Dempster.

I also name other Scottish legal organisations and individuals who were involved in blatant criminal activity in attempts to absolve the above Law Firms and their lawyers of the many crimes they committed against my family. They are:

The Law Society of Scotland and their Philip Yelland.
The Scottish Legal Services Ombudsman and their Garry Watson,
The Scottish Legal Complaints Commission.
And many more.

I believe this book is the first ever written which names and shames Law firms, the lawyers working in them, and other Scottish Legal organisations as criminals and criminal organisations. I have gone into some detail in connection with the many crimes Brodies and the other law firms and organisations perpetrated on my family and many other families to enable the reader to get some idea of the magnitude of the corruption within the Scottish Legal system.

Between the years 2000 and 2010 I publicly named and shamed dozens of other corrupt lawyers working within the Scottish Legal system via that well known champion of consumers of Scottish legal services 'Scotland Against Crooked Lawyers' which I founded in the year 2000. This was via monthly demonstrations mainly in Edinburgh and our handing out of approximately one hundred thousand leaflets to Members of the Scottish Parliament, and the Public at large.

These leaflets directly and unequivocaly accused these lawyers of being Crooks and Fraudsters. To my great disappointment not one of the accused lawyers and organisations ever took any action against me. The same applied to those courageous other people who stood four square with me

I feel obliged to inform the reader that I have written at length on the various frauds. I have had to do this in order to make the book credible. I just hope that readers of the book don't find all the detail boring and start skipping passages. Detailing all the various frauds will enable readers to, at least partially, comprehend the deceit which Brodies and the whole Scottish Legal apparatus practised on my family and many other Scottish families over the decades. This detail should fore-arm all readers of what lies in wait when dealing with lawyers. It won't save them altogether but it should limit the damage.

As a further assistance to the reader I have created an edited version of a 'Black Chain' which was requested of me in 1999 by a Scottish Advocate, John Mayer (now a writer of legal fiction) but which was, as will be revealed, just a further disingenuous act by one of the wig-lice of Edinburgh.

I very much hope that this book will go some way to achieving the abolition of the present irredeemably corrupt Scottish Legal System in its entirety and its replacement with a comprehensible, transparent and ethical system which the Public can understand, trust, and afford.

'The Time Has Come' as the Mandrill
said to the Lion in 'The Lion King'.

CAST OF MAIN CHARACTERS

Sir Robert Usher 2nd Bart of Norton and Wells, D.L. (of Caithness), J.P., M.F.H (1860-1933). Grandfather of Stuart Usher, author of this book.

Katherine, Lady Usher, (1868-1948). Wife of Sir Robert

Their Sons and Daughter-in-laws (where applicable). No Daughters survived to maturity.

Colonel Sir John Turnbull Usher, 3rd Bart of Norton and Wells, O.B.E., J.P., M.F.H., Royal Company of Archers, Major 9th Lancers, Brevet Colonel of the Lanarkshire Yeomanry., (1891- 1951). Usher Baronetcy Trustee.

Lieut-Commander Ronald James Usher, DSC., RN, (1892 – 1948). Usher Baronetcy Trustee.

Sir (Robert) Stuart Usher, Lt, Inniskillings Dragoons, 4th Bart of Norton and Wells (1898- 1962). UBT Trustee 1948 to 1962 and his wife **Gertrude Sampson**.

Major Alexander Balmer Usher of the 1st Lothian and Border Horse (1902-1940), unmarried, killed in action in France in the second World War..

William Dove Usher (father of Stuart Usher, author of this book) of Bedrule, (1904-1969). Usher Baronetcy Trustee 1962 to 1965 and his wife **Christa von Tevenar.**

Brigadier Thomas Clive Usher, D.S.O and Bar., M.C., R.A (1907-1982). Usher Baronetcy Trustee 1962 to 1982.

Valerie Stockwell, the wife of Brigadier Thomas Clive Usher.

James Greenshields Leadbetter WS, M.C., N.P., JP., (1891 – 1965). Nephew of Sir Robert Usher and Usher Baronetcy Trustee 1947 to 1965.

Robert Ronald Harry Usher, the Heir (1924-1947)

Sir Peter Lionel Usher, Down's Syndrome and and Mentally Incapacitated, 5th Bart of Norton and Wells (1931-1990). Died Instestate. Grandson of Sir Robert Usher.

Sir Robert Edward Usher, Downs Syndrome and Mentally Incapacitated, 6th Bart of Norton and Wells (1934-1994). Died Intestate. Grandson of Sir Robert Usher.

Sir William John Tevenar Usher, 7th Bart of Norton and Wells, (1940-1998). Grandson of Sir Robert Usher.

Stuart Alexander Usher, (1941-) the author of this book and brother of Sir William John Tevenar Usher. Grandson of Sir Robert Usher.

Hazel Jean Usher (1918 to 1995) and her sister **Margaret Daphne Usher** (1920 - 1995). Grandaughters of Sir Robert Usher.

Katherine Alice Usher (1920 -1978) and her sister **Jacquelin Usher** (1931-2014). Grandaughters of Sir Robert Usher.

Margaret Anne Usher (1941-). Grandaughter of Sir Robert Usher.

THE CROOKED LAWYERS:
Mackenzie & Black of Edinburgh, Usher family Law Agents from the nineteenth century until taken over by Brodies WS, of Edinburgh in 1972.
Brodies WS, but now **LLP**
Logan Mclure WS, lawyer and senior partner in Mackenzie & Black. Usher Baronetcy Trustee 1947 to 1988. Partner in Brodies 1972 to his retirement in the 1980s.
Thomas Greig Dempster WS, lawyer of Mackenzie & Black **WS** and later of Brodies WS.
David Sturrock WS, lawyer of Turnbull, Simpson and Sturrock WS, 1st ***Curator-Bonis*** to Sir Peter Usher (Incapax) for period 1982 to 1983.
Ian Taylor Carruthers WS, lawyer, of Brodies, 2nd *Curator-Bonis* to Sir Peter Usher (Incapax) for period 1983 until his (Carruthers) death in 1986.
Hugh John Stevens WS, lawyer, of Brodies WS, 3rd *Curator-Bonis* to Sir Peter Usher (Incapax) until Sir Peter's death in 1990.
David Henry Houldsworth WS, lawyer, of Brodies, 1st *Curator-Bonis* to the late Sir Robert Edward Usher (Incapax) from 1985 until Sir Robert's death in 1994.
Alastair Campbell WS, lawyer, Chairman of Brodies.
Hugh Drummond, WS, lawyer, Senior Partner of Brodies.
Alastair Shepherd WS (an ex Brodies lawyer) of HBJ Gateley Wareing and Company and more lately of Coulters.

OTHERS:
Charles John Usher (only a very distant relation to the family, though he pretended otherwise), the Wells Estate Manager.
Alice Sampson (married name Blamey) part-time Housekeeper and Niece of Gertrude Sampson. Minder of Downs Syndrome children Peter and Robert Usher.
Elizabeth Richards (née Usher), daughter of Robin Usher. If Elizabeth had been born a boy she would have came into the inheritance of the Usher Estates under the Usher Baronetcy Trust, for her lifetime

THE BLACK CHAIN

1911: Sir Robert Usher, 2nd Baronet of Norton and Wells establishes the Usher Baronetcy Trust, the purpose of which is to ensure the landed Estates and Mansion Houses belonging to him will devolve onto the heirs succeeding him in the Baronetcy for all time.

1924: Sir Robert's first grandson, Robin Usher, is born to his second son Ronald. He is now the Heir to the Baronetcy of his generation.

1931: Sir Robert's second grandson, Peter Lionel Usher, is born to his third son, Robert Stuart, in Argentina. Tragically Peter is Down's Syndrome and Mentally Incapacitated. Peter's condition is kept secret from his grandparents Sir Robert Usher and his wife Katherine, Lady Usher in Scotland.

1933: Sir Robert Usher dies, survived by his wife, Katherine Lady Usher, and their six sons: John Turnbull Usher, Ronald James Usher, Robert Stuart Usher, Alexander Balmer Usher, William Dove Usher and Thomas Clive Usher. John Turnbull Usher succeeds to the Baronetcy and becomes Sir John Turnbull Usher

1934: Sir Robert's third grandson, Robert Edward Usher, is born to Robert Stuart Usher in Argentina. Again, and tragically, this son is also Down's Syndrome and Mentally Incapacitated. Robert Edward's condition is also kept secret from the Usher family in Scotland.

1940: Sir Robert's fourth grandson, William John Tevenar Usher, is born to William Dove Usher in Tanganyika, East Africa. Old Sir Robert Usher's fourth son, Alexander Balmer Usher is killed in action in France in World War Two leaving no Issue and no Will. His brother William Dove Usher is given Bedrule farm adjoining the Wells Estate which had belonged to Alexander Balmer Usher.

1941: Another grandson, Stuart Alexander Usher (the author of this book) is born in Tanganyika.

1946: William Dove Usher returns home and moves into Bedrule farm.

1947: Robin Usher, Heir Apparent of his generation to the Usher Baronetcy Trust Estates and Assets, dies of cancer. Peter Lionel Usher, Incapax, in Argentina is now the Heir Apparent of his generation.

1948: Katherine, Lady Usher, wife of old Sir Robert Usher dies.

1948: Ronald Usher, second son of old Sir Robert Usher, dies of cancer. Peter Lionel Usher, Down's Syndrome and Mentally Incapacitated, in Argentina, is now the Heir Apparent.

1949: Robert Stuart Usher, third son of old Sir Robert Usher returns, bankrupt, from Argentina with his wife, Gertrude, and their two Down's Syndrome sons, Peter and Robert. He is given the tenancy of a farm on the Wells Estate and made a Trustee of the Usher Baronetcy Trust. Soon after he moves into Hallrule Mansion House on the Wells Estate with his wife, Gertrude and their two Sons, Peter and Robert.

1949: Sir John Usher and the other UBT Trustees, some of whom are lawyers, sell a lot of property on the Pitheavlis Estate in the City of Perth and divide up the proceeds between the four surviving sons of old Sir Robert Usher and the wife of the deceased Ronald Usher. This act breaks the Usher Baronetcy Trust.

1950: Sir John Turnbull Usher and the UBT Trustees dynamite Wells House against the wishes of William Dove Usher who is not a Trustee. William Dove Usher's family were the only route by which the ends and purposes of the UBT could be realised. This breaks the UBT for the second time.

1951: Sir John Turnbull Usher dies at Norton House on the Norton Estate near Edinburgh, also included in the UBT, leaving no male heir. Robert Stuart Usher succeeds him in the Baronetcy and becomes Sir Stuart Usher, 4th Bart of Norton and Wells.

1951 - 1955: Sir Stuart Usher and the other Trustees of the Usher Baronetcy Trust sell property on the Wells Estate. Norton House near Edinburgh is also sold and becomes an Hotel. This breaks the UBT for the third time.

1956: Sir Stuart Usher and the other Trustees give the site of the now destroyed Wells House, its Gardens, Stable block and three cottages and about eighty acres of surrounding parks to old Sir Robert's youngest son, Thomas Clive Usher who has no issue to perpetuate the Usher family of Norton and Wells. This breaks the UBT for the fourth time.

1962: Sir Stuart Usher falls from his horse and dies. The UBT Trustee Lawyers, Mackenzie & Black WS of Edinburgh inform William Dove Usher and other Usher family members that Sir Stuart has left no Will and that because of this the Usher Baronetcy Trust has come to an end. According to these Lawyers this meant that all the Estates, Properties and assets both moveable and immoveable held within the UBT had now devolved onto Sir Stuart's elder son, Peter Lionel Usher, who is Downs Syndrome and Mentally Incapacitated, as his own *personal* property. This being the case the Lawyers then inform William Dove Usher that one of their Lawyers would have to be appointed as a *Curator-Bonis* to look after Peter Lionel Usher's Estates and assets.

1962: William Dove Usher is made a Trustee of the UBT.

1965: William Dove Usher resigns as a Trustee and is replaced by his son, William John Tevenar Usher and Thomas Clive Usher.

1968: William Dove Usher and his family move to South Africa because they have been mislead into believing that the only way to save the UBT Estates is for WDU's two Sons, William John Tevenar Usher and Stuart Alexander Usher to make their fortunes and purchase whatever remains of the UBT Estates when they are sold on the Intestate Death of the survivor of Peter Lionel Usher or his brother Robert Edward Usher, both Mentally Incapacitated.

1972: Stuart Alexander Usher returns to Scotland to enforce an Agreement that Thomas Clive Usher give up his tenancy on a farm on the Wells Estate in 1972 to him and to agree a course of action which would guarantee an Usher future on all the Estates and Properties contained within the Usher Baronetcy Trust. Thomas Clive Usher breaks this Agreement by refusing to give up the tenancy to Stuart Alexander Usher, but assures him that he will vacate the farm in 1978 in favour of SAU. SAU stays at Hallrule House with the wife of the late Sir Stuart Usher, Gertrude Usher, and their two Mentally Incapacitated Sons Peter and Robert. It quickly becomes apparent to Stuart Alexander Usher that Gertrude Usher, Thomas Clive Usher and the Mackenzie Black lawyers, now part of Brodies WS of Edinburgh, do not want the UBT Estates and all its other assets to continue in the Usher family of Norton and Wells.

1982: William John Usher in his position as a Trustee of the Usher Baronetcy Trust flies to Scotland from Africa to sort the affairs of the Usher family of Norton and Wells. He meets with the UBT lawyers at Brodies WS and discovers that the UBT has *not* come to an end and that a *Curator-Bonis* had not been appointed as his parents and he himself, and his brother Stuart, had all been told by the UBT Lawyers in 1962. The UBT Lawyers refuse to give him the Accounts of the UBT. He meets with Gertrude, now Lady Usher, who refuses to help him ensure an Usher future for the UBT. He tries to meet his fellow Trustee, Thomas Clive Usher, but is refused on the grounds of the latter's illness. Thomas Clive Usher then dies, leaving now only two UBT Trustees, William John Usher and Logan McLure WS, an ex Mackenzie & Black lawyer who is now a Brodies WS lawyer.

1984: Gertrude Usher, the wife of Sir Stuart Usher, dies leaving her two Incapacitated sons, Sir Peter Usher and his brother Robert Usher living at Hallrule House. William John Usher and his brother Stuart Alexander Usher were not informed, at the time, of Gertrude Usher's death.

1984: The lawyers, Brodies WS, eventually advised WJU that a *Curator-Bonis* should now be appointed to look after Sir Peter's affairs and that WJU should sign over the Estates of Wells, Norton and Pitheavlis to the newly appointed *Curator-Bonis* of Sir Peter Usher - a Brodies lawyer called Ian Taylor Carruthers. WJU reluctantly signed over the Norton and Pitheavlis Estates from the UBT to Ian Taylor Carruthers but refused to sign over the Wells Estate. Sir Peter Usher, only now, is certified as an Incapax.

1986: Ian Taylor Carruthers died.

1986: Robert Edward Usher is certified as Mentally Incapacitated for the first time. Sir Peter Usher is certified as Mentally Incapacitated for the *second* time at the same time as Robert.

1987: Brodies WS asks WJU to again sign over the Estates of Wells, Norton and Pitheavlis to the new *Curator-Bonis*, Hugh John Stevens, another Brodies lawyer. WJU signs over the Estates because he is advised by the lawyers that he *has* to sign them over to Sir Peter's new *Curator-Bonis* although he does not understand this.

1988: WJU's fellow Trustee, Logan McLure of Brodies, dies.

1990: Sir Peter Usher Incapax, dies Intestate. He is succeeded by his brother, Robert Edward Usher, Incapax.

1994: Sir Robert Usher, Incapax, dies Intestate. He is succeeded by William John Tevenar Usher (the author's brother) as the 7th Baronet of Norton and Wells. He is now known as Sir John Usher. He is made the Executor of the late Sir Robert Edward Usher (Incapax) along with Mrs Jacqueline Wolfe-Murray his cousin.

1994: Stuart Alexander Usher (SAU, the author) returns to Scotland for good from South Africa armed with a Power of Attorney to act on behalf of Sir John Usher, his brother. SAU repeatedly catches out Sir Peter's *Curator-Bonis*, Hugh John Stevens WS, and Sir Robert's *Curator-Bonis*, David Henry Houldsworth WS, both of Brodies WS, lying on numerous occasions.

1994 - 1995 - 1996: The Wells Estate is sold and the proceeds are divided up between eight ultimate beneficiaries, only two of whom bear the name Usher - Sir John Usher and Stuart Alexander Usher.

1997 - 2006: Stuart Alexander Usher progressively discovers more and more of the systematic fraudulent activity used by Brodies against the Usher Baronetcy Trust over the decades. They made use of the Incapacity of Sir Peter Usher and his brother Sir Robert Usher as their protective shield against discovery. Some of the beneficiaries of this fraudulent activity included Thomas Clive Usher, his daughter Margaret Mactaggart, the Estate Manager, Charles John Usher (a very distant family relative) and Brodies themselves.

Stuart Alexander Usher then reported Brodies WS and other Scottish Law Firms who became embroiled in the Fraud to the Law Society of Scotland. The Law Society of Scotland cynically dismissed all his Complaints as having no merit by disregarding all the evidence of the systematic Fraud he had given them. Philip Yelland was the chief Law Society criminal involved in this. Stuart Usher then reported the Law Society of Scotland to the Scottish Legal Services Ombudsman, Garry Watson. Watson cynically dismissed all his Complaints against the Law Society of Scotland as baseless in the full knowledge that they were *not* baseless. Stuart Usher then reported Brodies WS to the Police. The Police agreed with him stating that the evidence he had given them showed 'plenty of skullduggery there' but declined to pursue the matter.

1998: Sir John Usher of Norton and Wells, the brother of Stuart Alexander Usher died. The end result of all this collective criminal activity by Brodies WS, Thomas Clive Usher, Gertrude, 'Lady Usher' (no Lady this), the Law Society of Scotland, the Legal Services Ombudsman and many others over the decades between the 1940s into the 2000s caused the ruination of my family - the Ushers of Norton and Wells.

1

THE ORIGINS OF THE USHER FAMILY

The Ushers were of Viking extraction and were among those Vikings who invaded Northern France under their King, Thorfinn Rollo, in about 940 AD. Charles the Simple, the French King, finally conceded defeat and granted Thorfinn Rollo Northern France and the hand of his daughter. From this time onwards these Vikings became known as Normans, short for Northmen. A descendant of King Thorfinn was William the Conqueror, Duke of Normandy who conquered England in 1066.

The first official record of an Usher in Britain is dated 1216 and refers to a Richard Ussier. Thereafter the name appears in varying forms such as le Usser, le Uscher, Hussar, Huscher, Ussher, and Usher.

Another early mention of an Usher refers to William le Usser in the Assize Rolls for Somerset, England in 1243.

The earliest record in Ireland refers to a Simon le Usher 'attorning' before King Edward the First of England in connection with matters to do with Wm de Valance, the Earl of Pembroke and Wexford, dated 1290 and again in 1295. This Irish sept of Ushers later became well-known in Ireland: one of them founded Trinity College, Dublin in 1591 and another, James, became the Archbishop of Armagh and the Primate of All Ireland in the 1600s.

Another notable member of the family, Thomas Ussher, became an Admiral of the Blue in the Napoleonic era. He transported Napoleon as a prisoner to the Island of Elba. Napoleon and Thomas struck up a friendship and Napoleon showered Thomas with gifts and named his boat 'Ussher.' Thomas also became a favourite of King George the Fourth and King William the Third.

The first mention of an Usher in Scotland occurred at approximately the same time, 1291, in connection with a Thomas the Usser; in the following year he is referred to as Thomas the Doorward: ie Ushering people through doorways. Thomas has always been a popular name in the Usher family — eg Thomas Usher & Son, Brewers of Edinburgh.

There were Ushers settled in Yorkshire in the thirteenth century. One of them, John le Uscher, was appointed Constable of Dublin Castle in February 1301 by King Edward the First of England. He retired in 1309.

Left:
Sir Robert Usher of Norton And Wells and his brothers Frederick and Francis Usher at a Meet of the Linlithgow and Stirlingshire Hounds outside Norton House

Below:
Sir Robert Usher with hounds at Norton House

Another early mention of the name was in connection with an Usher who was a favourite of King David II of Scotland in the fourteenth century. He married a daughter of Aymer de Macuswell, a powerful man of those days and a progenitor of the present family of Maxwell. After that the Ushers inter-married with the Ramsays and Wardrops. At much the same time there was an Usher who was Provost of Peebles in the Scottish Borders which is recorded in 'Exchange Rolls, Scot. 1330.' To-day there is a Wynd bearing the name Usher in Peebles. This was most probably named after Provost Usher or one of his descendants.

In the prefixes to the entries taken from the Parish Registers of Melrose in the Scottish Borders there appears the following:

> In the last Will and Testament of Gilbert Hately, Gattonside, dated 1547: To Laird Usher, my brither-in-law o' Faftenfield, a hunder merkis Scotis and my nobbler and the twae auld pricklers which I took frae the lads of the Border when they came ae nicht to harrie me.

In Pitcairn's Criminal Trials, III, 3, p.568 is an entry on the 21st of July 1624 relating to:

> 'Adie Uscher, borne in Birkinhaugh in Liddesdale, reived along with Robert Elliot of Redheugh and with his son Will Uscher aet sixteen so many sheep, oxen, cows and goats from Wm. Heron of Schewingscheill Castle.'

Schewingsheill Castle was in Northumberland, and 'reiving' is a Scottish Borders word for rustling livestock which was practised for centuries by families on both the Scottish and English sides of the border. Adie was hanged on the Burrowmuir of Edinburgh and his son Will 'nocht being past saxtene yeiris' of age was banished under pain of death. It is believed it was on the intercession of Scott of Buccleuch that Robert Elliot was pardoned.

There is a well known Border Ballad called 'The Wife of Usher's Well' of which the following is the first verse:

> There lived a wife at Ushers' Well,
> And a wealthy wife was she;
> She had three stout and stalwart sons,
> And sent them o'er the sea.

No one seems to know where Usher's Well was situated, though I think it dates from the 17th century and refers to an earlier age.

By the early sixteen hundreds the Usher family had proliferated in the Parish of Melrose. The name Usher appears on the very first page of the records of the Parish of Melrose. The first entry is 'George Usher b 14th December 1626 – m - Bessie Tait of Gallowshiels.' The Ushers belonged to

Johnstounburn House, one of the homes of Andrew Usher of Edinburgh

the villages of Darnick and Bridgend. A letter written by a James Curle, Melrose, dated Jan 1855, states:

> 'The family of Usher appear to have been large proprietors in Darnick for a period exceeding 250 years.'

The George Usher mentioned above was nine generations back from my generation.

In 1752 the lands of Toftfield (now Huntlyburn), near Darnick and Melrose were acquired by John Usher, a great grandson of George Usher, from a Charles Wilkinson, a writer in Melrose. It was here in Toftfield that a grandson of this John Usher was born on the 1st of April 1782. This grandson was called Andrew and was the third youngest of twelve children. Andrew went on to found the world famous Whisky Distilling and Blending Company of Andrew Usher & Co in 1813 as well as the famous Ushers Brewery of Edinburgh in 1831. He claimed that he 'fully maintained the character of an April Fool' in a narrative of his life which he wrote shortly before his death in 1855.

In 1816 the then John Usher of Toftfield, eldest brother of Andrew, sold the greater part of Toftfield to his neighbour the soon to be world-famous Sir Walter Scott. At this time Toftfield included Harleyburn, now Chiefswood. Sir Walter changed the name of Toftfield to Huntlyburn by which name it is known today. Also on Toftfield was Cauldshiels Loch and the Rhymer's Glen where Thomas the Rhymer in ancient times used to meet the Faerie Queen. The following poem alludes to one such meeting:

True Thomas lay on Huntlie bank
A ferlie he spied wi his e'e;
And there he saw a ladye bright
Come riding down by the Eildon tree.

On purchasing Toftfield Sir Walter told his publishing partner and friend John Ballantine: 'I have closed with Usher for his beautiful patrimony, which makes me a great Laird.' In 1819 Sir Walter commenced building his Abbotsford House close by the River Tweed. Abbotsford later became world famous and remains one of the major tourist attractions in Scotland to the present time.

John Usher and Sir Walter became fast and life-long friends. They shared a love of greyhound coursing with John being famed for his good greyhounds. Prior to his purchase of Toftfield Sir Walter was a frequent visitor, telling stories to John's children and thus winning their hearts. He was much taken with the second youngest son of John - also called John. This John was a precocious little fellow and Sir Walter encouraged him to repeat bits of poetry and to sing. When young John grew up poetry and song became the ruling passion of his life and he finds his place as a Poet in the tenth volume of Edward of Brechin's 'Modern Scots Poets'.

The Borders General Hospital is now situated on the site of Huntlyburn.

By far the most outstanding Usher of my Father's generation was Colonel Charles Milne Usher, D.S.O., O.B.E., Chevalier Legion d'Honneur, Croix de Guerre with Palm, and Citoyen d'honneur of the Town of Caen in France. He wrote our family book, 'The Usher Family in Scotland', published in 1955 and was a most colourful character.

He was one of a select band who played rugby for Scotland before and after the First World War and was a regular member of the XV between 1912 and 1922. In 1920 he, as Captain, had the honour of presenting the Scottish Rugby team to H.M. King George the Fifth at Twickenham, having had the same honour a fortnight previously in presenting the Army XV to the King, also as Captain, before a match against the Dominions. He was also an expert fencer with Sabre and Epee and represented Scotland in this sport at the Empire Games in New Zealand in 1950 at the age of 59. In addition he was a superb horseman and rode in numerous Point to Points.

He was much revered in France and legend has it that he once led the Scottish Rugby team onto the pitch at Colombes in Paris playing the bagpipes. The French government made him a Chevalier of the Legion d'Honneur and gave him the Croix de Guerre, with Palm. The Town of Caen made him an honorary citizen. In the Second World War at Dunkirk the troops he commanded were known as 'The Usherforce.'

2

THE SCOTTISH HOUSE OF USHER BEGINS ITS REMARKABLE RISE

The Andrew Usher who was born at Toftfield in 1782 first tried his hand as a young man in his brother Hugh's Counting House in London. This not being a success he was sent to Leith in 1800 to supervise the selling of corn from the warehouse of his elder brothers, John and Hugh. This, too, was not a success and instead he opened his own hosiery business in Edinburgh specializing in the wholesale trade. This progressed so well that he decided to move the business to London going into partnership with a Worcester manufacturer called Hardwick. Though this arrangement did very well Andrew was never really settled and in 1808 he was offered a share in Mr Dunlop's Spirit business in Edinburgh.

In 1813 Andrew commenced on his own as a Spirit Merchant in Edinburgh employing his brother-in-law, James Fairburn, as a travelling salesman.

In the 1820s Andrew was appointed by George Smith of the Glenlivet Distillery in the north-east of Scotland to sell his Glenlivet whisky. In 1823 Andrew purchased the Pear Tree House in the basement of which, in the year 1853 he was to produce the first ever blended whisky. By 1840, 'Messrs Usher controlled the whole output of the famous Glenlivet Distillery.' This Agreement lasted into the twentieth century. By 1900 Andrew Usher & Co were purchasing 110,000 gallons of Glenlivet whisky per year.

In 1831 Andrew set up his two elder sons, James and Thomas, as brewers in Merchant Street, Edinburgh. This business eventually grew to become the famous Edinburgh brewing firm of Thomas Usher & Co and, from 1959 to 1979, Usher Vaux. So, from 1831 onwards, there were the 'Whisky Ushers' and the 'Beer Ushers.' In the 1840s Andrew was experimenting hard with the blending of Highland Malts with the idea of producing a more uniform and palatable drink. Throughout this period he was steadily expanding his business. After a succession of office staff and colleagues Andrew took on his two youngest sons, Andrew and John, as partners in 1848. They were the two youngest sons of his twelve children. This proved to be a success from day one and with their help the business began to expand at a faster and faster rate.

Pear Tree House first home of Andrew Usher and Co. Edinburgh 1823

In 1853 the firm produced and marketed the very first blended whisky ever, which they called Usher's Old Vatted Glenlivet. Shortly before his death in 1855 Andrew wrote: 'By the united exertions of my two sons the business during the last seven years has far exceeded anything it ever did before.' He had founded two businesses which were still going strong forty two years later at the time of his death.

He could have had no idea that his two sons, Andrew and John, would be largely responsible for making whisky the world beating beverage it eventually became nor that Andrew II would be acclaimed as 'The Father of the modern Scottish Whisky Industry.' It could, however, be argued that Andrew I should be regarded as the Father of the modern Scottish Whisky Industry because he produced the first ever blended whisky.

In 1859 Andrew Usher & Co purchased the Glen Sciennes Malt Distillery in Edinburgh and renamed it the Edinburgh Distillery. Up until that time virtually all the whisky being produced in Scotland was for the local market. Whisky was virtually unheard of in England. However with some expert marketing the drink, slowly at first, and then with gathering momentum, spread abroad.

By the early 1880s blended whisky began to take the world by storm. Andrew Usher & Co quickly appointed whisky agents in all the principal countries of the world and sales rocketed.

In anticipation of the growing demand Andrew Usher & Co built the largest whisky maturing warehouses in the world at St Leonards in Edinburgh in the 1860s, serviced by the railways. One of these warehouses was 150 yards in length and lay adjacent to Usher's Brewery.

In 1877 Distiller's Company Limited was founded. To combat this and to secure their supplies of grain whisky Andrew and John decided that another Distillery should be built in Edinburgh. To this end they invited those whisky distillers who had not yet joined the Distiller's Company to join with them in building this new Distillery. This led to the founding of the North British Distillery Company in Edinburgh in 1885 with Andrew Usher ; William Sanderson of Vat 69; and John Crabbie, of Crabbie's Green Ginger, as the three founders. Andrew Usher was its first Chairman and John Crabbie the Vice Chairman. The first Managing Director of the company was William Sanderson. Other famous names in Scotch whisky were amongst the original shareholders and on the board of Directors: White Horse; Johnny Walker; Mackinley; MacDonald & Muir; Dewar; Crawford; Buchanan and Arthur Bell of Perth. This group were very powerful competitors to the Distiller's group, as indeed they had to be to survive. The North British Distillery was built in 1885 and after ten years despite large Capital outlays for more warehouses and newer machinery, the Company was embarrassingly 'cash rich.' By 1897 the they were producing three million gallons of whisky a year and had sold the whole of the following year's production in advance. It was now the largest and best equipped distillery in Scotland. Andrew remained Chairman for thirteen years until 1898 when he retired, shortly before he died. In its 1898 Obituary Notice of Andrew II *The Scotsman* wrote:

> 'Andrew II and John were excellent businessmen, upright and intelligent, far-seeing and resourceful, and under their skilful guidance the business grew until it is now reputed to be the largest of the kind in Scotland. The oldest distillery and Maltings were in the Sciennes (Edinburgh). To distilling they added Whisky buying and blending and developed an export trade which at the present moment includes agencies in every part of the civilised globe.'

The Scotsman report went on to relate how two friends of Andrew II and John had told them about their travels in Japan. This would have been in the 1890s when Japan was still emerging from its own brand of feudalism: Deep in the countryside of Japan, where very few Europeans had ever been, they entered a beautiful Japanese tea garden where they were attended by an equally beautiful Japanese maiden. Possibly in jest, they asked for whisky. Without turning a hair the maiden just nodded and off she went. She soon returned and served them, to their surprise and delight, with a bottle of Usher's OVG.

At much the same time *The Wine and Spirit Trade Record* wrote of Andrew Usher and Co:

> 'Blending with them is the result of generations of experience and it may be safely said that whisky which bears the name of the great firm of Usher is the best that skill and experience, combined with enormous capital, can procure.'

By now the firm of Andrew Usher & Co was exporting whisky to every major country in the world. Its Headquarter's was still in Andrew I's old house in West Nicholson Street, Edinburgh. This is now known as The Peartree House on account of the ancient trees which grow against its walls. At the present time there are no less than four Public Houses in the Peartree House: The Pear Tree, The Counting House, The Blind Poet and the Andrew Usher. All are well worth a visit; very convenient because you don't even have to move out of the building if you are pub crawling!

Andrew II was of a kindly disposition and highly thought of by people in all walks of life. He could, however, be a martinet: He usually lunched happily with his brother John in the office. One day in the early 1880s, John's son, Robert, was allowed to join them for lunch. This was not an immediate success because shortly thereafter Andrew II wrote to John stating: 'Although I have allowed your son, Robert, to lunch with us I wish it to be understood that he must not speak unless his opinion is asked. Yesterday he spoke several times when he had no right to do so.'

In 1929 Gordon Burn-Murdoch, one of Andrew II's sons-in-law, wrote a long tribute to Andrew II. In it he gives a description of him:

> He was thin hard, not an ounce of fat. Head like a Caesar, but finer, clean cut between a Caesar and a Pharaoh, very good, quiet carriage, in fact distinguished very much so, but in a very unostentatious manner, quicker than thought, I imagine or know, to see round your point of view and its possible fallacy.

Andrew Usher II of Edinburgh painted posthumously in c1899 by Edmund Brock

3

ANDREW AND JOHN USHER OF ANDREW USHER & CO, DISTILLERS OF EDINBURGH

Andrew and his family lived in Blackford House, Blackford, Edinburgh most of the time. His country houses and estates outside Edinburgh included Johnstounburn, near Humbie, just south of Edinburgh. This became a beautiful hotel for many years but is now in private ownership again.

Another of his estates was situated in the St Abbs and Coldingham areas of Berwickshire. He built a beautiful mansion house atop the cliff immediately north of St Abbs which overlooked the North Sea and the fishing settlement, then known as Coldingham Fore-Shore. In response to requests from the fishermen at Coldingham Fore-shore he let them have the land they wanted to build their houses on at a nominal price. This resulted in the establishment of the fishing village of St Abbs as we know it today. In response to further requests for assistance from the fishermen he had a new Harbour, a Church, a Manse, a School, and a Community Hall and some houses built for the village at his own expense. I visited St Abbs in 1998 and found the Church particularly impressive; actually rather too large for the village yet no expense had been spared. Andrew was a great Churchman and made one condition to his various benefactions in St Abbs; ironically that there should be no drinks licence in the village - a condition honoured to the present day.

At this point I record that Andrew II had the greatest misfortune to lose his two eldest children, Andrew and George, in 1858 when they were only five years and three years old respectively. However he was left with one son called Howard Graham who was born in 1866. His other three children, all by his first wife, Elizabeth Langmuir Miller, were all daughters. Elizabeth died in 1876 and in 1879 he married Marion Blackwood Murray and by her had another daughter in 1884 at the age of 58. However disaster struck in the mid 1880s. His only surviving son and heir, Howard, was smitten with exczema which progressively worsened. In those days sea water was thought to be good for curing exczema and to this end Andrew built a pump house half-way down the cliff near his house, Northfield, at St Abbs to pump seawater into the house in which Howard could bathe. My own son Richard and I saw the bath and the huge Victorian plumbing arrangements for the seawater in Northfield on our visit to St Abbs in 1998. It was plain to see that Andrew had fought with might and main to save Howard yet with hindsight we know that the condition in extreme cases can lead to blood poisoning - septicaemia - and the seawater may well, sadly, have been detrimental. Sad to say all Andrew's efforts to save Howard were in vain with Howard passing away in 1894.

Andrew's other establishments were Bielside House, West Barns, East Lothian and Hall Manor, Peebles, which was his favourite country retreat. He also owned property in the Highlands. He left all these Estates and properties to his daughters.

Both Andrew and John, staunch Christians, felt it their duty to do something for the community at large and one day in 1896 Andrew informed an Edinburgh jeweller called Aitchison: 'I have so much money that I do not know what to do with it.' Aitchison suggested that he build a City Hall for Edinburgh. Andrew thought this a splendid idea and later that year donated funds to the City Council of Edinburgh with which he stipulated it build a 'dignified' City Hall which should 'seat three thousand people,' at the same time expressing a wish that good music should be played and enjoyed in it. Andrew also expressed his love of music by including a Minstrel's Gallery in Northfield House atop the cliff overlooking St Abbs.

After many years of squabbling within the City Council as to where the Hall should be built a site was eventually selected in Lothian Road, Edinburgh in 1910 – twelve years after Andrew's death.

In 1911 King George V and Queen Mary laid two memorial stones for the Usher Hall, on which work had now commenced. This was done in the presence of Andrew's wife, Marion, Edinburgh Councillors and a large gathering of city burghers.

In 1914 the Usher Hall was opened by Andrew's widow, Marion. Since then and to the present day it has been the premier musical venue in Scotland and is the Edinburgh home of the Royal Scottish National Orchestra. All the major orchestras of the world have played in the Usher Hall, with many returning on numerous occasions. It has hosted many events including the bestowal of the Freedom of the City of Edinburgh onto Prince Philip, the Duke of Edinburgh in 1954. Commonwealth Games Boxing matches, political rallies and conferences, the Eurovision Song Contest in 1971 and, latterly, a whole host of Country and Western and other pop stars. It is also the venue of many University Graduation ceremonies. It is also much favoured for recording music on account of its outstanding acoustics which are generally regarded as among the finest in the world. In one of the main entrance halls stands a bust of Andrew II.

The Usher Hall, Edinburgh

In 1883 Andrew II's brother John purchased the Norton Estate near Ratho in West Lothian and followed that up by purchasing a lot of property in Wick and Pulteney Town in Caithness. In 1896 he purchased the Wells Estate in the Scottish Borders. In 1901 he purchased the Hallrule Estate, at the same time extending the Norton Estate by purchasing a neighbouring farm called Rathobyres.

John had been active in politics for many years and was greatly devoted to the Unionist cause. He was also a Free Churchman and a generous benefactor to his Church. John had been an avid supporter of Gladstone, but differed from him on the question of Ireland.

In 1898 John was approached by Mr Crole, a Director of Younger's Brewery in Scotland, and asked to help complete an endowment to establish a Chair of Public Health at Edinburgh University. This became the first Chair in Public Health in Britain. Mr Crole then informed John that a Chair without an Institute in which its purposes could be carried out was not of much use. To this end John then sent a Professor Hunter Stewart, who had already been appointed as the Chair's first professor, along with John's son-in-law, Thomas Leadbetter, an architect, to London and the Continent to study the best Institutes there to obtain design ideas. The result of all this was the John Usher Institute of Public Health in Warrender Road, Edinburgh, opened by Sir John in 1902. In 2002 the Usher Institute celebrated its Centenary and I was invited to attend the celebrations which stretched over three days. Leading Professors of Medicine from Britain and overseas who had been students at the Institute gave the most interesting lectures on various aspects of Public Health.

Some of Andrew Usher's various homes.

Above: Johnstounburn House, East Lothian
Below Left: Bielside, Dunbar
Below Right: Northfield House, St. Abbs

Some of Andrew Usher's various homes.

Above: Arthur Lodge, Edinburgh.

Below: Blackford House, Edinburgh

In 1899 John was created a Baronet and took the title of Usher of Norton and Wells. At this stage of his life he was referred to as the 'Croesus of Edinburgh.' He died in 1904 at the age of seventy-six, on holiday in Egypt.

John and Andrew II were largely responsible for making whisky the world conquering drink it became. Before the arrival of blending, Ireland produced more twice the quantity of whisky than Scotland did. In this regard Scotland's economy owes them both a debt of gratitude. In 2014 whisky contributed more than £3 billion to the British Gross Domestic Product - 2.5% of the total.

Above: Norton House.

Below: The Usher Health Institute, Ediburgh

4

THE BEER USHERS

Meanwhile the Beer Ushers were also thriving, though on nothing like the scale of the Whisky Ushers. In 1831 Andrew I had set up his eldest son James in a brewery in Merchant Street, Edinburgh. James was later joined in the brewery by Andrew's second son, Thomas. The firm then became known as James and Thomas Usher.

By 1860 the firm had expanded so much that it was deemed necessary to move to larger premises. To this end and in that year they purchased a site in St Leonards where they built a new brewery which they called the Park Brewery on account of its bordering Holyrood Park. It remained there until it was demolished in the early 1980s.

James is remembered for designing a very early steam plough in 1849 which was shown at the Great Exhibition of 1851. In 1861 the plough contributed to his early death in 1861. The plough was on display in the Meadows, Edinburgh that year. James had been unwell and unable to attend the Show so the Show authorities decided to run the plough to James's house for James to see. At the same time James, feeling better decided to go to the Show after all in his coach. The plough and the coach met in Lothian Road. The horse drawing the coach took exception to the appearance and noise of the steam plough and shied off overturning the coach, throwing James onto the road. James was much shaken by this and died shortly thereafter.

Thomas then took the helm in the brewery. He was a slim man of upright carriage and always presented a most distinguished appearance. He took life very calmly. He was also a generous man, as the following episode demonstrates:

He had a coachman who tried to commit suicide by jumping off the Dean bridge in Edinburgh. The poor man landed in a tree and only broke a leg. Thomas succeeded in getting the matter quashed and paid the coachman's fare to Australia to start a new life there. Many years later Thomas received a letter from this man in which he said that he had heard that many people had been ruined by the failure of the City of Glasgow bank. He had saved a few hundred pounds which he would gladly send to Thomas if he had

Thomas Usher, Brewer of Edinburgh ~~1862-1939.~~

1821 – 1896.

been caught by the failure of the bank. Fortunately Thomas had *not* been caught in the failure of the bank. This was a good example of a good turn being reciprocated and shows the essential decency of the two men concerned. Thomas died in 1896, his job for the brewery well done.

The firm of Thomas Usher and Company continued in the beer business until the brewery was sold to Vaux Brewery of Sunderland in 1959. It then became known as Usher Vaux. When it was sold Usher's Brewery employed about 260 people and had about three hundred tied public houses in Scotland. It also had an interest in twenty hotels and a group of top Edinburgh restaurants known as the 'Famous Five', one of which was the well known Hawes Inn in South Queensferry. Beer continued to be brewed in the brewery until 1980 at which time it was closed and soon thereafter demolished.

Some of Usher's best known brands were: 'Usher's IPA' (India Pale Ale); 'Usher's Golden Rule'; 'Usher's Gold Tankard'; and 'Usher's Amber ale.'

A Meet of the Jedforest Hunt in the 1930s. Lady Katherine Usher is on the right, at the front. The photograph shows the Northern Aspect of Wells House.

5

SIR ROBERT USHER TAKES THE HELM

On Sir John's death in Cairo in 1904 his eldest surviving son, Robert, succeeded him and inherited the Estates of Norton in Midlothian and Wells in Roxburghshire and a large number of feus in Pulteney Town, Caithness and other property in Wick. The feuing scheme in Pulteney town had been prepared by Thomas Telford, the great civil engineer.

Robert, now Sir Robert, continued to sit on the Board of Andrew Usher & Co with his two brothers Frederick and Francis and Sir Oliver Riddell who had worked for the firm to great effect all his working life.

Sir Robert was very keen on fox hunting and became Master of the Linlithgow and Stirlingshire Hunt in 1896 and remained Master for seventeen years, retiring in 1913. He was also a third proprietor of the hounds which were quartered at Golfhall, near Norton.

Sir Robert married Katherine Scott Turnbull of Abbey St Bathans, Berwickshire in 1890 and by the time of his Father's death in 1904 had produced five sons and two daughters. Sadly both daughters did not survive childhood.

In 1906 Sir Robert razed old Wells House, a huge place, to the ground because he found it uncomfortable and inconvenient and commenced building another very grand house in the Scottish Baronial style in its place. Electricity was supplied by a power plant built in the grounds and Wells oak was used for all the wall panelling. The new Wells House was completed in 1908.

Also in 1908 a Royal Commission gave its verdict on a case brought originally in 1906 by Islington Borough Council on whether Malt or Grain were the proper ingredients for Scotch Whisky, or whether a blend of both was acceptable. This became known as the 'What is Whisky?' debate. The whole of the Scottish Blended Whisky industry unanimously elected Sir Robert, to represent them. In this regard the *Wine and Spirit Trade Record* of October 1968 wrote:

Right: Sir Robert Usher, 2nd Baronet of Norton and Wells at Court In London.

Left: Katherine Lady Usher, wife of Sir Robert Usher at Court In London.

'It speaks volumes for the standing of the House of Usher in the blending trade that it was naturally the lot of an Usher to head the deputation.'

Mercifully the Commission ruled in favour of the blenders. If it had not done so the Scottish Whisky industry would not exist on the scale it does today.

In 1911 Sir Robert set up a Trust. The purpose of the Trust was to tie the Trust estates to the title holder. Sir Robert's instructions, as stated in his Trust Deed, were that all those succeeding him in the title should settle the estates and assets onto their heir in their Wills. His purpose in doing this was to ensure that the assets and estates in the Trust would remain within the Usher family of Norton and Wells, in the words of the Trust Deed, 'for all time.' By 1911 Sir Robert had 6 sons, ranging from John (b 1891) to Clive (b 1907).

In 1912 Andrew Usher and Company received the Royal Warrant appointing the firm as suppliers of whisky to the Sovereign.

In 1913 Sir Robert retired from the Mastership of the Linlithgow & Stirlingshire Hunt after 17 seasons as Master of Fox Hounds At this time he spent the winters at Norton, Midlothian, and the summers at Wells, commuting to Edinburgh as and when required. At this time Sir Robert was known as 'The Whisky King.'

In 1918 Sir Robert sold the firm to Distiller's Company Limited for a 'large undisclosed sum'. At that time whisky stocks were very scarce indeed - no doubt because of World War I. However Andrew Usher and Co. had a huge stock of approximately four million gallons of whisky in their bonded warehouses. This was therefore an important acquisition for Distillers in those difficult times.

In 1919 Sir Robert's youngest brother Francis purchased the Dunglass Estate from the Hall family in East Lothian and Berwickshire. Happily this estate was owned by Francis's grandson - also called Francis but known as Frank. Frank took little interest in the Usher family which I found rather odd. This was a shame because at least that Estate still remained in our family. He knew next to nothing about our family and never lifted a finger to help me with our branch of the family when I started the fight back against the notorious Edinburgh 'law firm', Brodies of Edinburgh, which had ruined us. Frank's affairs were still with Brodies in the late 1990s and were probably still there at the time of his death in 2009 despite his telling me in the mid 1960s that Dempster, a Mackenzie & Black and later a Brodies lawyer, had robbed his Father of £1,000 on his death-bed in 1954. I reminded him of this in late 1994. He told me, 'It still sticks in my gullet.'

He was an only child and did not follow his Father to Eton, but was educated in, of all places, France. I always suspected that 'something had been engineered' by the lawyers whereby his branch of the family had profited at the expense of our branch but could never find anything hard

Above: Dunglass House, 1826

Below: Rear of Dunglass House, late 1940s

on that. He was always reluctant to talk about our common family. Possibly he knew something and realised that silence was his best course of action. His wife did not let me know of his passing and I only heard of it many months later in Jedburgh. This made me even more suspicious about his side of the family profiting at the expense of ours. He left what remained of the Dunglass Estate to his adopted children, Simon and Katherine.

No history of our family would be complete without mention of the number of Masters of Foxhounds our family produced in the latter years of the nineteenth century and the first half of the twentieth century. This must stand as some sort of record.

Sir Robert Usher, 2nd Bart, was MFH of the Linlithgow and Stirlingshire hounds for a total of 17 seasons commencing in 1896 as already narrated. His younger brother, Frederick, was Joint Master of the L & S hounds with him for ten of those seasons. His youngest brother Frank James Usher was likewise Joint Master with him in the same Hunt for ten seasons. The Hunt history for this period records that everything to do with the Hunt was carried out on a most liberal scale by Messrs Usher. All damage to gates, fencing and land was paid for by them. In some weeks they were out hunting five days a week. Frederick was in charge of the hounds and improved the stock by careful breeding. The hounds became the envy of many Hound experts who visited the Hunt kennels.

In 1929 George Usher, a beer Usher, took over the Mastership of the L & S hounds. He was MFH for eighteen seasons, retiring in 1947. He in turn was succeeded by a daughter of Frederick Usher, Annette Usher, as MFH. She had already been MFH of the North Northumberland Hunt, the Ballymacaw in Ireland and the Berwickshire Hunt. She was, and still is, regarded as one of Scotland's outstanding foxhunting personalities of the twentieth century.

After resigning his joint Mastership of the L & S hounds in 1906 Frederick Usher became MFH of the Berwickshire Hunt for three years until his untimely death in 1909.

Col Sir John Turnbull Usher was MFH of the Jedforest Hunt, in which country the Wells Estate lay, for two seasons, 1932 and 1933.

6

WARNING CLOUDS ON THE HORIZON

In 1919 Sir Robert and Lady Usher were disappointed by their second son, Ronald, marrying his second cousin, Alice Usher, daughter of Harry Usher of Dunbar, a Beer Usher and an accountant. Worse was to follow. Shortly after this marriage, their eldest son and heir, John, married Alice's sister, Jean. John produced his first born, a girl whom they named Katherine Alice, in 1920. This would have been reason for great rejoicing in the family if only because it demonstrated that John and Jean were capable of producing children. But Sir Robert and Lady Usher were disappointed again because John and Jean did not have another child for another eleven years. Katherine was always an eccentric yet pleasant, outgoing and warm-hearted person with whom I always got on very well. She died in 1978.

In 1923 Sir Robert and his wife heaved a sigh of relief when their second son Ronald and his wife produced a son: a bonny, bouncing baby. They named him Robert Ronald Harry, although he was always known as Robin. If John and Jean failed to produce a son there was Robin onto whom the Trust estates could devolve.

Visits, at this time, to other members of the family were a regular feature of the calender. To Sir Robert's youngest sister, at nearby Spital-Tower, now called Towerburn. Also to his youngest brother Francis at Dunglass, the Cruikshanks at Johnstounburn which Andrew II's youngest daughter Mamie had inherited from Andrew II and where she lived with her husband, Colonel Chichester deWindt Cruikshank and also to his Aunt Marion at Blackford House, Blackford, Edinburgh until her death in 1925. Also to his brother Frederick's son, Neil, who had married Elizabeth the heiress of Lt Colonel Frederick Murray-Baillie of Broughton and Cally, Gatehouse of Fleet, Kirkcudbrightshire. The Estate was inherited by Elizabeth Murray-Usher in 1924 and she continued to let Cally House. Its last tenant was the Maharajah of Jind in the early 1930

Elizabeth Murray Usher sold the Estate in 1933 to the Forestry Commission. Cally House is now the fifty-six bedroom Cally Palace Hotel

Above: New Wells House.

Below: Spital Tower, house of May Usher, Sir Robert's sister. This was originally part of the Wells Estate

and has a delightful eighteen hole golf course as one of its amenities. Their son, James Murray Usher, lived near Cally for many years until his death in 2007. At its height the Cally Estate ran to tens of thousands of acres. There exists to this day a Murray Usher Foundation in the Fleet valley whose main purposes include the relief of poverty, the advancement of education, community development and the protection and development of the environment in the area. Its activities are listed as making grants, loans, gifts or pensions to individuals and organisations.

Other visits made by Sir Robert and Lady Usher were to Abbey St Bathans in Berwickshire and Synton House in Roxburgshire, the homes of his wife's family and connections.

On the 23rd of May 1927, Sir Robert placed the Estates of Norton and Wells into the Trust he had set up in 1911.

At that time the Norton Estate consisted of the mansion house of Norton, staff houses, a walled garden, about 50 acres of park and woodland, the Stable Block, and an indeterminate number of farms, houses and property in and around Ratho station and Ratho village. The Estate also included the Barony of Norton and possibly that of Hatton as well. I know the names of four farms on the Estate at that time: Norton Mains, Easter Norton, Rathobyres and Hillwood Dairy. To date I have not been able to discover the full extent of this Estate because all the Deeds and Papers I obtained from the Scottish Records Office refer to the plans of the Estate as being 'annexed hereto' but are *not* in fact 'annexed hereto.'

Wells estate at that time consisted of the Mansion houses of Wells and Hallrule. In addition there were eight farms on the Estate, numerous staff and farm cottages and smallholdings. There were also extensive woodlands, parks, gardens and about two miles of superb private fishing on the Rulewater. The Estate ran to about 6,000 acres. Sir Robert excluded the largest farm on the Estate, Bedrule, from being placed in the Trust and left it to his fourth son, Major Alexander Balmer Usher. On his being killed in World War Two in 1940 it passed to his brother, William Dove Usher, my Father. Bedrule was a Barony in its own right and also gave its name to the Parish of Bedrule. Bedrule's main claims to fame were that King Edward the First of England (Edward Longshanks, the Hammer of the Scots) visited Bedrule Castle in 1298 and that it was the birthplace of William Turnbull, the Bishop of Glasgow and Founder and First Chancellor of Glasgow Universiity in 1451. Bishop Turnbull was born at Bedrule in c 1400 and died in 1454 in Glasgow. Another Bedrule claim to fame is that the winner of the Grand National in 1979, Rubstic, lived and was trained there by John Leadbetter at Bedrule. Interestingly Rubstic was the smallest horse ever to win the Grand National.

But the whole remaining part of the Wells estate, one contiguous block, including the two mansion houses of Wells and Hallrule had been placed into the Trust.

Top: Western aspect of the-New Wells House, 1914

Left: Old Well House

Below: Hallrule House

By 1928 John had still not produced another child. On top of that he did not live in Scotland, which greatly annoyed old Sir Robert and Lady Usher. Sir Robert threatened him with disinheritance unless he came and lived in Scotland, cut down on the drink, and tried for another child. This had the required effect. John came home from England where he had been residing at Stratton House, Cirencester, Gloucestershire and took up residence at Hallrule House.

In 1931 another girl was born whom they christened Jacquelin. She was their last child.

Meanwhile Sir Robert's third son, Stuart, had grown up. He wanted to be a soldier and was sent to Sandhurst Military College. There he won the Saddle Award which, in some circles, was more coveted than the Sword of Honour. He joined the Inniskillings Dragoons before deciding that soldiering was not for him and moved to Argentina in the mid 1920s where he purchased a ranch near Rosario in Cordoba province and commenced ranching. He also played a great deal of Polo and was regarded as a crack player. In the late 1920s he met an Argentinian woman called Gertrude Sampson and married her in 1930 in Argentina.

Their first child, whom they named Peter Lionel, was born in 1931. To Stuart and Gertrude's grave disappointment they soon discovered that Peter was a Downs Syndrome baby. He was also mentally incapacitated, although I don't think his parents realised that at the time. Because of the intolerant nature of Society towards such children in those days Stuart and Gertrude concealed Peter's condition from Sir Robert and the family in Scotland. Financial difficulties then came Stuart's way and Sir Robert had to come to the rescue.

Readying himself for his final journey Sir Robert made his last Will and Testament on the 2nd of March 1932. As far as he was concerned he now had two grandsons: Robin and Peter; and four grand-daughters: Hazel, Katherine, Daphne and Jacquelin. However he did not know that one of his grandsons was Downs Syndrome and mentally incapacitated and therefore that the future of the Usher family of Norton and Wells and the Trust estates still depended upon Robin alone. If he had known that Peter was Downs Syndrome and Mentally Incapacitated he would have amended the Trust Deed to obviate any grandson who was incapable of administering the Estates, making a Will and so on.

In the winter of 1933 Sir Robert went to Cairo for a short break, fell ill and died in the British Hospital at Port Said in January 1933, thus emulating his Father, Sir John. Sir Robert was buried in the family burial ground in Bedrule Churchyard. Before the First World War he had carried out great extensions and improvements to the Church, transforming it into one of the five most beautiful Parish Churches in Scotland. John, now Colonel Sir John Turnbull Usher, succeeded him.

7

MY FATHER WILLIAM DOVE USHER

After the death of Sir Robert in January 1933 Stuart and Gertrude decided to have another child. This they accomplished, with another boy being born to them in April 1934. With odds yet to be calculated this boy was also Downs Syndrome and mentally incapacitated. They christened him Robert Edward. Again they decided to keep the condition of both boys secret from the Usher side of the family in Scotland.

When World War II broke out Uncle John sent his second daughter Jacquelin out to stay with Stuart in Argentina. She was the same age as Peter and instantly noticed that Peter and Robert were Down's Syndrome. On her return she would have told her parents about Peter and Robert and therefore Stuart made the decision to tell John, in confidence.

Sir Robert's fourth son, Alexander Balmer Usher, was killed in action in France in 1940. This was another major blow to the family because he was a highly regarded man. He farmed Bedrule and another large farm near Jedburgh called Whitton; the latter in partnership with a Leadbetter connection.

I now come to my father, William Dove Usher, born in 1904 and the fifth son of Sir Robert Usher. He was packed off to Uppingham School in Rutland, England in 1918 following all his elder brothers. He excelled at rugby and running. After Uppingham he went to Cambridge University in the early 1920s where he was told he would achieve his Blue in Running if he buckled down and took part in the training sessions. He refused to do so, however, on the grounds that his times were good enough as they were.

While at Cambridge he became quite a favourite of Rosa Lewis who was the Proprietrix of the Cavendish Hotel in London. This hotel was much favoured by high society. The life of Rosa Lewis is well documented in the book 'The Duchess of Jermyn Street,' by Daphne Fielding and another book on her called simply 'Rosa Lewis.' Father led a hectic social life in London often staying at the Cavendish. Rosa Lewis, very much a lady of her own ways, charged people she did not like double and charged people she *did*

Rosa Lewis 'The Duchess of Jermyn Street'

like nothing. I do not know what my father studied at Cambridge but, whatever it was, he did not apply himself and consequently failed. I suspect he was too busy consorting with the young the ladies of Cambridge and London. After Cambridge he was packed off to McGill University in Ontario, Canada where again he failed.

It was then decided to send him to Kenya and after some time there he moved to Tanganyika where he first farmed in the Dabaga area, also starting a transport business. He joined the Chunya gold rush and though he never struck gold he assured me he had a jolly time. He had a succession of baboons as pets, one of them called Big Bertie, although 'Big Bertie' was confusingly a lady baboon. One day my father threw a party at which there was a young lady with a baby among the guests. Pet baboons in those days had a box on top of a high pole in which to spend the night and sleep during the day as they pleased - a safe haven from leopards, their main enemies. Big Bertie spotted the baby, took an immediate fancy to it, seized it, and shot up the pole into her box with the baby under her arm. This, needless to say, had an electrifying effect on the baby's mother, no doubt fearing the worst. However she and the guests need not have worried as Big Bertie treated the baby very gently, carefully 'de-fleaing' it and showing it the greatest care in the world. The impasse lasted for some time until Big Bertie decided to bring the baby down. This she accomplished safely and laid it carefully on the ground.

On occasion people from Britain would visit my Father. One day a young lady on her first visit to Africa was dropped off at the end of the drive to my Father's house. She set off along this 'drive' which meandered through the rain forest. Suddenly 'a great ape' dropped from the foliage and grabbed her by the hand before she could even scream. It was Big Bertie again! Almost paralysed and ashen-faced with fear she let herself be led by Big Bertie to my Father's house. He had four such pet baboons in succession; two males, Big Willie and Little Willie and two females, Big Bertie and Little Bertie. Curiously the two males did not like women and the two females

My father, W.D. Usher, as a young man

My mother, C.E.M.C. Von Tevenar, as a young lady

did not like men. My father taught the males to drink out of a glass and it was their habit to join him in a sundowner with a glass of watered-down beer.

On another occasion the late Princess Alice, Duchess of Gloucester, visited him while on safari with her Uncle, Lord Francis Scott. Princess Alice, then Lady Alice Montagu-Douglas-Scott, and my Father had known each other since childhood in the Scottish Borders. Princess Alice recounts this visit in her Memoirs published in the early 1990s. My Father took her out for the day in his lorry with instructions from her uncle to be back in good time in the evening. In the event they got back very late because the lorry had 'broken down.' In her book Princess Alice wrote that she was never quite able to work out whether my Father's lorry actually broke down, as he claimed it had, or whether there was nothing wrong with it and that my Father was just pretending that it had broken down as an excuse so that they could be together for longer.

He eventually settled down to farming tea in the Mufindi area of the Southern Uplands of Tanganyika on his own account and later in partnership with Lord Francis Scott and others when farms in the area which were amalgamated into what became known as the Kidope Estate. Lord Francis was the youngest brother of the Duke of Buccleuch of the day and farmed in the White Highlands of Kenya. My Father became a stalwart of the Southern Highlands Club as well as the Mufindi Club. Lord Chesham and he had a lot to do with keeping the Southern Highlands Club running smoothly.

On the outbreak of the Second World War in 1939 my Father volunteered to join the Army but was turned down on the grounds that he was a 'Key Man' in Tanganyika. This meant that he was regarded as more important to the War Effort out of the Army than in it.

My Father married my mother, Christa Elizabeth Margaret Caroline von Tevenar in Mufindi in 1939. She was the elder daughter of a neighbouring farmer, Bruno von Tevenar, who had settled in German East Africa before the First World War. German East Africa became Tanganyika after the defeat of Germany in that war.

8

MY MOTHER'S FAMILY

My mother's family, von Tevenar, originated near the city of Essen in the present day Ruhr area of Germany. They were a noble family owning a water castle near Essen. Legend has it that they were originally one of the Robber Barons of the Rhine. By the early sixteenth century they had been forced to move into town, Essen, and go into 'trade'; disgraceful in those socially-regimented days, and had given up their water castle. In Essen they prospered with one of them Gerhard von Tevenar (1560-1644) becoming Mayor and Treasurer of Essen in c. 1600. He was also in partnership with a man called Krupp in a gun factory in Essen. This was very likely Arndt Krupp who joined the Merchant's Guild in Essen in 1587. With all the wars going on in Europe at the time the gun factory did very well. His son, also Gerhard, succeeded him in the factory, also in partnership with a Krupp. The business continued to expand with the outbreak of the Thirty Years War in Germany. Gerhard II made deals with the Great Elector of Brandenburg (Hohenzollern) for the supply of guns. This indicated that he was the major shareholder in the gun factory. Gerhard II was also a Senator and later the Treasurer of the city of Essen. Gerhard II's son, Johann, succeeded him in the gun factory and also became Senator and Treasurer of Essen.

In the early 1700s the von Tevenars sold their share in the gun factory to the Krupps. This gun factory was the foundation out of which grew the mighty Krupp industrial and armaments empire. By 1900 it had grown into the largest industrial enterprise in Europe and the largest armaments manufacturer in the world. In the 1800s it was always wholly owned by the chief Krupp of the day. No shareholders, partners, nor anything like that. This sole proprietorship tradition was eventually legislated into law known as 'Lex Krupp.' The single-owner Krupp of the day was known, not surprisingly, as the 'Cannon King'. The most famous gun they produced was called 'Big Bertha', after Bertha Krupp, the sole owner of the enterprise at the time. The largest gun they ever produced, called the 'Gustav', weighed over 1,300 tons and was the largest gun ever deployed on the battlefield.

The shell fired by this behemoth alone weighed seven tons . The Krupps became the wealthiest family in Germany for decades. Para-doxically, in spite of the enterprise being solely owned by one person, always a Krupp, and whether it was a man or a woman it did not matter, the Krupp enterprise was the first enterprise in the world to introduce Social Security and Welfare for its workers as a basic condition of employment. Unsurprisingly its workers were very loyal and some families worked for Krupp for three or four generations.

Shell of 'Gustav' on display at the Imperial War Museum

By the early eighteenth century the Tevenars had acquired estates near Essen and had taken to country life once more. By the mid-eighteenth century a successor to the von Tevenars, Johann Wilhelm (1724-1797) had moved to Magdeburg where he was appointed by King Frederick the Great of Prussia as its Governor and Representative of the King as head of the Church. Thereafter various descendants of the family moved around Germany as and when opportunity called, and prospered greatly. At some point in the early eighteenth century the famous composer, Johann Sebastian Bach, became related to the Tevenars. Sad to say the male line of the von Tevenars died out in my Mother's generation, although I have two lady cousins of the family still living. The elder, Adleheid, is married to Count von Schulenberg and lives in America and her younger sister, Gudrun, is a Professor of Philosophy at Birbeck College, London.

My grandmother von Tevenar came from a very famous German family; the Counts von Finckenstein. They were created Counts of the German Empire in 1710. They were essentially a military family and were close allies of the Hohenzollerns, the ruling dynasty in Prussia. In the Seven Years War (1756-1763) Prussia was simultaneously at War with Russia, France and Austria, the three great European powers of the time. King Frederick the Great wrote to my Great (five times over) Grandfather on the 10th of January 1757 entrusting him with the Affairs of State and the Royal family, should he be defeated. There was more than a distinct possibility of defeat as the King and his armies were fighting the three greatest European powers of the day, all at the same time, on three fronts and were hard-pressed. Happily King Frederick was not defeated and emerged victorious. The Prussian Royal family eventually became the Hohenzollern Emperors of Germany with the last of the line, Kaiser Bill, abdicating after the defeat of Germany in World War I.

Above: Gross Salau Schloss

Below: Finckenstein Palace

My Mother told me that either King Frederick the Great or his successor offered the chief Finckenstein of the time a Dukedom but he turned it down on the grounds that the Finckensteins were not wealthy enough to be Dukes. King Frederick had another good reason to be thankful to the Finckensteins: He was homosexual and as a young man had an affair with another young man called Katte. When his Father, also King Frederick, who was hot-tempered, discovered that the young Crown Prince Frederick was homosexual he wanted him executed. For a while nothing and no one could deter him. Family tradition has it that it was the intercession of Countess von Finckenstein with the German Emperor in Vienna which caused the Emperor to intercede on behalf of the young Frederick. Thankfully he succeeded in persuading the King that execution was too harsh. So the young Frederick was spared and went on to become Frederick the Great by turning Prussia into one of the major European powers.

Fifty years later Napoleon took over the main family seat, Finckenstein Palace, as his personal abode and HQ for a while after he had conquered Prussia at the Battle of Jena in 1806. It was here at Finckenstein Palace that he had his famous love affair with the Polish Countess Walewska. The famous fish dish, Sole Walewska, was named after her.

The Finckensteins continued to play a prominent part in the affairs of Prussia and Germany well into the twentieth century. In 1920 the German government produced a 450 page hardback book in blue and gold on the family history. More recently another book, with copious illustrations on the history of Finckenstein Palace was published. Sad to say Finckenstein Palace was looted and burned down by the Soviets at the end of WW2.

My Mother was born in Morogoro, German East Africa (now Tanzania) on the 28th of February, 1914 . After the end of WWI she was sent to Germany where she grew up. She and her sister, Lalai, were very beautiful young girls and on one occasion General Hindenburg, before he became President of Germany, spotted them and took them both onto his knee. She was quite proud of this. As one would expect she was brought up in the old German traditions of thrift, diligence and honesty. She followed these principles all her life and, naturally, imparted them to Johnny and myself. Speaking for both Johnny and myself she was successful on the honesty side with both of us but not so much on the diligence and thrift side of things. She was trained in art and painted some lovely pictures of scenes on our African farms and two views on Bedrule.

My father took her home to Wells in 1939 and introduced her to the rest of the family. All went well and thereafter they went to Loch Maree in the western the Highlands for their honeymoon and some fishing. Out on the loch one day a terrible storm arose without warning and at one stage they feared for their lives, so fierce was the tempest. But with my Father rowing with all his might and my Mother baling with all her might they eventually reached the shore, much shaken, but alive, thank God.

9

MY BROTHER JOHN AND I EMBARK ON OUR EARTHLY CAREERS

On the 18th of April 1940 my brother William John was born on the Kidope Estate in the Mufindi area of the Southern Uplands of Tanganyika. He was always known as Johnny in our family.

To mark his birth the Natives presented my parents with a leopard cub they had found in the forest. Though my parents appreciated the kind motivation behind the gift, and thought the cub very sweet they had recently lost two dogs to leopards and diplomatically decided against keeping him. My parents asked the natives to take them and the cub to where they had found it deep in the forest and released him in the hope that his mother would find him.

I commenced my earthly career on the 12th of July 1941. My first memory is of the terrible shrieking which the monkeys got up in the rainforest surrounding our house. I also have dim memories of my 'Aya' (Nanny), of having a fight with Johnny, and of a tree falling on my father's parked car.

The Kidope Estate consisted of at least three farms, Kidope, Kidope East and Kiperu. It ran to eight thousand acres with nine hundred acres under tea. Most of the rest of the land was undeveloped rain forest. The forest abounded with leopard, hyena, wild pig and antelope. Occasionally buffalo migrated through the Estate. Of monkeys there was no shortage either, mainly colobus, who moved around in large troops making a devil of a noise. They were the main prey of the leopards.

My Father was one of the Directors of the company and his main function was to manage the Estate. It had a labour force of about three hundred. During World War Two it was a desperate struggle to keep the company afloat for two main reasons: The shortage and unreliability of the labour, and the lack of maize meal with which to feed the labour. Tractors were unknown in Mufindi at the time, so oxen were used instead. On one occasion the workers speared one of the oxen to death and ate it. When my Father got to hear about this the workers made the utterly absurd excuse that a hyena had emerged from the forest and killed the ox. The workers then said they did not want the meat to go to waste and had therefore eaten it. My Father collected all the evidence and witnesses he needed and reported the culprits to the Police. Nothing, however, came of it.

With the difficulties of the war the company drifted deeper and deeper into debt and in 1946 it was sold to the Brooke-Bond tea company for £35,000. This was enough to settle all the creditors. But my Father, Lord Francis, and their partners all had to bear a substantial capital loss.

Johnny and I as boys with Peter the cat (I am on the left) in Tanganyika.

10

MY FATHER RETURNS TO SCOTLAND

We left for Scotland sometime in the summer of 1946 when I was five years old. My Father had inherited Bedrule farm which adjoined the Wells Estate from his brother, Major Alexander Balmer Usher of the First Lothian and Border Horse, who had been killed in action in France in 1940. Bedrule was about 1800 acres and had a large working Quarry on it called the Dunion. In addition there was a very pretty smallholding on the banks of the Rulewater which had been a Mill in years gone by and was called the Pirn Mill.

Of our trip to Scotland I recall seeing flying fish, the Gully Gully man - magician - who'd boarded the ship at Suez and impressed us greatly with his tricks, two of which included dragging a long line of flags out of his mouth and producing live chicks from seemingly nowhere! Johnny and I were entranced.

I remember my grandmother and her companion meeting us off the train in Edinburgh and our motoring down to Wells. At Wells Johnny and I were particularly impressed with the fire-places because the fire irons shone so beautifully. One morning Johnny and I had kippers for breakfast for the first time in our lives and loved them. Seeing this one of the servants, a japester, told us that the nearby Rulewater was full of kippers and we should try and catch some there. This we tried to do by means of bent nails embedded in plasticene and hanging them out on two pieces of string in the river, waiting with bated breath. Of course we caught nothing.

We moved into Bedrule in the autumn of 1946. It turned out to be a very cold winter much to the chagrin of my Mother who could not stand the chill. To make matters worse Bedrule did not have central heating at that time. With the help of roaring fires, however, we all survived that dread winter which turned out to be the most severe of the 20th century.

As you can imagine my mother suffered unpleasantries so soon after the end of the Second World War, ironically from civilians who had never seen active service themselves. Yet she was always treated well by the old soldiers and the military who knew how to behave in those circumstances.

Bedrule House with my son, Richard, in the foreground

She was endlessly patient, generous and outgoing and eventually won over the vast majority of people who had initially been hostile to her, by her patent decency and calm, dignified manner. She took an interest in and studied a wide range of subjects. For example on arrival at Bedrule she asked the Bedrule Schoolmaster, Mr Thomson, to teach her advanced mathematics. He declined on the grounds that he knew nothing about them. She always stoutly maintained that German women singers were infinitely superior to British women singers who, she claimed, screeched. But she much preferred British men singers to German men singers who she claimed sounded effeminate.

In the Spring of 1947 we were each given a pony. Johnny's was pure white and went by the rather inevitable and uninteresting name of Snowhite. Mine was a dun grey filly with a wall eye called Sheba. Snowhite was slow and predictable. Sheba was the opposite: fast and a touch unpredictable. We were taught riding by old Tom Scott who had been Headgroom at the Wells Stud and Stables and was now semi-retired. Out riding Sheba I would roar past Johnny which, of course, annoyed him greatly. The things we do when we are young! Actually I still enjoy doing that type of thing.

We had a Dutch governess called Miss Spapens who lived with us at Bedrule. She was beloved by both Johnny and myself, always cheerful, she entered our games with a will. Another person who made a great impression on us at this young age was Norton who also worked in the house at Bedrule as a sort of butler-cum-general dogsbody. Norton was English and spoke with a strong regional English accent. We used to have the most wonderful games of Hide and Seek with Norton and he appeared to enjoy them as much as we did, putting the fear of God into us by incanting: 'Fee, fy, foe, fum, I smell the blood of a Scots-mun' as he hunted us down. He was good sport who'd had a tough life and, I much later realised, enjoyed his carefree days at Bedrule with us.

Of course we also got to know the farm staff at Bedrule. They were a wonderful crew and we had such fun on the farm and visiting them in their cottages. One of them was old John Purves, the Bedrule gardner whose poor wife had been confined to her bed for the previous eight years with an illness the nature of which I do not know. I remember that she bore it bravely and always gave us boys a most cheery welcome. So life passed merrily along for us both at Bedrule.

The situation for the Usher family of Norton and Wells on New Year's day 1947 was as follows:

Dowager Lady Usher living alone at Wells House.

Colonel Sir John Usher and his wife Jean had moved out of Hallrule House and were now living in Norton House near Edinburgh. No male issue. Two daughters: Katherine and Jacquelin.

His brother Lt-Commander Ronald Usher RN, was farming Todshawheugh near Hawick. One male issue, Lieutenant Robin Usher RN, married with a pregnant wife, but no male issue as yet. Two daughters, Hazel and Daphne

Stuart Usher, still in the Argentine and still in financial difficulties. Two male issue, Peter and Robert, both Downs Syndrome and Mentally Incapacitated, but this not yet known in Scotland.

William Dove Usher, living at and farming Bedrule, adjoining the Wells Estate. Two male issue; Johnny and Stuart (myself).

Brigadier Thomas Clive Usher RA, still in the Army. No male issue. One daughter, Margaret.

Everything appeared to be calm, on the surface at least, but serious trouble was brewing underneath.

Bedrule Manse, Johnny's home at Bedrule (at that time owned by our father WD Usher).

11

THE GRIM REAPER STRIKES AND DISASTER ENSUES

Robert Ronald Harry (Robin) Usher, heir to the Estates, had served with distinction in the Second World War. He attained the rank of Lieutenant while serving on the submarine HMS *Telemachus*, was mentioned in Dispatches, and was awarded the 1939-1945 Star; the Burma Star; the African Star; the North Atlantic Star; and the Victory Medal with Oakleaves.

Having survived the War in early 1947 Robin was struck down with cancer. The cancer spread like wildfire and he died on 30th April 1947, aged only twenty-four, leaving his wife and a six month old daughter called Elizabeth. This was a major disaster for our family although no one, with the exception of Uncle John, knew this. As far as old Lady Usher, who was very much the Matriarch of the family, and other members of the family were concerned there were still four potential male heirs of the next generation to carry the family on, namely: Peter and Robert in Argentina and Johnny and myself at Bedrule. So she and everyone else would not have been unduly worried as far as the succession went. Someone told her at some stage during that year that Stuart's boys suffered from 'bad nerves' but whoever it was made no mention of either Downs Syndrome or Mental Incapacity. Naturally she hoped that Peter and Robert would grow out of their 'bad nerves' yet she must have wondered why Stuart had never brought them to visit. Little did she nor anyone else know what lay in store for them and the future of our family during the rest of 1947 and into 1948.

Stuart and Gertrude, still lying low in Argentina, now realised that, as far as the Usher family in Scotland were concerned, their elder son Peter was the heir of the next generation. If Stuart, in Argentina, owned up to the incapacity of his sons there would be absolutely no prospect of his succeeding to the Estates because his Mother would never agree to it. She was a firm Matriarch and her word was law. However this was not the only problem with which Stuart was grappling; he was now in serious, and deadly financial difficulties again.

The submarine HMS *Telemachus* on which Lieutenant Robert Ronald Harry (Robin) Usher, heir to the Estates, served with distinction. Photo taken post world War two.

He therefore returned to Scotland in the autumn of 1947 to ask for more money. At the same time he would have found out more about the succession. He would also have noted that Uncle John and his wife Jean were drinking heavily and would probably not live much longer. In November 1947, after Stuart returned to Argentina with what little money he had managed to lay his hands on, old Lady Usher made a new Will in which she left him some of her own furniture and belongings, including valuable jewellery which he was to 'hold and treat as family heirlooms and to give to Peter on the occasion of his marriage.' Of course she would never have done this had she known that Peter and Robert were both Downs Syndrome, mentally incapacitated, and would never marry. So Stuart had still not told her of Peter and Robert's conditions and nor had anyone else.

At the beginning of 1948 disaster struck yet again. The health of old Lady Usher herself began to fail and Lt-Commander Ronald Usher was diagnosed with cancer of the throat. Now the whole future of the Trust Estates was immediately endangered. The gravity of the situation caused someone who knew that Peter and Robert were Down's Syndrome and mentally incapacitated to decide that the secret could no longer be kept. That someone was almost certainly Uncle John who now told his Mother of the true conditions of Peter and Robert. As can well be imagined she was deeply shocked and instantly realised the deadly danger posed by Stuart's family to the future of the Usher Estates and its holdings in Scotland. She rose to the challenge, even in her weakened state, summoned my Father and told him that he, 'was to see to it that Stuart's boys never inherited the Title and Estates because your father would never have allowed that.' My father gave her his word that he would see to it that this never came to pass. Shortly thereafter on the 2nd June 1948 she died.

Uncle Ronald soon followed her. I saw him for what turned out to be the last time at the Wells Sawmill. He or my father had cracked some joke and were both roaring with laughter. My parents had always got on very well with Uncle Ronald. Many years later my mother told me she believed that if Uncle Ronald had lived a few more years none of the disasters which were subsequently visited upon our family would have occurred. As it was, Uncle Ronald succumbed to the cancer on 29th September 1948, not four months after his mother's death.

After Uncle Ronald's death his recently widowed daughter-in-law Jane, Robin's wife, arrived at Bedrule with her little baby girl, Elizabeth and stayed with us for sometime. Baby Elizabeth was born after Robin's death. Johnny and I were very fond of Jane as she tried bravely to maintain her naturally cheerful disposition in the face of the tragedies which had befallen her in quick succession. She was also very pretty and both Johnny and I sought and enjoyed her company. My mother looked after baby Elizabeth from time to time when the need arose. Jane and Elizabeth disappeared from our lives as suddenly as they had arrived and I was never to see Jane again, although I met Elizabeth in South Wales in 1996, forty-eight years later. No longer the bawling baby at Bedrule she had grown into a beautiful woman and became an inestimable help to me from 1998 to the present day.

The situation now was that the only route to the future for the Usher family of Norton and Wells lay through my father, and then Johnny and myself.

With Lady Usher and Uncle Ronald no longer with us Uncle Stuart, Sir Stuart Usher, 4th Bt of Norton and Wells, now brought his wife, Gertrude, and Peter and Robert to Wells in late 1948. They arrived with only the clothes in which they stood, so broke was he. He was immediately made a Trustee to replace Uncle Ronald alongside the existing Trustees, namely Uncle John, JGG Leadbetter WS, and Logan MacLure WS. As stated earlier, WS in Scotland stands for Writer to the Signet and denotes a member of a private society of Scottish lawyers, dating back to 1594. Ironically they are meant to uphold the highest standards of honesty and probity.

Uncle Stuart was given the tenancy of a farm called Town O'Rule on the Wells Estate to farm. Stuart knew little about farming in Scotland and had already been bankrupted twice during his Argentinian ranching operations. This therefore was an imprudent thing to have done; yet not only was it imprudent, it was illegal. One of the basic tenets of Scottish Law precludes a person from being a tenant on an Estate of which that person is also a

Trustee. This was just commonsense because of the huge conflict of interest thereby engendered. But on this matter the Writers to the Signet were silent.

With Lady Usher and Uncle Ronald out of the way this now dysfunctional group of Trustees wasted no time in reaching and executing some truly deplorable decisions. I use the word dysfunctional because that was exactly what they were: Uncle John drinking more than ever and unable to think straight. This made him easy prey for the lawyers. His wife Jean had by now descended into complete alcoholism and was in an even worse than Uncle John. Then came Uncle Stuart, an embittered man with two Downs Syndrome and, significantly at that particular time, also a bankrupt. On top of that he had a social climbing and avaricious wife in Gertrude, although that was not yet known to the rest of the family. Then there was Logan MacClure, a crooked lawyer acting in his own interest only, and finally another elderly bachelor lawyer called JGG Leadbetter who had been a parasite on his own Leadbetter family and then our family ever since he'd reached adulthood.

One of their first decisions was to rip the roof off Wells House. Their rationale for this was that it would save money by avoiding having to pay Roof Tax. When my Father heard about this proposed incredible piece of vandalism he was mortified, as you can well imagine. To save Wells House he offered to purchase it and, if possible, it's surrounds consisting of staff cottages, stables, gardens and Policies. Uncle John looked with favour on his plan. Drinker though he was, he knew his duty to his family. He put my father's proposal to the remaining two brothers, Stuart and Clive (who was still in the Army). Sir John soon reverted to my father with the bad news that both Stuart and Clive objected to him purchasing it, although he himself was in favour of it. This was a great disappointment to my father. He then suggested that Wells be converted into flats or a hotel as a means of saving it. Again he had the backing of Sir John but again this was opposed by Stuart and Clive and then the other Trustees.

But surely Uncle John should have been able to overcome all this opposition as the titular head of the family, I can imagine the reader thinking. If he had been a stronger character the odds were that he would have been able to do so. Unfortunately he was a weakling and was described as exactly that to me by a female first cousin of his in the early 1990s shortly before her own death at the great age of 90 plus. In these circumstances it appears that Uncle John was outvoted by the lawyers on the Usher Baronetcy Trust throwing their weight behind Stuart. As long as old Lady Usher, Uncle John and Uncle Ronald lived, the Estates were safe but, with Lady Usher and Ronald gone, Uncle John was now outnumbered and isolated.

At this point someone, most probably Uncle John or even my Father, told the Attlee government that the Trustees planned to destroy Wells House. The Attlee government were horrified at the sheer waste of the proposed destruction of Wells. To save it the government approached the Trustees with the proposal that they (the government) take Wells House over from the Trustees and rather put it to some good use for the country. To this end they suggested turning it into a Borstal home for boys; a glaringly better solution than simply destroying such a magnificent house. This would save the country an enormous amount of money from having to build a new and very large Borstal. Again, and incredibly, the Trustees, with the likely exception of Uncle John, would have none of it.

In this regard Dunglass House in East Lothian had already been dynamited in 1946. One of the Usher Baronetcy Trustees, that useless old parasite JGG Leadbetter again, had a hand in the dynamiting of Dunglass in that he was guardian to its heir at that time, Frank Usher, then only 8 years of age. And so did Logan MacClure, another of the Usher Baronetcy Trustees because he was the 'legal adviser' of its then owner, Francis Usher. Again, the Government had offered to save Dunglass by taking it over and converting it into a Police Training Academy. However this idiotic crew - one of whom, McClure, later proved himself to have been just another lawyer crook biding his time - had refused the Government's offer and simply dynamited this breath-takingly beautiful house. At that time Dunglass House had seventeen full-time house staff and eight full-time gardners.

Wasting little time in their programme of mismanagement the Trustees of Sir Robert Usher, as opposed to the Trustees of the Usher Baronetcy Trust, one of whom was the yet to be discovered 'death-bed thief' lawyer, Thomas Greig Dempster, commenced selling off heritable property. This included a town house in Grosvenor Crescent in Edinburgh in November 1948, and hundreds or possibly thousands of feus in the City of Perth in Dec 1948. These feus constituted part of the Pitheavlis estate. These Trustees dished the proceeds out to the four surviving brothers and the surviving issue of Ronald.

The Trustees then stated that the contents of Wells House should be sold but that members of the family should take whatever articles they wished at valuation. My Father did not approve of this at all because it would breach the Trust. However he eventually went along with it on the express condition that anyone taking furniture, paintings and so on should pay market value for them so as to not breach the Trust. Sir John agreed to this. When the four brothers and their respective wives had assembled at Wells for the choosing of the furniture my Father informed everyone that he felt that he should have the ancestral portraits. This was just plain common-sense because only he had the sons able to continue our family. No one contested the point, though he noted that Gertrude looked unhappy. My Father took this as recognition and acceptance by his brothers that he, with Johnny and myself, was the only route to the future for the Usher family of Norton and Wells and as such he and then Johnny would inherit the Trust

Estates on the death of either Uncle John or Uncle Stuart, *if* Stuart was allowed to succeed Uncle John. The four brothers and their respective wives then chose the various pieces they fancied and my Father got the ancestral portraits.

Sometime elapsed before my Father rang Uncle John enquiring about payment for what he had taken. Uncle John now effected an about-turn and stated that because Stuart could not pay no one else was to pay for what they had taken. My Father was furious because this meant that a lot of the beautiful furniture, paintings and the like had passed out of the Trust for nothing and therefore was in breach of it. Sir John also deplored this but told him that he had been advised by the lawyers that this was the best way to do it. This now meant that everything that had been taken, with the exception of what my Father had taken, would pass out of our family, for nothing.

So the Trustees went ahead and took the roof off Wells in 1949. It quickly became a ruin. What an end to our most beautiful Borders home and the main seat of our family of Norton and Wells. The most hurtful thing about it was there was no real financial need for it.

So why did the Trustees act in this vandal-like manner, the reader may well ask? Largely because Sir John was outvoted. Also because of Stuart's total ignorance of economics; *vide* his ranching 'achievements' in the Argentine. And the lawyers advising them? MacClure was just another legal mechanic who stood to make more money by causing confusion and destruction in our family than by acting in good faith, as both Johnny and I later discovered.

But there was more to it than just that; a lot more. This will become apparent later in the book at the various times that Johnny and I became aware of it as we grew older.

Both Wells and Dunglass houses were colossal assets, which only needed prudent managing, and a modicum of commonsense. To build these houses today would cost tens of millions of pounds. Put brutally the so-called Trustees sent millions of pounds up in smoke; millions which should have been put to good use, if not for our family, at least for the country.

Another meeting of the Trustees was held on 28th October 1949. Stuart now moaned that the rent he paid for Town O'Rule farm was too high. This is a classic example of what happens when a Trustee is also the tenant of the same Trust. The Trustees agreed to lower his rent from its already absurdly low figure to an even lower one. Stuart appears to have been incapable of making a success of anything. One would have thought that his rotten experiences in the Argentine would have taught him a thing or two but, alas, this does not appear to have been the case. It was now also agreed that Stuart and his family occupy Hallrule House at the risible rental of £50 per year. During World War Two Hallrule House had been utilised as a Girls' School.

With the Trustees behaving like vandals and Uncle John rendered powerless to stop them this must have been rather a depressing time for both him and my parents.

In February 1950 Uncle John's wife, Jean, died at Norton at the very young age of fifty seven. Ex-house staff of Hallrule told me that she had an even worse drink problem than Uncle John.

Uncle John, now living alone at Norton, drank more than ever. A meeting of the Trustees took place at the offices of Mackenzie & Black lawyers in Castle Street, Edinburgh on 8th February 1951. Wells had by now been dynamited and lay in ruins. The Trust estates were losing money fast. One obvious reason for this was that the Trustees had hardly, if ever, raised the rents on the Estates since Uncle John had succeeded to them in 1933. That alone was bound to lead to financial meltdown.

I suspect Uncle John realized that he had let his Father and family down very badly and this made him drink ever more heavily, thereby hastening his death. He died on the 5th of May 1951 at the age of 59. He left instructions that his Ashes were to be taken to the summit of Ruberslaw, an extinct volcano which lay on the western edge of the Wells Estate, and 'scattered to the winds.' In the event his wishes were blithely disregarded by his Executors and Trustees, most of whom were the same crew of crooks and idiots. They were too lazy to climb Ruberslaw and instead scattered his Ashes beside a wood on the lower slopes of the mountain. In retrospect it was a pity that old Sir Robert had not disinherited Uncle John as he had threatened to do in the late 1920s and settled the Trust Estates onto Uncle Ronald who was much more competent and, even more importantly, not a weakling.

The lawyers, however, saw to it that Uncle Stuart succeeded John and the situation now became critical. A lot depended on Stuart's mood improving. The situation could still be retrieved by the Trustees agreeing to amend the Trust Deed so that neither Peter nor Robert, both Down's Syndrome and Mentally Incapacitated, could inherit what remained of the Trust Estates.

12

RETURN TO TANGANYIKA

In these unhappy circumstances my father decided to return to Tanganyika again for a while. He hoped that his absenting himself would have a calming effect on things and help Uncle Stuart get over his bitterness at life and, as we later discovered, his jealousy of my father.

When our parents told us we were going out to Tanganyika in 1950 Johnny and I were delighted because this was just more excitement. My father sold the Wolseley car we had and purchased a 1938 Buick V8 in Glasgow because these pre-war American V8s were the best cars at coping with the extremely bumpy and dusty Tanganyika roads. We said good-bye to Miss Spapens, Norton, and the Bedrule crew and off we went to London where we stayed at Browns Hotel in Dover Street. In our absence my Father appointed a farmer called John Scott who farmed near Hawick to manage the day to day running of Bedrule.

While in London my Father took Johnny and myself to the Cavendish Hotel in Jermyn Street, to meet Rosa Lewis. We were greeted by Edith Jeffrey, her long time companion, who showed us into a sitting room and asked us to wait while she went to fetch Rosa. While she was out of the room my Father told us that we were going to meet a famous lady and we were to be on our best behaviour. Of course Johnny and I had no idea how famous Rosa was. When she eventually arrived with Edith we were introduced. She was tall, grey haired and red faced. She spoke to us briefly before going off to the far end of the room with my Father, leaving Johnny and myself with Edith who gave us a coca-cola each and kept us company.

When I grew up, I realised why my Father had taken us to meet Rosa and was very glad he had done so. If ever there was a larger than life character it was Rosa Lewis. Although she was of relatively humble birth and always spoke with a Cockney accent she was a snob *par excellance*. The people who stayed at the Cavendish read like a roll-call of Debretts or Burkes. In Daphne Fielding's biography the author relates how Rosa would overlook the most terrible indiscretions, *if* she liked you. Nor did Rosa hesitate in referring to the great and the mighty in rather disparaging terms like 'Old Shrimp Whiskers' or 'Snivelling Dick' and '. . . knew him before he was born.

Pots of money. They gave him a gold cigarette case when his trousers fell down in Piccadilly,' plus: 'he is a damned old woodcock in tights,' and so on. She also did a lot of cooking for King Edward and at the major Houses of England on gastronomic occasions. On the recommendation of King Edward she was engaged by the Kaiser to cook on his yacht, the *Hohenzollern,* during his cruise to England in 1907. The Kaiser gave her a tip of £100, a brooch and a portrait of himself by Laszlo. She was to die in 1952 aged 85.

We sailed out of the Pool of London, as I recall, on the Union Castle Line ship, the SS *Landovery Castle,* sometime in 1950. We had a most enjoyable voyage out to Capetown playing deck tennis and ping-pong among other things. I was getting too big for my boots at this stage in my life and on two occasions my poor father had to placate the irate parents with whose children I had been a little 'rough'.

The ship stopped at the island of St Helena. Of course we did a tour of the island and also visited Longwood House where the French Emperor Napoleon had been held prisoner until his death.

After landing at Capetown we motored half-way up Africa in the Buick. The car went like a cheetah and we had many a race against what my Father deemed to be cars as fast or even faster than the Buick, mainly Packards and the odd Cadillac. Arriving in Mufindi we first stayed with my Grandmother von Tevenar.

We did not go back to the Kidope Estate because it had now been sold but went to another of my Father's farms which had not been part of the Kidope Estate. It was called Itona - about seven miles from Kidope. The Farm Manager there was a man called Jopps; a most pleasant man. At five thousand feet in altitude, most of the farm was heavily forested and consisted of 2,200 acres. The farm was stiff with leopard, monkeys and forest antelope, just like Kidope. We led an idyllic life of riding, trout fishing, forest walking to spot game, camping in the forest with the farm policeman to guard us, swimming and boating in a lovely lake which my father had engineered on the farm, about 8 acres and surrounded on every side by the primaeval forest.

Visiting the natives in their huts for hours on end, where we were always most hospitably received, we developed a taste for the native beer called Pombe. A youth called Gaga was assigned to be my playmate and Johnny's was called Katoto. We had the most wonderful house staff. In particular there was Lupa, about four foot nine in height, who was the chief house-servant and Mpishi, the cook and Chegele the water carrier. My father's Headman was called Makwaya; a venerable and dignified man who always wore a fez and carried a 'kiboko' which was a rhino-hide whip. Then there was Wazi, the farm Policeman, who had worked for my father for many years. He would prowl around the farm armed with an old 303 but no ammunition, and a kiboko. Every now and then he would turn up at the house with a poacher he had caught and present him to my father in the most military style imaginable. Wazi had been in the army at some stage and liked to practise his military prowess on poachers. On these occasions my father warned the poacher to desist and that if he were caught again he would receive a beating. I think these poachers were outsiders who came into the area from time to time. Wazi did not tolerate strangers poaching on his territory. Wazi was a Muslim and so was Lupa. Curiously Wazi was a Yao, a tribe inhabiting a region of Nyasland, now Malawi, about five hundred miles south of Mufindi.

We were sent off to Mbeya School which was at the extreme southern end of Tanganyika. It was about 80 miles from Itona. Because of the vast distances which the pupils had to travel there were only two terms a year. The School drew pupils from places as far as 500 miles away. As I recall the numbers of boys and girls were about the same. The Headmaster, Mr. Wallington, was a large well covered man with a florid face who operated a strict regime of discipline. Canings were carried out by him on a daily basis and I averaged about four per term. Mr Wallington allowed you to select which cane, out of five, with which to be beaten. Boys received six cuts to their bare bum while girls received only four and were allowed to keep their panties on. Wallington did not play at these beatings. Sometimes he drew blood and the bruising lasted for days. The school ran like clockwork and had a sort of *Beau-Geste* feel about it. Despite this we were all given a lot of leeway and generally speaking were very happy. There was very little bullying at Mbeya because Mr Wallington came down like a ton of bricks on would-be bullies. Aspirant bullies would come out of Mr Wallington's House much chastened and chastised, ruefully rubbing their backsides. Most of us, and that included the girls, became expert tree climbers, insect collectors, feather collectors, and so on. Much trading and bartering went on in these items. Football, Cricket, and Hockey were the main sports at Mbeya. Boxing was the secondary sport. All were fiercely contested

Mbeya School. Tanganyika in 2005

between the Houses and the greatest possible suspense reigned at these matches. The houses were called Livingstone, Burton, and Stanley after the three great explorers of Africa. Johnny was in Livingstone whose colour was yellow and I was in Stanley whose colour was blue. Both Johnny and I always carried fond memories of Mbeya School. When Mr Wallington and his wife left the School they went back to England where Mr Wallington became a vicar in the west of England somewhere. He and his wife made the perfect Headmaster and Mistress. They had a most ravishing daughter called Sarah who was in her late teens. She was a beauty and I regarded her as a Goddess.

From time to time a large group of boys and girls were taken down to the river near the School where we played all the sorts of games which children of that age always used to play. For example we would gather into the group to which we belonged, either Cavalier or Roundhead, and ambush each other. Tiring of this one day, another boy and I wandered off into a bush clad area on the banks of the river some distance upstream. There we found a large and very dead dark blue and yellow snake, four to five foot long and quite thick. Downstream from us four or five girls were sitting on a branch of a large tree which stretched out over the river, dangling their legs in the water. This gave me an idea. I suggested that we put the snake crossways into the river and let it float down and, hopefully, wrap itself round the girls' legs. My friend was keen on this plan so we carefully placed the snake across the current, which was quite swift. Letting go we watched and waited with bated breath as it floated off. Suddenly the whole branch of the tree with the girls on it erupted into a maelstrom of flailing legs, arms, bodies and branches, accompanied by the terrified shrieks of the girls, two of whom fell into the river. My friend and I thought this very funny indeed and laughed like blazes. This proved a big mistake. We were instantly spotted and in no time at all surrounded by a now extremely irate group of girls including the dripping wet two who had fallen into the river. The girls threatened us with the most dire punishment. Oddly, the end result was that the girls reported only me to Mr Wallington, but not my friend; not very fair at all. I was given a severe dressing down by Mr Wallington after which he concluded the matter in his usual manner, six cuts on the bare bum.

My Grandmother Tevenar died on 1st June 1952. I remember looking at the sheets of her bed the next day and being very sad. She had been a wonderful Grandmother to us. Her house staff were always immaculately dressed in white, and always wore red fezes on their heads.

From Scotland, in 1953, news came to us that the Trustees, with the lawyers leading them by the nose, had agreed to the sale of Norton House and its adjacent stables, staff cottages and the like in 1953 for a pittance. A baffling decision which caused my father, reluctantly, to return to Bedrule. With Sir John, his only ally, now dead he realised it was simply too dangerous to leave the Estates at the mercy of Uncle Stuart and the lawyers.

13

RETURN TO BEDRULE

So once again we packed our bags and off we went in the Buick to Mombasa for the long journey back to Scotland.. Just before we left Johnny and I went down with malaria. He got over his quite quickly, but I didn't. To hasten it away I was given a special pill. It sounds inconceivable, but some inner voice told me not to take it. Seeing my reluctance to take it my mother urged me to do so. I therefore did so, but reluctantly. But whatever it was that warning turned out to be correct. That pill was to have a profound effect of a bad nature on me for many years. I believe a number of children who took it died. I didn't die, but got the most terrible jaundice and felt most dreadful. But that did not stop our travelling. I lay in the back of the Buick for the three or four hundred mile trip to Mombasa with overnight stops at Dodoma, Arusha and Voi. Voi was close to the Tsavo game reserve so we spent a day in the Reserve. We watched many elephants at the small lake below Mudanda Rock and other game. Unfortunately we did not see any lion. This was the area in which the book: 'The Man-eaters of Tsavo' was set and where many of the indentured Indian labour had fallen prey to these Tsavo lions. It must have been a nightmare for them, poor people.

At Mombasa we embarked on a very opulent, to us anyway, French ship called the *Marechal Joffre*. It was a most beautiful and comfortable ship. The dining room, as one would expect with the French, was particularly beautiful and the food matched it. I was too weak to even go swimming in the pool for the early part of the voyage. However once through Suez and on the Mediterranean I felt a little better and pestered my parents for a swim. By now the crew had emptied the swimming pool as it was thought to be too cold to swim in those northern climes! Eventually my Father spoke to a ship's officer about refilling the pool. The officer could not have been more obliging and straightaway arranged for it to be filled. By now however a bit of a storm had blown up causing the ship to pitch ever more violently. When the pool was about a quarter full the water merely rushed from one

Myself, Johnny and mother at Itona farm, Tanganyika just prior to our return to Bedrule.

end of the pool to the other. And the storm got worse and worse. By now Johnny and I were having second thoughts about swimming but, with the pool nearing a third full, our parents insisted that we pop in. Pop in we did and what a battle it was to avoid having our brains dashed out against the walls of the pool as a veritable wall of water sped from one end of the pool to the other. The crew thought this a rare spectacle and crowded round laughing! We got out as soon as we properly could, timing our arrival at the pool steps on a rushing wave of water with the precision of a Swiss clock and scampering to safety. We were treated like heroes by the crew!

Eventually we landed safely at Marseille. We went to a wonderful restaurant there and had the Marseille speciality 'Bouillabaise', and how we all enjoyed it. We then 'did' Paris for a few days before travelling to London, where we stayed at Brown's Hotel again. My Father then bought another pre-war Buick V8, 1939 model, and off to Scotland we went in it.

Back in Bedrule we renewed our acquaintances with the people we remembered from our childhood. Norton, Jack Bell, Willie Smith, Auld Ale (old Alice), the Foxes and so on. Sad to say old Purves and his wife had both passed away in our absence.

We were immediately packed off to Prep School at Warriston, Moffat, in Dumfrieshire. Warriston was a quiet sheltered school compared to Mbeya school where the beatings you got from Mr Elbourne were a pale reflection of those dished out by Mr Wallington! Johnny and I were very happy at Warriston. We loved the long walks to the various exciting places and woods around Moffat. One of my most vivid memories of Warriston was the swimming pool at the girls part of Warriston School, Parkside. This pool, even in mid-summer, was bitterly cold. I still had not got over my jaundice and even worse had developed a bad rash which worried me no end.

At Bedrule we took up all our old pastimes of riding, walking and helping out on the farm. Our parents told us that Uncle John and Aunt Jean had died at Norton and that Norton had been sold and was now a Hotel. Also that a new Uncle (Stuart) and Aunt were now living at Hallrule. We had never heard of this Uncle before.

We were then told that their children, Peter and Robert were quite a few years older than us, were not normal and we would be meeting them soon. On the way to Hallrule we were told to be pleasant and to play with Peter and Robert if they felt like playing, although by then Peter was 22 , Robert 19 and I was not yet 12. With some trepidation we arrived at Hallrule where we met Uncle Stuart, Gertie, Peter and Robert. Peter and Robert were of jovial dispositions and jabbered away at us, and would then - for no apparent reason - laugh like blazes. We went along with this and laughed as well. In time as we got to know them better we could understand them a little better. To us Uncle Stuart seemed a cold distant figure. He was tall, thin and bald, like all of our family. Gertrude was a large, amply covered woman. I never took to her from the first time I met her although I can give no specific reason for this. Still, life rolled on.

I used to walk over to Spital Tower to visit my Great Aunt May, Sir Robert's youngest sister. She was invariably in the drawing room sitting in front of a nice cosy fire. She was by then well into her 80s but this did not stop us getting on very well. She always rang for scones and tea with a little brass bell. These scones and jam were the among the most enjoyable I have ever had. I greatly admired two large china lions which had their paws resting on two globes of the world and pointed them out to her. She said that she too had always liked those lions. To me, despite her age, she seemed such a friendly straightforward old Aunt. Also a cheerful one, but in a quiet way. She eventually died in 1955. Thereafter her son the same JGG Leadbetter WS, who was by now expert at blowing up large and beautiful houses, having been instrumental in the destruction of both Wells and Dunglass Houses, leased Spital Tower to a Mr Case who was the headmaster of Blanerne School in Berwickshire. Mr Case then moved the whole School over from Berwickshire into Spital Tower.

Mr Case had the singular distinction of having removed his own appendix with a pen-knife during an attack of appendicitus while on active service in the War. A remarkable feat. Spital Tower remained a School for a few years before closing down in the mid-sixties. Thereafter it was purchased by a Mr Rea who converted it into apartments and it is today known as Towerburn. My parents told me that Aunt May had Spital Tower built in 1912. Her husband was an architect called Thomas Leadbetter, - the same Leadbetter who had been sent off to London and the Continent with Professor Hunter Stewart by Sir John Usher in the late 1890s to study the best institutes for design ideas for the proposed Usher Health Institute in Edinburgh.

At other times I walked over the ruins of Wells House. The Portico at the entrance still stood and on it were displayed the arms of our family. This was eventually knocked down in the late fifties or early sixties. I don't actually know why I kept going to Wells because these visits always left me feeling slightly sad, however something always drew me back there. Possibly I was drawn by the knowledge that this had been the main seat of our family and, as such, I felt a subconcious duty to maintain a contact with it, young though I was, and ruin though it was.

After Warriston we were sent to my father's old School, Uppingham in Rutland, England, which we enjoyed. Johnny made the first Rugby fifteen. I failed to achieve anything of note at Uppingham - mainly because I was still afflicted with the aftermath of the jaundice and often felt weak and dizzy. To make matters worse I also developed bronchitis at this time and suffered badly from it. Regrettably I was rather a disruptive boy and received quite a few beatings as a consequence. However compared to Wallington's beatings these beatings were tame affairs.

As we grew up my parents from time to time told Johnny and I what a tragedy both the destruction of Wells and the sale of Norton had been. I never thought too much about this at the time but later realised that they were sowing seeds in our minds for the future. In that they certainly succeeded. Thereafter I continued to walk over the ruins of Wells with a sad air.

Johnny and I led a pretty carefree life at Bedrule at this time. We helped out at busy times like hay making and harvest time on the farm. We were pretty old fashioned at Bedrule and still made hay by reaping it and stacking it first into kyles and then into hayricks in the fields before carting it to the farmyard by trailers. We still had a few Clydesdale cart horses as well as tractors. We had eight full time farm workers, including two shepherds.

In the winter we helped Jack Bell, who was the Bedrule Groom and Cattleman, to exercise the horses. Sometimes we rode over Bedrule Hill which was about 700 acres and had wonderful gallops there. At other times we did the Estate ride. This was about a five mile ride through the Wells estate. Jack taught us a lot about trees, plants and the like. We hunted with the Buccleuch and Jedforest foxhounds in the Christmas holidays. My horses were Silver and Siam — both greys. At the beginning I had some nasty moments hunting. In particular I recall one day with the Buccleuch in the hills west of Hawick. Silver must have been full of oats that day and delighted in scaring the wits out of me by running away down steep hillsides, of which there were no shortage in that part of the country. He'd break into a gallop and head for what seemed a certain and violent collision with a stone dyke at the bottom of the hill. In the way that horses do he always managed to skid to a stop with his breast against the dyke and me hanging onto his neck or half over his head! It was nerve wracking stuff!

Likewise Johnny's horse, Sheila, once ran away with him after a meet at Bedrule. The only way to stop her was to steer her in the direction of Spital Tower, Aunt May's abode. She fairly tore down the drive towards the house, which was very large, and came to a screeching halt with inches to spare. Johnny was much shaken by this. But at other times we had wonderful runs. I cannot recall ever once falling off hunting, although my horse sometimes came down under me. The most spectacular of these falls was when Major-General Younger of Ravenswood, near Melrose, and I collided at right angles at speed whilst hunting with the Buccleuch! Both our horses went down. Mercifully he got up intact. He gave me a frosty look and I apologised and told him that he seemed to come from nowhere. He took it pretty well and after making sure that he was alright we both remounted and off we went again. I never could understand how that happened because in hunting people are usually headed in the same direction.

Uncle Stuart also invited us to shoots on Wells. I was keen on shooting but Johnny never took to it. At that time the shooting on Wells was excellent but after myximatosis was introduced into Britain in the mid fifties the shooting went rapidly downhill as foxes were forced to prey more on pheasants and partridges rather than rabbits. Of course I also shot on Bedrule itself, walking up with our sausage dog called Fupi (Swahili for 'short') who was very adept at putting up pheasants. I was quite happy if I got two birds and never shot more than that in this form of shooting. Basically shooting for the pot. There was also a grouse moor on the Estate where we shot every year.

However my favourite sport by a long way was fishing. The Wells Estate game-keeper, Glover, taught me fishing on the Estate private water on Rulewater. Glover was a keen fisherman himself. He had a daughter called Morag who married a man called Reg Mouland. On the strength of this my Father gave Reg Mouland a job as a tractorman at Bedrule where he worked for many years. Morag and he had two daughters called Sally and Molly who were a few years younger than me and grew up at Bedrule. I still see them from time to time today which is a nice link to the past.

Above Left: Sir Stuart Usher, 4th Bart Of Norton And Wells, after life's disappointments had taken their toll. Above right: Sir Stuart as a young officer in the Inniskilling Dragoons. Below Left: Sir Stuart's sons, Pete (standing) and Robert, Both Down's Syndrome and Mentally Incapacitated. Below right: Peter when younger.

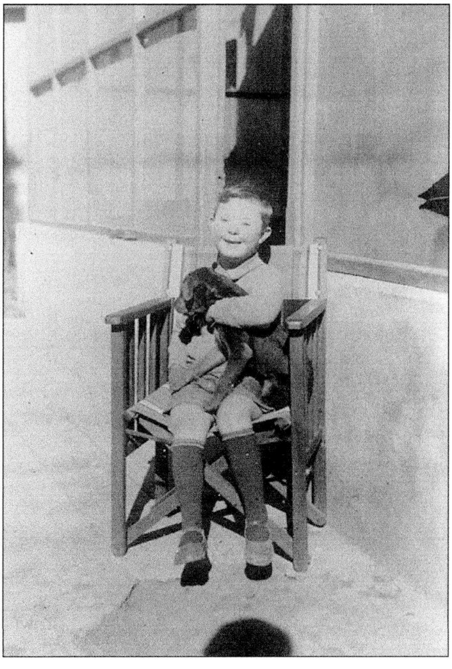

From time to time my Father took a beat on one of the local salmon rivers like the Tweed or the Border Esk. He and I then shared the day's fishing between us. The biggest salmon I caught was a twenty-two and a half pounder on the Tweed on the Hendersyde beat. I caught my first salmon on the Lennel Beat, just below Coldstream. In the summer I spent what I now regard as the happiest days of my life on the Wells Estate private waters, on Rulewater, trout fishing. The fishing was marvellous. Even on bad fishing days, such as low water and still, thundery conditions I seldom came home empty handed. Again I never took more than what I was told was a fair bag; seven, mainly trout and the odd grayling. They averaged about half a pound with the odd one pounder every now and then. Trout fishing in those surroundings was just idyllic, the scents of the air, the pastoral quiet with only the gurgle of the river and the rustling of leaves on the trees to break the almost heavenly silence. I seemed to become one with nature, the river, the trees, the very earth itself on those halcyon days; until I got my fly caught in a high branch of a tree, that is. That always pulled me back to the grim realities of life!

On Sundays it was *de rigeur* that we went to Church at Church. Uncle Stuart, Gertie and 'the boys', Peter and Robert, as they were always known although they were now grown up, often attended Church as well. The Leadbetters of Spital Tower and Knowesouth were also regular churchgoers. After Church everyone joined us for drinks at Bedrule before returning to their respective abodes.

The social side of things consisted of lots of private dances, Balls and Huntballs in the winter and cocktail parties in the summer. Without fail we would go to Peter and Robert's birthday parties at Hallrule which were made great affairs for their sakes as they were both very jolly and looked forward to them for weeks. The same went for Christmas when the whole family gathered at Hallrule for dinner. After dinner Peter always made a speech. He did his best but ninety percent of what he said was incomprehensible. Uncle Stuart always had to stop Peter's speeches otherwise he would have gone on and on and on. But we all gave him a good clap at the end of it. After dinner we would play charades in the drawing room. My Mother and Johnny were particularly good at this.

In 1956 another uncle called Clive retired from the Army and took up residence in one of the cottages in the Wells stables with his wife, Valerie, and daughter, Margaret. In addition to being given residency he was also given the tenancy of Dykes farm on the Estate. He was the youngest of Sir Robert's six sons.

At that time I thought Uncle Clive quite exciting. He had done very well in the War, was a Brigadier and had won the DSO and Bar and MC. I was now old enough to feel proud of family achievements from the wider filial point of view. We had met Clive on a few occasions in the past when he had stayed with us at Bedrule, but never his wife, Valerie, whom he never brought with him. His daughter Margaret also stayed with us at Bedrule for some time when Clive was posted to India with the Army in the 50s so as not to interfere with her schooling.

Before meeting Valerie my Father told us that she was half Red Indian but we were to pretend that we didn't notice and, above all, to say nothing about it. The only Indians Johnny and I had ever come across in our lives had been the Indian shopkeepers in Tanganyika. Europeans and Indians hardly ever mixed socially in those days anywhere in Africa. So we followed his instructions to the tee.

Valerie was an attractive, slightly-built, slim woman with jet black hair and small dark eyes, as one would expect. I loved her North American accent because at the time I was much taken with all things American. I was also a great admirer of Buffalo Bill and the Pony Express. For some reason I also had a soft spot for the Sioux Indians.

However marrying across what was called 'the colour line' was frowned upon in those days and both Clive and Valerie suffered the consequences. Some years later my Father told us that Clive had held a cocktail party soon after settling into the cottage at Wells Stables in 1956 on his retirement from the Army. His purpose in doing so was to launch himself and his wife Valerie and daughter Margaret into 'Society'. Of course my parents attended and soon the usual cocktails loosened many tongues in the way alcohol always does. Suddenly one of the local, less discreet, worthies piped up in a loud voice; 'Who is the squaw?', pointing to a framed photograph of a Native American woman on an occasional table. The animated conversation quickly dried up and everyone waited for an answer. None was forthcoming. Conversation soon started again and shortly thereafter my Father glanced at the table again to have another look at the photograph. It was no longer there! Some swift and unseen hand, almost certainly Clive's, had removed it to stop any further comment.

Yet life at Bedrule in the fifties was very pleasant and all seemed well - on the surface. But underneath it there was an underlying tension of which Johnny and I slowly became aware. As we grew up we became more and more aware that the cause of the tension emanated from Uncle Stuart and Clive. However our parents shielded Johnny and I as any decent parents would. So life for us was generally carefree and happy.

At this time our old cousin Mary, Great Aunt May's elder daughter, used to visit us a lot at Bedrule. She never married but was a very pleasant person, if somewhat strait-laced. She had a lot to do with the Bedrule Women's Guild and was always dropping in at Bedrule with baskets of flowers, cakes and biscuits and became great friends with my Mother.

14

THE COVERT ATTACK COMMENCES

In 1954 Uncle Stuart and the Usher Baronetcy Trustees, McLure and Leadbetter, sold a farm called Fodderlie on the Wells Estate to an Englishman called Edward Bird. This farm bordered Bedrule. They effected this sale without informing my Father. Of course my Father soon heard about it from local people and was absolutely furious as he would have bid for it in an attempt to keep it in the family — not to mention that his acquiring it would have enlarged his farming operation to well over 2,300 acres because Fodderlie bordered Bedrule. If he'd had any hopes that Uncle Stuart was getting over his bitterness and jealousy they would have been dashed at this point. Stuart's one aim in life now appeared to be to get 'revenge' on my Father and the world in general for his own failures in life, being bankrupted twice, and fathering two Downs Syndrome and Mentally Incapacitated sons. Because of this Stuart posed, and would continue to pose, a deadly danger to the future of our whole family until he realised that this way of getting revenge was a betrayal of *his own* Father and would simply compound his own feelings of failure and never cure his bitterness at life.

The same thing happened two years later in 1956 with the sale of a most attractive small-holding called Hallrule Mill to its tenant, William Donald. Again without informing my Father who would have tried to purchase that as well. Again my Father was furious. None of these sales were necessary because there were still ample cash funds in the Trust. Of course the Estate continued to be most dreadfully mismanaged throughout the 50s.

In 1959 my Father suddenly informed us that Uncle Stuart had given Clive the whole Wells Stables block, which included two cottages, the site of the ruin of Wells House, the informal gardens, the formal garden and the Head Gardner's cottage, and the surrounding parkland of about 50 acres. He was absolutely furious about it. He now at last told us more about the family Trust and that its main purpose was to stop our family Estates of Wells and Norton from passing out of our family.

My mother also entered the fray and said that she knew the day that Clive arrived back in Rulewater it would go ill for the whole Usher family because

A peaceful area around Bedrule.

Clive had a 'chip on his shoulder'. My Father then went on to explain that Uncle Stuart giving all this property to Clive had broken the Usher Baronetcy Trust. With Clive having only one daughter all these properties were now set to pass out of our family unless something was done about it or Clive, on his death, left them to my Father or to Johnny. Father then recounted all the damage that had already been done since the death of Lady Usher and Uncle Ronald. Wells House blown up, the dam creating the beautiful lake near Wells blown up, Norton House sold for next to nothing, Dunglass House blown up and various farms and small holdings already sold.

This made both Johnny and myself uneasy. By now, as teenagers, we realised - and although our parents had never actually told us - that we were the only route to the future for our family. Seeing the main seat of our family, ruin though it was, going to Clive, of all people, and in those deceitful circumstances, appalled us.

It took Johnny and I many years to realise why Stuart behaved in this anti-social manner towards my Father. The main motivation appeared to be plain old-fashioned jealousy arising from his fathering two Downs Syndrome sons. Also his going bankrupt twice did not help. And finally it had become apparent to everyone that his wife, Gertrude, was not *comme-il-faut*; a large, lumbering, uncouth, uneducated woman. However Stuart was not the only one who had been taken over by the green-eyed monster.

Clive also suffered from the same disease. In his case it arose from his being short in stature and weedy, quite unlike his five brothers who were all six footers. It also arose from his not being accepted in Society because of his wife being half Red Indian. Marriage across the colour line was simply not accepted in those far off days. In contrast to both Clive and Stuart my Father was very popular with all grades of society. This, combined with his cross line marriage and being a weed, appears to have driven Clive in particular into a great jealousy of my Father.

Clive however had another compelling reason, in his eyes, to have a down on my Father and the world in general of which none of us were aware at the time. I shall record this later on in the book when I discovered it because I am trying to write this book chronologically.

I also think that both Stuart and Clive resented my Father being given Bedrule shortly after Uncle Sandy's death in 1940 while they got nothing. This had been effected at the instance of old Lady Usher and must have therefore have been agreed by Uncle John, Uncle Ronald and the lawyers. I presume their giving Bedrule to my Father in preference to Stuart, his elder brother, was based on Stuart's having gone bust and because Stuart had never brought his family home to meet his Mother and the rest of the family. This was the price of 'lying low and awaiting development'. Clive had no basis whatever for being jealous on account of my Father being given Bedrule because 1) he was outranked by my Father and 2) he had no issue to carry on the Usher ownership of Bedrule and the Wells, Norton and Pitheavlis Estates.. He had never even been in the frame, as Uncle Stuart had been.

By this time I had already gone off Clive a bit because, dimwit though I still was in many ways, I had noticed that he was always trying to be the 'Big Man' to get attention.. I no longer respected him in the way that I still respected Uncle Stuart. Stuart never tried to act the 'Big Man' at all. He did at least have something to be bitter about; Peter and Robert, but that was not his fault. Young people can be quite good at spotting 'Who is Who in the Zoo'.

It was about this time that my Father told me that Uncle Stuart had caught syphilis in Egypt. Curious how Egypt kept cropping up almost as a curse to our family just about every time one of our family visited that country. Like Anthony Eden at that time I did not at all like the Egyptian leader, Nasser, so Egypt was not my favourite country.

'God almighty,' I thought, 'Uncle Stuart seemed to have staggered from one disaster to the next ever since he left Sandhurst. He would have been ten times better off had he had stayed in the Army.' Of course the syphilis was just another reason for him to be bitter at life.

In 1960 my Father told us that Uncle Stuart had suddenly become more amenable and friendly towards him and had told him that nothing further would be sold without letting him know in advance. Possibly Stuart's need for revenge had finally been satiated by his giving Clive the Wells properties. Another possible reason was that he might have finally realised that he had let his Father and his extended family down very badly indeed all his life and now wanted to make amends. Possibly a combination of both.

Symptomatic of Uncle Stuart's improved attitude was in 1961 my Father told me that Uncle Stuart wanted me to go to the lawyers' offices Edinburgh with him to sign a document in connection with the cottages at Hallrule farm. So off I went to Edinburgh with Uncle Stuart in his Rover car. This Rover was a very slow and unexciting car compared to my Father's new light blue 5.8 litre Buick. However I made no comment on the car for obvious reasons. He was very pleasant and more forthcoming than he had ever been in the past. I signed the document in front of him and TG Dempster the lawyer without reading it. However Dempster (the yet to be discovered deathbed thief) did not tell me what the document was about other than that it was in connection with the Hallrule cottages and nor did he give me a copy of it. However I trusted Dempster at the time and assumed that my signing them had something to do with my becoming the tenant of Hallrule farm at some future date about which my Father had already told me. Uncle Stuart and I then had a most pleasant lunch at the Conservative Club in Princes Street.

Many years later, when the mango was really hitting the fan, I realised the significance of my signing that document. It indicated that Uncle Stuart wanted to leave a written record that I, and no one else, should succeed him in the Tenancy if I wanted to. In doing this he must have obtained the assent of the other lawyer Trustees. When I asked Brodies for a copy of that document in the late 1990s they denied all knowledge of my ever having signed any document in connection with the Hallrule cottages and informed me that they did not have such a document. Of course I then really kicked myself that I had never obtained a copy of it. But at the time I signed the document it never remotely occurred to me that I should ask for a copy because I trusted both Uncle Stuart and Dempster

Also symptomatic of Stuart's change of mind was that he, Gertie and my parents and Johnny and myself with our respective partners went to the Buccleuch Huntball together in the autumn of 1961. I do not recall Stuart dancing with Gertie at all. She had absolutely no idea of Scottish reels, foxtrots and the like so he kept her firmly in her seat! And Clive and Valerie? They did not come. They *would* have been invited. At the time I attached no significance to their absence but many years later, as I discovered more and more, I realised that their absence was significant.

So, why had they not come? There were a number of reasons: Firstly that Uncle Stuart and Clive might have fallen out over Stuart's securing the Estates for an Usher posterity. Secondly that Clive feared being unfairly embarrassed again regarding his wife as he had been at his abortive Cocktail party in 1956 and, Thirdly, that he might be publicly humiliated over a dark secret from his days in the Army which Johnny discovered only in 1982.

In the mid sixties my Father told me that Clive was a Socialist. This came as a great shock to me as I had always regarded all of our family as staunch Tories. However Clive hid his Socialism and, to outsiders, appeared to be a Tory and, indeed, was active for the Tories at election times.

Throughout these years everyone in the area assumed that when Uncle Stuart died the Estates would devolve onto either my Father or Johnny as it would be impossible for them to devolve onto Peter and Robert because of their Down's Syndrome. Sometimes our Bedrule workers and Estate workers told me that they knew that Johnny would inherit the Estates one day because it would be impossible for them to be inherited by Peter and Robert because of their Downs Syndrome. I went along with this as a 'no brainer.'

I left Uppingham in 1959 at the age of 18. I was then sent to Canada and worked for a distant Usher connection in Alberta. This was the first time that I had been out into the big wide world on my own. This connection, also called WD Usher (like my Father) owned a surveying company and the work I did for the company entailed going out with a small group of surveyors as one of the bush-cutters, holding the surveying pole and taping out great distances and digging holes. This trip opened my eyes a little on what a hard place the world could be.

On my return Johnny and I were sent to the Royal Agricultural College at Cirencester to study Estate Management. Johnny lasted a year before being turfed out - he was too much of a party man! I was then sent to the RAC and, regrettably, met the same fate. One of the main reasons for this was that I saw no need to spend years on studying how to manage an estate or estates. I felt that commonsense was all that was needed.

Of course my Father was absolutely livid with both Johnny and myself for being turfed out of the Royal Agricultural College. It might have been a different story if our parents had impressed the importance of qualifications onto us at the time, but they never did. If I had known that qualifications would come to be regarded as much more important than commonsense of course I would have applied myself.

15

DOOMSDAY

By now Johnny had matured into an extremely good looking young man. A girl of our age told me Johnny was one of the best looking young men in Scotland. In addition he had a presence about him and our peers sought his company and regarded him as a sort of model to be emulated. He was polished, fit and healthy, and deported himself well. He always presented a very well-groomed appearance and took great care in his dress. In addition he was pretty competent all round and had plenty of commonsense. With all these attributes our family were very fortunate in having him as the heir. In fact as far as heirs go he was in the very top bracket. All too often, and very regrettably, heirs tend to be spoilt, stupid and pig-headed. By looks, temperament, habit and conduct he far outshone both Uncle John and Uncle Stuart. He also far outshone me.

I was not one hundred percent well. My illness manifested itself in shortness of breath, a constant feeling of tiredness which wrestled with a determination to achieve. Deep down I suspected this was related to the malaria which I'd contracted years earlier. Nevertheless I had a high opinion of myself and on the rare occasions when I suddenly did feel well I felt I could conquer the world.

There was nothing I liked better than to don my, rather tatty, jerkin and tramp around Bedrule and the Estate in all weathers. Wind, rain or snow never deterred me. I found such weather made me feel closer to nature with the roaring of the wind through the trees or on the heather and bracken out on the hills. These activities left me with an abiding love and affinity for Hill, Glen, Burn and River. Despite this, perhaps, eccentric activity I was nevertheless regarded as 'clever', mainly because I was a voracious hunter and absorber of knowledge. My parents, though regarding me as a bit peculiar, realised I had the potential to 'get somewhere in life,' if only I could channel my talents in the right direction.

Johnny married Rosemary Houldsworth, the younger daughter of Colonel Sir Reginald Houldsworth Bt, of Kirkbride, Ayrshire, in 1962. The wedding was a great affair in Ayrshire. Uncle Stuart came over for it but without Gertie. This was another indication that he had 'come right' and was now reconciled to the fact that we were the only route to the future for our family

Johnny's wedding

although at the time, again, I did not fully realise this. I now believe Johnny *did* realise its import. And Clive and Val? Not a sign of them.

Further disaster struck our family in November 1962. Uncle Stuart dropped off his horse and died while hunting with the Buccleuch foxhounds near Hawick. He was only sixty-four years old. His death was obviously regrettable in itself but we and everyone else outside our family did not expect the terrible news that soon followed. The news was that his Will could not be found. 'They hunted high and low all over Hallrule for his Will but could not find it,' my Father told us. This therefore meant that Stuart had died Intestate. A few days later the lawyers told my Father that because Stuart had died Intestate the Usher Baronetcy Trust had come to an end and that meant that the the Downs Syndrome and Mentally Incapacitated Peter had personally inherited the Wells and Norton Estates and all the other assets in the Usher Baronetcy Trust.

The inconceivable had come to pass. We were all utterly horrified and my Father was in tears about it. He had given his word to his Mother that he would never allow this to happen and now, only fourteen years after her death, it had indeed come to pass.

The lawyers then informed him that because Peter was now the new sole owner of all the assets in the Usher Baronetcy Trust, and was Mentally Incapacitated a *Curator-Bonis* would have to be appointed to manage his affairs and that they had just the man for that job: Thomas Dempster. Dempster had been the man who had done most of the legal donkey work for the Usher Baronetcy Trust. On top of that he was the personal law agent of both Uncle Stuart and Clive and, crucially, my Father as well. A few years later Frank Usher of Dunglass, my second cousin, told me that Dempster had robbed his Father, Francis Usher of Dunglass, of £1,000 on his deathbed and how furious he, Frank, had been about it and that he had never forgiven Dempster.

The lawyers further informed my Father that if Peter, now Sir Peter, survived his mother Gertrude, which was unlikely, he would be incapable of making a Will so he too would die Intestate and all the Usher Baronetcy Trust assets would then have to pass to Robert, if Robert survived him. Robert would likewise be incapable of making a Will and for this reason what remained of the Usher Baronetcy Trust assets on his death would have to be liquidated and the proceeds divided up between an indeterminate number of ultimate beneficiaries only two of whom would bear the name Usher, namely Johnny and myself, if we survived my father as well as Peter and Robert. In this scenario there would be two sets of Death Duties to be paid; one on Peter's death and another on Robert's death. At that time Death Duties stood at 60% of the total value of the Estate of a deceased person. Worse was to follow.

In the event of Gertrude outliving Peter and Robert, the Estates would have to be liquidated and the proceeds, after Death Duties at 60% had been paid, would have to be shared equally between the ultimate beneficiaries of the Usher family *and* Gertrude's Sampson family in Argentina. The odds at the time were that Gertrude would outlive Peter and Robert because people with Downs Syndrome at that time were not, generally speaking, expected to reach their half century.

You can imagine the dreadful impact this had on us all at Bedrule. It threw me into a rage and much the same went for my parents and Johnny. My whole being revolted against the Estates passing out of our family in the relatively near future. The greatest revulsion was the possibility of having to share what little remained of the Estates with the Sampsons. Deep down I harboured suspicions about Uncle Stuart's Will being 'unfindable' but never said a word about it and in fact, at the time, shied away from entertaining such 'awful' thoughts.

This was the worst possible scenario for our family, Usher of Norton and Wells and guaranteed our ruination in the coming decades unless we, the Ushers of Bedrule and the only route to the future for our family since 1948 managed to do something about it. This was the very thing that old Sir Robert Usher had done his best to prevent by establishing his Trust in 1911 and placing the Estates in them.

On hearing this Doomsday scenario my Father had a heart attack and was hospitalised. This was the first of a series of heart attacks in the ensuing months. My Mother was devastated and so were Johnny and I. The lawyers were to blame for all this as the one thing that any honest lawyer does for his client is to make sure he makes a Will. All this for me was a very steep learning curve.

Recovering from his first heart attack my Father determined to get another set of lawyers onto finding if there was any way in which the Estates could be saved for an Usher posterity. To this end he appointed a Jedburgh lawyer called Robert Anderson WS. Anderson's brief was to find a way in which the wishes of old Sir Robert Usher, as per his 1911 Trust, could be carried out.

Anderson soon reported back to my Father: The Estates could be saved in only one way: Peter would have to make a Will in which he left all the Usher Baronetcy Trust assets to my Father or, failing him, Johnny. However before this could be done Peter would have to be certified mentally incapacitated. A Will on the fore-going basis would then be presented and explained to Peter in the presence of a psychiatrist who would have to be satisfied that Peter understood and agreed the contents of the Will. But before this could be done permission would have to be sought from Gertrude.

Father immediately put the plan into action. First of all he approached Gertrude for her co-operation. She appeared amenable and seemed to understand that unless this was done our family would be ruined. He then approached the other Trustees, Logan McLure and JGG Leadbetter. They were also amenable. He then approached Clive, probably thinking he was bound to agree because he had already got the go ahead from the Trustees and Gertie. To his horror Clive refused to agree to this plan. The lawyers then advised the plan could not go ahead because Clive was against it.

This, I much later realised, was absolute nonsense, though I don't think my father realised it at the time. Clive was not yet a Trustee of the Usher Baronetcy Trust and therefore he had no locus on the matter. I therefore suspected that the Trustees, McLure and Leadbetter, and possibly Gertie, had simply feigned their agreement to my Father but were in fact against the plan. My Father was misled into believing that because Clive was against the plan it could not be implemented: this was the easiest way out for Logan McLure and JGG Leadbetter because they would not have to show their hand by voting against the plan in a formal vote.

Clive's refusal and the lawyers malafide advice therefore meant that the Estates would have to continue along the road on which they were now already set and pass out of our family as described above, unless there was some radical change of mind on the part of those who could now best be described as the enemies of our family of Usher of Norton and Wells.

My Father decided to let things be in the meantime because he felt that Clive would soon do the honourable thing by respecting old Sir Robert's wishes and thereby save the Estates for an Usher posterity. However Clive opposing him yet again was a bitter disappointment. My father became depressed again and had another heart attack. Obviously we all now regarded Clive as an even greater and deadlier threat to our family than Stuart had ever been. We knew what motivated him but had never thought that he would take matters this far. He appeared to be quite happy to betray the present and previous generations of our - and *his* - family and the principles it stood for. That included betraying his parents. For what? A bit of transient 'revenge'? Or the yet to be discovered dark secret from his Army days. At the time it seemed inconceivable.

In 1963, Clive asked my Father for his permission - as a Trustee - if he could take over the lease of Hallrule farm from Stuart. In view of Clive's past record of objections to every effort of my Father to save the Estates and his having been the sole beneficiary, of all the six brothers and their issue, of the Trust being broken in 1959, my Father refused. However Clive pleaded and pleaded with him and my Father eventually relented but on the express condition that he vacate the farm after ten years in my favour. Clive agreed to this. They shook hands on this, sealing the bond of a Gentleman's Agreement. This was the sequel to my signing the documents in connection with the Hallrule cottages in 1961 with Uncle Stuart. Another probable reason for my Father relenting was that he might have, in exchange, got an assurance from Clive that he (Clive) would henceforth carry out his filial duty to save the Estates for an Usher posterity. If so, this might have entailed getting the Trustees to agree that the Estates be conveyed to Johnny from Peter at some future date, most probably on my Father's death, or arranging for a Will to be made for Peter, as already narrated or possibly in some other way. If he did in fact get this assurance from Clive he never mentioned it to us.

A few days after my Father had made the Gentleman's Agreement with Clive, Johnny suggested to my Father that it would be wise to have it in writing to make it absolutely water-tight. Johnny was always quite careful like that. My Father was quite annoyed by this suggestion and told Johnny, with some asperity: 'It would be a sad day if I could not trust my own brother to honour a Gentleman's Agreement.'

The only trouble with Gentlemen's Agreements is that they only work if both Parties to them are gentlemen. By now my Father should have known better. Much later, yet again, I realised that this episode demonstrated how completely Clive, Gertrude and the lawyers had led my Father up the garden path.

During the years 1963 to 1965, with all his heart attacks and all the drama caused by Uncle Stuart's death my Father was finding it impossible to run Bedrule properly. To get the ship back on course it was decided that Johnny give up his Farm Manager job at Kirkbride in Ayrshire and come and manage Bedrule. This he did. In a matter of three years and on a shoestring budget he turned the farm around completely and by 1968 it turned in a healthy profit of £14,000 - the equivalent of about £200,000 in today's money. My Father was now a shadow of his former self - a sick and unhappy man.

By necessity a great deal of timber was starting to be cut on the Estate and father could not bear to see this. Thereafter he avoided taking the Wells road out of Rulewater and used the back road out of Bedrule instead.

On two occasions in 1964 and 1965 or thereabouts he came into the house weeping. Of course I made myself scarce but later asked my Mother what had happened. She told me that he had been trying to get Uncle Clive to co-operate with him in making a plan to save our Estates for an Usher posterity. On both occasions Clive had refused to even discuss the matter. With hindsight again this was the probable sequel of my Father's wishful thinking in relenting to let Clive have the tenancy of Hallrule farm for ten years as already narrated. It appeared now that Clive had been officially made the tenant of Hallrule farm he felt it safe to break whatever v l erbal assurances he had made to get the tenancy. So Johnny had been vindicated about getting the 'Gentleman's Agreement' signed after all.

In 1967 - I was 26 years of age - I popped into Hallrule in the evenings from time to time to sound Gertrude out as to the future of the Estates. The first time I brought the subject up she steered the conversation away from it. On one occasion we got onto the subject of the dynamiting of Wells and the sale of furniture from it. She had been furious that so much furniture had been sold from Wells. I eventually plucked up enough courage to tell her that the Estates passing out of our family in the not too distant future seemed a very heavy price to pay merely because Uncle Stuart had not made a Will. That flushed her out alright! Visibly annoyed she made no comment on my statement other than to say: 'The Estates are nothing to do with you and I will not discuss them with you,' looking daggers at me.

Not wanting a dust-up with her at that stage I got out of it as best I could. When I told my Father about this he told me not to go to Hallrule any more. I never did and had no desire to either, but began to realize more and more, that the future of the Estates lay wholly in the hands of people who stood to gain the most from their break up. This upset and worried me most terribly.

One day I climbed our hill called Blacklaw which lay wholly on Bedrule to clear my head. From the top of Blacklaw I had a magnificent view of most of the Estate and that great Border landmark, Ruberslaw, directly opposite me. I had done this often before, but this time it was to be utterly different. As I stood there on the summit of Blacklaw thinking of all this passing out of our family, as it was now destined to do, my emotions suddenly welled up from deep inside and the tears sprang to my eyes. 'Never, ever as long as I live will I let all this pass out of our family,' I solemnly swore. When I finished and recovered myself I realized, for the first time in my life, that I now had at least one firm goal in life - one which I would never abandon. This seemed to electrify me in some way. As I ran across Blacklaw towards Fulton well over a mile away I felt the strength of ten men flowing through my body. It was truly awe-inspiring. In many ways that was the best day of my life.

At this time of my life one of our employees told me that the local people regarded me as 'the Tramp of Rulewater' (after the Rule river which ran through the Estate) when talking about me. They did so because of my constant walking around Bedrule and the Estate in rotten weather in shabby clothes. I did this for three main reasons: firstly because I thought this would toughen me up and conquer my various afflictions; secondly it made me feel closer to nature and the raw elements; and thirdly this was the best way of controlling the constant worries I had about the Wells Estate passing out of our family and the terrible effect that this was having on my parents.

In 1968 we discovered that under some new laws which the Wilson government had passed there would be huge death duties to pay on Bedrule if my Father died in Britain. My parents and Johnny had long discussions on what should be done. I was not included in these discussions partly to shield me and partly because they thought I was not mature enough. When the discussions were over, Johnny told me what they had decided: My parents and he were simply not prepared to accept this new development on top of the Estates being set to pass out of our family without doing something about it. Their solution was that we should sell Bedrule and go to South Africa, where death duties were much lower. This would give Johnny and me a much better chance of making our fortunes. When we had made our fortunes we would purchase back firstly Bedrule, and then what remained of the Wells Estate when the dread day came for for it to be sold. What did I think of the plan?

I immediately gave him the go-ahead because I thought this offered the best chance of keeping the Estates in our family. I also grieved for the unhappy state my Father was in and hoped he would regain his old elan when he was away from all the misery he had been through with this ghastly business. We would not be beholden to Clive, Gertie, the lawyers and the other parasites anymore.

Bedrule was therefore put on the market and sold lock stock and barrel in very quick order in about May 1968. The Dunion Quarry soon followed being sold to the firm which leased it and had a large infrastructure there. Also Bedrule Manse in which Johnny and his family lived. Our selling Bedrule came as a great surprise to people in the locality, not least to Clive and Gertie, so confident were they that they had us over a barrel through the intestacy of Uncle Stuart and the Down's Syndrome and Mental Incapacity of Peter and Robert. They expected us to simply roll over and let our beautiful Estates just slip away out of our family for the benefit of their own personal families without a fight. No chance as far as we were concerned!

Shortly before leaving for South Africa I went to Hallrule to say good-bye to Peter and Robert; also Gertie, but in her case it would not be good-bye, but good riddance. In the drawing room at Hallrule she told me how sad it was that my father had sold Bedrule and gone abroad at this late stage in his life. I agreed that it was indeed sad but that I would be back in 5 years time to take over the tenancy of Hallrule farm and would live half the year at Hallrule farm, very close to Hallrule House, and the other half in South Africa where I would make my fortune. She just looked at me for a short while, tossed her head, and then said: 'You will never come back.' Just like that. Dictating has always annoyed me, and the more so this time coming from her, of all people. I therefore flatly contradicted her by saying that there was nothing more certain than my return and in addition to taking over Hallrule Farm I told her that we would also get Bedrule back in the family as well, by hook or by crook. She just stood there shaking her head, looking uncomfortable. I also felt like ramming it down her throat that we would also get the whole Wells Estate back in the family as well when the dread day came for it to be sold. However I held back on that as I felt it that would be counter-productive. Having got the message over to her good and solid I bade her farewell without further ado and made for Peter and Robert in their own room to bid my genuine farewells to them.

Gertie however must have felt sufficiently exercised by my statements to call me back. She then had the temerity to tell me that the blame for the Downs Syndrome of Peter and Robert lay with the Usher family, not her family. This was too much for me: I told her, icily, that she had neither the basis or the right to make such a statement and pointed out to her that Downs Syndrome was unknown in our family. She then told me that it was unknown in her family too - so where had it come from? I responded to that by saying: 'Then it is a mystery and is just one of those things which, unfortunately, happen from time to time and for which there is no ready explanation.' She did not like this at all and just stood there, shaking her head again. I was now so annoyed that I just said 'Good-bye' and left the room without further ado.

Peter and Robert were their usual jovial selves as I told them, purposely in Gertie's hearing, because she was now hobbling after me, that Johnny and I would be back at Bedrule in five years time and we would be seeing them again. They both nodded in agreement and appeared happy about that. Gertie just stood there, trying to look normal, but looking anything but. Throughout this I was mindful of my Father's instructions that I must not have an open breach with her as he still harboured hopes that she and Clive would have a change of heart and do the honourable thing.

Before bidding Gertie Good Riddance, as above, I told Clive that I would be back in five years time and expected that it would take Johnny and myself between ten and fifteen years to amass enough money to buy back both Bedrule and the Estates. He just nodded, looked vaguely uneasy, and got off the subject as quickly as possible. At the time I was disappointed in his reaction. I should have been forewarned.

16

BACK TO AFRICA

My parents flew to South Africa in the summer of 1968. Johnny and his family went by ship. By now he and his wife Rosemary had three children: Andrew, Caroline and Michael.

In September I flew out to join my parents in Durban. Johnny bought a farm of 600 acres in the Natal Midlands. My parents bought a nice place on the outskirts of Pietermaritzburg. I went on a long tour around South Africa and Rhodesia as it then was. I decided that I preferred Rhodesia and took a job as a Farm Manager near Glendale, about 40 miles northeast of Salisbury.

In 1969, just before I took up this post, my Father died. He had perked up a bit in Durban but was then diagnosed with cancer of the prostate. He was put on heavy medication and told that it would have to be operated on. Two days before the operation he suddenly had a heart attack just after he had retired for the night. He died in my arms. His last words to me were that I was to fight for the Estates as hard as I could as his Father would want that. I swore that I would. I was mortified and swore a terrible vengeance on those who had caused him such dreadful unhappiness for the last seven years of his life. My poor Mother was likewise distraught and for the first time in my life I saw her weeping.

He had been a good Father in many ways, but in some ways not so good. I think the trouble was that he had caught the tail end of the Victorian era. As such he could not express himself in a warm manner towards his children. He could be warm alright, when playing tennis or deck coits at Bedrule. But when it came to more serious things like giving us advice on life he was rather distant. This is something that all children need; even if they do not agree, or welcome it, at the time. I certainly needed such advice and his encouraging me to conduct myself in a better manner than I did at the time would have been a great help to me. Just then I was not aware of this but much later in life became so.

Prior to he and my mother leaving for South Africa in 1968 he came into my bedroom at Bedrule as I was about to turn in for the night and sat down on the bed; something he had never done before. He said: 'I could have been a better Father to you and could have done much better in my life. I drank too much and I am sorry for that.' I told him not to worry about it but thanked him for apologising despite not really understanding why he had apologised. But I could not bear to see him so unhappy in the last years of his life and now wish like blazes that I had been a better son to him and given him the support he so desperately needed, but never asked for. But I never did; to my now eternal regret.

He was what was known as a 'Gentleman Farmer' in those days. Gentleman farmers never actually worked on their farms as this was not done in those days. This resulted in their being rather impractical. On top of that my Father was no good at bookwork and the like. I think he despised that type of thing, as indeed I did myself. All in all he spent too much time socialising and had too much of a fondness for drink - mainly whisky and always Usher's Old Vatted Glenlivet.

But he was deadly honest in all his dealings. He was also a generous man who would always help someone in trouble if he could. He loved salmon and trout fishing and following, by car, the Buccleuch Fox hounds in the winter. He shot only occasionally and eventually gave it up because he came to regard it as cruel. He was also extremely distinguished looking and deported himself very well. One lady told me that he had the most exquisite and elegant hands she had ever seen. So, my fellow man, if you have half decent hands and are having difficulty in attracting the ladies, look to your hands to do the job. Just flash them before a pretty lady and watch her swoon! He was also very popular with people of all walks of life. The same 'hand' lady also told me that one of the reasons for his popularity was that he never betrayed a confidence.

To this day I grieve for him. Unlikely though it may seem I felt his presence for about ten years after his death. In my dreams I would suddenly come across him in the garden and we would chat briefly. It seems too incredible but I firmly believe that he 'hung around' my mother and myself for years before finally disappearing altogether.

I will now do a short resume of myself at this time because it had a vital bearing on the course of my future life.

I was now twenty-eight years of age. I had long recovered from the shortness of breath that had afflicted me in my younger years but often felt weak and out of sorts. I still suspected the pill I had been given when we'd left Tanganyika in 1953 at the age of 11. In years to come later I was to realise that I had always had a low level form of malaria but also that this might be coupled with an organo-phosphorous poison in my system, from the sheep dipping at Bedrule during which, unlike the shepherds, I'd never wore any form of protective clothing. Combined, this caused me invariably to feel liverish and out of sorts. This in turn caused me to sometimes behave in an awkward and tactless manner to my many good friends. As far as my years in South Africa were concerned I drank too much and suffered the consequences. I also never drank enough water to combat becoming dehydrated in the dreadful heat of the country. This also made me feel rotten. It seems very odd indeed that I never realised the importance of keeping oneself well hydrated in all those years.

Looking back on my life there must have been plenty of people who thought I was distinctly odd but nevertheless they bore it stoically. I take this opportunity to fully apologise to anyone and everyone who I may have offended in my life.

17

I HEAD HOME

During 1972, at the age of thirty-one, I had been in correspondence with Clive in connection with my replacing him as the tenant of Hallrule Farm as per the Gentleman's Agreement he had with my father. There appeared to be some doubt about the matter so I decided to fly home to clear the air once and for all. I would also ascertain the lay of the land as far as Clive and Gertrude were concerned in connection with saving the Estates.

I stayed with Gertrude because I disliked her less than Clive. Gertrude, on the face of it, was welcoming and tried to make me feel at home. A welcome change to the last time I had seen her. Peter and Robert were their usual jovial selves, though Peter appeared to be more pre-occupied than he had been when we left. Katherine, Uncle John's elder daughter, was also living at Hallrule at this time. She helped out with the boys and the house in general. We were both glad to see each other as we had always got on very well. She also liked a good joke and prank and we enjoyed playing them on each other.

I eventually touched lightly on the future of the Estates with Gertrude. As before she steered the conversation away from this by saying that 'nothing could be done about them now.' I left it at that and decided to concentrate my efforts on Clive instead.

I went see Clive and put it to him that it was manifestly absurd for the Estates to be forcibly sold just because Stuart had not made a Will. Not to mention the two sets of Death Duties they faced, unless something was done about it, and soon. He asked me what I thought should be done in a rather dismissive manner.

I had thought up a plan which would result in the Estates being saved for our family (the Usher family of Norton and Wells) and which would not cause any upheaval as far as most of the people connected with, and living on them, were concerned. No change whatever as far as Gertie and her boys and he himself were concerned. I therefore put my plan to him:

That the Estates be sold to Johnny at a nominal price as he already had the sons to continue the family. Johnny would then be the owner of the Estates. If required Johnny would sign documents guaranteeing Gertrude and the boys living at Hallrule House for the rest of their lives or for as long as they wanted to, with an appropriate income and the like. If necessary Johnny would refrain from anything to do with the management of the Estates until the survivor of Gertrude and her two sons had died. This plan would have the added and very favourable advantage of saving two, or possibly three, sets of death duties depending on who died first and in what order. In essence my plan was that there would be no change in the *modus operandi* of the Estates' management and affairs, with the very important exception that the Estates would now belong to Johnny.

As soon as I finished explaining my plan to him, Clive immediately responded by stating: 'I think it is a bad plan.' Just like that. He made no other comment whatever and showed absolutely no regret about the Estates passing out of our family in the not too distant future. Of course I was very disappointed. I asked him what was so bad about my plan? As always when people have no credible answer to a straightforward question they change the subject. Clive did exactly that now by incanting a variation of Gertrude's words: 'The Estates are nothing to do with you. You have no rights in them and I do not have to give you reasons on any matters to do with them.'

In a further attempt to gain his co-operation I told him that I personally would be happy to walk the world as a tramp with a song in my heart in gratitude from the day the Estates had been conveyed to Johnny. He now pulled rank on me by glaring at me and saying: 'I will not discuss the matter any further with you. You have no rights in the Estates or here.' I then informed him that as he did not want the Estates to be sold to Johnny on the basis of no change for the people living on them, like himself, the only conclusion I could draw was that he had something against Johnny personally. He just stood looking uncomfortable. As the silence had become pregnant I upped the ante: 'As you appear to hold some grudge against Johnny, are you agreeable to the Estates being sold to Johnny's eldest son, Andrew, instead of Johnny? Surely you could have no objection to that?' Andrew was only ten years old at the time. His response to that was: 'I repeat I will not discuss this any more with you.'

Of course I was absolutely seething but had to conceal this because there remained the matter of his handing over the Hallrule tenancy to me. To have had a flaming row with him at that point would have been the kiss of death to my getting the tenancy. So I told him that I would put my plan to Dempster, the lawyer who Mackenzie & Black had told us had been appointed the *Curator-Bonis* to Peter. Dempster was now working for Brodies WS as Mackenzie & Black WS had recently been taken over by Brodies. I continued, 'I am sure he will think it a good plan. The only thing which needs to be sorted out is the purchase price and the mechanics of the conveyance. This would carry out your own Father's wishes.' He had no answer to this other than to incant his usual 'You have no rights here.'

I then told him that as both Johnny and I were the only route to the future for our family it was perfectly evident that it was our filial and moral duty to protect our family and, as such, narrow legal rights did not come into the equation. Duty over rode everything in its own right. That stumped him alright; he simply turned on his heel and walked off without answering.

I immediately made an appointment to see Dempster, the death bed thief, now at Brodies WS lawyers in Edinburgh the next morning.

Passing the Wells Stables on the way to Edinburgh next morning I decided to pop in and see if Clive was there and, if so, tell him that I was on the way to see Dempster. Not that I thought it would do any good but I wanted him to know that I was not giving up on it. Sure enough he was at home so I told him. To my great surprise Clive now piped up and told me that he now considered my plan to be 'a good plan' but said no more. I was delighted and welcomed his complete about- turn on my plan. However I wondered how he could effect a 180 degree turn so quickly.

An hour and a half later I was seated opposite Dempster in his office at Brodies in Edinburgh. I had met him a few times before, both at Bedrule and in Edinburgh. He was your usual Edinburgh lawyer in appearance and manner, — grey haired, dark suited and exuding a dry 'give away nothing' air.

'I know you stole £1,000 all those years ago from Francis Usher of Dunglass on his deathbed. That makes you a deathbed thief. But you don't know that I know that,' I thought to myself.

I put my plan to him and very quickly noted that he was uncomfortable and tense: He sat bolt upright with his hands under the desk looking at me but every now and then glancing momentarily downwards. What on earth was he doing? I decided to catch him ou.! I dropped a packet of Vicks cough sweets onto the carpet and, quick as light, bent down to retrieve them, at the same time looking to see why he had been glancing down. And catch him out I did in spectacular style. He quickly tucked his knees up in an attempt to stop me from seeing what he had been doing, but too late! His hands were now as still as death but clasped between them was a short pencil and, on his knees, a small notebook on which he had been writing notes of what I had been saying. Of course I immediately realised that Clive had rung him to warn him of my plan.

Straightening up I informed him that he was at liberty to make notes openly on top of the desk and asked *why* had he been doing so secretly? Caught out, he blushed, laid his notebook on the desk, and asked me to carry on, thereby evading my question.? I therefore asked him again to answer my question. Again he refused to do so by asking me to carry on giving him my plan. So as not to provoke a major bust up, I did not rub his nose in it anymore and finished putting my plan to him, during which time he made no further notes. He kept batting my plan aside by raising legal objections to it. I told him that I did not accept his 'legal objections' on the grounds of commonsense and told him there had been many precedents of large organisations being sold for a pound to expedite matters in similar circumstances. 'My plan is simplicity itself,' I told him. His demeanor became cooler and cooler. He simply kept incanting that my plan could not be legally executed. Ignorant of the law as I was at the time I knew this was nonsense and that he was lying through his teeth.

When it became apparent that I wasn't getting anywhere with him on my plan I changed tack and asked him for a copy of my Grandfather's Will, which I had never seen. He pointed to four large leather bound volumes stacked on a shelf to the right of his desk and informed me that one of them was my Grandfather's. When I asked him if I could see it he instantly replied, 'No, you may not see it. It is nothing to do with you and is not your business.' What utter balderdash. He was fully aware that Wills become public documents after the death of the Testator. This was the same old mantra of Gertie's and Clive's. It now dawned on me that he had advised Gertie and Clive to use that mantra as a shield to block me. I pointed out to him that only through my Brother and myself could the Usher family of Norton and Wells continue with what remained of its possessions into the future, as per my Grandfather's Will and Trust. Of course he had been fully aware of that since Robin's death in 1947. He just sat there looking ever more uncomfortable. I then got up and made for the door, now openly angry. He leapt up and tried to mollify me. I recovered some of my composure and asked him to use what influence he had with Clive and Gertie to see to it that the Estates were transferred to Johnny forthwith, thereby fulfilling old Sir Robert Usher's wishes. He now changed his tune by agreeing to 'see what I can do.' I didn't believe him, but was pleased that I had at least forced him to change his tune.

I then asked Dempster to make sure that Clive honoured the Gentleman's Agreement he had with my Father by getting out of Hallrule Farm in my favour. He now said that the tenancy had never been for me, but for Johnny. I corrected him on that, but added that if I was for some reason unacceptable, I did not at all mind Johnny getting the tenancy as this would maintain an Usher presence in Rulewater, if only as tenants. He made some placatory noises but again I did not believe a word of it. Shortly thereafter I bade him a frosty farewell and left.

Again I was absolutely seething but was proud that I had not had an open breach with him. I also realised that Dempster had advised Clive to change his 'bad plan' statement to a 'good plan' statement; to keep his and everyone elses' backs covered. Dempster would have seen the danger that Clive's 'bad plan' statement posed to them all in the future. Also to leave me to him (Dempster) to handle.

Why had Dempster taken notes secretly? To construct a misleading 'record' against me is the short answer. For example he could 'note' that I wanted the Estates to be conveyed to me personally and that I wanted to 'rob' Peter and Robert or some other such rubbish, to cast me as the villain of the piece and so on. I made no notes in his presence because I wanted him to think that I had no record of the meeting. It would then be his written notes against my spoken word as far as he was concerned. But of course I immediately made my own notes as soon as I got back to my car.

Back on the Estate I tackled Clive about my taking over Hallrule Farm from him. He now stated that he wanted to farm it for another five years and would vacate it in my favour in 1978, if that was alright with me? Of course it wasn't alright with me but I felt that I did not have much option so I made a show of 'reluctant acceptance.' He then gave me his solemn assurance that he would vacate the farm in my favour in 1978. Curious though it may seem I believed him. Of course his giving me his solemn assurance that he would vacate the farm in my favour in 1978 was an admission that his earlier statements about my having 'no rights in the Estate' were nonsense.

I also asked him to let me know if he ever thought of giving up his tenancy on Dykes farm because I would like to take that farm over from him as well. Again he agreed to do so. This later proved to be another of the 'Big Man's' lies because in the 1990s I discovered that he had already given up that tenancy very shortly *before* my visit.

Just before I left I warned him that I wanted to raise a matter which he would very probably not at all like but which I felt obliged to tell him. I then asked him if he wanted to hear me out.

'Yes, Yes, I want to hear it,' he responded rather testily, but now all ears. With some trepidation I told him that I felt it was his duty to leave all the Wells properties which Uncle Stuart had 'given' him, making no mention of this being illegal and breaching the Trust, to Johnny in his Will as this would carry out his Father's wishes. He just looked at me for a few seconds in a combination of disbelief and alarm and then, shaking his head in the negative, said he would not do so and walked away. That was the last time I ever saw him.

When I got back to Hallrule I told Cousin Katherine of my dislike of Clive. She immediately came back at me with: 'He (Clive) is a nasty piece of work. The other day he made a nasty remark to me which made my hands itch. They always do that when people are nasty to me.' Poor Katherine. I now regret that I hadn't pursued the matter further with her.

What about Peter in all this and what was he like? Well, Peter was Peter. Here is something which will give you an idea of his mentality: One evening, in the presence of Peter, Gertie told me that her dog, Mustard, had tripped her as she was coming down the front stairs and that she had fallen heavily, rolled down the stairs and fractured her leg. She then told me, with a reproachful glance at Peter, that Peter had seen this and had laughed. Peter just sat there looking somewhat discomfited, as well he might. I made a few sympathetic noises about it. A day or two later I told Peter at the bottom of the same stairs that Gertie had better watch out that Mustard did not trip her up there again. At this Peter exploded into laughter until the tears ran down his cheeks! At the time his reaction did not strike me at all unusual; par for the course rather. Later on when I discovered the full extent of Gertie's rotten character I could not have agreed more with Peter and would have joined him in the laughing. As far as I am now concerned it was a pity that she had not broken her neck there and then; and well done Mustard!

Robert had much the same sense of humour as Peter. However Robert was more active and spent hours in his 'study' dancing the Sword Dance to Scottish music. Peter was more sedentary and contemplative. Peter was also a devoted viewer of 'Blue Peter' on television. I sometimes thought that the reason for his liking Blue Peter so much was the 'Peter' part of it.

Peter and Robert were merely the 'useful tools' which the Lawyers, Clive, Gertie, and the Estate Manager (Charles John Usher, only a very distant relative via an Usher born in 1738) used to enrich themselves.

After two and a half month's stay in Scotland I flew back to South Africa. I re-organized my long term planning to cover the next 5 years so as to be ready to take over the tenancy of Hallrule farm in 1978.

Track at Town O'Rule Farm

18

CLIVE USHER IN COLLUSION WITH BRODIES

In 1977 I again wrote to Clive to set the date for his vacating Hallrule farm in my favour. In direct contradiction to the solemn assurance he had given me in 1973 he now stated that he would not vacate the farm in 1978 because he still wanted to continue farming it. He now promised that he would vacate it in 1983 in my favour. I remonstrated with him, but to no avail. I had long discussions with Johnny about this second blatant breach of trust. As a fellow Trustee of the Usher Baronetcy Trust with Clive and Logan McClure of Brodies, Johnny did what he could but, again to no avail. Of course I was absolutely devastated and accepted that I had been a fool to have ever believed a word the man said. In the years to come I slowly learnt that the best way to deal with crooks was to figuratively 'smack them between the eyes,' very fast, and very hard! Johnny likewise was shocked to the core and consequently refused to renew Clive's tenancy on Hallrule farm beyond 1978. We had been advised by friends in Scotland that we should at all costs get this tenancy because it would put us in a very strong position for purchasing at least that *one* farm on the Estate if and when the Estate was sold.

At this time Johnny told me that he had discovered that Dempster had never been appointed the *Curator-Bonis* to Peter as we had been told he had in 1962. And Dempster had allowed me to continue to believe he *was* Peter's *Curator-Bonis* at our meeting in 1973. Clive, Gertie and Valerie had likewise never told us that Dempster had never been appointed *Curator-Bonis* to Peter. Both Johnny and I failed to realise the great importance of this deception in 1977. A great pity.

In January 1980 Johnny suddenly received a document for his signature from Brodies. This document was to make Valerie and and his daughter Margaret, now Mrs Mactaggart, joint tenants with Clive in Hallrule farm. By now of course Clive was farming the farm illegally because Johnny had not renewed his lease in 1978 as already narrated. He was now nothing more that a squatter on the farm. Of course Johnny refused to sign this new document and informed Brodies accordingly. Also in 1979 - unknown to us at the time - Clive had already made his Will. In this Will he 'left' the tenancy of Hallrule farm to his daughter Margaret, as I was subsequently to discover when I obtained a copy of it from the National Archives in the 1990s. So, although he had blithely broken his word to my Father, Johnny and me, in fact and in law he had no tenancy to leave.

In the face of Johnny's refusal to sign this document Brodies sent another document to Johnny for his signature later that month. This document was to extend the tenancy from 1978 to 1983, for Clive only, actually the same extension that Johnny had already told Clive he would never sign. So Clive and Brodies had dropped their dirty little ploy of getting his wife and daughter into the tenancy. This evidently was exercising both Clive and Brodies a great deal.

At this time there were now only three Trustees of the Usher Baronetcy Trust: Johnny, Logan McLure now of Brodies, and Clive. There had to be two Trustee signatures on the lease to make it legal. This was the root of the problem facing Clive and Brodies. The difficulty was that Scots Law precluded a Trustee of a Trust Estate from signing a lease that made himself a tenant of a Trust Estate of which he himself was a Trustee. Therefore the lease *had* to be signed by Johnny and MacLure. So Johnny, by letter dated 4th February 1980, wrote to Clive informing him that he would not sign the new lease on the grounds of his having repeatedly broken the Gentleman's Agreement he had with my Father, that the tenancy was to go to me.

In 1981 Brodies, on behalf of Clive and his daughter, Mrs Mactaggart, sent Johnny a *further* document for his signature. This document sought to have Clive's daughter, Mrs Mactaggart, of *all* people, assumed as a *new* Trustee of the Usher Baronetcy Trust. We were staggered. To have the daughter of a squatter appointed a Trustee would have been an even greater breach of the Law, Commonsense and Ethics. It was also an outrageous attack on my Grandfather, the Usher family, the Usher Baronetcy Trust, my deceased Father and Johnny and myself personally. Of course, Johnny refused to sign, yet again, saying 'I will not give in to that twister any more. Dad was an idiot to have believed a word he ever said and so were we. Clive is a lying cheat.'

Brodies and Clive now thought better of their various devices and traps. By letter dated 17th November 1981 Clive, at long last and nine years late, acknowledged the Gentleman's Agreement. In his letter he stated that Johnny:

> '. . .must appreciate that I had hoped one of my grandsons would farm Hallrule, but I am perfectly agreeable to going out in May 1983.'

He went onto to state that Andrew, Johnny's eldest son, should be the tenant. Andrew at this time was twenty years old and had been brought up in Natal, since the age of 5. Clive then went on to state that I would not be a suitable tenant and would advise the Trustees to that effect. Of course he *would* say that, just wouldn't he? I put it that down to his getting his revenge on me for having kept reminding him over the years of his duty to save the Estates for an Usher future.

In this same letter he also stated that Andrew being the new tenant would fulfil his Father's wishes. That was an admission that all of our efforts to keep an Usher presence on the Wells Estate for all those years were now vindicated. Remember that I had put exactly that to him in connection with the whole estate in 1973 and he had sabotaged it. Of course Johnny and I were delighted that, at long last, he had agreed, in writing, to vacate the farm.

Thereafter more correspondence between Johnny and Clive followed in which Clive gave Johnny a list of his own valuation of the stock and machinery on the farm. This came to more than £184,000 which, inevitably with him, was a gross exaggeration He then started prevaricating about Andrew. Then we heard from friends that he had fallen ill, looked terrible and was worried that his defrauding the Estate for so many years would soon be exposed.

Near the summit of Rubers Law looking down to farmland between Billerwell Farm and Hallrule Farm

19

JOHNNY TRIES TO SAVE THE ESTATES

I was married on the 12th of December 1981 at the age of forty to Gillian Creeke. Nine years younger than myself Gillian was the younger daughter of Dr Herbert Anthony Creeke MD, Fellow of the Royal College of Surgeons MRCS, LCS who was a Dental Surgeon who'd worked at Guy's Hospital in London for many years. The Creekes originally came from Burnley in Lancashire where they owned a cotton mill in the 1800s. Unlike the Ushers of late, they were a studious family and Gillian's grandfather became the philatelist to Queen Victoria. Dr Creeke and his wife left England in 1950, the year in which Gillian was born, for South Africa because the sun, it was thought, would be better for Mrs Creeke's delicate health. Gillian, pretty and candid, has stuck with me through more than 35 turbulent years. I doubt many women would have - and that is the mark of Gillian. Most would have abandoned me because of all the misery and poverty caused by my struggle to save the family Estates. The only sure thing in my life is that Gillian loves me, imperfect as I am, and we share one most important thing in common and that is we are both deadly honest with each other - the bedrock on which our marriage has endured.

To sort matters out once and for all with the Trust busting crook Clive we decided that it would be best if Johnny went to see him in person to agree the mechanics of the handover of the tenancy and have everything signed and sealed before Clive died. Also, but without telling Clive, to make further enquiry into the management of the Estates and to try and secure their future in our family. Clive agreed to meet him about the mechanics of the handover and a date in early November 1982 was set for the meeting. Johnny flew over towards the end of October 1982.

On 6th November of that year Johnny wrote to us stating that when he'd arrived at the Wells Stables he'd found Val and the Estate Manager, Charles John Usher (still claiming to be a close relative) waiting for him, but no Clive. Val told him that Clive had been hospitalised and was too ill to see him and that he had now decided that neither Johnny nor Andrew were to have the tenancy after all. Clive had this time broken his written assurance as

Love conquers all. Myself and my wife, happily married after 37 years. Gillian is the younger daughter of the late Dr Herbert Anthony Creeke MD, Fellow of the Royal College of Surgeons MRCS, LCS

opposed to having repeatedly verbally broken the Gentleman's Agreement in the past. The Estate Manager then had the cheek to inform Johnny that he did not have the necessary experience to farm Hallrule. This of course was rich given Clive's complete ignorance of farming when he had retired from the Army in 1956. At that time he used to come to Bedrule for farming lessons from my Father after he had been given the tenancy of Dykes farm. It was all arrant nonsense for the singular purpose of keeping us out of the farm and out of the Estate. Johnny informed them that he was totally shocked at Clive's repeated dishonesty, reminding them that Clive should have been out of the farm nine years ago in 1973 and that his occupation of the farm was unlawful and that he was just a squatter there. He also informed them he would fight them to the bitter end.

Johnny now determined to put matters right and to this end made an appointment with another large firm of Edinburgh lawyers called Tods Murray because he no longer trusted Brodies. There he dealt with a lawyer called Mike Simpson. Simpson told him that morally the whole thing 'stank to high heaven' and even more so because Clive as a Trustee of the UBT was only paying between a quarter and a fifth of the rent he should be paying for the farm. He also told Johnny that he was obliged to do something about it as fingers could be pointed at him, as a Trustee of the UBT, at some later stage if he continued to let Clive get away with his risible rental. And that

Clive should be forced to pay all the shortfalls in rent, and whatever else, retrospectively over the decades.

To this end Johnny had a meeting with Brodies on the 8th November 1982 in connection with the UBT Estates. Brodies, in their capacity as the UBT lawyers, were represented by Ian Taylor Carruthers WS and not Dempster. Whether Johnny asked why Dempster was not present I do not know. If he had not asked he should have done so, as we both much later realised that Dempster's absence must have had something to do with protecting Dempster and Brodies themselves and so on.

The purpose of this meeting was to look at all the Estate records and Accounts for the period 1962 - the year that Peter had, as we had then been told, inherited the estates - until 1982. Carruthers stated that Brodies did not have any accounts and records for this twenty year period. Johnny was dumbfounded. So where were these accounts? Carruthers told him that the Estate Accounts were prepared by John G Welch and Co, Chartered Accountants of Hawick in the Scottish Borders and that they should have them running back for many years. With regard to the rents he suggested Johnny should approach the Estate Manager to find out what they were on the Wells Estate.

At the time he accepted Carruthers dealing with him, but he later realized that he should have insisted on seeing his co-Trustee, MacLure, instead, whom he had never met. MacLure had never made any move to meet Johnny at the numerous meetings which Johnny had with first Mackenzie & Black and latterly with Brodies over the years in the 60s, 70s and now 80s. As a lawyer and fellow Trustee of Johnny's it was incumbent on him to have been present at any meeting at which Usher Baronetcy Trust affairs were to be discussed. It was only in 1998 that we realised the reason why MacLure had never attended any of these meetings: To avoid answering the awkward questions which he knew Johnny would ask him, like: 'Where are the Estate Accounts and why was I never sent them?' and 'Why was I never informed of anything to do with the Estates?' It was much safer for MacLure to let a junior lawyer such as Carruthers lead Johnny up the garden path rather than he himself doing so. So Johnny at the time did not have the faintest idea that this was the reason why Carruthers was seated opposite him that day rather than MacLure. Nor did the deceit end there. Also unknown to him at the time was that Carruthers was Gertie's personal law agent. Carruthers was therefore in the ideal position to see how much Johnny knew and what Johnny's intentions were and then report back to Gertie and Clive. In essence his main function was to spy on Johnny on behalf of Gertie and Clive and of course Brodies themselves.

On 9th November 1982 Carruthers wrote to Johnny enclosing a record of recent 'intrommissions' of the Trustees - gobbledygooky meaning 'paying themselves.' So Brodies had some records after all. But only the ones which suited them!

So back to Edinburgh went Johnny to tackle Carruthers again on 11th November 1982. He again asked for the UBT Estates accounts, but Carruthers again denied that Brodies had them; but this time he was decidedly more uncomfortable than at their first meeting. Johnny remonstrated with him but Carruthers, looking ever more uncomfortable, kept up the denial. When eventually Johnny had him cornered Carruthers suddenly caved in. He told Johnny that the Estates accounts had never been audited! How on earth could that be? What on earth was going on and, even worse, what had been going on over the last twenty, thirty, forty or even fifty years? Brodies, with their own in house 'Brodies Accountancy Services' department, portrayed themselves as one of the top law firms in Scotland in Estate Agency and Accountancy and yet here they were telling him that the UBT Estates Accounts had never been audited. Johnny now suspected the worst.

Johnny then went and stayed with his father-in-Law, Sir Reginald Houldsworth; Bt, at Kirkbride in Ayrshire. He had kept Sir Reginald abreast of Clive's refusal to get out of Hallrule farm at the agreed time in 1973 and 1978 on earlier visits and Sir Reginald had taken a very dim view of this. Johnny now told him that Clive had done it for the third time and showed him Clive's letter of 1981 in which he had agreed to vacate the farm in 1983. Sir Reginald was horrified and only now told Johnny that, 'Clive was never accepted by his fellow Officers in the War because they regarded him as not being straight.' This was just a polite way of saying that his fellow Officers regarded him as a crook and had therefore, ostracised him. I wished to blazes that Sir Reginald had told Johnny that years before. It would have saved us both a lot of trouble and heart-ache.

Johnny also told Reggie about the unsatisfactory nature of his meetings with Brodies and their constant evasions, their refusal to give him the Accounts of the Estates and their final admission that the Accounts had never even been audited. This also shocked Reggie. Little did Reggie know that in a few years time his own Kirkbride estate would be lost to him in tragic and and quite possibly similar lawyer-engineered circumstances.

Johnny then received a curious letter from Carruthers of Brodies, dated 11th November 1982, at Kirkbride. Enclosed with the letter was just one set of unaudited Accounts for the year ending March 1982. The letter stated this set of accounts was not audited and that 'this may appear somewhat irregular, but the Estate Manager's records are immaculately kept. . . and there never has been any cause for concern.' He then apologised to Johnny for 'suggesting' that these accounts were not available at their first meeting with Johnny, making the excuse , 'I quite innocently forgot.' *Quite innocently forgot*? Of course this letter aroused Johnny's suspicions far more than allaying them. From this and his previous meetings he deduced that no audited accounts had ever been produced for the Estates since our leaving in 1968 at the very least and most probably far longer. He also concluded that this incredible state of affairs had left the field wide-open for Brodies, Clive, the Estate Manager, and Gertrude to plunder and pillage our Family Estates and Investments at will. In the event from that day to the present, more than thirty years later, Brodies steadfastly denied Johnny - until his death in 1998 - and then myself access to any Estate records. That said it all as far as I was concerned.

On the 18th November 1982 as Johnny was about to board his flight back to South Africa he heard that Clive had died the previous day. This left him no time to cancel his flight.

It has since transpired that Clive had been cheating the Estate ever since my Father had agreed to his becoming the tenant of Hallrule farm in 1963. With the proceeds of his cheating he'd bought race horses and raced them all over the country. Ironically the only winner I ever heard that he had was a horse called Fiddler on the Hoof. He wrote to me about this rare win shortly before his death, in an attempt to mollify me. I did not reply. Actually the name 'Fiddler on the Hoof' would have suited Clive much more than his poor horse. Horses do not fiddle people.

Bridge over the Rule Water at Hallrule

20

BRODIES TOGETHER WITH TODS MURRAY, LAWYERS OF EDINBURGH, DEPLOY THEIR WEAPONS OF MASS DECEPTION AGAINST JOHNNY

As soon as Johnny arrived back in South Africa we had a meeting to go over what had happened on his trip. He told me that he could not understand how it was that there was no *Curator-Bonis* in position because we had been told that Dempster was to be appointed the *Curator-Bonis* to Peter when he succeeded to the Estates in 1962. And how was it that the set of Accounts (1982-1983) which Carruthers had given him were still in the name of the Usher Baronetcy Trust which the lawyers told us had terminated in 1962? How then was it that Peter still didn't have a *Curator-Bonis* twenty years later?

We decided to follow things up once we got the Hallrule tenancy sorted out. Believe it or not we still clung to the hope that things could not possibly be as bad as they appeared to be. Johnny was particularly perturbed by Brodies refusal to give him the Estate Accounts and that they were unaudited.

On the nineteenth of November 1982 Johnny wrote to his new lawyer Mike Simpson of Tods Murray. Edinburgh, instructing him to contact the only other remaining Trustee of the UBT, MacLure of Brodies, with a view to getting Clive's widow and daughter to honour the Gentleman's Agreement on Hallrule farm. At the same time reminding MacLure that the new lease, to run from 1978-1983 on Hallrule farm still remained unsigned. Also that another Trustee independent of Brodies and family should now be appointed.

On 29th November 1982 Logan MacLure wrote to Johnny, no doubt having received the letter from Mike Simpson of Tods Murray. In this letter MacClure informed Johnny that Hallrule farm belonged to Peter. This was a statement of the obvious as we had always been told that Peter had succeeded to the Estates in 1962. He went on to suggest that a *Curator-Bonis* be appointed to Peter to decide who should get the tenancy. But never a word about our being told that Dempster would be appointed the *Curator-Bonis* twenty years previously. MacClure was fully aware of that because he was a UBT Trustee at that time. He also suggested that Johnny consult other solicitors on the Hallrule tenancy issue because Clive had let him have a copy of his letter of the 17th of November 1981 in which he had agreed to give up the tenancy to Johnny in 1983. This showed that Carruthers had not even told MacLure that Johnny had already consulted other solicitors, or if he had in fact done so, MacLure was feigning ignorance of it.

On the 9th of February 1983 Johnny received a letter from Hugh Stevens of Brodies, *another* change of lawyer by Brodies, stating that Gertie had 'instructed' Brodies to appoint a *Curator-Bonis* for Peter, but, very significantly, made no mention of who the *Curator-Bonis* was to be.

Less than a week later, on the 15th of February 1983 Johnny received a letter from Hugh Stevens of Brodies which informed him that the First Order appointing the Estate Manager, Charles John Usher of Courthill, to be Peter's *Curator-Bonis* had *already* been made by the Court. Brodies were evidently hoping like hell that Johnny would not respond in time to beat the time limit for objections. Outraged at this latest bit of Brodies deceit Johnny instantly objected to this on the grounds that the Estate Manager would be in a terrible Conflict of Interest situation. He made his objection through Mike Simpson of Tods Murray to Brodies at his own personal expense as with all the other meetings and correspondence he had with Tods Murray.

On 6th April 1983 Mike Simpson of Tods Murray wrote to Johnny saying that Brodies had now agreed to withdraw the candidature of the Estate Manager to be Sir Peter's *Curator-Bonis,* although Gertie had taken 'some persuading' on the matter. Simpson noted that there had been enough of the principle of *Auctor in Rem Suam* with Clive already being both Trustee and Tenant of the UBT estates. *Auctor in Rem Suam* translates into 'Actor in his own cause' breaching one of the basic tenets of Scots Law, as already stated. It's worth reinforcing the point that, despite pretending otherwise, Charles John Usher was not in any real sense any relation to our family. This whole performance was yet another example of Brodies having executed an unlawful, criminal act which perverted and confounded the very Trust of which they themselves were the Law Agents.

On 7th May 1983 Johnny wrote to Clive's wife Valerie appealing to her better nature to honour the agreement with regard to the tenancy of Hallrule Farm. He informed her that he had told his father-in-law and others of Clive's breaking this Gentleman's Agreement. Valerie took the easy way out by never replying to his letter; instead she simply forwarded it to Brodies. Almost certainly she would have also shown Johnny's letter to Gertie to keep her in the picture and as a warning of the dangers that lay ahead for them both.

On 11th June 1983 Carruthers of Brodies wrote another letter to Johnny. Brodies had by now installed Carruthers as Peter's *Curator-Bonis* thereby disregarding Johnny's request that the *Curator-Bonis* should be someone independent of both Brodies and the Usher family. In his letter Carruthers stated that it was quite clear from Clive's letter of 17th November 1981 that Clive wished the tenancy to go to his daughter. This was a breathtaking misrepresentation of that letter which made it clear that Clive had finally agreed in writing to honour the Gentleman's agreement he had made with my Father with the one notable difference that the tenancy was to go to Johnny's son Andrew and not me. Carruthers, again deliberately, made no mention of the fact that the lease had not been renewed by Johnny in 1978 when it had expired - an event which could not have been more relevant and one that meant that Clive had no tenancy to leave in the first place.

Carruthers and Logan MacLure of Brodies then simply acquiesced in Clive's daughter, Margaret Mactaggart, occupying Hallrule farm as a squatter. This illegal state of affairs continued until 1995 when she was allowed to purchase the farm at a small fraction of its open market value.

Her son David then squatted there in her place after she had what I regard as a hovel built for herself on the site of our beautiful Wells House. She lives there to this day, knowingly and illegally, and will continue to do so until forced out.

On 13th June 1983 Mike Simpson of Tods Murray wrote to Johnny claiming he had only just received his letter of 17th May 1983 though the normal postage time from South Africa was five days. He stated that he had tried to get Johnny's preferred candidate, Sturrock of Jedburgh be made *Curator-Bonis* to Peter but that 'the family would not go along with that suggestion.' What family? Johnny and I were Peter's only family apart from his mother Gertie and brother Robert. More of the egregious Sturrock later but suffice it to say now that he, too, would have been a catastrophic choice as we were to find out later.

Johnny continued to write letters to Tods Murray in connection with the tenancy issue but received no reply until the 1st December 1983 when Simpson responded stating that a letter,

> 'from as long ago as September has just surfaced from under a pile of papers in my room where it had inadvertently been misplaced.'

Again how terribly convenient. The more time that passed the less chance we had of obtaining the tenancy. This is a further example of the many Weapons of Mass Deception which Scottish lawyers routinely deploy to sabotage their clients.

At the end of 1983 I asked Johnny bluntly if he trusted Simpson as I did not now trust him at all. He said he now only half-trusted him. I replied that if Simpson was hunting with the hounds and running with the fox we, the only remaining Usher family of Norton and Wells, were in very serious trouble indeed. He agreed but asked what more he could do? These lawyers were recommended to him and the cost was ruinous. We agreed that there was something radically wrong when a Trustee had to pay alternative lawyers out of his own pocket for advice on the behaviour of the lawyers who were the Law Agents of the Trust as well as one of his fellow Trustees. One can only hope the reader has so far managed to follow this sinister theatre of the absurd.

After several moments of pregnant silence Johnny then told me he had totally lost faith in Scottish lawyers and felt, frankly, like washing his hands of the whole thing. I encouraged him to soldier on as our giving up now was what Brodies was hoping and praying for. From then on I had to constantly encourage him not to give up. In my darker moments part of me flirted with the idea of surrender; I had done my best, I told myself. Yet I always came out of such reveries more convinced than ever that I would never be able to ever look myself squarely in the eye again.

From that time onwards Johnny decided that all further correspondence with the lawyers, both Brodies and Tods Murray would be carried out through his South African lawyer, Andrew Ewing of Hillcrest, Durban whom he trusted.

In June 1984 Brodies sent Johnny three Dispositions for signature. These Dispositions were to convey the Estates of Wells, Norton and Pitheavlis from the Usher Baronetcy Trust to Peter.

Johnny and I had always believed Pitheavlis was in the Trust because my father told us it was. We therefore thought it quite normal that these Dispositions included Pitheavlis. It was only in November 2004 that I established that Sir Robert Usher, in 1927, had not placed the Pitheavlis Estate in the Usher Baronetcy Trust. When and by what authority then *had* the Pitheavlis Estate been placed in the Trust? I have established from a County of Perth record that it was placed in the UBT in 1971 by the Trustees of the late Sir Robert Usher, which was a separate entity from the Usher Baronetcy Trust. In January 1954 there remained only one Trustee of the late Sir Robert Usher and he was none other than that foul death-bed thief lawyer, Thomas Greig Dempster. He had been the sole surviving Trustee since the death of Sir John in 1951 and in that capacity had been selling Usher property from the Pitheavlis Estate unilaterally. A most unhealthy situation and, up to that time, the only instance of a sole Executor selling property in this way.

Something however must have made Dempster uncomfortable because in February 1954 he appointed a new Executor. Needless to say the new Executor was not a member of our family but none other than the egregious Logan MacClure, Johnny's co-Trustee of the UBT! No doubt Dempster, with MacClure concurring, thought that having a UBT Trustee on board would help to muddy the waters to anyone with the temerity to make inquiry into what he had been doing with the Pitheavlis properties for all those years. These two lawyers, with no family representation, continued apace selling property on the Pitheavlis Estate until December 1971 at which time they suddenly placed what remained of the Pitheavlis Estate into the Usher Baronetcy Trust. Why, I do not know, and it remains a mystery to me to

Pitheavlis Castle

this day. I therefore regard the manner in which the Pitheavlis Estate was 'handled' by the lawyers as fraudulent and that they gained financially from this practice. In addition it indicates to me that these lawyers convinced my father that Pitheavlis was a consituent part of the Usher Baronetcy Trust.

Without consulting me and partly on the advice of his South African lawyer, Ewing, Johnny signed the Norton and Pitheavlis Estates away to Peter but did not sign away the Wells Estate. This meant that Johnny, as a UBT Trustee, had signed away Norton and Pitheavlis without knowing of what they consisted. He told me, rather sheepishly, a few weeks later what he had done. I was furious, as you may well imagine. When we calmed down a bit he told me that he could not bring himself to sign the Wells Disposition because it was the main seat of our family and we had lived most of our young years at Bedrule which adjoined the Wells Estate. That mollified me a little. But I still told him that he had made a big mistake and we would both come to rue it one day. How could he possibly sign over assets of which he was a Trustee without establishing what those assets were? It was lunacy as far as I was concerned. I rationalised his doing so because firstly, at the time, like me, he still believed that Peter owned the Estates and that he was therefore obliged to sign them over to Peter by law. And secondly that he'd had enough of paying three sets of lawyers.

However the matter did not end there. On 19th February 1999, after Johnny's untimely and early death in 1998, I procured copies of the three 1984 dispositions along with a newer set of dispositions transferring the three Estates *again* to Peter in August 1987. With regard to the 1984 Dispositions I, to my horror, discovered that Johnny appeared to *have* signed the Wells Estate over to Peter in 1984 but could find no trace of Norton and Pitheavlis having been signed over. This was the exact opposite of what Johnny had told me. This mystified me. But his signature was there alright. What on earth had happened?

On closer inspection there was something fishy about this 1984 Disposition of Wells: I had made a copy of the unsigned Wells Disposition sent to Johnny in South Africa in 1984 and had brought it home with me. So I compared it with the one which I obtained from the National Archives of Scotland. The wording over the 8 pages was exactly the same as the one I had from South Africa. However the last page of the National Archives one was different in that Brodies had inserted a lengthy final paragraph in an area that had originally been marked 'Please Leave Blank.' With the Norton and Pitheavlis Dispositions of 1984 I expect that the same blank area with the same words had also been left. However I did not get copies of those in South Africa because they had already been sent back to Brodies duly signed. So I looked at the Norton and Pitheavlis Scottish Dispositions of 1987 to see if Brodies had inserted a similar lengthy final paragraph as they had with the Wells Disposition of 1984 in the blank space. They had indeed. However when I compared the 1987 Norton and Pitheavlis inserted paragraphs to the Wells inserted para of 1984 there was a difference: The text of the Norton and Pitheavlis Dispositions were laid out neatly with line following line with no alterations or additional insertions. The Wells Disposition was also laid out line after line but jammed between the original lines and in a smaller font to make it fit between the existing lines was some additional text dated 22nd June 1984 - the date Johnny was portrayed as having signed it. This meant that the 'jammed between the original lines' text must have been added at some time *after* the original text had been laid out.

I immediately smelt a rat. Johnny had told me that he had *not* signed the 1984 Wells Disposition and here was that Disposition with what appeared to be his signature on it but with that one very telling giveaway insertion which had been inserted between the lines of the original text at some later date, *after* Johnny had signed it. But how was his signature and the other signatures to be explained? One explanation was that Brodies had simply substituted the signatures on the final page of either the Norton or Pitheavlis Dispositions which Johnny told me that he had signed in 1984 onto the final page of 1984 Wells Disposition which Johnny told me that he had not signed. I therefore went to the National Archives to get the signed Norton and Pitheavlis 1984 Dispositions. Lo and behold there was no record of them! That indicated that Brodies had indeed used one of their final pages with Johnny's signature on it for the 1984 Wells disposition. Having used the one Brodies appear to have decided to simply get rid of the other one (either

Norton or Pitheavlis) as their best option, otherwise they would be unable to explain why one of them had been signed by Johnny and not the other.

But why did Brodies make that insertion between the lines instead of laying out neatly as in the other dispositions. The answer to that is that they had to because there was no room to add that insertion without causing the text to run into the area reserved for the signatures. They could not draft a new last page with all the lines present and correct stating the date that Johnny had signed it on that date with no insertions because this would have caused the text to run into the signatures at the bottom of the last page that had been taken from either the Norton or the Pitheavilis Dispositions. As it stood the text already ran so far down that it had to take avoiding action to dodge one of the witness's signatures! When it did end MacLures signature was hard up against the last line; quite unlike all the other Dispositions. This explained Brodies inserting the false date between the lines of the existing text, otherwise it would have run into MacLures signature. I showed this to a lawyer called Tom Murray in the summer of 1999 and he straightaway said: 'That's fraud.' He was the best possible person to have told me that because I subsequently discovered that he was a big time fraudster himself. It takes a thief to catch a thief!

Finally why should the one thing that Johnny told me that he had not done be jammed in between the lines making out that he had done it? It appeared therefore that Brodies effected this fraud to enable them to get their hands onto the Wells Estate in 1984, and to hell with Johnny not having signed it over to Peter.

As already stated the 1987 Dispositions conveyed the Estates of Norton and Pitheavlis to Peter again, according to Johnny's statement to me. And this time also the Wells Estate. But according to Brodies only Johnny had signed over Wells in 1984. So why did Brodies get Johnny to sign the Wells Estate signed over to Peter *again* in 1987 if he had already done so in 1984 as they had made it appear in this fraudulent 1984 Wells Disposition? Their doing so must have been that they realised their fraudulent 1984 Disposition would not stand close inspection. Another point: If Johnny had in fact signed the Wells disposition in 1984 there would have been no reason for him to sign it over to Peter again in 1987. With regard to the Norton and Pitheavlis Estates it appears that Brodies decided they had to get new ones signed because 1) They had used one of their final pages to fabricate the 1984 Wells disposition and 2) to maintain the fiction that Johnny had never signed them over to Peter in 1984, which Johnny said he had. In effect standing the truth of what had really occurred on its head! I was furious with myself that I had not checked all this out with Johnny before he died. All this vindicated Johnny's statement to me that he had not signed the Wells Estate over to Peter in 1984.

As a matter of interest Brodies got Peter himself to sell property at Wells in 1985 for a truly risibly low price on the strength of what I now regarded as the fraudulent 1984 Disposition. But Peter's actual selling property begged another very important and altogether different question: If he was capable of selling property what stopped Brodies drawing up a Will for him which adhered to the terms of old Sir Robert's 1911 Trust and his signing it? Nothing whatever, other than Peter leaving the Estates to Johnny on his death which was of course the very last thing that Brodies wanted. However Brodies must have had second thoughts or got cold feet about selling property in Peter's name because in 1986 they effected another transaction in the name of Peter's *Curator-Bonis*. After Peter died in 1990 Brodies continued to sell property but now in the name of his Brodies appointed Executor, Houldsworth of Brodies who was none other than Robert's *Curator-Bonis*.

On 7th November 1984 Gertrude died at the age of eighty-three. Brodies kept quiet about her death so, as far as we knew at that time, she still lived. Keeping us in the dark as always.

By letter dated the 18th of February 1986 Mike Simpson of Tods Murray responded to Andrew Ewing, Johnny's South African lawyer, agreeing that Johnny had the right, as a Trustee of the Usher Baronetcy Trust, to have an Inventory of the UBT assets before they were transferred from the UBT to Peter in 1984 and 1987. This was just stating the obvious; a bit like saying the water in the sea is salty. But it had cost Johnny a packet and years to get Simpson to admit this. So the question remained: Why had Carruthers refused to give him an Inventory of the UBT assets and UBT accounts when he was in Scotland for exactly that purpose in 1982?

March 1986. Carruthers of Brodies died unexpectedly. That may have left one less crook in Scotland, thank God, but there were plenty of others to take his place. Johnny then naively invited Simpson of Tods Murray even though he did not trust him, to become the *Curator-Bonis* to Peter in the place of Carruthers mainly because we wanted to get the Curatorship away from Brodies at all costs and Simpson was the lesser of the two evils. Simpson declined. In retrospect, thank God, otherwise we would undoubtedly have had both Brodies and Tods Murray defrauding their client - the hapless and unknowing Peter - for all their worth. Simpson would have loved to have taken the post for the money but declined because he knew the post posed great danger to him and his rotten firm of Tods Murray because of his past dishonesty in his dealings with Johnny. Another very probable reason was that Brodies told him: 'Hands off, Simpson: Peter the Idiot and the Usher family are *our* prey.'

In December 1986 Andrew Ewing wrote to Simpson enquiring who Peter's new Curator was and asked for a copy of Gertie's Will, of whose death we had only recently heard via the grapevine.

By letter dated the 15th of January 1987 Simpson responded to Ewing's letter and informed Johnny that Brodies had simply gone ahead and appointed *two* new *Curator-Bonis's*, one for Peter and one for Robert in

August 1986, five months earlier. This therefore was yet another of Brodies' nasty *fait accomplis* in order to retain their deadly control of the Estates and all the other Usher Baronetcy Trust assets. Peter's new *Curator-Bonis* was Hugh Stevens of Brodies. Robert's was David Houldsworth, also of Brodies. What a scandal and what a calamity for our family this was to prove to be. Simpson went on blithely to state that Hugh Stevens had informed him that Gertie had left her whole personal estate in life rent to Robert and, on his death, her estate was to be shared equally between her Argentinian niece, the Hallrule Housekeeper Alice Blamey, and the Estate Manager, Charles John Usher (no relation).

On 25th June 1987 Johnny at last and most reluctantly signed the Wells Estate over to Peter. Likewise Norton and Pitheavlis, for the second time as far as he was concerned. This time he did tell me before signing them away. Again I disagreed with him. He argued that because Peter owned the Estates and he had a Curator he had to sign Wells over to Peter because that was the law. 'So what?' I said. 'You did not sign Wells over in 1984 and the Estate carried on much as usual, so why sign it over now?' So we argued about it. He told me not to worry too much because Brodies would not dare to do anything untoward because they knew we were now watching them. Neither he nor I could still understand why Brodies wanted Johnny's signatures on the Dispositions if Peter had owned the Estate since 1962 as Brodies claimed. This was basically conveying heritable Estates to the person who already owned them. Usually if something does not add up it is because it does not add up. On top of that Johnny was signing away family Trust assets, the extent and location of which he was only partially aware, to the Downs Syndrome and Mentally Incapacitated Peter who, among many other things, would not be allowed to make a Will.

I eventually deferred to Johnny for two reasons: The first was that he had been a Trustee, albeit one that both MacClure and Clive and their law Agents, Brodies, never consulted - I never had been a Trustee. And secondly he was my elder brother and had been the senior non Incapax heir of our generation since the death of Robin in 1947. It was therefore Johnny's call. So we agreed to disagree. In the event it was proved spectacularly that if Johnny had stuck it out for another year or so and 'awaited developments', as Uncle Stuart had done fifty years earlier, things could have been very different.

By letter dated 22nd July 1987 Simpson informed Andrew Ewing that Stevens had informed him that he, Stevens, would refuse to provide Johnny or anyone else any Accounts of Peter's Curatory Estate; just as Carruthers had refused to hand over any Accounts or Statement of the Usher Baronetcy Trust Estates and Assets in 1982. To justify withholding this vital information Stevens stated that he regarded himself as 'standing in Sir Peter's shoes and that if Sir Peter was capable he would not let other people know what his assets were.' This was the usual Brodies twaddle particularly to Johnny who had finally signed the Estates over to Peter less than a month earlier. Stevens could never have made that statement had Johnny not signed them over.

Colonel Sir John Turnbull Usher, Bart (Uncle John). The Royal Company of Archers 1938. Sir John was the eldest son of the orginal Sir Robert.

21

SIR PETER USHER Bt DIES INTESTATE, AS PLANNED BY BRODIES. SIR ROBERT USHER Bt DIES INTESTATE, AS PLANNED BY BRODIES

On the 1st of June 1990 Peter died, Intestate, as planned since Uncle Stuart's death in 1962 or since Robin's death in 1947 by Brodies *et al.* Things were certainly going according to a script which spelt death to our family of Usher of Norton and Wells. Robert, equally Incapax, now succeeded to the Title and the UBT estates and assets.

In response to a request by Johnny's South African lawyer, Ewing, for the Accounts and Inventory of Peter's Estate another Tods Murray lawyer called David McLetchie responded by letter dated 17th July 1990. McLetchie informed Ewing that Stevens of Brodies had agreed to let him have the Inventory of Sir Peter's Estate in two to three weeks time. This Inventory would record the closing balance of Peter's Estate, but would not include the opening balance - ie what assets had been conveyed to him in 1984 and 1987. Without an Opening Inventory the Closing Inventory only was utterly meaningless. We would not be a whit the wiser. Nevertheless it was *seven* months before we received it. As always *something* was going on behind the scenes. One explanation for the delay was that seven months could have been the deadline for objections to be made on Peter's Estate. Another explanation was creative accounting by Brodies.

In November 1990 my Mother received a letter out of the blue from Alice Blamey, Gertie's Argentinian niece and Hallrule Housekeeper. This letter, dated 16th November 1990, was very disturbing indeed. Mrs Blamey stated that Carruthers of Brodies, Gertie's personal Law Agent and Peter's Curator, along with the Estate Manager had 'forced' Gertie to make a new Will. In terms of this new Will, Gertie's Estate was to be equally shared between herself (Mrs Blamey) and the Estate Manager, CJ Usher, on Robert's death. She added ambiguously: 'This is all very much Gertie's fault.'

Mrs Blamey wrote us another letter dated 18th May 1993. In this one she stated that Carruthers of Brodies and the Estate Manager had 'tricked' Gertie into signing away her rights as joint tenant, with the Estate Manager, of Town O'Rule farm to the Estate Manager. And that Gertie had meant to leave her share in Town O'Rule farm to her (Mrs Blamey). She then went on to inform us that the Estate Manager had made off with the heirloom jewellery and that Stevens and the Estate Manager had laughed at her when she had asked them what was to happen to all the Usher Trust silver.

We were aghast and furious at this litany of bad news. As always our family was the victim of daylight robbery and try as we might we could not stop it. I did not, however, for a minute believe that Gertie had not understood what she was signing. She was far too cunning for that. I swore again that such disgusting behaviour would never go unpunished as long as I lived.

My Mother instantly wrote to Stevens of Brodies in an attempt to save our personal silver which my Father had been foolhardy enough to lend to Uncle Stuart in 1950 and which we now feared Gertie had stolen. Also the heirloom jewellery which should have come to Johnny but which the Estate Manager, CJ Usher, had stolen. We contemplated reporting Brodies and the Estate Manager to the Police but decided against it as this would alert Brodies to the fact that Mrs Blamey had spilt the beans to us. Snookered again; always snookered. We felt as though we were caught in a terrible vice from which there was no escape.

As expected all my Mother received were dissembling replies from Stevens of Brodies stating that nothing could now be done about our personal silver being returned to us and that everything had been done legally and properly. Just another Brodies lie on just another Brodies day of defrauding.

In July 1992 we were informed that Robert had suffered a stroke and had been taken to the local hospital in Hawick.

On 30th July 1992 Ewing, Johnny's South African lawyer wrote again to Simpson of Tods Murray still trying to obtain a statement of the Assets remaining in the Usher Baronetcy Trust from Brodies. This effort had now gone on for ten years.

In August 1992 we heard from Alan Bailey, Great Aunt May's grandson, that Brodies were putting parts of the Estate up for sale to pay Peter's death duties. Alan sent out plans of the properties for sale. Brodies, it goes without saying, had appointed themselves as the Selling Agents because they also had a convenient in-house Estate Agency. The parts for sale included Dykes farm in which Clive had been a tenant from 1956 to 1973. In 1998 I discovered Brodies described Dykes farm as '*formerly* part of a large private estate' in their Sales Brochure of 1992. On the face of it this meant that Brodies were selling Dykes farm on behalf of someone else who had already purchased it from the Usher Baronetcy Trust or Peter and were concealing this by portraying it as being sold on behalf of the Usher Baronetcy Trust or Peter. This has remained a mystery to me ever since. Whatever else it might have been it was just another example of yet another Brodies engineered mystery; most likely another Brodies's fraud.

As luck would have it a very charming lady called Mrs Tweedie and her three very pretty daughters had lived in Dykes farmhouse in the late 1950s and early 60s. Of course the two elder daughters, who were about my age, soon caught my eye so I invited them to dances and outings with me. I therefore contacted Mrs Tweedie, who was now living in Dumfries, in 1998 to see if I could glean any information. She told me that a friend of hers who lived very close to the Estate had told Clive that she (Mrs Tweedie) was looking for accommodation in the area. Clive met her and told her that he would let her live in Dykes farmhouse rent free. Of course she accepted this offer and lived there with her daughters for five years. She assumed absolutely that the farm belonged to Clive because he never told her that he did not own Dykes farm. This was just another Clive lie by omission to make himself appear as 'The Big Man' in the area. Letting Mrs Tweedie live at Dykes for five years free of charge was another example of him betraying his own Usher family. By that time the Wells Estate was operating at a great and rapidly increasing loss which had to be financed from the Trust cash reserves. A reasonable rent from Dykes farmhouse would have been most welcome.

Of course Brodies never mentioned a word of these proposed sales to Johnny, a Trustee of the UBT and me. It was the same old story: Brodies, the Estate Manager, Valerie and the Mactaggarts colluding to enrich themselves and excluding us.

In September 1994 MacLetchie of Tods Murray informed us that Robert had died. The years of our and the Usher family being denied would now surely soon be over.

Dykes Farm House

22

MY MOTHER AND JOHNNY SEND ME TO SCOTLAND

Brodies wrote, in 1994, to the beneficiaries, of whom there were eight, stating that a meeting would be held at their offices in Edinburgh on the 26th of October for the purpose of electing Executors to the late Sir Robert Usher, Incapax.

For more than 20 years during my time in Africa I had been largely involved in the construction industry. In 1970, I purchased a small company called Midas Construction in Pietermaritzburg, Natal the main function of which was the building and selling of houses. Initially I had a work force of about ten; we built and successfully sold many individually designed houses, making a good profit. The company also built a lovely new and commodious house for Johnny on the basis of his paying the wages of the men during the time it took to build and his supplying all the building materials.

In 1976 I purchased an additional business called Wonder Concrete. Wonder Concrete's main function was the manufacture of concrete walls and the erection of them around houses and factories. Such was the demand for concrete walls of all types and varieties at the time that the business was successful and expanded greatly. At its height it employed 65 people.

Once or twice a year I held a great party for all my employees to celebrate all their hard work. On two occasions I gave the work force a surprise by taking them all down to the beach in Durban for a day out in the sea.

The business continued to thrive until the mid 1980s when through increased competition and, I have to admit, mismanagement on my part, the business started to go downhill. By the early 1990s I decided to close.

Following Brodies' letter to the beneficiaries and after much discussion between my Mother, Johnny and myself it was decided that I was now in the better position to represent the interests of our Usher family of Norton and Wells than Johnny. Johnny, now Sir John, was too tied up with his own business interests in South Africa to be able to drop everything and fly to Scotland at short notice.

I therefore flew over on 25th October 1994. I decided to stay at Hallrule farm with the Mactaggarts, much as I disliked the idea. The rationale for this was that I wanted to sound out the views of Valerie and the Mactaggarts on the contents of Hallrule House now belonging, according to Brodies, to the Estate Manager and Gertie's Argentinian niece.

As I motored onto Bedrule, which lay adjoining Wells estate, tears unexpectedly sprang to my eyes. It was raining lightly as I drove through Bedrule and then onto the Estate. Through avenues of Oak and Beech I sped until I arrived at Hallrule Farmhouse about 3 miles from Bedrule at 10pm. Inside I found Valerie and the Mactaggarts waiting for me in the kitchen. I gave no indication of my contempt at their usurping our family by squatting at Hallrule farm. This, not being in my nature, took some doing.

We soon got onto the subject of the contents of Hallrule House going to outsiders in terms of Gertie's Will. As I half-expected they were also furious about it and said that whoever became Executors must make sure that the contents were immediately returned to the soon to be created Executry. Mrs Mactaggart then quickly jumped in by telling me that Gertie had told her she would leave the 'Cat Picture' to her and that she bitterly resented that it was to be sold with the proceeds going to the Estate Manager and Mrs Blamey. I immediately told them all that Gertie had never owned the contents, and therefore had no right to leave them to anyone.

As people do on occasions like that we warmed to each other, largely because we had identified a matter of common interest. I had never really spoken much to Alan Mactaggart in my life because we had never moved in the same circles. He came from a family who used to work in the sheepwool industry. I actually got on with him rather better than I expected. I think this had something to do with all the beer Mrs Mactaggart kept giving me, which was a clever move on her part. Mactaggart sympathized with my anger at the Estates having to be sold and told me that if he were in my shoes he would fight like blazes to keep them in the family. In connection with Stuart leaving no Will he repeatedly impressed on me that it was the duty of every man to make a Will in good time because his father had told him that if someone died without leaving a Will it invariably resulted in a huge quarrel amongst the next generation and that this was most unfair on them. And that Stuart dying without a Will had been a great tragedy for our family.

Mrs Mactaggart, though, was more reserved and generally kept quiet, knowing of course that her Father had swindled me out of the tenancy of Hallrule Farm. She never, either, made one statement of regret about our beautiful Wells Estate having to be sold, thereby causing our family to lose its last remaining seat in Scotland. The only issue which aroused her was the fact that the Estate Manager and Mrs Blamey now supposedly owned the contents and that she would not be getting her 'Cat Picture.'

However I was there to get information and make allies of them in the short term until we got the contents of Hallrule House back into the ownership of the Executry so conducted myself accordingly. After we had rescued the contents I would then show my hand and set about them in no uncertain terms.

They all warned me to be very careful of the Estate Manager because he was 'very cunning.' Though I thought it was a case of a bunch of kettles calling a pot black I agreed with them that I would tread carefully, adding however that he held absolutely no terrors for me and that I would sort him out in short order when the time came to do so. They appeared delighted about that.

On Tuesday, 26th October 1994 Mrs Mactaggart drove me to Edinburgh in her spanking-new, purple BMW. On the way she was at pains to assure me there was no money in farming and how her life at Hallrule farm was just one long hard slog. The inference was, of course, that I should consider myself lucky that I was not farming it. I changed the subject to horses and horse racing, the only things which really interested her. Near Edinburgh we stopped while I purchased a small tape-recorder to secretly record the meeting with Brodies. Mrs Mactaggart heartily approved of this saying she didn't trust Brodies as far as she could throw them.

At the appointed time of 11am we walked into Brodies Offices in Atholl Crescent. A large oil painting of what appeared to be the original Brodie hung on one of the walls with lesser portraits on the other walls. I readied myself for the meeting as best I could, although, at that time, I was an innocent abroad regarding how deep ran the mendacity of lawyers. A short while later a medium-sized plumpish man in a dark suit came into the reception area and introduced himself as Hugh Stevens. Stevens told us that David Houldsworth would be joining us shortly, before ushering us into a small interview room where the Meeting was to take place.

Stevens was polite, exuding an air of, 'We are a highly respected law firm and have nothng to hide so *don't* ask awkward questions.' No doubt he was hoping like hell that Johnny and I had given up and that I would be a pushover. Tea and biscuits were served; all part of the softening up process.

I then realised I hadn't turned the tape-recorder on and excused myself saying that Nature called. In the Gents I did a quick test run and, all being well, hid the recorder in my breastpocket. Back with the others, Stevens opened the meeting.

He stated that the purpose of the meeting was to appoint Executors to the late Sir Robert Usher Incapax who had died without making a Will because he was incapable of making one. Under the laws of Intestacy the beneficiaries would now have to elect Executors. He had heard from some of the other beneficiaries that they did not wish to become Executors. He had heard from one beneficiary, Jacquelin Wolfe-Murray, that she *would* like to be an Executor. He then asked us if we wished to become Executors. I told him that Johnny would like to be an Executor as he had been a Trustee for many years and had a greater knowledge of the subject than anyone else.

He then asked Mrs Mactaggart if she would like to be one. She almost imperceptibly mumbled 'No.' Johnny and I had decided that only one of us should become Executor on the grounds that if we both became Executors this would alarm Brodies, Valerie, Mrs Mactaggart *and* the Estate Manager, and would cause them to close ranks against us sooner rather than, as we would prefer, later. At the time this appeared to be plain commonsense to both of us and I happily went along with it - another huge mistake - and one of the biggest. The upshot was that Johnny and Mrs Wolfe-Murray were elected to be the Executors. This business finished Stevens went off to fetch Houldsworth.

Houldsworth was more the typical lawyer type than Stevens, who had worked for the Inland Revenue before joining Brodies, possibly head-hunted by Brodies. Of the two I preferred Stevens. Houldsworth was more inclined to talk in the deliberately unfathomable legal-speak which the legal profession delights in. I was on a steep learning curve and, distrusting lawyers more and more, I naturally preferred the one who used less legal-speak.

Once we were all seated I asked if I could bring up some points which I felt they should all be aware of at the very outset. I was given the go-ahead. This was the part that I had looked forward. I knew that Brodies and Mrs Mactaggart would not at all like what I was going to say. But say it I had to. I also hoped that their reaction would yield me useful information.

'The very first thing I would like to inform you all is that *none* of us would be sitting around this table here to-day if my Grandparents' wishes with regard to the Estates had been adhered to.' I then told them about my Grandmother's exhortation to my Father: 'You are to see to it that Stuart's boys (Peter and Robert) do *not* inherit the Estates. Your Father would never approve of them doing so.' And that my Father had given her his word that he would never allow this to happen. I related this slowly, using the exact words that my Grandmother had used. All this was met by a stony silence and a slight shifting of uneasy posteriors and downcast eyes. I then went on: 'I don't propose to go into the Whys and Wherefores of my Father's failure to avert this disaster at this juncture.' Now that I had what appeared to be their undivided, albeit discomfited, attention I brought up my second point which would, as far as I was concerned, catch Brodies out, hook line and sinker.

Addressing Stevens and Houldsworth directly I asked them: 'Please tell me from whom Lady Gertrude Usher acquired her *personal fortune*?' I put heavy emphasis onto the words 'personal fortune' as both Johnny and myself had been incensed by the contents of Hallrule House, all Usher Baronetcy Trust property, being described by Brodies as part of 'Lady Gertrude's personal fortune,' in one of their brainwashing letters to us.

Stevens hesitated slightly before responding: 'Presumably she inherited the property from her husband, Sir Stuart.' I was not sufficiently *au fait* at catching lawyers out at that early stage so failed to tackle him on his use of the word 'presumably.' But I saw that I had him worried.

I therefore, instead, came back with the clincher: 'But that cannot be because Sir Stuart died without making a Will. So, from whom did she acquire this fortune?'

Stevens cleared his throat nervously and shifted in his chair before deciding discretion was the better part of valour. 'I do not at present know the answer to that question but will make enquiry.'

As Brodies had been Gertrude's personal Law Agents as well as the Usher Baronetcy Trust law Agents - a flagrant conflict of interest in itself - and as his immediate predecessor, Carruthers, had been both Peter's *Curator-Bonis and* Gertie's personal lawyer, Stevens' answer was simply not credible.

At this point Mrs Mactaggart piped up on her favourite subject: the *Cat Picture*. 'Aunt Gertie always told me that she would leave that picture to me. How come that John Usher of Courthill and Alice Blamey now own it?' Stevens explained to her that those were the terms of Lady Usher's Will. Of course I immediately jumped in again by stating the obvious; that Gertrude had no right to leave *any* assets which did not belong to her to anyone. I asked Stevens if she had also appropriated the Usher Trust Silver, the Bust of Sir John Usher and the full length portrait of Sir Robert Usher in hunting pink; and whether *these* were to be shared between her part-time housekeeper and the Estate Manager? The now sweating Stevens told us that only the portrait of Sir Robert and the portrait of Sir Walter Scott by Sir Henry Raeburn and some Usher silver still remained in the Curatory, but that everything else in Hallrule House had belonged to Gertie and was now the property of the Estate Manager and Mrs Blamey.

Obviously I thanked God for the small mercies of the two family portraits and some silver being saved but was furious that Gertrude, with Brodies colluding, had appropriated all the other Usher Baronetcy Trust contents of the house to herself and particularly the bust of my great grandfather, Sir John Usher, and the remainder of the Usher silver.

I stared long and hard at Stevens before moving on to the third point: 'Perhaps you could enlighten me? Did Sir John Usher *own* the estates after the death of his father, Sir Robert in 1933, and after *he* died in 1952, did Sir Stuart own them until his death in 1962 or were they owned by the Usher Baronetcy Trust for the whole of that period?'

Stevens replied: 'I do not know the answer to that but will make inquiry.' He knew, as his reddening face suggested, that he was on dangerous ground and the less he said the better. If he didn't know, of course he *should* have known, and if he *did* know, then he was lying. It had to be one or the other. Almost certainly it was the latter.

So the meeting went on. Mrs Mactaggart made virtually no contribution to the meeting other than to witter on about the Cat picture. However she backed me in insisting that the contents be taken away from Mrs Blamey and the Estate Manager, and placed into the soon to be created Executry. I noted, however, that she had been all eyes and ears and had taken in more than she wanted me to think.

I arranged another meeting with Brodies for two days later, on Thursday, 28th October 1995 at 2 00pm and thereafter we departed.

On the way back to Hallrule farm she told me that it would be the 'talk of the Borders chattering classes,' if she did not get the *Cat Picture*. This puzzled me. Why on earth should anyone be remotely interested in her being or not being left a picture by her Aunt? I therefore filed this episode in the back of my mind. Good job too, because in 1996 I discovered a 1988 Christies Inventory in which the *Cat Picture* had been marked as 'Missing.' Mrs Mactaggart's statement about the 'chattering classes' then immediately sprang to mind and I deduced that she had stolen it from Hallrule House after Gertie's death in 1984. I therefore researched the matter further and procured a 1990 Christies Valuation for Probate for Peter. Lo and behold the *Cat Picture*, valued at £1200 for probate, was now back in Hallrule. She must therefore have returned the picture sometime between 1988 and 1990 because she felt it too dangerous to keep.

Back at Hallrule I rang Tods Murray and fixed an appointment with David MacLetchie for 10.00 am on Thursday the 28th of October to bring him up to date before my 2.00pm appointment with Brodies in the afternoon. I then climbed Ruberslaw, a great landmark of Rulewater and the Scottish Borders. Its northern, and by far its prettiest, flank lay almost wholly on the Wells Estate. The climb did me a power of good, as it never failed to do. Standing on the summit I could see the whole Estate below me. I looked straight across the valley to Bedrule and picked out all the places I loved the most as a child and still loved. I also looked straight across to the summit of Blacklaw and remembered the vow I had made up there all those years ago in 1968. I therefore reconfirmed my vow from the summit of Ruberslaw. Having done so I again felt much invigorated as I ran down to Wells and visited some of my favourite fishing spots on the Rulewater. Arriving back at Hallrule Farm I felt like a new man.

On Wednesday, 27th October 1994. I did something which I had looked forward to for a long time; I went to Bedrule Church. It held so many happy memories for me. I thanked God for my home-coming and asked Him to look with favour on my efforts in connection with the future of my family. I then inspected my Father's gravestone in our burial ground. I then went back into the Church to reminisce and recapture old memories there. Sir Robert had carried out extensive additions and improvements to the Church in 1914 turning it into, I am told, one of the five most beautiful Parish Churches in Scotland.

One of the most significant events of the Second World War was triggered by a Bedrule Parish Navy man called Lt Francis Anthony Blair Fasson GC (Posthumous). He was the War Hero who recovered the vital documents from a sinking German U-Boat off Port Said which enabled Bletchley Park to break the German secret Enigma code. He and two others, Able-Seamen Glazier and Brown, from the Destroyer HMS *Petard* had swum to the stricken U-boat and recovered the documents. Fasson and Glazier then went down again into the U-Boat to try and rescue some transmitting machinery. Unfortunately the submarine then suddenly took its final death dive, taking Fasson and Glazier with it. Thankfully Brown managed to make it back to HMS *Petard.* Some WW2 historians hold that this episode was the turning point of the second world war. If you ever visit Bedrule Church please look out for the Memorial to Lt Fasson in the main body of the Church to your left as you enter.

Another notable Bedrule man was Archbishop William Turnbull who founded Glasgow University in 1451. He is remembered on an escutcheon high up at the end of the nave of the Church

I then noticed that a scroll which used to hang in our family pews was missing. This scroll listed the previous owners of Bedrule and other landowners in the Parish of Bedrule over the last 600 years or so. The Red Comyn, the Earls of Douglas, the Turnbulls, the Elliots and the Ushers. For many years Bedrule has been regarded as the Mecca for all Turnbulls the world over because they regard Bedrule as their ancestral home. They visit in a steady stream the year round and I now wish that I, as a young man, had taken more interest in them and shown them the ruins of Bedrule Castle which lay nearby. Katherine, Lady Usher was a Turnbull by birth. This scroll also identified the various coats of arms of these families which were displayed around the Church just below the ceiling. I thought this scroll being missing was odd. I then looked around the rest of the Church to see if I could locate it but could not find it. But I did find a new Scroll which hung near the altar of the Church. This scroll had been beautifully illuminated and painted. However I was perturbed to see that the entry for our family had been curtailed to just 'Usher of Norton', instead of 'Usher of Norton and Wells' as it had appeared, correctly, on the old missing scroll.

'Ahaa, Gotcha,' I said to myself. Clive strikes again. Clive had simply removed the old Scroll and had the new one made as part of his attempt to erase all memory of our family and Wells in an attempt to conceal the uncomfortable fact that he and his ghastly family were no more than squatters on the Estate. Also to make it look as though he, Clive, had inherited Wells from his father in the normal fashion when in fact he had never done so. How could he? The whole Wells Estate had been placed in the Usher Baronetcy Trust, of which he himself was a Trustee. In effect this was an attempt by him and Valerie to bury the past and put himself in the clear. 'Well, Well, Well, we'll see about that, you cunning swine,' I swore to myself. This had parallels to Wilkie Collins' gripping book 'The Woman in White.'

Bedrule Church

Leaving the Church I walked up to Bedrule House for the part that I half dreaded, and looked forward to most, in equal measure. I was warmly welcomed by its new incumbents, John and Adele Richardson. They showed me proudly over the house. I was much moved as I re-visited the beloved abode of my so-happy childhood and was filled with warm memories of Norton, Miss Spapens, John Purves, 'Auld Ale' (Alice) and everyone else. And of later times I thought of Jack Bell, Jock and Willie Fox, Reg Mouland, Agnes Easton, Mrs Jardine, Mrs Laidlaw, Bob Thompson, and Willie Smith.

Richardson then showed me around the almost completely revamped farm. It was quite apparent that Bedrule was being very efficiently farmed and was up to the minute in modernization. I welcomed this though the farmyard did not have the romance about it that it had in my day - only to be expected. In my day the farm buildings were all very old with lots of nooks and crannies - rather like the farmyards in fairy tale books. Romantic and evocative.

With the exception of one new cottage the village had not changed much. I then had a very pleasant lunch with the Craigs who lived at Pirn-Mill, just below Bedrule, before visiting Jack Bell in the nearby village of Denholm. He was a wonderful man who'd worked at Wells Stables in my grandfather's time and remained with our family until we left in 1968.

On 28th October 1994 at just before ten on this Thursday morning I walked into the offices of Tods Murray in Queen Street, Edinburgh. Their premises were nothing like as salubrious as those of Brodies. I soon met David MacLetchie who was a well-built man, keen on rugby; perhaps unusual for a lawyer. This heartened me because I had always assumed that a man who was keen on rugby was a good man. Nevertheless I remained *en guarde*.

I asked McLetchie when the Trust had been set up by my grandfather. 1911 was the answer. I then tackled him about whether Uncle John and then Uncle Stuart *owned* the Trust assets between 1933 to 1962 or whether the Trust owned them - the question that Brodies had steadfastly refused to answer. Significantly he responded *immediately* that the Trust owned them in this period and that Uncle John and Uncle Stuart had been entitled only to the income from the Estates plus the income from funds within the Trust. Of course the only place McLetchie could have gleaned this information was from Brodies. I then asked him about heirloom jewellery and he gave some answers on that. He had been 'unable' to get a copy of Gertie's Will because Brodies had 'refused to release it'. This was of less importance, now, because of his answer that Stuart had never owned any of the Usher Baronetcy Trust Assets; so his wife, Gertie, could never have inherited them from him even if he *had* made a Will. We then talked more about rugby before I bade him farewell and left to meet Jacquelin Wolfe-Murray for lunch at the Caledonian Hotel in Princes Street.

I hadn't seen Jacquelin for 35 years. She was the younger of the two daughters of Uncle John. My last memory of her had been of her kissing her prospective husband, Mike Wolfe-Murray, in the drawing room at Bedrule in the 1950s. All very romantic. Before I left South Africa Johnny had received a fax from Alan Bailey which contained advice from Mrs Blamey to the effect that we were to be very careful of Jacquelin because she had been spreading stories about the Estate Manager having defrauded the Trust Estates. So she, Jacquelin, already knew that he was a crook. It was precisely because of this that Johnny and I agreed to her being appointed an Executor.

I found her waiting in the lounge of the Caledonian and it was good to see her after all those years. It was also a pleasure to be back in the good old Caledonian, which had always been my family's favourite hotel in Edinburgh and of which I had many pleasant memories. We brought each other up to date on our lives and I then filled her in on the meeting that Mrs Mactaggart and I had attended with Brodies two days previously. I was very pleased to hear that she too was adamant that the contents of Hallrule House be taken out of Gertrude's so called *Trust* and placed into Robert's Executry. She confirmed that she considered the Estate Manager a crook. She was also at pains to tell me that whenever she had happened to meet Dempster, the Death bed thief and now of Brodies, in Edinburgh and had asked him about what was happening to the Estates he had always brushed her off with his usual lie: 'It's none of your business.' She and Mike Wolfe-

Murray had divorced many years previously after having produced three daughters.

After lunch we went to Brodies. Stevens opened the proceedings by telling us that Uncle Stuart *had* left a Will *after all.* Well, you could have knocked me over with a feather. For 32 years my family was led to believe that Uncle Stuart had left no Will; that this was the cause of the Estates going to Peter, who had been both Downs Sydrome and Incapax. The lack of a Will was ultimately the cause of my father selling Bedrule and going to South Africa, taking Johnny and me with him. The silence was broken by my audible gasp, but instead of showing any sign of compassion, and while he had me proverbially 'on the ropes', Stevens hit me with the news that Stuart had left, in his Will, all his personal effects and furniture to his wife Gertie.

It seems important to me at this crucial stage to fast forward some four years to 1998 when I had some dealings with a Glasgow lawyer called David Lyle of David A. Lyle and Company. I told him that originally Mackenzie and Black had informed the family that Uncle Stuart had died intestate. At this he expostulated that it was inconceivable that a man in Stuart's position, as the Titleholder, an Usher Baronetcy Trustee and the father of two Downs Syndrome and mentally incapacitated sons, would leave no Will given that the whole future of the Trust Estates depended upon him doing so. In addition Sir Stuart would want to make what provision he could for his wife and two sons. Lyle then went to great lengths to warn me that photocopies of Wills, even if signed, should never be relied upon as being authentic. The only way to be sure of the authenticity of *any* Will in Scotland was to see the original and then have a copy of it made in one's presence. That got me thinking.

After Stevens confessed to me that Stuart *had* after all left a Will, as opposed to the lawyers in 1962 claiming he had *not* left a Will, I made it my business to procure a copy of his Will. It was *unsigned.* Significantly, at the time the Will was made, the Executors listed were MacClure, Clive, and Leadbetter, in that order. MacClure and Leadbetter were also Usher Baronetcy Trustees at the time. I have already established that MacClure and Clive were crooks. But Leadbetter, was *he* a crook? He most certainly *was* a crook: under the heading of 'Crimes of Omission'. Crimes of Omission mean that any person who knows that a crime is about to be commited, is being commited or has been commited and does not inform the Police of the crime. Leadbetter, a *lawyer* I remind the reader, was fully aware that the Usher Baronetcy Trust was being repeatedly defrauded and broken and had been ever since he had become a Trustee of it - yet he never reported this to the Police. By not reporting this to the Police he became an accessory and complicit in the crime. In view of what Mr Lyle told me about Wills the question then arises: As an Executor of Stuart's Will *and* a Trustee of the Usher Baronetcy Trust did Leadbetter believe that Stuart had died Intestate because his Will could not be *found* as claimed by the lawyers in Edinburgh? I am certain that he did not believe that at all. But instead of making a stand he took the easy way out by keeping quiet. A further question then arises in connection with Stuart's Intestacy: *If* Leadbetter had always acted in good faith as a Trustee of the Usher Baronetcy Trust he would have made sure that Stuart, who was his cousin, had made a Will that was current on his death and not hidden it so well that it could not be found. I therefore regard Leadbetter as an accomplice to the breaking and defrauding of the Usher Baronetcy Trust. I delve further into Stuart's purported Intestacy later in this chapter.

However, Stuart's unsigned Will is dated 1955 and has this passage in it:

> 'And in the event of my said wife predeceasing me and my sons being still in minority I bind my said Trustees to be their Tutors and Guardians.'

The main point here is that this purported Will claims to have been 'subscribed to' by Stuart on 19th October 1955. Yet, in 1955 Peter was twenty -five years old and Robert was twenty-one; therefore they were *not* in their minority when Uncle Stuart had purportedly signed this Will in 1955, as claimed by Brodies. This is hugely important. The Will *must* therefore have been drafted *before* both Peter and Robert reached their 18th birthdays. The year that Robert came of age was in April 1952. When I checked with the National Archives to see if this purported Will of Stuart *had* been registered I discovered that it *had* been, but was unsigned. I therefore believe that Stuart had made a later Will than 1955 but that Will has been deliberately destroyed by the then lawyers, Mackenzie and Black; most probably by the death-bed thief Thomas Dempster.

This might be a good moment to quote part of the 1911 Trust Deed of Sir Robert Usher which states:

> I declare it to be my earnest desire that each heir should resettle the Trust Estate for the life-rent, use and enjoyment of himself and the heirs succeeding him in the Baronetcy in similar terms to those above set forth and so on throughout the course of the succession to the Baronetcy so that the *Trust Estate may in all time be preserved* and retained for the maintenance of the said title and the benefit of the Baronet at the time [italics mine].

Obviously this Trust Deed was created on the assumption that the heir would be *capable* of making a Will and resettling the Estates. The effect of any person inheriting the Trust Estates and assets who was *incapable* of making a Will would be catastrophic, as events were now proving. This was the very reason that caused my grandmother, Katherine Lady Usher, to enjoin my Father to ensure that Uncle Stuart's mentally incapacitated sons Peter and Robert did *not* inherit.

Why, then, had the lawyers lodged Stuart's unsigned Will of 1955 in the Sheriff Court in September 1963, *ten months* after his death? This appears to have been a very risky thing to have done in view of their original claim that Stuart's Will could not be found.

The answer appears to be this: The lawyers *had to* because, under the laws of Intestacy, the *assets* of an Intestate deceased person have to be shared between his wife and issue. As already narrated Stuart had next to no *assets* of his own. This meant that Gertie, Peter and Robert would become destitute in a matter of weeks. The only way to overcome this was to register the unsigned Will as his only and last Will and to make it appear that Peter had inherited the Trust Estates, thereby securing the financial futures of all the malefactors, including the lawyers. How the lawyers managed to have the Court accept an unsigned Will is anybody's guess. But managed it they somehow did.

Why then *was* Uncle Stuart's 1955 Will unsigned? The only plausible explanation is that he was not happy with its wording and had therefore refused to sign it. By far the most devastating clause in the 1955 Will was that Peter *was* to inherit the Estates with no mention of his being Downs Syndrome and Mentally Incapacitated. If Stuart subsequently decided that he did *not* want Peter to inherit the Estates why did he not simply have a new Will drafted which reflected such revised and common-sense wishes? It appears that the lawyers advised Stuart that to do this he would have to obtain the agreement of his fellow Usher Baronetcy Trustees to vary the 1911 Deed to make it possible for him to by-pass Peter and Robert and settle the Estates onto his brother (my Father) instead, on the grounds that this was the only way for the Estates to be 'preserved and retained' as stated in the 1911 Sir Robert Usher Trust Deed. Of course Sir Stuart would need to do this in a manner that guaranteed the future of Gertie, Peter and Robert for the rest of their lives. This would be something that my Father would have insisted upon as a matter of course.

It appears, however, that the Usher Baronetcy Trustees would *not* agree to the Trust Deed being amended unless they got something from the Trust in return. So now Uncle Stuart was in the most unenviable position of desperately wanting to make a new Will which would give effect to his Father's wishes as expressed in the Trust Deed but not being allowed to do so unless he gave some of its assets away, which was illegal. This would entail him breaching the Trust of which he was the Principal Trustee. The situation was one of out and out blackmail. Of course the lawyers, and Clive, and Gertrude would have exerted all the pressure they could on him to sign the 1955 Will as it stood because they all saw meal tickets for the rest of their lives in his so doing. Despite all this pressure Stuart, being an honourable man at heart, stood firm. He must have realised that if he settled the Trust Estates and other assets onto Peter for his lifetime, the Trust Estates would be defrauded, and inevitably lost to our family on Peter's death, or on Robert's death if Robert survived him. Which was exactly what came to pass in 1995.

So, for Sir Stuart, how to break the impasse? He saw only one way to do it and that was to negotiat a *quid pro quo* with MacClure, Clive and Gertie. The upshot was that Uncle Stuart was forced to agree to 'give' Clive the properties in the vicinity of Wells House in 1959 and to promise Gertie the Contents of Hallrule House on his death as the price of their agreement for the Trust Deed to be amended. Obviously both of these arrangements breached the Trust but, to Uncle Stuart at the time, this appeared to be the lesser of two evils and the only way to break the impasse.

What about JGG Leadbetter WS, also an Usher Baronetcy Trustee at the time? He, being a lawyer, the odds were that he, too, would have insisted that he get *something* in return for his agreement that the Trust Deed be amended. But I have never discovered anything to date in this regard. If, in fact, he had *not* asked for anything it appears that he nevertheless agreed to the Trust being breached in this manner.

Having got the agreement, on the face of it, of his fellow Usher Baronetcy Trustees it appears that the necessary amendments were made to the Trust Deed in either 1959 or 1960 and thereafter Stuart made his final Will which by-passed Peter and Robert in favour of my Father, but which also made provision for Gertrude, Peter and Robert to be looked after for the rest of their lives.

This must have been a great relief to Stuart. Hence his suddenly improved attitude to my father, his taking me to the lawyers to sign the documents in connection with the Hallrule cottages, and accompanying us to the Buccleuch Huntball in 1961 as well as his attending Johnny's wedding in Ayrshire - significantly, without Clive and Val at the Ball and without Gertie and Clive and Val at Johnny's wedding. He was now over sixty years old and to have been without a Will for all that time had been very risky indeed because he could have died at anytime for any number of reasons.

Uncle Stuart, unfortunately, suddenly dropped off his horse and died whilst hunting with the Buccleuch Hunt near Hawick in November 1962. However fifty or more years later and my trust in lawyers having long been utterly extinguished, as the reader will readily appreciate, I therefore revisited the events surrounding Stuart's death.

First of all let us take the lawyers' statement to my father following Uncle Stuart's unexpected death in 1962: 'No Will could be found. They hunted high and low for it at Hallrule but could not find it. This means that Stuart has died intestate.' And a few days later: 'His dying intestate means that the Trust has come to an end and the Estates and all the assets now belong to Peter personally.'

My Parents had accepted this explanation at the time, so had Johnny and I. But now and with the benefit of first-hand experience of Brodies' subsequent frauds, the ambiguity of those carefully crafted words suddenly struck home: They did *not* mean that Stuart had left *no* Will, only that no Will could be *found* at *Hallrule*. Why then had they used such carefully crafted words to establish Stuart's 'intestacy.' One reason was that if they stated categorically that he had left *no* Will they, as the Usher Baronetcy Trust lawyers *and* Stuart's personal lawyers, would be held responsible by all and sundry for not seeing to it that he *had* made a Will. However their wording that 'no Will could be found at Hallrule' implied that Stuart *had* made a Will but had hidden it so well that it could not be found. It also implied that the lawyers did not have either the original nor a copy of his new Will; a most unusual state of affairs. So unusual as to be not credible. Also his hiding it without even telling wife Gertrude where he had hidden it implied that Stuart had made his Will by himself without telling anyone and had hidden it in a place where it could not be found - again without telling anyone. This is so unlikely, it has to be untrue.

Much more likely was that the lawyers had drawn up a *new* Will for Stuart which gave effect to his Father's Trust Deed and which he *had* signed and retained the original themselves and might have or might not have given Stuart a copy of it. If they had given Stuart a copy of it is just possible that Stuart had hidden because he did not want Gertrude to know that he had made a new Will, for obvious reasons. Alternatively Gertie was aware of the new Will and had feigned agreement with its contents. In the event of the lawyers not having given Stuart a copy of it, this meant that only the original of Stuart's new Will existed and over this the lawyers had full control.

So what happened to Stuart's new Will after his death? The answer which most closely fits the train of events is that the lawyers, with Gertie and Clive colluding, destroyed the original and Gertie destroyed any copy at Hallrule if a copy existed. If Stuart had not asked for a copy of his new Will (quite possible) all the lawyers had to do was to destroy the original in their keeping. Which specific lawyer actually destroyed the new Will? Most likely it was Dempster, the Deathbed Thief, on the instructions of Logan McLure and Clive Usher, and possibly James Leadbetter of Spital Tower. I name these three as Stuart's most likely Executors and Trustees as they were the ones he appointed his Executors and Trustees in his abortive 1955 Will.

And what specifically were the benefits for the conspirators to have Peter, through Stuart's Will being destroyed, becoming the Proprietor of the Estates?

In addition to Clive and Gertrude getting meal tickets for the rest of their lives, the lawyers would be in an infinitely stronger position to defraud the Estates as and when they pleased for as long as they pleased. On top of that it would make the concealment of all the past frauds much easier to maintain. For example Uncle Stuart 'giving' Clive the properties around Wells House itself. It also made Gertrude being 'given' the contents of Hallrule after Stuart's death in 1962 much easier to conceal.

The last time I spoke at any length to Uncle Stuart was at a Cocktail party at Bedrule in the summer of 1962 shortly before he died which he attended again, significantly I now realise, without Gertrude. He was in good humour and I complimented him on his having given up smoking. He laughed and said it was eleven months since his last cigarette and that he had never felt better.

Sir Stuart had *not* died Intestate. He was made to *appear* Intestate by the collusion of Clive, Gertrude and the lawyers. The destruction of Uncle Stuart's Will of course bound the conspirators together in an unholy alliance of mutual criminal self-aggrandisement and eternal silence. By inferring that Stuart had left no Will the conspirators deflected all the blame for Peter inheriting the Estates and their ultimate loss to our family onto the deceased Uncle Stuart alone. This also gave the lawyers and Gertie, Clive and Leadbetter their 'keep out of jail' cards. Uncle Stuart has therefore carried the blame, opprobrium and contempt it engendered for him in our family of Bedrule and the whole neighbourhood for more than fifty years up to the present time as I write these words. I fervently hope that this book exonerates him.

What about the Tax Authorities? It appears that the lawyers told them absolutely nothing about Stuart's purported intestacy nor that Peter was Downs Syndrome as well as mentally incapacitated . So, as far as the Tax Authorities were concerned, Peter was a normal heir who had inherited the Usher Baronetcy Trust assets in the normal way and that the Trust continued to exist and function in a normal manner. That of course was another explanation for the Estate Accounts still being in the name of the Usher Baronetcy Trust until the mid 1980s, though the Trust had supposedly come to an end upon Sir Stuart's death in the early 1960s Actually it is likely the Tax Authorities remained in complete ignorance of the real state of affairs with the Trust until I informed them of just one aspect of the fraud on a cold, blustery April day in 1996 which I cover in more detail later in this book.

Of course the lawyers were aware that someone, one day, might discover this unsigned 1955 Will. But in the short term they must have felt pretty confident that no one would. Why should anyone check when they had all been brainwashed into believing that Stuart had died Intestate. However the lawyers delayed presenting the unsigned 1955 version to the Sheriff Court for ten months after Stuart's death as a further precaution. They would also have noted my Father's heart attacks and no doubt hoped that one of them would, sooner rather than later, kill him.

The more time passed, the less chance of discovery. By the time of Peter's death in 1990 and Robert's death in 1994 Brodies would have been almost certain that no one would discover the bogus 1955 Will. I might never have discovered it myself if Stevens had not told me that Stuart *had* left a Will at our meeting on 28th October 1994 in a bungled attempt to justify Gertrude's 'ownership' of the contents of Hallrule House.

The revelations in this passage of the book will come as another very unpleasant shock to Brodies. In essence it was a very skilfully concealed example of Will Fraud which took half a century to discover: *Though the mills of God grind slowly;Yet they grind exceeding small,* according to Longfellow.

Back to 1994 when Brodies' lawyer Stevens had just let this very large (bogus Will) cat out of the bag. As I shook my head in disbelief he followed up with the news that the value of Uncle Stuart's possessions only came to a few hundred pounds. I looked toward Jacquelin but she was equally baffled. I knew of course that the contents of Hallrule House were worth hundreds of thousands of pounds, so, gathering my wits I repeated a slightly different version of the question I had asked him at our previous meeting: 'From whom, then, and how, did Gertie become possessed of the vast majority of the Contents of Hallrule House, given that Stuart only owned a few hundred pounds worth of personal effects and furniture?' This time Stevens had done his homework and was ready for me:

'This came about as follows. The Capital Taxes office contacted Tommy Dempster in 1963 and asked him why the contents of Hallrule House no longer appeared in the Usher Baronetcy Inventory, as they always had done in the past. Dempster told them that Gertie owned them with a view to saving the Estate paying death duties. This was most probably an inaccurate statement by him.' Those were Stevens' exact words.

I did *not* respond by asking Stevens to confirm that Dempster had lied to the Capital Tax Office on a matter of great import to the Usher Baronetcy Trust and the Usher family concerning their great losses. This Dempster lie was just another attempt by him to illegally convey Usher Baronetcy Trust assetts to someone whom he very well knew had no right to them. The lie was also designed to give credence to the falsehood that the Usher Baronetcy Trust had ceased to exist on the death of Stuart. The 'most probably' part of Steven's statement was a good example of lawyers always leaving themselves a little wriggle room. I was later to catch Stevens and Brodies out on this point in the most spectacular style, as the reader will see. There followed a general discussion on the implications of this revelation by Stevens and how we should most easily remove the contents from *'Gertrude's Trust'* which Brodies themselves had now set up, and place them into the ownership of the yet to be constituted Executry.

Stevens was also at pains, now, to correct another statement that he had made at our first meeting to the effect that Gertrude had made a *new* Will shortly before her death in 1984. 'Turns out,' he chuckled, as if this were some jolly reminiscence, 'this was not so. The last Will she made was *not* a few months before her death but quite some time *before* and *that* had been her last Will. The Will had differed from an earlier one only in a *minor, legal* and *technical* way.' He seemed unnaturally emphatic about this, so I filed it in my mind just as I had with Mrs Mactaggart's 'chattering classes' remark about the Cat Picture.

I then asked Stevens for a copy of Sir Robert Usher's (died 1933) Will. Stevens claimed that Brodies did not have one. 'It was lost, unfortunately, in one of the moves of office or perhaps it was never brought over to Brodies Offices in Rothesay Terrace from Mackenzie & Black's offices in Heriot Row when this firm took over in 1972.' A credit to his profession, Stevens never so much as blushed as he said this. But I knew, at least, that the latter part of his statement was not possible because Dempster had pointed out Sir Robert's leather bound Will to me in 1973 in Brodies offices in Rothesay Terrace. Of course I did not believe a word that Stevens told me, and neither did Stevens. I had already heard that my family had been far and away Mackenzie & Black's biggest clients and that they had very few other clients. As such it was incredible that they would *lose* the Will of the leading member of a family which was paying their salaries. Brodies had the Will alright.

Instead of reaching for his tie and calling him a liar I told him that old Sir Robert's Will was certainly in existence in 1973 because Dempster had pointed it out to me but had refused to allow me to peruse it. 'When I *now* undoubtedly have the *right* to inspect the Will you tell me it has been *lost*?' His only response was to stutter that it was, 'all so unfortunate.'

Both Jacquelin and myself were at pains to tell Stevens that, had the family known earlier that the contents were being treated as Gertie's 'personal fortune' as a consequence of Dempster's so-called 'inaccurate statement' we would all have objected in the strongest possible terms. Stevens just sat there, his eyes darting about the room like a chameleon.

I then told Stevens that the Estate Manager (Charles John Usher, who was no relation) being a tenant of one of the farms, Town O'Rule, on the Estate was unlawfully serving two diametrically opposed and irreconcilable interests; his own and the Estate's. What had Stevens to say about that? He told us that nothing untoward was possible as the Accountant of Court went through all the accounts with a 'fine toothcomb'. His response did not satisfy me at all as it had not answered my question. I did not push the point at that time however as I needed his further co-operation on the contents issue. Thereafter the meeting closed. I made another appointment to see Stevens three days later on 31st October 1994 at 9.00am.

In the meantime Jacquelin startled me by telling me that *she* had a copy of Sir Robert's (1933) Will albeit unsigned which she was happy for me to have. In addition she had a copy of Katherine Lady Usher's (1948) Will which I could also have. This was welcome news and I looked forward to studying them both.

So, what about old Sir Robert's 1933 Will which had been made in 1932? If I may fast forward once again, briefly, to 2004 I applied for and obtained a copy of this Will from the National Archives. The copy from the National Archives appeared to have been properly signed by Sir Robert and the wording accorded with the unsigned copy I'd been given by Jacquelin. So all seemed in order. However in 2011, I requested the National Archives for yet another copy of Sir Robert's Will which I received on 6th October 2011 and this time it was *unsigned*. My instincts tell me there is an innocent explanation for this as the wording of the copies are identical; but of course it makes me uneasy. However I keep in mind the advice of Mr Lyle the Glasgow lawyer that one cannot entirely rely on the authenticity of any Will until you see the original. It may seem to the reader that as all these copies concur - apart from the signature - that I should accept them as authentic but we should keep two events firmly in mind : Firstly, Dempster's blank refusal to let me even look at what appeared to be the original *leather bound* original in 1974, and secondly: Steven's statement in 1994 the Will had been lost.

On 29th October 1994 I went to a Meet of the Jedforest hounds at Spital Tower, old Aunt May's abode. To my disappointment and incomprehension the property's name had now been changed to Towerburn. It had been converted into nine flats which were inhabited by elderly retired people. Apart from a few alterations it looked much the same. It was a most beautiful house in appearance with corbelled corners and other fancy stonework. The same quality had been applied to its interior; everything solid and exuding quality. It was nice to be back there and see the hounds and hunters, both equine and human. I recognized few of the hunters as most of those who had hunted in my day had either moved away or been appropriated by the Grim Reaper.

On 31st October 1994 I met Stevens again at Brodies offices. He and I were the only ones present. Unlike the previous meetings this one was held in what looked like the Brodies Boardroom upstairs. When you have a lawyer on the backfoot you don't allow him to butter you up in the boardroom so I immediately hit him with the question: 'By what right did Gertrude dispose of the contents to outsiders?' Stevens's reply was: 'It is now virtually certain that she did *not* have the right to do so.' For a very pleasant change he had given a 'virtually' straight answer to a dead straight question.

I expressed my delight at his unusual veracity. Johnny and I had vowed that we would never allow Brodies, Gertie and the Estate Manager to get away with that particular piece of chicanery.

'Well, that is the big one,' I said to Stevens. He agreed with me. The reader might be surprised that at the time I regarded this as the 'Big One,' but it was because I felt this first victory was the 'Big One' in the sense that it would set the precedent for us to win the far bigger battles which I knew lay ahead. Stevens, blushing in the face of my praise, now seemed to think that Johnny and I would from now on let things rest because Brodies had allowed us this small victory. He could not have been more wrong.

While Stevens was still basking in his new-found philanthropy I asked him for copies of both Uncle Stuart's and Gertie's Wills, which he agreed to procure for me. However, he bounced back by asking me for a copy of Sir Robert's (d 1933) Will. I agreed to him taking a copy and he further pushed his luck by asking for a copy of Lady Katherine's (d 1948) Will. Again I agreed. Nevertheless it struck me as very odd that Brodies did not have copies of both these Wills. Had they 'lost' Lady Katherine's Will as well? Or did they believe both had been destroyed?

I then informed Stevens that the heirloom jewellery should, by right of succession, have gone to Johnny in terms of Lady Katherine Usher's Will. So why the blazes did the Estate Manager now have them? In his customary evasive manner he responded by informing me that the Estate Manager had returned them to him (Stevens) because he (The Estate Manager) did 'not want to be accused of having something which he should not have.' In essence this was a roundabout, 'cover my back' admission by the Estate Manager that he *had* stolen them. Of course I was delighted that our objections had frightened the Estate Manager into returning the stolen heirloom jewellery. It would only be a question of time, I thought, before I had the heirloom jewellery for Johnny. To encourage him further I then tackled Stevens about the massive conflict of interest arising if 'we', the Executors and beneficiaries, found ourselves in dispute with the beneficiaries of Gertrude's Will and 'Trust' which Brodies themselves had set up. This seemed inevitable unless the Estate Manager and Mrs Blamey gave up the contents without demur. Particularly so because one of the Executors and Trustees of Gertie's Trust had been Carruthers of Brodies who had, on his death, been replaced by another Brodies man called Page, who worked in Brodies Taxation Department. Just to turn the screw I pointed out to Stevens that Carruthers was the specific Brodies man who had set up Gertrude's so called 'Trust' and subsequently appointed *himself* as Trustee. To complicate matters even further, if such a thing were possible, Carruthers had *also* been Sir Peter's Curator.

Stevens, having recovered at least half his composure, was evidently expecting this. He replied: 'In that case I suggest Brodies represent the interests of the Executry and that Mr Page would have to resign as Trustee of the Gertrude Usher Trust, leaving the Estate Manager as the sole Trustee. The Estate Manager would then have to find himself another lawyer as Brodies could not continue to act as his Law Agents because Brodies can only represent the interests of the Executry.' Impressive footwork but it failed to address the basic fact that Brodies were as a matter of fact *already* embroiled in many flagrant Conflict of Interest situations - all of their *own* construct. But Stevens knew this and was once again stuttering.

He added that, 'We' (now Brodies and the Executors) must work nicely together in the Executry but if it was felt that Brodies would still be in a Conflict of Interest then the Executry must instruct other lawyers'. At this point I rammed it home to him that Brodies had been in many monumental Conflict of Interest situations for decades in their acting as Law Agents for Clive, Law Agents for Gertie, and Law Agents for the Estate Manager - all on the one hand; and yet were the law agents for the Usher Baronetcy Trust on the other hand. Why had they knowingly placed themselves in these totally illegal situations in the first place? And why had they continued with it for decades as though it were perfectly acceptable? Stevens had no credible answer to this and maintained an uneasy silence during which he had the grace to blush further.

Having made my point I then asked him about the implications of changing to another set of lawyers. He informed me that this would be a very expensive business indeed as the new lawyers would have to first acquaint themselves with the background and history of the Estates, the Usher Baronetcy Trust, the Curatories, and so on. This he said would be a monumental task for any new lawyers. There would also be the extra costs of communicating between three parties instead of two: that is the Executors, to New Lawyers, to Brodies and vice-versa. Further that as Brodies had all the documentation to hand and a first rate knowledge of the whole background (another lie but I let it pass) then employing new lawyers did not make any sense.

I was certainly not happy with this appalling state of affairs but came to the conclusion that the devil you know is better than the one you don't know. In this regard look at how deceitful Tods Murray had been with Johnny. Finally it occurred to me that if we did not allow Brodies to 'act' for us they would then continue to act for the Estate Manager and, as such, would be acting against the Executry, with all the documentation of the Curatories and Usher Baronetcy Trust to hand. This would put them into an even more powerful position to lead any new lawyers we appointed up the garden path in the seemingly unlikely event that any new lawyers would act in good faith; again *vide* Tods Murray. The implications of instructing new lawyers therefore appeared to me at the time even worse than staying with Brodies.

I therefore agreed that they continue as the Law Agents for the Executry, purely as the lesser of the two evils, and told him so in those words. He did not like this at all but said nothing. I then set up another meeting with Stevens for 9.30 am three days later because I had not finished with him yet.

As time went on I discovered that I was continually faced with choices whereby the lesser of two evils was always the only option. On 4th November 1994 there was again only myself and Stevens present at this meeting. Stevens opened this meeting by stating that all the silver had now been removed from Hallrule by Christies in the interest of security and he wanted to take the paintings out of their frames for the same reason . The removal of the silver should have raised my suspicions more than it did because he had not consulted me about it. Yet again I was presented with a *fait-accompli.* I told Stevens that I did not like the idea of the paintings being removed from their frames. He then informed me that the head of Christies, in Scotland, Alexander Meddowes, had said he knew Johnny and me and that this was his idea. This recalled Meddowes to mind.

Stevens then said that he had told the Estate Manager and Mrs Blamey that 'we' did not accept that the contents belonged to them. At the time I presumed that the 'we' included Brodies as well. He then informed me that the Tax implications appeared to be very serious for the Executry if the contents were taken out of Gertrude's Trust and placed into the Executry-to-be because the Tax authorities would charge the Executry interest for the intervening 32 years on the Contents at their penal rate for non-payment of taxes. This would come to an astronomical sum. He suggested very strongly that we should not go back to 1962 and re-open the matter with the Tax Authorities. Rather we should try and reach some accommodation with the Estate Manager and Mrs Blamey and pay Gertrude's Trust back that portion of death duties it had already paid (£40,000) and settle the outstanding portion on the contents. We did some quick calculations on this and it appeared that the accommodation route would be better for the executry, although I was careful not to commit myself, just a preliminary conclusion. Only much later I realised that this was a further fraud to conceal an existing fraud. So as not to fall out with him and Brodies I did not tell him my belief that this was a consequence of their Dempster's lie in 1962 and that being the case Brodies themselves should pay the whole outstanding amount of Tax, including the penal rate of interest for the 32 years.

I made it clear that the contents issue was not to hold up the liquidation of the Estates and the beneficiaries payments. Stevens agreed and assured me that the it would be dealt with as a separate issue and as such would not in any way hold up the beneficiaries receiving their inheritances. That, inevitably, turned out to be another, monumental lie.

I then contacted Meddowes of Christies in Glasgow who invited me to lunch there. I motored over to Glasgow. I myself could not recall ever meeting him but knew that Johnny and his wife Rosemary had met him. Meddowes was a medium-sized man with large eyes and curly black hair. Over lunch I asked him how paintings could be removed from their frames and put back into them without being damaged. 'Very simple indeed. All you do is bend the nails backwards and remove the paintings. To replace you just pop the painting into position and bend the nails back into their old positions. That's it.' He told me this with such confidence that I agreed that they should be removed thus. However I later felt more and more uneasy about it.

On the way back to the Borders, I had to pass near Norton. As I approached it I suddenly decided that I would spend the night there to see if I could glean some information from the locals. We had all visited Uncle John there in the late 1940s and I had gone there from time to time as a young man after it had become a hotel although such visits had aroused feelings of great hostility in me about its having passed out of our family. I now took a far greater interest in Norton than I had ever done, in the way that people do when they have lost something. I was also pleased that it now had a wealthy owner in Richard Branson and was part of the Virgin Group of Hotels. Branson had greatly extended the house and I particularly liked the way the stables had been converted into a very pleasant Gourmet Pub called 'The Gathering.' I engaged one or two locals in conversation there but got no useful information other than I should consult an old man who still lived in the area and who would remember Uncle John.

After a very hearty breakfast the next morning I motored off to Haddington. This, for a change, was on pleasant business. When I left in 1968 there was a particularly striking bronze bust at Bedrule which I had always loved. It was of a beautiful young woman, but who she was I did not know. At the time she was to be sold with other excess furniture and possessions which had been stored in a room called the 'Glory Hole' at Bedrule as my Father felt we could not take everything with us to South Africa. I determined to save her. I was going to store her at Hallrule where Katherine, elder sister of Jacquelin, was living at the time and could keep an eye on her for me. However an inner small voice whispered to me: 'Don't leave her at Hallrule.' I thought of other places but none seemed safe enough. I then decided that the National Portrait Gallery of Scotland in Queen Street, Edinburgh was the safest place for her. There I met the very helpful Curator and Head of the Gallery, Mr O'Connor. He identified the bust from their records as being of Nellie Faa Blyth, the last Gypsy Queen, by the celebrated Scottish sculptor, Pittendrigh Macgillivary and told me that she was a very fine piece indeed. I was elated. Years later I was to discover that the bust had been commissioned by my great grandfather, Sir John Usher of Norton & Wells. Mr O'Connor told me that the Museum would be delighted to store her for me until my return in 1973, as then planned.

When I *did* return on my abortive trip to ask Clive to vacate Hallrule farm in 1973 I popped into the National Portrait Gallery to see my beloved Nellie. Mr O'Connor told me that the Gallery was having a big revamp and he could no longer store Nellie for me there, but that he liked her very much himself and would be more than happy to look after her for me until my eventual home-coming which at that time I thought would be be 1978. I told him that he was very welcome to look after Nellie for me until then. Due to Clive's chicanery on the Hallrule farm tenancy, as already narrated, I did not come home in 1978. However my sister-in-law, Rosemary, visited Scotland regularly so I asked her to contact Mr O'Connor at the Museum. She told me that Mr O'Connor had retired and that she had been unable to trace him. I became worried about Nellie, and began to think the worst. In the early 1990s I asked my nephew, Andrew, to try to see if *he* could locate Mr O'Connor's whereabouts. I did not hear anything from him until I landed at Heathrow on 24th October 1994. Andrew then told me that he had at last discovered that Mrs O'Connor was living in Haddington, East Lothian but that unfortunately Mr O'Connor had passed away some years previously. However Mrs O'Connor still had Nellie safe and sound and I was free to come and collect her at any time. I was over the moon! And here I was in 1994 on my way to collect her. Such a pleasant change from being led up the garden path by crooked lawyers like Brodies.

I met Mrs O'Connor at the Jane Welch House in Haddington where she lived. Jane Welch was the wife of the famous nineteenth century Scottish Author, Historian and Philosopher, Robert Carlyle and was born in this house. Mrs O'Connor turned out to be a most charming lady, as was her Mother. And Lo and Behold, there sat my beloved Nellie on a sideboard looking as serene and beautiful as ever, except now she had a cigarette dangling from her lips. Mrs O'Connor explained that this was her son's doing, because it amused him. I was not too enamoured with the cigarette because it detracted from Nellie's beautiful femininity; but I saw the funny side of it alright. Mrs O'Connor and I had a very pleasant lunch together in a local eating establishment. We enjoyed our lunch and I thanked her and her whole family very much indeed for having kept Nellie safe all those years before leavinng with my beloved Nellie.

On my way back to the Borders I dropped in at the Johnstounburn Hotel which was on the way. This was the Johnstounburn which had belonged to Andrew II in the late 1800s. Johnny and I had been taken there at a young age to visit an old great Aunt, Mamie Cruickshank, the youngest daughter of Andrew II, who still lived there. Again it was nice to re-visit a place I hadn't seen for so many decades. I was hospitably received by the manager and had a good look over the house, stable block and walled garden. An alteration which Andrew Usher had made was pointed out to me. Also his initials, along with his wife's carved into a stone on the front wall of the hotel.

On Saturday 6th November I motored to North Berwick for lunch with Lord and Lady Stodart. Lady Stodart was Hazel, the elder daughter of Lieut Commander Ronald Usher, RN, and eldest sister of the Robin Usher who had so tragically died of cancer in 1947. I hadn't seen Hazel, who was my Godmother, for about 30 years. We had a most pleasant lunch. She asked if there was any way by which the Wells Estate could be saved for an Usher future. I told her that, as things stood at present, there wasn't and that my father, then Johnny and I, had fought hard for years to that very end but had always been opposed by the other Trustees (McLure, Leadbetter and Clive) as well as by Brodies and Gertrude. She still deplored the Estate being sold, but made no comment on the parties who had opposed us. But I was much bucked by her loyalty to our family and thought the more of her for it. I also noted that she seemed to be under some sort of strain. It proved to be the last time I ever saw Hazel because she died in 1995, just before I arrived back in Scotland for good.

In the afternoon I motored down to Coldstream to meet with Jacquelin at Rosiebank House where she was temporarily staying. My main purpose was to agree a common strategy with her as to how we were to work together to the greatest advantage for the Executry. Also to find out more about our family in the years when she was young because she was ten years older than me.

We exchanged our experiences in the past with Brodies and in particular Dempster. I told her about his taking secret notes at my meeting with him in 1974 and she was not surprised by this, expressing her strong dislike and mistrust of him, Brodies, the Estate Manager, and Gertie.

To my great suprise she then told me that the Estate Manager and Mrs Blamey had agreed to toss coins for the Contents of Hallrule House which Gertrude had purportedly 'left' them in her Will. The first item up for the tossing was, of all things, the Usher heirloom jewellery.

Apparently, up went the coin for the Heirloom jewellery and down it came in the Estate Manager's favour. The consequence was both predictable and immediate: Mrs Blamey lost her temper and said she would toss no more coins, thereby summarily breaking their bargain. The Estate Manager however was delighted, grabbed the jewellery and hared off as fast as his spindly legs could carry him. I swore again I would retrieve the jewellery for Johnny.

She also told me that she had 'always stuck up for Johnny.' I took this to mean that she had always deplored the Estates going to Peter and Robert and that they should have gone to my Father on Stuart's death in 1962.

Jacquelin then told me that at the age of nine, she had been sent out to Argentina to stay with Uncle Stuart and Gertrude on Stuart's Estanzia near Rosario, Cordoba province, for safety in case Hitler invaded Britain. She went on to tell me how she had suffered at Gertrude's hands and how treacherous she was and that her nickname was 'The Cobra' because she would suddenly strike out like a cobra at anyone who she thought had slighted her

Jacquelin then told me that my father was the favourite of the six sons, particularly of his mother, Katherine. Again this came as a great surprise to me. She told me how, as a young man, he had been dispatched to Baden Baden in Germany to get some of its famous healing waters and bring it home to Wells. He was told to go to Baden Baden via Paris as it was thought he should see this great city to broaden his horizons. Apparently he never got beyond Paris so bewitching did he find the French Capital. He spent the money which was meant for the whole trip in Paris and came home empty-handed. Much later I came to realize that his being his mother's s favourite son might have been another factor in Stuart and Clive's jealousy of him.

On 8th November 1994 I had my last meeting with Stevens at Brodies. The meeting was spent going over and re-inforcing the positive aspects of our previous meetings. I made it clear that the Executry's immediate aim was to get the contents of Hallrule House into the Executry as soon as possible. He wholly concurred with me. I also asked him to send the farm leases and all other information connected with the Estates to us in South Afgrica for the period of the Curatories for a start. Again he agreed to do so.

Near the conclusion of the meeting he informed me that all the Estate accounts were still in Peter's name (Peter had died in 1990) but that this was purely a mechanical book-keeping exercise to keep things simple and that Brodies had obtained permission from the Accountant of Court for this. This struck me as odd because I was not aware of this at the time so why had he not told me before? Something was exercising him so I memorised this episode, as I had with the "cat picture" and Gertrude's "last Will" episodes. It took me years before I discovered the real reason which was, inevitably, another skeleton in Brodies' extensive closet and his telling me this at that time was an attempt to limit the damage in the event of my finding out later.

On 9th November 1994 I went to Hallrule House, as opposed to Hallrule farmhouse, and breakfasted there with the Brodies land agent, J Carnegie-Arbuthnott. I asked him if the Estate Manager could in any way enrich himself out of the Estate, in view of his being both the Estate Manager and a Tenant. I knew the answer to that already but wanted to get Arbuthnott's reaction. His answer was an unconvincingly skeletal 'No.' Nothing further. I immediately knew, he was lying.

I then visited every room of consequence in the house, noting various objects in the various rooms, and tried to memorize them. In particular I noted the Bust of old Sir John Usher, still languishing in the laundry room in the basement where it had been when I stayed at Hallrule in 1973. Again it took many years before the penny dropped as to the reason for it being hidden away in the basement like that for all those years. Up until the time we left for South Africa in 1968 it had always proudly stood in the entrance hall of Hallrule, where it had always been from my first memories of Hallrule. The only plausible explanation for the Bust being banished to the basement, *after* we had left please note, was that it was a calculated attempt by Gertie to expunge all memory of Sir John and to make it easier for her to steal it; out of sight and out of mind. This is just one of the many ways stealth fraudsters work. Brodies could always conceal the identity of the Bust in the Inventory of her Estate by describing it as simply as a ' Bust' or 'Statue' without stating that it was of Sir John. Who would be any the wiser? Hardly anyone, but of the few who did know I happened to be one.

I arrived in London that evening and stayed with my nephew, Andrew. I confided my fears about the paintings being taken out of their frames to him. He did not like this idea either and suggested that I contact Johnny in Natal about it. When I got Johnny on the telephone he told me that he did not at all trust Meddowes. On no account were the paintings to be taken out of their frames.

On 10th November 1994, I passed on the instruction to Jacquelin that the paintings should not be taken out of their frames under any circumstances and further they should not be allowed out of the house. She entirely agreed with me. I then contacted Stevens at Brodies with the same instructions and asked him to make sure that Mrs Lancashire, the Hallrule housekeeper, did not let any paintings be removed from Hallrule. He assured me he would let her know.

I then rang up Mrs Blamey, Gertrude's niece, in Wales where she now lived to say 'Good-bye.' I didn't expect any trouble from her in view of the fact that she had been the one person decent enough to warn us of what Gertrude, the Estate Manager and Brodies had been up to at Hallrule and in connection with the Estates. I was wrong. She immediately challenged me as to why we were contesting Gertrude's Will. I quietly drew her attention to the fact that Gertrude had no right to leave property, in her Will, which did not belong to her. She then warned me that in any dispute only the lawyers would get rich and 'we' could all end up with nothing.

I asked her how much silver Robert had been left with and about our Bedrule silver as she had always appeared honest about this, but she now refused to co-operate. Up until this point I had planned to put it to Johnny that we should allow her to keep half of what Gertie had 'left' her, if the other beneficiaries were agreeable, as she had always appeared to have been so decent about things - warning us and the like. Her reaction now made me drop this idea altogether.

I then flew out to South Africa, so ending my sixteen day trip. What a trip it had been!

23

BACK TO SOUTH AFRICA

Back in South Africa in time for Christmas 1994 I immediately wrote up the salient points of the meetings with Brodies, Tods Murray and all the other parties from the notes that I'd made and also while they were fresh in my mind. I also straightaway re-iterated to Stevens that he make sure Mrs Lancashire did not let anyone remove the paintings from their frames. I also asked Johnny to re-inforce this to Stevens which Johnny did in no uncertain terms by telling him that 'Alex Meddowes is not the type of person to whom I would entrust the family silver.' Johnny was the last person to make such a statement unless he had good reason for doing so.

Shortly after my arrival back in South Africa Brodies sent us a document headed 'Position Paper as at 7th November 1994' in connection with the late Sir Robert Usher' and a 'Note of Beneficiaries Meeting,' a supposed Resume of the meeting we had on 26th October 1094.

I shall deal with the 'Position Paper' first: This paper dealt with the Contents of Hallrule House at length. Among other things it stated, and I quote *ad verbatim*: 'It is important to note that the Lady Gertrude Usher's Trust which has, on the face of it, held most of the Contents since her death has paid inheritance tax both on her death and the death of Sir Peter Usher in 1990 on one half of those contents. Any arrangement come to now in respect of the contents would have to take into consideration that the beneficiaries of Lady Usher's estate have lost out by having had to pay the tax which should have been paid by Sir Peter but also on any capital appreciation which has been lost due to those payments of tax having been made in error.'

Johnny and I were very pleased that Brodies had now, for the first time admitted *in writing* that the contents of Hallrule House had never belonged to Gertie. It is important to remember that the contents had been treated as hers since Dempster, the egregious Death Bed Thief, had lied to the Capital Tax Office in 1962 and as such would have appeared in her personal accounts.

With regard to the 'Note of Beneficiaries Meeting,' this made only small mention of the Contents of Hallrule House issue and but went to great length in describing other matters. At the Meeting these other matters had been only briefly discussed while the Hallrule Contents had been discussed at great length. Stevens' Note was therefore was not an accurate reflection of the meeting but instead an attempt by him and Brodies to divert the discourse away from the matter they had conceded.

Still we thought 'One step at a time' and the 'Big One' right now was to win the Contents battle. After we'd won that battle, the precedent would be set to win the other much bigger battles which lay ahead.

In the months that followed we received the Statements of Accounts of Sir Robert's Curatory for the period from Peter's death in 1990 until Robert's death in 1994. Of course we asked for the Accounts for the whole period of Peter's Curatory from its inception in 1983, but Brodies, as always, adamantly refused to supply them.

On 21st December 1994 we received copies of the Leases of the four remaining farms on the Estate. There *had* been five remaining farms but two of them had, for some reason, been merged into one. We never did receive a copy of the lease of another farm called Dykes in which Clive had been a tenant for the period 1956-1972. Dykes was sold in 1992. Still, we puzzled over who had farmed it, if anyone, after Clive's death until it was sold. Johnny and I had enough to study in the meantime with the four leases so we decided to leave Dykes for the time being. The farms concerned were Town O'Rule, Hallrule, Hawthornside and Billerwell. The leases went back to the 1960s or before on all the farms with the exception of Town O'Rule, where it only went back to November 1985. This was the farm in which the Estate Manager was the tenant. The reader will forgive me for immediately scenting a rat.

The very first thing we noted on these leases was that Brodies, with their finely-honed instinct for danger, had doubled and trebled the rentals on the tenants of these farms as soon as possible after their man Carruthers took over as *Curator-Bonis* in 1983, shortly *after* Clive's death. And Clive's unsigned lease of 1978 on Hallrule farm was still up for renewal, so as soon as Brodies had engineered Mrs Mactaggart's squattership there in 1983 they increased the rental from £4,000 to £11,000 per annum in one fell swoop, clearly demonstrating that the rental Clive had been charging himself (as a Trustee) had been risibly low. Further, there was no record that he had ever *paid* even this risible rent, because Brodies refused to let Johnny see the Estate Accounts. In 1982, from the one set of unaudited accounts which Johnny *had* managed to get from Carruthers, the annual rental for Town O'Rule farm was only £2,650. Suddenly, in 1985, this rental rose to £14,000. Mysteriously this lease was in the name of a 'Mr Marley.' And yet the Estate Manager actually farmed Town O'Rule. How on earth could that be? Remember that although the Estate Manager's name is Charles John Usher, he is no relation to our family. Nor is there any record that this Estate Manager, like Clive, had actually paid even the risible rent of £2,650 for Town 'O Rule.

From these leases it is perfectly apparent that the rentals which Clive and the Estate Manager had been paying were miles below market value at the time Carruthers became Peter's *Curator-Bonis*. Later I was to discover other ways in which both Clive and the Estate Manager had been enriching themselves at the expense of the Usher Baronetcy Trust. Throughout the 1970s and early 80s, Clive and the Estate Manager were paying far lower rentals for their farms than were being charged to the tenants of Hawthorneside and Billerwell farms even though Hallrule and Town O'Rule were more valuable farms in agricultural and infrastructure terms. To cap it all Clive and Logan MacLure of Brodies had effected these frauds without ever sending Johnny any of these leases for his signature. After we had digested this information Johnny's reaction was: 'How can this be? The whole lot of them are swindling swine. No wonder they've consistently refused to supply me with any records; telling me it was none of my business. It was always my business. Clive colluded with Brodies and the Estate Manager to betray our family and enrich themselves and to hell with the Trust and everyone else.

We agreed, however, that it would not be wise to bring things to a head until after the Estate had been sold as Brodies would sabotage the sale and annul any progress we had made on the Contents issue. Hindsight again makes one realise that the artificially low rentals would play a critical and prejudicial role on the price the Estate would eventually realise.

At this time we were constantly sending Jacquelin faxes via Alan Bailey's office near Spital Tower which we knew she received. However she never replied.

On 27th December 1994, however, Jacquelin phoned me in South Africa. She now suggested that the best way to resolve the Contents issue was for the Executry to recompense Gertie's Trust the £40,000 that Gertrude's Trust had already paid in Death Duties on the Contents but that the Executry should not pay any interest because the whole thing was Brodies' fault for setting up the fraudulent Trust in the first place. I agreed that this might be a way out of the impasse, although it seemed rather harsh that we should have to pay £40,000 to conceal a lie perpetrated by Dempster in 1962 and perpetuated by Brodies ever since.

On the 13th January 1995 Brodies sent us a seven page Report on the Contents issue, the latest Accounts, and a Receipt Form for the Estate for Johnny to sign. Crucially the Accounts and Receipt Form did not show or make any reference to the Contents of Hallrule House as ever belonging to Robert nor to Peter before him. Johnny was therefore most reluctant to sign the Receipt Form. We eventually decided that he should sign it but only on condition that any other assets found to be missing from the Accounts would then be added back to them. Our reason for doing so was that we did not want the contents issue to hold up the transfer of the Estate and whatever else Robert 'owned' in Scotland onto to Johnny and Jacquelin and thereby delay the commencement of the Executry. So Johnny eventually did sign it subject to those conditions which he inserted in writing on the Receipt Form itself. I was later to discover that Brodies withheld this Receipt from the Accountant of Court. More of that and the very serious consequences arising from it later.

Brodies had quickly realised, however, the serious implications of their earlier written admission that the contents of Hallrule House did not belong to Gertrude and decided it was too dangerous to maintain. So in this Report they effected a complete 180 degree *volte-face* by now claiming that Gertie had acquired the Contents legally after all and therefore the Executry had no right to them. Just like that.

The Report first 'assumed' that Stuart had 'acquired' these contents in 1949, but gave no evidence of how and on what basis this acquisition had been been effected. They then would have passed to Gertrude in terms of Stuart's Will. Brodies then went on to 'suggest' that Sir Stuart had at one time purchased these contents. What they studiously avoided mentioning was the fact that Uncle Stuart had been a Trustee of the Usher Baronetcy Trust from 1949 until his death in 1962. This meant that it would have been utterly unlawful for him to purchase the contents of Hallrule House. In addition he had returned home from Argentina absolutely broke.

The Report had been deceitfully drafted for the singular purpose of pulling the wool over the eyes of its readers in addition to being an absolute perversion of what the record showed. It was enough to deceive most of the beneficiaries for a while, but certainly not Johnny nor myself. Of course Brodies knew this and banked on our having difficulty in getting the other beneficiaries to believe us, let alone to do anything about it.

Between January and April in 1995 when I left South Africa for good we had the Accountancy Department of our South African lawyers to carry out an in depth study of the Curatory Accounts since Peter's death in 1990 until Robert's death in 1994. The Accountant who carried out the in-depth study concluded that: 'These Accounts are a minefield.'

As we caught Brodies out more and more they resorted to intimidation by informing us that the more questions we asked the higher their account would be. The inference here was: 'You accept the situation as it stands, fraudulent though it be, or we will charge you more and more until there is nothing left for any of you to inherit.' This was like having a metaphorical gun held to your head, and such intimidation by Brodies was an admission of their own fraud from which they benefited twice: firstly from the fraud itself and secondly by charging the victims of the fraud to deal with their objections to the fraud. Naturally this made us more determined than ever not to let them get away with it.

I then detected a change in Jacquelin's attitude on the phone. She seemed to have lost her earlier enthusiasm to have the contents conveyed to the Executry. This and the Brodies *volte-face* forced us to the realisation that it would be impossible for Johnny to do his job as Executor properly from South Africa. We therefore decided that I should go to Scotland to act as Executor in Johnny's place and armed with his Power of Attorney, because he was not in a position to leave his business at that time. I was in a much better situation in that regard.

Of course I was delighted that I would, at long last, be returning to Scotland and looked very much forward to exposing Brodies, Clive, Gertie et al in their decades old fraud against our Usher family of Norton and Wells and thereafter getting matters put to rights. By now my wife Gillian and I had two beautiful children, Katherine and Richard. I notified Gillian's family of our intention and eventually got their go-ahead.

'The Time has Come,' as the Mandrill said to Simba, in *The Lion King*.

The view from Brodies proposed spanking-new Offices at Capital Square, Edinburgh which might well have been partially paid for by money defrauded from the Usher Baronetcy Trust.

24

HOME IN SCOTLAND FOR GOOD

On 5th April 1995. I left South Africa twenty-one years later than planned. My family were to follow once I had organised where we were to live and where the children were to go to school. Arriving in London I stayed with my nephew Andrew. On the 11th of that month I went to the Dorchester Hotel where the Estate Agents Savill's were doing a promotion for the sale of what remained of our beautiful Wells Estate There were large wall-type pictures of the Estate, Hallrule House and the like. I soon espied Jacquelin and waved to her. She looked apprehensive and averted her eyes. I instantly knew that our suppositions about her in South Africa had some basis. I approached her but she moved away. I tried once more but got the same reaction. Thereafter I didn't bother to try again that evening and did not speak to her until I saw her in Scotland a few days later.

The next day I motored up to Scotland. As I crossed the Border at Carter Bar on the A68 little did I know that I was destined to spend many years selling fast food from a kiosk on that most beautiful but foul- weathered spot. Ruberslaw, Blacklaw and the Dunion, three of the highest hills on the Wells Estate and Bedrule loomed into view. I looked at each in turn and said to myself 'I have not forgotten you my old friends. We will never part.' I stayed with Alan Bailey near Spital Tower who had kindly agreed to having me for a short time until I found alternative accommodation.

Despite now being outnumbered by Brodies and Jacquelin I felt confident that once I told people of what Johnny and I had already found out about the successive Incapaxes, Peter and Robert, being defrauded we would get plenty of allies and so expose and quickly defeat Brodies and whoever else had been involved in the ruination of our family. Little did I then realize that was not the way of the Scottish 'Legal Justice' system and the world at all.

On the 14th of April I went over to Hallrule farm to test the waters with the Mactaggarts. I soon espied Mrs Mactaggart exercising a horse in a lunging ring. I greeted her. No response whatever as she continued to exercise the horse. When she had finished she walked over to me and, without any form of greeting, coolly asked me where I was staying. I told her. She immediately shot back: 'You can't go around Scotland sponging on people.' I shot back at her: 'I am not in the habit of going around Scotland sponging on people.' I nearly added added that her very presence before me was proof that *she* was the sponger and had been sponging on our family, like her father, for very many years. She then asked, rather too casually, if Johnny was coming back as well? I told her, 'Not right now,' whereupon she said: 'There is no point in him coming back at all as there is nothing here for him to come back to.' I just kept cool on that one and told her he would be back in his own good time.

She then again started bleating how hard farming was again; more brainwashing, the same tactic she had used when I had stayed with her in October the previous year, and how poor they were and so on. This did not fit at all with what the new owner of Bedrule told me a short while later, which was that he had made a six figure profit on Bedrule farm! Mrs Mactaggart was, as usual, lying through her teeth.

'No time for tea I am afraid,' she said. 'We're down to the boards here.' As if I would stay for tea with her in such circumstances. Still wanting to keep her onside I took my leave as soon as I politely could. However, with one exception I was not to speak to Mrs Mactaggart again until 1999 when I met her in the streets of Jedburgh and metaphorically floored her.

I quickly realized that the telephone lines had been humming with the news that I was home. The Old Empire was now represented only by Johnny and myself whereas the Usurpers were more numerous, one of whom, Brodies, was very powerful. But we had a just cause and our opponents only the avaricious grasp of the thief.

I then went to see Valerie at Wells Stables. She was still very much in favour of our contesting Gertie's Will, which was all I wanted to ascertain, so I did not tarry there. I then went for lunch with Cousin Daphne, the younger daughter of Lt-Commander Ronald Usher RN, at New Headshaw, Ashkirk, near Hawick. She always was a charming girl and lady, now well into her seventies. We regretted having seen little of Daphne as we grew up as my mother had always spoken highly of her so I looked forward to seeing her again. Over lunch she told me how outraged she was that the contents of Hallrule House were now part of Gertrude's estate. I filled her in as to what else we had discovered. How tiny the rentals had been and other matters which did not seem at all in order. She was not a bit surprised and said: 'Typical Brodies and typical John Usher of Courthill.' This was the Estate Manager. She cautioned that it was useless to fight Brodies because the lawyers always won, no matter how good your case was. She also told me that she regarded Mrs Mactaggart as a swindler because she, Mrs Mactaggart, had swindled her on a horse deal. I sympathised and told her that I already knew Mrs Mactaggart was a twister but that was to be expected with such a crooked father. I later discovered that Daphne had

had a difficult life which she had borne with great fortitude. Her elder sister Hazel had died very recently and we commiserated on her passing.

I then went to stay for a few days at Chesters, near Ancrum which Jacquelin was housesitting for its owners. I had often been at Chesters as a young man so looked forward to staying there. Helen Ogilvie, the daughter had recently married a distant cousin of mine called Timothy Usher, of the brewing side of the family. They lived on a nearby farm and had got Jacquelin to look after the mansion house for a bit.

Jacquelin also had her daughter, Dorinda and her young Australian husband called Hancock, staying at the time. Jacquelin made an effort to be pleasant, unlike our meeting at the Dorchester in London. She could not however disguise her unease. I brought up the Contents issue with her. She looked apprehensive and then said that she was 'now not so keen to contest the ownership of the contents.' When I asked her what had changed her mind she echoed Brodies: 'Stuart had bought them for Gertie.' She knew this was a bald lie and she knew that I knew it was a bald lie. She became agitated, just like Gertie all those years ago, and in the end refused to talk about it. I let it be for the time being in the hope that she would realise the futility of maintaining this patent fiction and make common cause with us again. The next day I tackled her again but to no avail.

On my suggestion we agreed a time for a meeting on the evening of Sat 15th April 1995. By then I would still only have been in the country 10 days. At this meeting I planned to raise some other matters which did not appear to be above board and also try to get her onside again. However she called the meeting off at the last minute. We then set it for the next evening, Sunday 16th. Again she called off at the last minute. We then set it for Monday 17th April. At the same time I told her I did not know why she was so frightened of having the meeting and would she please tell me why. She did not answer but agreed to stick by this latest arrangement. And indeed she was there for the meeting with her daughter Dorinda. I told her that this was confidential business and Dorinda should remove herself. She insisted that she stay. Fearing that she would abort the meeting if I insisted on Dorinda removing herself I reluctantly gave way. The first thing I brought up was in connection with some cottages at Hallrule, the ones in connection with which I had signed the papers in the presence of Uncle Stuart and Dempster back in 1962.

'I know nothing about them,' was her flat answer.

I then brought up the matter of the Policies of about 30 acres around Hallrule House about which I was not satisfied. She now glared at me and then jumped up and marched out of the room saying that she was not prepared to be treated like an idiot. I was dumbfounded. Then Dorinda piped up and told me that her mother did not want me to 'go back over old ground' in any way as this 'might upset the sale of the estate.' Also that 'people were apprehensive of you and your coming home.' A very revealing remark and one which vindicated both Johnny and myself.

Dorinda then apologised for her mother's behaviour. I quietly told her that it was the duty of an Executor to see that things had been run properly and to ingather the estate of the deceased person to whom she had been appointed as one of the Executors and the more so when the deceased person was a registered Incapax. Dorinda had no credible answer to any of these statements and just sat there looking uncomfortable. Realising the futility of discussing matters further with her and her mother I brought the meeting to an end.

It was now quite apparent that Jacquelin had been well and truly 'got at' by Brodies and had simply changed sides. But how had they got at her: Skeleton in her cupboard? Bribery? Jacquelin had been very short of money for years, so bribery was a distinct possibility. At the time I could hardly bring myself to think that she would rat on the beneficiaries so quickly. So, whatever it was, it must have been sufficiently powerful to have convinced her that she would be better off ditching the beneficiaries and joining Brodies. As events unfolded I, and much later all the other beneficiaries, were to discover that she was rotten to the core and had been regarded as such for many years by many people in the Borders and the Edinburgh areas.

Later in the week Jacquelin came out with the incredible statement: 'There is no longer a Wells Estate - it no longer exists.' Again I was dumbfounded and asked: 'If that is indeed the case, what is it that we are proposing to sell and why is it called the Wells Estate in all the correspondence I have seen, not to mention the fact that everyone else refers to it as 'The Wells Estate.' She answered this by saying that we were selling the 'Hallrule Estate' - a name by which it has never been known by anyone. This again made me think of Wells being expunged from the Scroll in Bedrule Church and was another pointer to Wells being purposely buried from memory with the aim of putting Clive and his squatter family in the clear, inter many other alias. No wonder all the secrecy over the last thirty years. This was one of the most miserable weekends of my life. It slowly dawned on me that Brodies and their allies would be no pushover and that Johnny and I were in for the fight of our lives.

On 18th April 1995, Johnny's birthday, I had a meeting with Stevens at Brodies. I asked a whole lot more questions but got little other than the usual lying twaddle. When I got back to Chesters in the evening Jacquelin looked worried and asked me what I had been discussing with Stevens. By now I did not trust her as far as I could throw her, so gave her a meaningless 'Brodies' type reply. She then said 'There is no need for you to have any more meetings with Brodies because I, with John Usher [the Estate Manager] and Hugh Stevens have organized everything and everything is now cut and dried.' Just like that. As well as attempting to exclude me she was now acting as though Johnny did not exist. I told her that was not how it worked and decided from that moment I would not share with her anything I discovered in the future because she would simply pass such information on to Brodies - for their benefit, and not that of the beneficiaries. I then left Chesters and returned to the relative harmony of Bailey's house near Spital Tower.

On Friday 21st April 1995 I had a meeting in the afternoon with a retired lawyer called Patrick Murray, who was well into his 70s and who lived in the neighbouring parish of Cavers. He worshipped at Bedrule Church and was its Treasurer. When he first arrived at Cavers in the late 60s he had become the Treasurer of Cavers Church. However the Cavers churchgoers did not take to him at all, which he told me he had hurt him very much. Hence his moving to Bedrule Church.

He told me that he had always been fascinated by the Usher family and had lived near Norton as a young man. Also that we (the Usher family) had fingers in all sorts of pies in Edinburgh. 'It was all circles within circles,' was the phrase he used, giving emphasis to it by drawing imaginary circles in the air with his hands to describe our interests in Edinburgh. I let him carry on because this was all news to me. He then told me that he had heard that Sir Robert Usher had sold the business for £7 million in 1918 and that Sir Robert had told some of his friends: 'That's a million pounds each for my six sons, and a million for Lady Usher.' £7 million in 1918 would translate into approximately £700 million in 1995.

I showed him some of the most damning documentation I had on the Usher Baronetcy Trust Estates. He was shocked to the core and described what I had shown him as resembling 'the Augean Stables.' This refers of course to Greek mythology and the task of cleaning a place or situation which had become exceedingly filthy from long neglect or corrpution. He then said he would go to Edinburgh and consult the law firm Murray, Beith and Murray, in which he had been a partner. He also suggested that I use Murray, Beith and Murray against Brodies.

That evening I told Alan Bailey, who was a nephew of JGG Leadbetter, one of the Usher Baronetcy Trustees already alluded to in the book, of my Meeting with Murray. I knew Murray had been the lawyer of Alan's Mother, Jean Leadbetter - youngest sister of JGG Leadbetter - and therefore I presumed that Murray, Beith & Murray were now Alan Bailey's Law Agents. When I told him about Sir Robert Usher selling the business for £7 million in 1918 Alan Bailey made the rather interesting comment: 'Yes, I *know* he sold it for seven million and he was a fool. He could have got double that for the business.' This of course made it certain that JGG Leadbetter, his uncle, had *known* this.

I had two more meetings with Murray at which he was as helpful as could be. He also consulted Murray, Beith and Murray as promised. He arranged for me to meet a Mr Pollock, one of their lawyers, which I duly did. Pollock was also shocked at what I showed him. He told me that Patrick Murray had always followed the affairs of our family very closely indeed and was 'obsessed by the Usher family.'

At one of our subsequent meetings Murray told me that he had protested at what he described as Clive's 'sleight of hand' in moving money from the Bedrule Church fund, which was in a good financial state, to the Denholm Church Fund which was the opposite. And that Clive had dismissed his concerns with the words that 'he was not to worry about it.' So he had done nothing, but had always felt bad about it, and thereafter never trusted Clive again. Of course I told him that Clive was a swindling thief and that his fellow officers in the War had despised him and also about his farming Hallrule as a squatter with no lease, his breaking the Gentleman's Agreement and so on. He expressed his displeasure at all this and gave me his sympathies for which I was very thankful.

However at our fourth and final meeting Murray was suddenly a changed man. Ashen, he told me I should drop everything and that he would not help me anymore. He also stated that I should cease my attacks on Gertrude and Clive. He asked me for my word that I would never divulge anything of what he had told me, and what had passed between us, at our meetings and without pause went on to add that I was to never to even mention our meetings at all. I assured him that he had my word, but that I was only bound by it while he was alive. He died in 2001. I concluded he had been 'got at' by powerful people in the Scottish Legal establishment. They must have put the fear of God into him.

25

MORE WEAPONS OF MASS DECEPTION

On Saturday 24th April 1995 I went to Bedrule Church. I always found solace there and it usually bucked me up. When I had finished in the Church I paid my respects at my Father's grave.

The next day I had another meeting with Stevens at Brodies. Stevens appeared anxious and adopted an aggressive 'gloves-off' approach, beginning right away with intimidation. He 'advised' me with all the gravitas he could muster that if the Estate Manager felt threatened by us on the Contents issue he had every right to remove the contents of Hallrule House and take them to Courthill, *another* farm in which he was a tenant, near Hawick. Stevens asked me if this worried me? I assured him that it did not; that the Estate Manager had no such right and would do no such thing. I knew that his speciality, like that of Brodies, was stealth fraud as opposed to daylight robbery. Caught on the back foot Stevens began stuttering and suggested I ask Jacquelin if she would agree to our jointly approaching the Estate Manager *and* Mrs Blamey with a view to seeing what they might be prepared to concede voluntarily. I agreed to this, just for starters, because I felt it would set the precedent for us to get the whole lot.

On 27th April 1995 I attended the Brodies proposed meeting with Jacquelin at Hallrule House to discuss the best way to approach the Estate Manager on the matter. I suggested we ask the Estate Manager give up all the contents which were presently in Gertie's Trust. Jacquelin instantly refused: another example of her fighting *against* the interests of the Executry. I then suggested that he give up the five most celebrated paintings, the bust of old Sir John Usher and all 'Gertrude's' silver to Johnny alone as he was now the head of our branch of the family and because this would partially fulfil the purposes of the Usher Baronetcy Trust. Predictably she did not like this idea at all but agreed to approach the Estate Manager with the proposal. I then suggested that Johnny should also be given all the silver and the portrait of Sir Walter Scott by Sir Henry Raeburn and the painting of old Sir Robert Usher by Fiddes Watt which *were* actually back where they belonged, in the Executry. Again she did not look happy, but agreed to think about it.

The next day I had a follow-up meeting with Jacquelin at Hallrule on the above. When we had finished discussing this matter I kept quiet because I believed this offered the best chance of her spilling the beans on other topics. She was one of that breed who simply could not resist showing off.

I was not disappointed; in fact I struck gold. Jacquelin suddenly piped up in her usual attention-seeking way that Mrs Mactaggart had told her in the early 1980s that Gertrude had told her (Mrs Mactaggart) that she, Gertrude, had left the whole Wells Estate to her (Mrs Mactaggart) and to herself (Jacquelin). I was both gobsmacked and delighted at this pearl of information. If Brodies had been a fly-on-the-wall I suspect they would have immediately assumed their human form and brained Jacquelin there and then. The implications of this pearl of information needed thinking through so I politely ended our meeting and repaired back to Alan Bailey's place near Spital Tower. Of course the Estates had never belonged to Gertrude in exactly the same way that the Contents had never belonged to her. On the face of it the Estates had belonged to Peter since 1984 but that was as a consequence of Brodies' fraud as already narrated. But Peter had certainly never owned them before Gertrude's death in 1984. They still belonged to the Usher Baronetcy Trust. In this circumstance it would have been quite impossible for Gertrude to have left Wells Estate to Jacquelin, Mrs Mactaggart, or anyone else without the collusion of Brodies' MacClure and Clive (two of the Usher Baronetcy Trustees). This plan could only have been hatched by Clive and MacClure and put to Gertrude. She, no doubt with delight, agreed to it. Brodies then drafted her Will in either the late 70s or early 80s in which she 'left' the Estates to Mrs Mactaggart and Jacquelin in as equal Shares as could be managed and the Contents of Hallrule House to the Estate Manager and Mrs Blamey, her niece, on the same terms.

But what about the explosive objections which would erupt from Johnny (the other Trustee) and myself were this to eventuate? Brodies reckoned they could handle us by their usual methods of lie, lie, dodge, dodge, *fait acomplis*, smokescreens, and magic mirrors. Judging by their performance in connection with the Contents of Hallrule House to date they would have had a pretty fair chance of success too. They would plead 'confidentiality', then lie and dissemble for years, paying themselves out of the Executry for the 'honour' of doing so. They could also count on everyone else living off the Estates to back them up. Against this formidable array of crooks and fraudsters, realistically, stood only Johnny and I, thousands of miles away in South Africa.

Clive's, McClure's, Gertrude's and Brodies' rationale on embarking on this utterly fraudulent course of action was that they all judged this to be their best 'stay out of gaol' and at the same time 'get rich quick' card.

With regard to this 'stay out of gaol' card let's take Clive first: As a 'Trustee' of the Usher Baronetcy Trust he had illegally and unlawfully broken the Trust and used his position to make it appear that he had every right to the properties he now occupied on the Estate when in fact he had *no* such rights whatever and was now nothing more than a squatter. Secondly Gertie: She had 'acquired' the Contents of Hallrule House by fraud in collusion with her lawyer, the death bed thief, Dempster of Brodies. Thirdly McClure: He had agreed to and supported these fraudulent plans. The same went for Brodies.

There would be colossal material gains for all the beneficiaries of this fraudulent Will. Gertrude's family and the Estate Manager would share the Contents of Hallrule House. Clive's daughter, Mrs Mactaggart, would get half of the Wells Estate and Jacquelin would get the other half thereby becoming instant multi millionairesess. Brodies would get what remained of Norton and Pitheavlis (only they knew the extent of these) and on top of that they would handle everything from start to finish through their 'Legal', 'Accountancy', and 'Estate Agency' departments; and monstrously overcharge for so doing. Clive, if he outlived Gertrude, would get to carry on farming Hallrule Farm as a squatter with his daughter, Mrs MacTaggart, as his landlady. It was all too perfect.

But what about the undoubted howls of protest which would explode from all the other beneficiaries, namely: Katherine's issue in Australia, Neil and Anne, and Hazel and Daphne, Elizabeth Richards in Wales and Johnny and myself. When push came to shove Brodies knew that, with the exception of Johnny and myself, it was highly unlikely indeed that any of these parties would take them, Brodies, to court for fraud. With regard to Johnny and myself they knew we would want to play by the rules - a weakness in their eyes - and could overcome us by their usual methods of deceit, legal-speak, brainwashing, intimidation, smoke, magic mirrors, and intimidation. Remember for them the prize was incredibly high.

Brodies would have factored all this into their calculations when deciding whether or not to take the gamble. So when did they get an inkling that their base plan might not succeed as easily as they hoped? The simple answer to that was Johnny's trip to Scotland in 1982, as earlier narrated. He had caught Carruthers out about the Estate Accounts, re-iterating his passion for the Estates to go on in the Usher family, trying to tackle Clive eleven days before his death, his exchanges with Val and his sharp exchanges with Gertrude when he had warned her that it was incumbent upon her to do what she could to save the Estates for an Usher future. And thereafter his pursuit of explanations from Brodies, stopping the Estate Manager becoming Peter's *Curator-Bonis,* asking awkward questions to which Brodies either gave no credible answers or simply refused to answer, and so on. All this made Brodies realise that their Grand Fraud Plan with Clive, McClure and Gertrude was altogether too dangerous.

At this point Brodies, again, had a piece of good fortune. Clive died just at the right time on 17th November 1982. Almost certainly Brodies and McClure informed Clive a few days before he died that Johnny was onto him and them. And Brodies will have heaved a sigh of relief at Clive's death because it made things much easier for them. Crooks often double-cross each other when the opportunity arises and Clive's death was just such an opportunity. Brodies and Gertrude now did exactly that to the late and great double-crosser himself, Clive. With him safely out of the way Brodies and Gertrude reneged on the 'Gertrude Will' plan by cutting Mrs Mactaggart and Jacquelin out of it altogether but left Gertrude's part of the deal intact. She was after all still alive. If she felt in need of any justification it would have been something along the lines of: 'Clive, you made one big miscalculation and that was you thought you would outlive me because you were seven years younger than me. Well you didn't outlive me so I will now double-cross you in the same way that you double-crossed so many in your life. One thing is certain and that is that I would never have betrayed my own family of Sampson like you betrayed your own flesh and blood, the Ushers. You were an even bigger crook than I am: so to hell with you'! Brodies then destroyed Gertrude's fraudulent Will in which she left the Estates to Mrs Mactaggart and Jacquelin and made her another new Will. This *second* new Will was the one about which Mrs Blamey had spilt the beans to us, as already narrated, when Gertrude told Mrs Blamey that she 'had not understood a word of it' and that she had been 'forced' to make it.

It was only now that I made the connection between *this* Will to Steven's statement to me at my meeting with him on 28th October 1994. At that meeting he had corrected an earlier statement of his that Gertrude had made a new Will shortly before her death in 1984. His correction was that she had *not* made any new Will shortly before her death but that the old Will had been altered only in a minor and technical way for tax purposes. So Stevens had lied at our 28th October 1994 meeting because she *had* in fact made the new Will. Actually I suspect that Brodies had made *two* new Wills for Gertrude - not just the one - and used the version would which suited them.

Mrs Mactaggart and Jacquelin as the new 'owners' of the Estates? How appalling! They were both, and still are, out and out twisters and a rank disgrace to our family. Thank God we would, at least, spared that.

> An ape is an ape, a varlet's a varlet,
> though they be clad in silk or scarlet.

Before the end of the month I was informed that a cottage had come empty on the Estate and I could move in there. I could now make arrangements for my wife Gillian, daughter Katherine and son Richard to come over from South Africa to join me.

On 3rd May 1995 I met Jacquelin at Hallrule at 3.00 pm. This assignation was to prepare for my meeting with the Estate Manager at 4.00pm. She told me that he would only give up the Bust of old Sir John Usher (d 1904) and nothing else. Of course this told me that she had already told him what I was going to ask for, which I had specifically asked her not to tell him. She also kept referring to the painting of Sir Walter Scott by Sir Henry Raeburn as 'belonging' to him. She had done this a number of times in relation to the very few other assets which Gertie had not stolen and of which there was no question of their belonging to the Executry of which she was one of the Executors. All she seemed to care about now was how best to conceal the pillaging of the Estates. For some reason that I had yet to fathom, she was now keen that the Estate Manager, whom she had formerly regarded as a crook, and Mrs Blamey, whom she also professed to loath, keep the Contents, even though this would mean a large financial loss to her personally. The likelihood that she had been bribed or blackmailed by Brodies, and possibly others, already latent in my mind, now grew.

At 4.00 pm the Estate Manager, Charles John Usher (no relation) arrived. The first thing I asked him was if he had any objection to my taping our conversation. He immediately went on guard and, after a slight hesitation, always a give-away, said he was not prepared to have it tape-recorded because, 'I do not like tape recorders.' Another dead giveaway. I then let the matter drop as I feared he might flee the scene if I were too hard on him at the outset. I asked him for the five paintings, the silver, and the Bust. He refused to concede anything except the Bust which he said he would 'donate' to Johnny. How *gracious* of him!

He then went on to state that because Gertrude had left all these items to him and Mrs Blamey he was not prepared to give up anything else. Like Jacquelin he was uncomfortable and evasive. Nor had he accepted my invitation to sit down. He stood in the doorway shifting his weight from foot to foot throughout while I was seated. It then dawned on me that he thought I might attack him; hence his position for a quick getaway. He knew that I had every justification to attack him but misjudged his man. I had no plans for that type of action but only because I thought it would damage me more than him, purely in a PR sense, and mean that Johnny might not get the bust. Also I did not want to humiliate him too much for tactical reasons and so ended the meeting quite quickly. I had got the bust and quite sufficient in the way of body language to tell me that, cunning as he was, he had been unable to conceal that he was a very, very frightened man. I later learned that if I had flattened him there and then (the idea of which I relished) many people would have been delighted because he was widely regarded as a consummate stealer and concealer in the Borders of Scotland.

On 17th May 1995 I received a note from Mrs Blamey inviting me to drinks that evening at Wells Stables where she was staying with Valerie. 'Something brewing,' I thought. I didn't even bother to reply as I now despised them so much and wanted to keep them on tenterhooks wondering whether or not I would make an appearance.

I pitched up unannounced and purposely late, looking forward to seeing how they would react. I was also pretty sure they would let things slip which were not in their interest to let slip. Mrs Blamey approached me with great apprehension, as well she might. She made as good a job of breaking the ice as anyone could have in those circumstances and we were soon settled in the sitting room which, in my day, had been a stable.

My opening gambit was to inform them that Johnny and I regarded the proposed sale of the Wells Estate and the other Estates as an absolute catastrophe for our Usher family of Norton and Wells. I knew they would not like that at all, and nor was I disappointed. They gave each other the briefest of glances which I was not meant to see, and just sat in silence, looking down, one on each side of the blazing fire. To push the moment home to them I also remained silent. Time passed. When the silence was becoming embarrassingly pregnant I let them out of their misery by moving onto another subject. I regret now that I did not insist on them giving their views on the matter as they would probably have given more away. At the time I was not sufficiently adept at pushing home an advantage in situations like that. In time, on a steep learning curve, I became more practiced.

I then moved onto the Contents issue. Mrs Blamey informed me that there were two silver tea-sets in Gertrude's Trust, from which she herself stood to benefit, but which rightfully belonged to Robert's Executry. Also that there were two Coronation cups in the Executry which should be in the Gertrude's Trust. She then said she would write to Stevens and get it put right.

Suddenly Valerie piped up for the first time and told me that she had my old shotgun. That was nonsense because I had left my shotgun at Hallrule when I left and Johnny had left his at Clive's. This gun was Johnny's. I played along with her on the shotgun being mine and got it off her there and then before she changed her mind! Valerie then told me that my encyclopaedias had been found at Hallrule and were ready for me to collect. Sometime previously I had told Jacquelin that I had left these encyclopaedias at Hallrule when I left for South Africa. She had been dismissive about them then and I feared the worst that they also had been stolen by Gertrude. Now however I thought it more than odd that Valerie told me that they had been found. When I collected them from Hallrule I realized that the only reason that 'they' had agreed to return them was that I had written my name and address on every single one of them; too risky to sell them at the Auction where they would readily be recognised as mine. Anyway I was very pleased to get them back. For most of my life I have been somewhat careless with my own things and would never normally have put my name in all these beautiful old leather bound encyclopaedias but I now recalled that that same inner small voice had warned me to do so before dropping them off at Hallrule. Thank God I did and here I was, twenty six years later, reaping the benefit of heeding that unspoken warning.

We discussed various other things but I got no further useful information. I was reasonably happy with the information I had picked up. I deduced that their purpose in asking me for drinks was to mollify me by returning what Val either thought or feigned was my gun, the encyclopaedias and the two silver tea-sets to Robert's Executry. Some chance! If Johnny and I had not made our stand on the Contents issue I believe that Val would have simply kept Johnny's gun and Jacquelin would have made off with my encyclopaedias and I would never have been told about the two silver tea-sets. However the most significant thing by far about this drinks party was neither of them expressing one word of regret at the impending sale of the Wells Estate and it passing out of our family. That showed beyond any shadow of doubt that they had always put fraudulent personal gain ahead of family loyalty.

I arranged to meet Alice next morning so that she could show me other items in the Christies Inventory which she said had got 'mixed up', as she put it, between the Gertrude's Trust and the Curatory. 'Mixed up', be damned; 'Stolen' was the right word.

Next morning I went to the Stables just after 8.30. The front door was open but no-one was yet out of bed. 'Hmm, nice, easy living in Rulewater these days,' I thought. There was a swallow in the sitting room desperately trying to get out so I made good its escape. I returned at 9.25 and found Alice, but no sign of Valerie. She, wisely from her point of view, was 'constructively' still in bed. Alice and I discussed the Silver Tea sets and the Coronation Cups. She told me that she would send me a copy of her letter to Brodies in which she would ask them to make the necessary exchanges. In the event Alice never did send me copies of her correspondence to Brodies. I believe that she wrote to them but that Brodies, Valerie and the rest had simply put the frighteners onto her. For the record I never included Mrs Blamey in the same class of shysterdom as the others although I now knew she could not resist the opportunity of self enrichment.

On 31st May 95 I contacted Stevens by telephone and reminded him that he had promised me copies of the pre 1984 leases for Town O'Rule farm of which the Estate Manager had been the tenant. Stevens promised me again that he would do so.

It was about this time that one of the Estate staff informed me that Clive was nasty to Peter from time to time. On one occasion he had looked contemptuously at Peter and said: 'Just look at you', implying that he was a disgrace, before walking off. Peter had just stood there looking most uncomfortable but said nothing. He would have certainly realised that Clive was being nasty to him. It was therefore very likely that he would have been just as nasty to Robert. For Peter and Robert's sake it was a blessing that Gertrude outlived Clive. Without her to protect them he would have made their lives a misery. The great irony of it was that it was precisely Peter and Robert's existence which enabled him to become relatively wealthy.

26

THE ACCOUNTANT OF COURT TWISTS AND TURNS LIKE THE DEVIL.

On 2nd June 1995 I had a meeting at the Accountant of Court's Office in Parliament Square, Edinburgh and met the man who Brodies told me had been overseeing and auditing the Curatory Accounts; a Mr Walker. Mr Walker looked the part of a person who had worked in public sector accounting for many years. Medium height, well fed and the figure to show for it. By now I had become more aware of the importance of taking particular note of people's reactions when I first met them. Mr Walker immediately struck me as ill at ease.

I asked him for the accounts of Peter and Robert's Curatories. He then asked me why I wanted them. 'To see that everything has been done correctly by Brodies,' was my immediate response. He did not like this and tried to put me off. I stood my ground and eventually he agreed to get them. He shuffled off and returned with a bundle of papers. To my amazement these were not the Accounts of the Curatories at all. They were just the Borders Regional Council rates assessments in connection with the Wells Estate. And nothing whatever on Norton or Pitheavlis. I was dumbfounded, yet again, and told him that I had not come all that way just to see the Wells Estate Rates Assesments. I now informed him that I wanted *all* the records of the Curatories from their inceptions. His answer to that was: 'Why? Don't you trust us?' Again I was astounded! I told him that I did not distrust him but that I did distrust Brodies. He then refused to give me any further records, stating that I should get them from Brodies. I told him that Brodies had always refused to give them to me and had notified me and all the other beneficiaries in writing that the Accounts were available for inspection at his offices. No answer. 'Here we go again,' I thought.

I then asked him some specific questions in connection with the Estate Manager and how much he was getting paid by the estate. He gave me this information verbally and then told me that his office had put a stop to the Estate Manager awarding himself hefty increases year after year since 1982. 'Aha, after Clive's death; While he was alive he must have been watching the Estate Manager to make sure that he was not making more than he himself was making from his own various frauds. That would never do,' I thought. Mr Walker told me that his Office had got into long correspondence with Brodies about stopping the Estate Manager awarding himself these yearly increases. Brodies wanted the increases to continue, no doubt because they were also the Estate Manager's personal law agents, but had eventually agreed to the increases being stopped, but nearly ten years later, in 1991.

It goes without saying that I was most disappointed at the tenor and content of the meeting. At that time I was no good at all at stopping lawyers and people like Walker dictating the course and tenor of meetings.

On 7th June 1995 I contacted Stevens again to get copies of the Town O'Rule Farm leases pre 1985. He now reneaged on his assurance to me that he would send them 'soon' by stating that there was no point in my having them as they would be 'the same as the other leases.' What utter rubbish. I persisted. As I slowly cornered him he changed his tune by telling me that he could not find them, but that he would have 'another look.' He had them alright but did not want me to see them.

On 11th June 1995 I contacted Walker of the Accountant of Court offices in a further attempt to get the Town O'Rule leases. He also agreed to 'try' and get me copies.

On 14th June 1995 I contacted Walker again. He now informed me that he *had* copies of the leases but that he was not allowed to let me see them - because 'it was against the law'. This was patently absurd. However he told me what the rents had been for the year 1983-1984.

I nevertheless sensed that Walker was, beneath the surface, somehow sympathetic to me. But I also realised that Brodies were leaning on him very heavily indeed to stop him showing me *anything* pre-1990, the year of Peter's death.

On 19th June 1995 Chris Hall of Langley Taylor, Estate Agents of Edinburgh came down to Wells at my behest to give me some 'advice' on the various Estate properties. We looked around the various farms, cottages and woodlands. When we came to West Lees farm house we were met by a most unpleasant man called Clark. The tenant of West Lees, Cameron Thomson, had sublet the Farmhouse, in flagrant breach of the terms of his lease, to this most unpleasant man. On the odd occasion on which I had walked over West Lees Clark had subjected me to verbal abuse and tried to stop me walking there. I always simply told him to get out of my way and that I would go where I pleased. This occasion was no different to the others. He started to interfere with us. I told him to get out of my way as usual, which he eventually did. We then looked around the place. This episode epitomised how the tail wagged the dog, and had done, for very many years on the Wells Estate. In our day it would have been quite unthinkable to have people like him living on the Estate.

I suspect that this sub-letting of their farm houses, which the Estate Manager allowed the tenants to practice, alone covered the tiny rentals they were paying for their whole farms. Of course I never even bothered to ask any of them what they were getting for these very 'nice little earner' sublets because I realized that they, the tenants, would not give me any information and had probably been warned not to do so by the Estate Manager. I also realised that the tenants were apprehensive of me.

Having finished this bit of 'pleasant' business at West Lees we then went to Hallrule. I expected a cool reception there. When we arrived there was a potential purchaser called Devereaux and his family there with Jacquelin and the Estate Manager. After the West Lees episode Chris Hall was somewhat twitchy. I informed Jacquelin that I was going to look around the house. She appeared most unhappy and nervous at this but reluctantly agreed. Prior to this occasion I had once before arranged to meet her there so that I could look around the house. On that occasion she had shadowed me like a dog from room to room. I had then decided that I would never step foot into Hallrule House again without someone accompanying me as I feared some dirty tricks campaign being started by Brodies, herself, and the Estate Manager. I had also once been refused entry by, of all people, the housekeeper, Mrs Lancashire. As always we, the Usher family, were being kept at bay.

On this occasion Jacquelin suddenly rushed past me and stood guard at the door to the Morning room and announced that I could not go in there because the Estate Manager (the Estate Thief should have been his designation) was in negotiations with Devereaux. I had half a mind to just push her aside and go in anyway because she had no right to keep me, acting as Executor on Johnny's Power of Attorney, away from either the Estate Manager or Devereaux. However I decided not to push past her because I had Hall with me and instead I continued around the house with him. When we came downstairs she again took up her position outside the same door, managing to look both guilty and idiotic at the same time. 'Hardly surprising,' I thought. 'You are guilty and an idiot.' I then marched out of the house in defiant mode to show her who was who. Hall had by now become so nervous as to be of little further use so I dismissed him. It goes without saying that I had never been informed of this meeting with Devereaux and I therefore regarded it as yet another of Brodies and Jacquelin's *fait accomplis*.

Having got rid of Hall I went to the Cross Keys pub in nearby Denholm to catch up on the latest news regarding Wells from the locals and have a beer while I was about it. As luck would have it I found none other than MacTaggart at the bar. He informed me that the Closing Date for the reception of Sealed Offers to purchase the estate had been set for 12th of July. Not a word of this had been passed to Johnny or myself. I feigned that I was already aware of this to Mactaggart, finished my beer and went straight back to my cottage near Wells to give Johnny this latest bit of bad news. As expected Johnny was as furious as I was. He told me that he would get onto Brodies straightaway to demand an apology from them for keeping him and me in the dark. This he did and then came back to me quite shortly thereafter and told me that he had received verbal apologies from both Stevens and J Carnegie Arbuthnott of Brodies but had insisted that they put their apologies to him in writing. He duly received a written apology from Carnegie-Arbuthnott of Brodies, but none from Stevens nor Houldsworth who were the persons 'handling' the Executry affairs and giving Carnegie-Arbuthnott the orders. Crafty of them, but so very typical of Brodies. Dodge, lie, dodge and lie; again and again.

On 20th June 1995 I contacted Stevens again about the Town O'Rule lease and also about another bit of Estate amenity grass and woodland ground of about forty acres adjoining Rulewater called Roughside, now apparently in the possession of the egregious Mrs Mactaggart. He told me that he hadn't found the leases yet but had a man hunting for them full time. 'And charging the Executry £150 an hour for hunting out something the whereabouts of which you are perfectly aware, or have destroyed,' I thought.

I then asked him why he had not let Johnny and I know about the Closing Date. After a slight hesitation he decided that discretion was the better part of valour and apologized for not letting us know. However I was not going to let him off so easily and demanded to be put through to the equally slippery Carnegie-Arbuthnott for an apology from him as well. Carnegie-Arbuthnott duly apologised as well and told me that Johnny had given him a 'flea in the ear' about it. This episode demonstrated that Brodies were operating a strategy of ignoring us in order to do things *their* way. In this regard they had all they needed in the very slavish and wholly dishonest Jacquelin. 'Their way' was, of course, a 'the concealment of fraud way.'

On the 21st June 1995. I contacted Angus Cheape, a colleague of Chris Hall, of Langley Taylor Estate Agents of Edinburgh to discuss the level of rentals on the Wells estate. I asked him what he thought of the rentals. He immediately answered that they were 'astonishingly low'. This despite Brodies either trebling or quadrupling them in 1984. But they were now, in his words, *still* 'astonishingly low.' That of course meant that rentals had been more like only 10% of open market rate and not the 20% that we had hitherto thought.

On 27th June 1995 I contacted Stevens yet again about the Town O'Rule leases. He told me his man was still hunting for them.

At the end of June I decided that I would try to get for Johnny all the assets which, by some miracle, had not been stolen and placed in Gerrude's fraudulent Trust. These assets consisted of the portrait of Sir Walter Scott by one of the most famous Scottish painters of the day, Sir Henry Raeburn; a portrait of Sir Robert Usher in hunting pink, and a great deal of Silver. I did this on the grounds that they should have gone to Johnny on his succeeding to the Baronetcy. To this end I wrote to all the beneficiaries asking them if they would give up their claim to these Executry assets in favour of Johnny to mark his succession to the Baronetcy and notified Brodies of my doing so. Of course Jacquelin did not like this idea at all. However all the other beneficiaries agreed to Johnny having them. When she saw that she was outnumbered seven to one she eventually agreed to Johnny having the two portraits and Silver to the probate value of £7,000 only. This Silver included our Bedrule Silver which my Father had loaned to Stuart in 1950. I eventually collected the portraits and items of Silver to a value as near as possible to £7,000, based on Christie's probate valuations, in early September 1995. One of the pieces I rescued for Johnny was a beautiful Georgian candelabra. As he was short of money he asked me to sell the candelabra. I contacted some Edinburgh shops who specialised in that trade and was told that I could expect between three and four thousand pounds for it. The same inner small voice warned me that this was not a fair price at all. So I eventually took it to Hamilton and Inches, the famous jewellers in George Street, Edinburgh. The silver specialist I dealt with there straightaway offered me £15,000 for it. Of course I was over the moon and immediately sold it to him for that price.

Front of the sale catalogue - showing Brodies, now not only as the conveyancing lawyers, but also as the joint estate selling agents.

27

BEAUTIFUL WELLS ESTATE IS SOLD.

The 12th of July 1995 was my birthday - and the day which saw the opening of the sealed bids for the Wells Estate. For me the worst possible birthday present and something I had sworn I would never allow. I arose early and went for my last walk through the woods on the Estate while it still belonged to my family. I swore again that I would fight with might and main to somehow put things right. I also entertained the most hostile thoughts imaginable towards the people I held responsible for the Wells Estate, in particular, passing out of our family in these utterly fraudulent circumstances.

I then drove to Brodies in Edinburgh for the opening of the bids. When I arrived Jacquelin and Mrs Mactaggart were already there. She immediately informed me that she would be present when the bids were opened. I immediately informed her that she certainly would *not* be present because she was not an Executor and therefore had no right to be present. She told me she had permission from Jacquelin to be present. I replied that she would need permission from both Executors and that I would not agree to it. I then informed both Houldsworth of Brodies - there was no sign of Stevens - and Jacquelin that I would not allow Mrs Mactaggart to be present. Houldsworth conceded that it would be irregular on the grounds that one beneficiary could not be treated in a different way to the others. So why had he tried it on? It was plain, however, that he would have preferred Mrs Mactaggart to be present. Why?

Jacquelin then pleaded that Mrs Mactaggart be allowed to be present. She suggested a scheme whereby I would allow Mrs Mactaggart to stand at the far end of the room where she could not actually *see* any bids and the Executors - Jacquelin and I - would whisper to each other about the merits and otherwise of each bid. Houldsworth expressed sympathy to these pleadings. In response to all this theatre I warned them that I would not agree to any of their pleadings under any circumstances and would scupper the whole process rather than have her, of all people, watching and listening from the wings. Faced with this Houldsworth advised Jacquelin that Mrs Mactaggart should not be allowed in the room.

When I walked into the room I was surprised that the bids were already open and lying on the table, but foolishy did not query this straightaway. Of these bids there were only two for the Estate as a whole and one bid from a consortium of the tenants which had been orchestrated by Richard Landale of Sale & Co, Estate Agents of Glendale, Northumberland. There were also a whole lot of individual bids for individual lots, two of which bids were mine.

The consortium bid from the tenants was conditional in that it had to be accepted as a whole and as it stood or not at all. Brodies misleadingly 'advised' me that this condition forced the Executors to disregard all individual bids, as any acceptance of even one of them would lead to the consortium bid being withdrawn. This meant that my bids for parts of the estate would have to be disregarded, although one of my bids was more than 250% higher than the average of the other four bids for the same property. I was the only bidder for one of the other lots. I was bitterly disappointed at this but of course had to put the interests of the beneficiaries ahead of my own.

Houldsworth then 'advised' that we accept the tenant's consortium bid because the two bids for the Estate as a whole had some conditions on them which made them less desirable than the consortium bid - despite the consortium bid being £40,000 lower than even the lesser of the two bids a whole.

The consortium bid consisted of all the tenants on the Estate bidding for the farms which they tenanted as well as all those who were renting cottages bidding for these cottages. This absorbed most of the Estate. There remained the woodlands and other odd pieces of ground, including the piece of ground I had bid for, and also the cottage I was renting on a short lease. There was an individual offer for all these properties from a neighbouring farmer called Reddihough who was also part of the consortium.

New Wells House, completed in 1908

I was not at all happy with the consortium bid mainly because I did not want the Estate to go to tenants who had been paying a tiny fraction of Open Market place rental for their various farms and cottages for decades. I also knew that they had bid only 40% of the Open Market value for the properties they were tenanting. They did this on the strength of their tenancies being 'Protected Tenancies.' Both Johnny and I wanted the Estate to be sold to a wealthy sole owner because this would make it much easier for us to recover it from a single new owner than from a host of recent tenants, the proposed 'new owners' once we had exposed the fraud.

After much pressure from Brodies I reluctantly agreed to accept the consortium bid providing Johnny would agree. To that effect I telephoned Johnny for his final go ahead, which he gave. This meant the sitting tenants acquired all the properties they tenanted or rented at 40% of Open Market Value. Of course the tenants were delighted. Those who purchased their farms on that disastrous day were instantly many hundreds of thousands of pounds wealthier than they had been the day before. For example, and in round terms, the Mactaggarts bid £380,000 for Hallrule farm as one of the members of the consortium. The minute their bid was accepted the freehold of the farm was instantly £1 million on the open market. Of course the banks had been falling over themselves to provide loans on this basis to all these tenants

With hindsight it may seem obvious to the reader that the sale of the Estate to the tenants had been orchestrated by Brodies and Landale of Sale and Co to enable the tenants get their farms and houses at the 60% discount, thereby ensuring their co-operation with Brodies. As already stated this would make it infinitely more difficult for Johnny and me to get the sales reversed. I can only say in my defence at the time that I did not fully comprehend the deceit that the Brodies orchestrated tenants consortium bid was based on.

It took me years before I realised the significance of the three bids lying already opened on the table when I walked into the room. This was illegal because they should only have been opened in the presence of *both* Executors. This in turn meant that Brodies could have opened these 'sealed' bids days or weeks before the closing date. If this had in fact occurred this would then have enabled Brodies to inform Landale to tailor the consortium bid accordingly. Brodies could also have simply withheld or destroyed any 'sealed' bids for the Estate as a whole which were much higher and better than the aggregate of the consortium 60% discounted bids. I should have realised all this and therefore should have aborted the sale of the Estate the moment I saw that the 'sealed' bids had been opened in my absence. But I didn't and somehow Brodies knew I wouldn't. This again sickened to the pit of my stomach.

Sometime later I was told by an acquaintance that a man called Cowan had bid for the Estate as a whole with virtually no conditions. I told him there had been no bid from anyone called Cowan. This made it highly likely that Brodies had destroyed Cowan's and any other bids for the Estate as a whole which were higher than the consortium bid. Most likely Brodies had opened the 'sealed' bids as soon as they arrived.

But what would Brodies do if those would-be purchasers of the Estate as a whole made enquiry about their bids? Easiest thing in the world for the habitual liars they were and still are: If the sealed bid had been sent by unregistered mail Brodies would simply tell such enquirer that the bid had never arrived and therefore must have got lost in the post. If it had been sent by registered mail all Brodies would need to say, no doubt with saintly sympathy, was: 'Your bid was not the best bid. We are sorry that you were unsuccessful on this occasion and wish you success in any bids you may make on properties being sold through us in the future.' The would-be purchaser would have no prospect of success in proving that Brodies had either withheld or destroyed his/her sealed bid.

Was Jacquelin in on it? I don't know. The point is rather academic because if they had included her she would have kept her mouth shut and if they hadn't included her she would never have queried the bids lying open when she arrived.

Another manifestation of this orchestration was Brodies constantly brainwashing me over the previous months that they did *not* put much store on the consortium bid and expected the Estate to go as a whole which would be the best outcome as far as they were concerned. I realised that this had been yet another of their brainwashing lies to conceal their orchestrating the sale of the Estate to the tenants. Without this orchestration the tenants would never have thought of getting together as a consortium to get the Estate on the cheap, let alone to actually manage to do so. This made it almost certain that the tenants consortium bid was Brodies' idea alone and to conceal this they got the crooked Richard Landale to advise the tenants accordingly.

It was only in 2015 that it dawned on me that the bids for the Estate as a whole could never have been so close to the tenant's consortium bid other than by Brodies' orchestration. No one in their right mind would bid for the whole Estate at a 60% discount of its Open Market value if they really wanted it. They would bid on the basis of its Open Market value and if their bid was successful they would have immediately raised the rents to Open Market levels.

The final nail in the coffin of that disastrous day was that Mrs Mactaggart had wormed her way into the far end of the room at some stage without my noticing her. I was so distracted that I did not insist she remove herself.

On 15th July 1995 Gillian, Katherine and Richard landed at Edinburgh Airport from South Africa. Katherine was ten and Richard eight years old. They had not been able to leave South Africa earlier because of complications in ending their schooling there. But it was now the end of the summer term and this was to be the start of a new life for us all. When

I'd left South Africa I thought we would have matters sorted out relatively quickly and settle down on a nice property on the Estate and lead a pleasant country life. How wrong I was. Our life was made a nightmare by Brodies, the Scottish 'legal system' *et al.*

Thankfully Gillian got a job at a Primary School near Wells on the strength of her South African qualifications so that stabilised our finances. We sent Katherine and Richard to the Denholm State Junior School and thereafter to Jedburgh High School.

On 17th July 1995 by chance I met the Estate Manager in the Bank of Scotland in Hawick where I had been invited to celebrate the tercentenary of the bank. I asked him if he recalled the Gentleman's Agreement my father had with Clive on my getting the tenancy of Hallrule farm in 1973. As usual the cunning fellow did not give a candid answer but stated that he recalled *something* about it and left it at that, waiting for *me* to give him clues as to the best way forward for *him*, Valerie, the Mactaggarts and Brodies. I simply kept quiet until the silence became embarrassing; for him, not me. I enjoy seeing crooks squirm. He eventually piped up by suggesting that I phone him about it and scuttled off saying he was in a hurry.

On 18th July 1995 the Estate Manager phoned me, ostensibly about an electrician who was to come and sort out an electrical problem in the cottage. I kept things skeletal to see if he would bring up the Gentleman's Agreement business again. sure enough did. He asked me to tell him about it, which I did in no uncertain terms. He then said, 'Yes I heard talk about it; Yes I did, and I can't say that I *didn't* hear about it, because I *did* hear about it.' Those were his exact words. His talking in this convoluted manner confirmed that he was trying to avoid being trapped. He then asked 'Did you get the Gentlemen's Agreement in writing?' Like the greenhorn idiot I was I told him we did not. He saw his salvation and seized it: 'If you have not got it in writing there is nothing you can do.' Of course I, too late, stuttered that of course a Gentlemen's Agreement by its very nature was not in writing . . .' but he was gone.

On 20th July 1995 I discovered another bit of deceit by Clive. I went to the National Archives in Edinburgh to do some research on disposals of Usher Trust properties. I discovered that Mrs Mactaggart had 'purchased' a further 40 acres of the Wells Estate in 1973, called Roughside, which adjoined the 80 acres or so that Clive had been 'given' in 1959. This purchase therefore enlarged Clive's family holding on the Trust Estate.

Mrs Mactaggart had, on the face of it, purchased this most attractive forty acres of permanent pasture with ornamental hardwoods and about half a mile of the Rulewater, for the risible price of £2,250. But it did not end there, because Clive, as a Trustee, had effected the sale to his own daughter. This was another flagrant breach of Scots Law - a Trustee is absolutely precluded from selling any land of which he is a Trustee to his immediate family. And MacLure, Johnny's fellow Trustee, had sanctioned this totally fraudulent transaction. I wrote, 'On the face of it, because the question arises: Had Mrs Mactaggart ever actually paid even *this* risible sum for the land?' We did not know because Brodies refused to show us any Trust Accounts for 1962 to 1982 and we do not know to this day as I edit this book for the umpteenth time in 2018.

This, in turn, aroused my suspicions on the land and cottages which we had been told that Stuart had *given* Clive in 1959 so I checked that out as well. Sure enough Stuart had *not* given them to him at all, according to the Land Registry. It was recorded that Clive had *purchased* this glorious holding for just £4,000. This was again a risibly low sum for three very nice cottages, extensive and very well appointed Stables, the formal garden, the informal gardens, including the bowling green and the site of Wells House itself, in all about 80 acres? Such a sum was simply not credible. Had my father known at the time that this core part of the Estate was to be sold then he would have bid for them.

And finally, to cap it all, by either giving *or* selling these properties to Clive, the Trustees at the time, Stuart, McClure and Leadbetter flagrantly breached the Trust which they had the fiduciary duty to uphold. It wasn't until some years later that I deduced that Stuart had been forced into this particular piece of chicanery.

On 6th August 1995 I discovered a further deceit in connection with the orchestrated and fraudulent sale of the Estate. I contacted a local farmer called Reddihough who had bought up those pieces of the Estate (the woodlands, etc) as a member of the 'tenant's consortium" despite his not being a tenant. This was another of Brodies deceits which I had not noticed at the opening of the 'sealed' bids. Amongst Reddihough's purchases was some land for which I had bid more than two and a half times the bid he had made. I now wanted to purchase this land from him. Reddihough then told me that he had already sold it on to a Mr Nicholson who lived across the river from this land thus enlarging Mr Nicholson's holding by including that part of the river as well. Nicholson lived in what had once been the Bedrule Manse, before my father purchased it from the Church for Johnny to live in with his young family in the mid 1960s. It was a lovely house because, in support of the church, old Sir Robert Usher had extended it greatly into quite an imposing place. Reddihough suggested that I contact Nicholson. But here was the rub: Nicholson was a very great friend of Houldsworth of Brodies, Robert's Curator Bonis. On top of that Nicholson worked for the stockbroking firm of Lawrie & Bell which handled the Usher stock broking investments on the instructions of Brodies.

I further discovered that Nicholson had also purchased other Estate land adjoining the Manse in the past and now owned several acres there. Before I became aware of all this I had contacted Nicholson to have a chat but had been given short shrift by his wife. This of course aroused my suspicions at that time. It was after this that I discovered his close association with

Houldsworth. Of course my suspicions were now further aroused. Nicholson worked in Edinburgh, living there in a flat during the working week.

On finishing my call to Reddihough I relieved myself in the loo. This took three minutes at the most. I then called Nicholson in Edinburgh. The receptionist asked my name. I told her 'Usher', my steep learning curve teaching me to keep things skeletal and not volunteering any information that I had not been asked for. On hearing 'Usher', she immediately blurted out: 'Oh, Stuart Usher. Yes we were expecting a call from you?' Of course I instantly asked her how on earth she knew that I was going to call her office? Unfazed she answered that someone had just phoned and had asked her to tell Mr Nicholson to expect a call from Stuart Usher. That someone could only have been Reddihough. His calling Nicholson immediately after the end of my call to him showed that he, Reddihough, had realised the importance of warning Nicholson that I was going to phone him so that he, Nicholson, could prepare himself and make it more difficult for me to catch him out.

The receptionist then told me that Nicholson was out but would be back at 2.30 and would return my call. He failed to do so. So I phoned again at 3.20 and, disguising my voice, asked for Nicholson again. I was learning fast that this was the only way to get through to Edinburgh professional crooks like Nicholson when they feared exposure. It worked. She told me that she would put me through to him and asked for my name. I sprang my trap by giving it in full in my normal voice. Deafening silence from her. Recovering herself she then lied; 'Sorry, he's just gone out again.'! She then assured me he *would* return my call. He failed to do so. At 6.20pm I phoned again. I got a man this time, probably a cleaner or janitor. He told me that Nicholson had gone home to his flat in Edinburgh. I asked for Nicholson's home telephone number fully expecting him to refuse on the grounds of confidentiality. To my great and pleasant surprise he gave it to me without demur. I then rang Nicholson and got him almost at once.

On hearing it was me Nicholson inhaled sharply. No 'Good Evening' - just silence. Crooks do that when suprised! I let the silence run. After a while, during which time I could almost hear his brain cogitating feverishly, he eventually acknowledged me. I then asked him if he would sell me the piece of ground (for which my bid had been two and a half times higher than Reddihough's) which he had purchased from Reddihough. Silence again, as he thought of the best way out of it. He then piped up by incanting: 'How unfortunate everything is. How unfortunate everything is,' and became apologetic. But he had not answered my question. When he had finished his thoroughly insincere incantations I asked him the same question again. He now informed me that he wouldn't sell it to me because he wanted to keep it as it was, undeveloped. He then said he had told Houldsworth a long time ago that he wanted that ground. I told him that this was rather peculiar because Reddihough himself had told me that he (Nicholson) had told him (Reddihough) that he did not want that ground before the sale of the Estate. Another long silence He eventually responded with more incantations of regret thereby again evading my question. I got nowhere with him and ended the call.

So Reddihough had lied to me about Nicholson not wanting that ground. Nicholson had wanted that ground alright and had told Reddihough. This was further confirmation that Brodies, the tenants and people like Nicholson and Reddihough had been in cahoots for months to acquire Estate land on the cheap. Also to keep Johnny and me out. And the worst of it was they had succeeded.

It was the end of my hopes of acquiring any property on the Estate. The ground I had bid for was about an acre, beside the river and with plenty of trees, an idyllic spot. Of course it made me ever more determined to expose Brodies and their partners in crime, such as Nicholson and Reddihough.

On 29th August 1995 I had a meeting with Duncan Thompson of the Scottish Landowner's Federation at their Maritime Street, Leith offices. He was most charming and helped as much as he could. He confirmed that Clive being both a Trustee and a Tenant breached a basic tenet of Scottish Law. Also that I might have a case against Clive on his breaking the Gentleman's Agreement. He did not tell me anything I did not already know but his trying to be helpful was a very pleasant change.

On 31st August 1995 I contacted Stevens again about the Usher Baronetcy Trust records and the Minute Book of the meetings of the UBT Trustees. He now informed me that no Minute Book of the UBT existed and that most of the UBT 'stuff' had been either 'lost or burnt' (his exact words). Charming, and how incredibly unhelpful to the Executry and us and how terribly convenient for Brodies, Clive, Gertie, Valerie, the Mactaggarts, and whoever else - for example Nicholson.

One of the Church Elders had now found the old Scroll in the Vestry. I therefore put it back onto its old nail in our family pews. When I asked the Session Clerk, Roger Hemming, why, and by whose authority, it had been removed and the new misleading one displayed in its stead he told me that he did not know and had never understood it.

28

LAND AGENTS AND TURNCOATS

At this time I started trying to get a firm of Land Agents to carry out an in-depth study and thereafter produce a report on the level of the rentals for the farms and cottages on the Estate as compared to the going rate on properly managed Estates. I contacted many such firms and individuals but not a single one of them wanted to become involved. The most common reasons they gave for not wanting to get involved were either 1) They did not want to offend Brodies because they did business with them and 2) They knew the Estate Manager. Or a combination of the two.

I then tried Rental Arbiters in the form of local farmers and the like. I got absolutely nowhere for much the same reasons. After that I tried the Scottish Office and the various state organizations involved with Agriculture. No success there either. Just the same uncomfortable silences and evasions. I then tried the Scottish Farmer and various other Agricultural publications. They either did not have records which would be of assistance to me or, in the rare event of having them, pleaded confidentiality.

Eventually an Ayrshire Land Agent had the decency to warn me that I would get nowhere with any Land Agents and lawyers with my enquiries about anything to do with our properties in Scotland. He warned me that they would all combine against me to protect each other as this was the price of their remaining 'respected professionals.' Of course I found this profoundly discouraging and began thinking more and more: 'What sort of country had Britain, and Scotland in particular, become in my absence. Or had it always been like that?' Of course I'd never had any idea that such a network existed, but now I knew alright. It dawned on me that professionals all over Scotland were perfectly aware that our Estates were being plundered by those who had been entrusted to protect them, but everyone was keeping quiet. I began to despise and loathe 'professionals' more and more. Local farmers privately volunteered that they regarded the Wells Estate rentals as 'a joke.' However they, likewise, did not want to get involved. I continued the hunt.

On the 19th September 1995 I at last had what I thought was a breakthrough. I contacted a Land-agent called Wemyss of FBR Ltd, Kelso in the Sccottish Borders. The first thing I did was to inform him of the identity of the people involved in the management of the Wells Estate, Brodies, the Estate Manager, and in the past Clive and MacClure. He was very positive about taking it on and told me that he was not a bit worried about the personalities or bodies involved. He was adamant that he would produce his report entirely on the merits of the case without fear or favour to anyone. He estimated that it would take him about two weeks to produce and would cost about £600. I was delighted with his business-like attitude which focused on the job to be done rather than who was involved, as all the other land agents had been. I therefore supplied him with the records needed to produce his report, copies of leases and the like.

However, as so often in my pursuit, my elation was misplaced. Wemyss wrote to me on 11th October 1995 summarily breaking our agreed terms of his investigation 'on the grounds of the various parties involved.' This was the very thing that he had assured me that did not worry him at all! I concluded that he must have been got at, and in no uncertain terms, in much the same way that Jacquelin and Murray the lawyer had been got at before him. He then suggested that I contact an Arbiter. I did so but again got nowhere. The fear of getting involved saw to that. I was back to square one..

On the twenty-first of September 1995 I had a meeting with Kenneth Oliver, a well known Hawick Auctioneer and race-horse owner and trainer at his home near Denholm to see if he knew anything about the Wells Estate debacle. In particular I thought his firm might have had something to do with the valuation of Uncle Stuart's estate and the contents of Hallrule House. I also told him that the Estate Manager had stolen the heirloom jewellery and gave him a general outline as to what appeared to have been happening on the Estates over the last three decades. He was shocked and then told me he too had heard of all sorts of very bad things in connection with the management of the Wells Estate for a long, long time: I was very pleased to hear that coming from him because he was a popular man who had the respect of the whole Borders community. He then went on to say: 'What a disaster the whole thing is. There has never been anything like it in the Borders before.'

He then suggested that I contact a man called Donald Inch who used to work for him to see if he knew anything about the valuation of Stuart's estate. I therefore contacted Donald Inch who lived near Newcastleton. He immediately told me that he himself had done the valuation of Stuart's estate. I was over the moon about that and felt that here at last I would get the proof I needed to force Brodies to give up their various patent fictions on the Contents issue. We arranged a luncheon date for Sunday 24th September 1995.

As arranged Gillian, my daughter Katherine, son Richard and I took Donald Inch and his daughter to lunch at a lovely hotel which straddled the Border between the 'Auld Enemies' on the Hawick to Carlisle road. He was as helpful as could be and gave me a written statement to the effect that the contents of Hallrule which he valued as belonging to Uncle Stuart made up only a tiny percentage of the contents of Hallrule House. That was exactly our position and made a complete mockery of Brodies claim that Uncle Stuart had left the vast majority of the Contents to Gertie in his Will. Again I was over the moon about that. But I had been over the moon about things before only to be brought crashing down to earth by people effecting 180 degree turns. So I now kept my feet firmly on the ground.

I then told him of some of the more glaring examples of the 'mismanagement' of the Estates and he volunteered his further assistance on these matters as well. I also told him about the Gentleman's Agreement with Clive and how Clive had repeatedly ratted on it. In this regard his father, Ewart Inch, who had lived in Hallrule Farmhouse for a few years in the early 70s had told me on my 1973 visit to Scotland that Gentlemens' Agreements only worked if both parties to any Agreement were Gentlemen and that he himself had never regarded Clive as a Gentleman at all. How right he was.

So we all had a lovely lunch and we all departed in the best of spirits looking forward to working with him on all the aspects of the 'management' of the Estates.

Lo and behold a short while later he informed me that he now 'did not want to get involved' and would be of no further assistance to me. Just like that. Jacquelin, Murray, Wemyss and now Inch. As far as Donald Inch was concerned I dismissed him as yet another flaky 'professional'; too frightened to do the honourable thing. That is exactly how tyrannies arise.

'The only thing necessary for evil to triumph is that good men do nothing'. Left: Andrew Wemyss of FBR Land Agents.

29

LAST STAND ON THE CONTENTS OF HALLRULE HOUSE

By 28th September 1995 Johnny had written to all the beneficiaries informing them that he was going to make a stand on the Contents issue and asking for their backing.

To this end I arranged to meet Mrs Mactaggart on this day to ascertain whether she would support Johnny. On the odd occasion all summer when I had spoken to her in passing, usually from my car, she had made it clear that she wanted the contents back in the executry. However at this meeting she now informed me that, 'it will be impossible to get Gertie's Will revoked,' and was therefore against Johnny making a stand She then said that she had no clear perception of who owned the contents. I went over the history of the Contents again with her and reminded her that she had fully agreed with our position all year, so something must have changed her mind. What was it? She now shifted ground and stated that she had no view about it and had, 'never been interested in that type of thing.' I recounted the facts of the matter to her, yet again. She then feigned a more positive attitude and told me she would 'think about it.' As I was bringing the meeting to a close she suddenly said that it was, 'a disgrace that the Contents were going to outsiders.' This made it abundantly clear that she could not be relied upon in any way.

On 29th September 1995 I had a meeting at Hallrule House with Jacquelin at 10.00am for the same reasons that I'd had the meeting with Mrs Mactaggart. Jacquelin greeted me with feigned warmth, before launching into a twenty minute discourse (yes, I *did* time her) on all the reasons why we should allow the Estate Manager and Mrs Blamey keep the Contents. I kept quiet and let her do the all the talking - actually jabbering - because this offered the best chance of her letting another cat out of the bag. 'You cannot undo the past,' was one of her favourite incantations during this discourse. By now I felt I had become reasonably adept at spotting the difference between an impassioned relater of the truth and the anxious defence of a fraud. When she'd finished I gave her the facts of the matter yet again and reminded her that the duty of the Executors was to ingather the estate of the Deceased person and distribute it to the beneficiaries. And that if the Executors discovered that the Estate of Robert or Peter had been defrauded it was the duty of the Executors to recover the assets of which it had been defrauded - citing the contents of Hallrule House as a prime example. Like Mrs Mactaggart she then said she would think it over and come back to me.

However nothing could disguise the fact that our making a stand on the Contents was the last thing she and Mrs Mactaggart wanted. Jacquelin knew that the Contents had been removed by fraud and she knew that I knew that she knew. The same applied to Mrs Mactaggart. In this regard Jacqueline wrote to Johnny (always studiously avoiding me) on 3rd October 1995 in response to the letter from him on the subject: She ended this letter with this statement; 'Morally it may be wrong but history is made up of things that should never have happened.' Another admission that Gertrude, with Brodies help, had simply defrauded the Usher Baronetcy Trust using her son, the hapless and mentally incapacitated Peter, as a shield to protect herself from discovery.

On 2nd October 1995 I made my first inquiries to lawyers about taking our case on a No Win No Fee basis.

On 3rd October 1995 we had Valerie to our place, the ex-staff cottage near Wells, for drinks. My purpose in doing so was to glean more information to use against Brodies, the Estate Manager, her daughter Mrs Mactaggart *et al* She didn't disappoint me. A couple of stiff whiskies soon had her singing like a canary. She told me: 'Gertie was always apprehensive of you, you know.' I told her that I was never aware of that and asked why Gertrude was apprehensive of me? She evaded answering this by making a variation of the statement. Of course I was inwardly delighted at this pearl of information; Gertrude must have accepted me at my word that I would be back all those years ago in 1968 when I had bade her 'good riddance' at Hallrule. And that this had worried her all those years. This made me a very happy chappy indeed

I then informed Valerie that Johnny had written to all the beneficiaries about making a stand on the Contents of Hallrule. She instantly responded: 'I know - and no-one thinks much of it at all.' She, also, had been keen at the start that the contents to be returned to the Executry but was now, like Mrs Mactaggart, suddenly opposed. Losing the argument in the same way as Mrs Mactaggart and Jacquelin had, she suddenly became angry and let yet another very useful cat out of the bag: 'The lawyers bogged up on the Usher Wills. Also on Gertie's Will but you cannot do anything about it now as it would cost a fortune. You must stop always trying to find out what happened. Just stop going back!'

Well, well, well: 'Bogged up on the Usher Wills.' I was delighted with that admission, but it wasn't a 'bog up'; it was a blatant and ongoing fraud. The 'just stop going back' part was all very well for her and her family squatting on Hallrule farm and at Wells as a consequence of just one aspect of the overall fraud. I presume she would have explained all this away as just another 'bog up'. This did not sit at all well with me. She soon became so agitated that I politely asked her to leave. This she did without further ado. I was never to speak to her again. She exeated this world in November 2002. However I attended her funeral; not to mourn her, but in the hope of gleaning further useful information.

That said I never regarded her in the same league as Clive and Gertrude in the Crooked Stakes . I suspect she, at the start anyway, deplored Clive's crookery but then just stuck it out with him because she was his wife. In this regard Clive had informed Uncle Stuart in the late nineteen forties that he intended to walk out on Valerie. Stuart had made short work of Clive by telling him: 'If you do that, you will never cross my doorstep again.' So Clive did not walk out on her. Well done Uncle Stuart.

Significantly she'd arranged for herself to be buried in the open part of Bedrule Churchyard and not in the private Usher burial ground next to Clive. It appeared that she wanted to have nothing whatever further to do with him. I took my hat off to her for that.

On 23rd October 1995 Gillian and I went to the Assembly Rooms in George Street, Edinburgh where Christies were hosting a Preview of the Contents of Hallrule House. Jacqueline was there, loudly proclaiming to anyone who would listen, that she was the Executor. I am glad to say that no one paid much attention to her. An indescribable grief overwhelmed me to see our family's last remaining possessions flaunted before the public prior to being knocked down to the highest bidder with the proceeds going to the Estate Manager and Gertrude's niece, Alice Blamey, who both knew full well they had no right to them. Gillian and I, sickened, drifted away.

On 24st October 1995 Gillian and I gathered our strength and went to the auction. The rooms were heaving with people. With little enthusiasm we bid as high as we possibly could for numerous pieces, - particularly any silver pieces with the family crest on them but were successful with only two. In all it cost almost us £2,000 for just three pieces. To add insult to injury the auctioneer was Meddowes. Again in our naivety we sat in the front row of seats instead of the back where I could have kept a much better eye on him. After the auction some decent person told me that in such auctions unscrupulous auctioneers were not above acknowledging phantom bids from the back of the room; what I understand now is known as 'bouncing them off the wall.' Out in front we were sitting ducks for this despicable practice.

After the auction finished a haggard looking Mrs Blamey of whose presence I had been unaware, approached us and asked if we would give her a lift back to Wells Stables. We simply shook our heads in disgust and she walked away disconsolately. It was the last we ever saw of her.

On the way home I regretted that we had not given her a lift home because she might have given us, wittingly or unwittingly, some further useful information. I knew that she loathed both Brodies and the Estate Manager and suspected she despised the Mactaggarts. So this was another opportunity missed. Also there had been something apologetic and despairing in the manner in which she had approached us. Fool that I had been. But Gillian and I felt so angry and hurt at the time that we were not thinking clearly.

On 25th October 1995 I contacted Mr Love of Ker & Macallister, Auctioneers of Glasgow. This firm had collected the contents of Hallrule House which were deemed not worthy of the Christie sale; cupboards, pictures, engravings, silver plate, china and the like. I asked him for a list of the items which had been collected. Mr Love informed me that some items on the list they'd received from Christies and which they were to collect from Hallrule House were missing. They had only been able to collect what remained. He informed me that only Christies had this original list. So I then approached Christies for this list to establish which items had gone missing. Meddowes informed me that Brodies had the list. I then approached Brodies for the list. Brodies then informed me that Christies had it. I was like a rag doll being thrown around by perverts. When they'd had their fun Meddowes finally sent me the list of items which were eventually auctioned by Ker & Macallister at their Glasgow premises. This was *not* of course the original list. When I again approached Mr Love he had was now, all of a sudden, evasive and unhelpful. The usual reaction when I had someone cornered.

So what happened to the missing items? They must have been stolen. By whom? Almost certainly Jacquelin because she was living at Hallrule House at the time. Had she allowed the Estate Manager and Mrs Mactaggart in on the theft? I don't know but she might well have done so as a means of control and potential blackmail over them on the principle of: 'If I am caught out on this I will spill the beans on you two as well. We are all thieves in this so you better keep your mouths shut'.

Hallrule:
sharing the spoils

30

BRODIES AND THE COURT OF SESSION

On 23rd November 1995 I went to the Accountant of Courts offices in Edinburgh to inspect the Curatory Accounts which Brodies had notified me were awaiting my inspection there. When I asked Mr Walker for these Curatory Accounts he told me: 'You have already seen them.' I was stunned. Of course I'd never seen them - why would Brodies write informing me the Accounts were ready to be inspected at the Accountant of Courts offices if I'd already seen them? It was Alice in Wonderland. Walker then changed tack by informing me that, actually, it would be a 'monumental task' to produce the accounts. Next he told me I would have to pay them £1 per sheet to see them. When I asked him how much this would be in total he estimated £200. Next he came out with a total contradiction: 'But then again we might not charge you at all.' Just another example of the total dysfunctionality of the Scottish 'Legal' system. It was also another example of the arrogance and contempt with which it treats members of the public who exercise their basic societal rights.

Walker then volunteered that his Department were aware that, 'Parts of the Usher Estate had gone to Robert via Lady Usher's Trust but we cannot understand how or why.'

'Aha!' I thought, 'Thank you very much for telling me that, my friend.'

He went on: 'Brodies told us that it was all perfectly legal. So we left it at that.' I then told him that the one of the *parts* of the 'Usher Estate', he had just referred to were the Contents of Hallrule House, and that was exactly why I was there on that day and that I, like him and his Department, 'cannot understand how or why this had been done.' I then informed him that I had demanded that Brodies freeze the proceeds from the sale of the Contents with a view to having them returned to the Executry. He now became more guarded. However it did not stop him having another shot at Brodies by saying: 'Uh Oh. They've got it wrong again,' in connection with some other aspect of the Estate's affairs. Of course this Brodies getting it 'wrong again' was not the correct term at all. 'Uh Oh Brodies are defrauding again,' was the correct term.

Walker then asked me to come back in four days time with a written request to see the accounts and to deliver this to him personally. The apparatchik had spoken, but the constant back and forth to Edinburgh was taking its toll on us financially.

On 27th November 1995, as requested by Walker, I delivered my written request to see the Accounts, to him personally. In this written request I asked to see the Accounts from the inception of the Curatory in 1983 until 31st March 1991. After that date I *had* the Accounts from Brodies. Again he said it would be a 'huge task' and that now I definitely *would* have to pay for them. I then left. As I was walking towards the car I realized that I had not inspected the accounts that were supposedly ready for inspection. I went back to do so. When I asked Mr Walker for these he told me that they were not, after all, ready but 'would take another hour or so to get ready.'

He then informed me that because I had inspected the Accounts from Peter's death in 1990 to Robert's death in 1994, I would then *not* be supplied the accounts for which I had asked. Again I was flabbergasted and informed him accordingly. He told me I should get these accounts from Brodies. I replied that he had seen Brodies' letter to the beneficiaries stating we were to inspect them at his Offices. He then said the Accountant of Court would write to me on the matter and told me that the accounts I had asked for would now cost £300. I then asked him for a copy of the letter I had already given him as I had, my head in a spin, forgotten to make a copy of it for my own records. He refused this perfectly simple request on the grounds that he was 'not allowed' to give me a copy. Yet another bald and this time patently absurd lie.

I then arranged to meet him on 5th December 1995 to inspect the accounts and forthwith marched out of that accursed building, thinking with regard to Alice in Wonderland that Walker was the March hare. What sort of legal system *was* this? Whatever it was it was quite apparent that it was an utterly dysfunctional one manned by liars. It was also clearly evident that the Accountant of Court had failed dismally to protect the interests of their successive Wards of Court, Peter and Robert and it was this failure that was causing Walker to conduct himself in such a bizarre and dishonest manner.

On 5th December 1995 I took the Gillian with me to act as a witness to Walker's constant obstructions and evasions. When we arrived we were told to wait on the stair landing outside the offices. This we did for almost a quarter of an hour before Walker appeared, looking more agitated than ever. He failed to greet us but instead demanded how we had 'got into the building.' He then continued; 'You have no right to be in the building so tell me how you got past the security'. Of course both Gillian and I were much taken aback. I responded, with a degree of heat, that I had never had a moment's bother with the security staff before and we were there as per the arrangement which *he* had made with us to inspect the accounts as per Houldsworth of Brodies letter. He then said we should make an appointment; and then changed his mind and said they would take about an hour to produce. We agreed to return in one hour's time. He then said he would see what he could do and asked us to wait. Within 5 minutes he came back with them. We were still on the landing - a most inhospitable place to do business. He then argued that I had already seen the Accounts before giving in and allowing me to peruse them. I immediately saw that they were the same accounts that Brodies had sent to us in South Africa which covered the period 1991-1994 which I had already told him that I had seen. These were not the 1983 to 1991 Accounts for which I had asked. Walker now just stood there looking embarrassed.

To relieve the tension I informed him that Johnny had put a stop to the Estate Manager becoming Peter's Curator. Mr Walker's answer was as interesting as it was revealing: 'A good job too; otherwise there would have been no Estate left by now.' Gillian and I were very pleased to hear this admission. He then informed us that the Accountant of Court, 'will freeze the remaining monies (well over half) from being paid out to the beneficiaries because of your objections.' Of course I challenged him on that in the strongest terms possible. However he was adamant and now stated: 'As you have objected to the Discharge of Mr Houldsworth, the Accountant of Court has (*fait acompli*) frozen all the proceeds now payable to the beneficiaries and they will remain frozen until a Court hearing takes place.' Again I was flabbergasted at this latest piece of nonsense and and told him so in no uncertain terms that I had *not* objected to the Discharge of Houldsworth. Walker's statement was just another of his blatant lies.

I then told him, for the umpteenth time, that all I wanted to do was to inspect the Accounts of the Curatory from 1983 to 1991. How could I possibly give a Discharge to Houdsworth without, at the very least, seeing the Opening and Closing balances of the Curatory? It would be patent lunacy. Walker repudiated this. He then went on to say that we now had 42 days from 15th November 1995 in which to make representations. Also that there were two sets of accounts. One for Robert and another for Peter. I then asked him if his offices had the vouchers for the Curatories. He said they did not but that Brodies had them and were obliged to show them to us. Despite repeated requests and efforts by Johnny and myself Brodies had always absolutely refused to let us see any Accounts, let alone vouchers, pre 1990. However Brodies had recently admitted to me that they held 'bundles' of records. Walker then said it would take about a week to get all the Curatory Accounts ready.

On 6th December 1995 Stevens at last sent me three further Inventory Valuations. He had written to me on 6th July that he was trying to 'uncover any older valuations of silver.' The valuations he now sent had taken him five months to 'uncover'. One valuation was for 'Lady [Gertrude] Usher's' Silver, dated 25th January 1985, three months after her death carried out by Ingles, Jewellers of Hawick. Another was for 'her' furniture, paintings, *objets d'art* etcetera, carried out by Phillips Auctioneers of Edinburgh and dated 10th January 1985. Both were done for Probate purposes. Later Brodies claimed that Andrew Oliver of Hawick had done the Probate Inventory Valuations and this is confirmed by Gertrude's 'Confirmation of Estate'. But Stevens did not send me that Valuation, no doubt because it contained information Brodies did not want me to have. The third Valuation he did send me was in connection with 'Peter's [purported] Silver' and this was done on the 12th of July 1990 - forty-one days after his death by Christies this time, again, for probate purposes.

It is now obvious that Stevens and the other Brodies lawyers involved had known about the two pre-1990 Valuations all along but had not sent them to me for fear that I would compare them with the valuations done by Christies in 1990 and 1994. They might well have commissioned these pre-1990 Valuations themselves. If not then the only other person, with the perceived only authority to have done so was the Estate Manager. But much more likely it was Brodies. Of course I did compare these earlier valuations with the Christies valuations and discovered that no less than sixty-four items that appeared in them were missing from the Christies 1990 and 1994 valuations. Some person, or persons, had therefore been helping themselves to items from Hallrule after Gertie's death in 1984 while Peter and Robert were living there alone and then again after Peter's death in 1990 when Robert was living there alone, and again after Robert's eventual death when the house stood empty except for the Housekeeper, Mrs Lancashire, and her husband. Who was the thief or thieves? Suspect No 1 is the Estate Manager as he had access to the house. Suspects No 2. Valerie and Mrs Mactaggart. Suspect No 3 Alice Blamey, Gertrude's niece. They all had access to the house so I suspect they all helped themselves. It might well have become a 'robbing derby' between them as each party noticed items disappearing. Remember the Mactaggarts and Alice Blamey loathed the Estate Manager and he loathed them. The rationale would have been along the lines of: 'That thieving so and so has stolen that lovely piece of china so I will steal something as well'. Crooks don't tolerate other crooks getting more than they themselves in the 'Robbing Stakes'.

I was sickened at this revelation but looking back I realize that I had, yet again, been naive and slow on the uptake. It was some time before it struck me that another reason Brodies had not sent me these Inventories and Valuations earlier was because they feared if the had sent them *before* the Contents were removed from Hallrule House I would have checked them against what was actually in the house before their removal and discovered that these items were missing, as per the pre 1990 Inventories. Of course I could not do this *now* because the Contents had been removed by the Shore Porter's Society on 20th October 1995. So Brodies had simply waited until the Contents had already been removed and sold before sending them to me. This made it certain that Brodies had been aware that many items had been stolen from Hallrule in the period between Gertrude's death in 1984 and Peter and Robert's respective deaths on 1990 and 1994. Had they reported the thefts to the Police? No, they hadn't. I therefore concluded that the Brodies lawyers who had access to Hallrule, Carruthers, Stevens and Houldsworth, were accessories to the theft. It is also quite likely that these lawyers also partook in the 'Robbing Stakes' themselves.

The final twist to this particular catalogue of deceit was that this day (6th December 1995) that Stevens finally sent me the Valuations was the very day that the deadline for my inspecting the Curatory Accounts at the Accountant of Court's Offices expired. This meant, on the face of it, that it was too late for me to lodge any objections in connection with the missing items. Brodies sending me the Inventories on that day was an extra safe-guard. And Jacquelin? She claimed she was too 'busy' to help me. I was shortly to discover that that she had indeed been busy, concocting false expenses claims (ie stealing)!

With hindsight and as I was later advised by ex Estate staff I should have just marched into Hallrule and made my own inventory of what was there shortly after my home-coming in April of 1995. However at that stage I did not even remotely suspect the theft of items had been going on since at least Gertrude's death in 1984. Nor could I have had any idea that Jacquelin either already had, or would very soon, burn lots of Estate and Family records held at Hallrule. One of the staff gave me something that he had managed to save from this conflagration. This honourable staff member suspected that all these records were being burnt by Jacqueline, not for 'tidying up' purposes as claimed by Jacquelin, but to get rid of incriminating evidence. It later became obvious that she had burnt the Wells Estate records that had remained in the Hallrule House, on the instructions of Brodies. Likewise her living at Hallrule House had been on the instructions of Brodies whose real, but hidden purpose, was to keep me out of it just in case I thought of making an Inventory or noticed things going missing, not to mention discovering the Estate records which she later burnt, *et al.*

The Ingles and Phillips Valuations also best explained her extreme twitchiness whenever I went to Hallrule before the Contents were removed, which should have warned me to make my own inventory. Twenty-twenty hindsight vision is a wonderful thing. While no excuse for my lack of incision I was handling so many things at once, many of which contradicted each other, that my mind was in a whirl of disbelief and confusion.

On 12th December 1995, I telephoned Walker of the Accountant of Court's office. After much difficulty I got him on the phone, and informed him that I would give him the cheque for £307 which he had asked for when I came to collect the accounts. He now moved the goal posts yet again by stating that he would only start getting the accounts ready *after* I had given him the cheque. I protested, but to no avail. As you can imagine by now I heartily disliked the Accountant of Court's Office. However some inner voice told me to be patient with Walker. He had shown his contempt of Brodies on a number of occasions and I hoped to build on that.

On the 18th December 1995 I attended a meeting at Brodies. Present were Stevens, Jacquelin and myself. The main purpose of the meeting was to discuss Jacquelin's fraudulent charges on the Executry of just under £2,000 which I had recently uncovered. It was now quite apparent that her attitude to the Executry was one of self-interest only and to hell with the other beneficiaries. And Stevens role at the meeting was to limit the damage to both Brodies and her. Of course my aim was to force her to repay the money and at the same time further embarrass Brodies and her.

Her fraudulent charges on the executry included having her car repaired and valeted. Also fuel so far in excess of what she could possibly have used as to be farcical. When the bills were presented for payment the Estate Manager had settled them from the Wells Estate Account without question. Neither Johnny nor I had behaved in this secret and deceitful manner and nor would have any half-decent person. So I was damned if I was going to let her get away with it. She tried to huff, puff and bluff her way out of it by telling me that she felt 'quite justified' in charging thus. When that fell flat she changed tack by trying to soft soap me: 'I do not regard the executry as a soft touch,' and so on. She had regarded the executry as exactly that, so was lying through her teeth. And from that day on I regarded her as a thief. For their part Brodies had tried to conceal her theft by informing the beneficiaries the payment had been made to her in appreciation of 'all the worthwhile work' she had done at Hallrule House. She had done very little at Hallrule other than to burn the Estate and Family records there and play the Grand Dame *et al*. Of course Brodies did consider this very worthwhile work. Sometime later I discovered that she had Estate staff to do garden work at Chesters House, which she was meant to do herself as part of her keep when she was staying at Chesters, and then pretend to do some weeding in the Hallrule House gardens. She, Brodies, and the Estate Manager would have got clean away with this fraud had I not seen through Brodies attempt at disguising her theft as 'a token of appreciation' in their usual dishonest manner. After it became plain that I had no intention of backing down on these fraudulent charges we moved onto other matters in connection with the Estate which were of great import to the beneficiaries. At which point Jacquelin lost all interest in the proceedings.

I asked Stevens for explanations on the Interim accounts from Brodies from 26th October 1994 to Dec 1995 which they had recently sent us. Accounts can be drawn up in a way that can, and often do, mislead even expert Accountants; and I was no expert Accountant. Noticing Jacquelin nodding off I decided to wake her up.

'Jacquelin', I barked; 'Have you studied these most recent Accounts?' She gave me the answer I expected: 'No, I haven't. I have been too busy.' 'Too busy stealing and concealing, and doing everything that Brodies tells you to do, and to blazes with the beneficiaries,' I thought.

On 19th December 1995 I faxed the Estate Manager asking for a meeting so that we could go through the Accounts from 1962 to 1995. We agreed to meet on Thursday 28th December 1995.

On 26th December I faxed again to confirm the meeting. However his wife, Eve, now told me that the Estate Manager could not meet me on the 28th, as agreed, but that she would meet me instead. The usual evasion. However I agreed to meet her; not that I thought she would be of much use, but rather that she might inadvertantly reveal some useful information.

On 27th December 1995 the Estate Manager replied by fax and stated that he would be happy to show me the Accounts any time after the 8th January 1996. The next day, the 28th December his wife rang and summarily cancelled our meeting for that day.

At last I now received the Curatory Accounts from the Accountant of Court, but only from 1986 to 1991 but not from the inception of the Curatory in 1983 as I had requested. But at least it was something pre 1990 which Brodies had so far adamantly refused to let me have.

On 31st December 1995 I faxed the Estate Manager again asking for another date for the Meeting. The next day, New Year's Day, he telephoned me and told me he would meet me on Thursday 4th January at 4.30pm. On the 3rd of January he rang again and cancelled the meeting, stating he would ring me the next day to fix a new date. He never did ring . I therefore phoned him on the morning of the 5th to fix yet another appointment. I got his wife Eve. She now said he, like Jacquelin, was 'too busy' to speak to me. Too busy be damned; he was avoiding me like the plague. I then rang again at 3.00 pm and he answered the phone. He immediately became angry and impolite and told me to stop bothering him. White collar thieves like the Estate Manager always try to huff, puff and bluff their way out of meetings which promise to expose them for what they truly are; thieves, leeches and fraudsters. He then tried intimidation by telling me he would charge me for the time. When he had finished his bluster I, very politely, asked him to turn his fax on and said no more. I had long realised that talk is cheap and the way to catch these criminals out was to have everything in writing. I then faxed him a letter requesting another appointment. He faxed me back suggesting Wednesday 10th January 1996 at 8.45am, thereby conceding that his intimidation had failed. I confirmed this by a further fax.

On 8th January I had a meeting with David MacRobert of MacRoberts of Glasgow. He appeared to be sympathetic and helpful, but with my past experiences of lawyers I proceeded with caution. MacRobert told me that Brodies could not lawfully withhold payment to the beneficiaries of *existing* proceeds on the grounds of my trying to recover assets which appeared to have been stolen or were otherwise missing. That was *exactly* what Brodies were doing. On the more complicated areas of fraud he advised me to get a QC's Opinion. I tackled him on his acting for me against Brodies and the various other parties on a No-win No-fee basis. He replied that he was not prepared to do so but was willing to act for me at half-price and that if we won he would expect to be recompensed from any damages awarded. This struck me as the best I could hope for in the circumstances providing he would act in good faith. That was the question. At least it promised some sort of action.

On the 9th January 1996 I contacted Stevens on the phone about the Usher Baronetcy Trust 'Minutes of Meetings'. He now confirmed that no Minutes had 'survived' other than the ones from the late 40s and early 50s in connection with Wells House and it contents. Again how terribly convenient for Brodies. This was the period which covered Stuart's and his two incapacitated sons holding the Baronetcy (1951 to 1994). From this I deduced that no Minutes of Meetings had ever been taken since the early 1950s or, if they had, Brodies were withholding them or had destroyed them.

Stevens then informed me that he was aware that I was to have a meeting with the Estate Manager. So the wires had been humming. He warned me that I would experience 'resistance' from the Estate Manager in connection with the accounts from the early 60s, 70s and 80s, which he, the Estate Manager, held. So Stevens knew there was a lot to hide. It also explained the Estate Manager's constant breaking of appointments to meet me, his constant evasions and his half-denials that he held these Estate records.

Stevens then went on to claim that he deplored all the secrecy of the past because this had led to the problems 'we' were now experiencing. I informed him that Brodies were entirely responsible for the never ending secrecy. With lawyers one must always nip in the bud any attempt by them at shifting blame away from themselves onto nebulous third parties.

At long last and after all the previous cancellations, intimidation, twisting and turning and lying by the Estate Manager I had my meeting with him at his home near Hawick on Wednesday the 10th of January. As always at important meetings I took Gillian with me for witness purposes. He informed me that he 'did not really know' if he had the Accounts for period 1963-1993. On my pressing him he changed this to he 'I think I might have them' , but only from 1975 onwards. As he twisted and turned again - it was like wrestling with a snake - he told me that I should get them from Brodies. I informed him that Johnny had tried to do exactly that for many years but that Brodies had always refused to let him have them, despite Johnny being a Trustee of the Usher Baronetcy Trust. And that Stevens of Brodies had just told me that I should get them from *him*. This was turning into the usual farce as it had done, for example, with Walker, the Accountant of Court. But the Estate Manager still refused to let me have copies of those accounts. This confirmed these accounts were too explosive for *anyone* to see, least of all by Johnny and myself. Exercising self-restraint I asked him if he would let me inspect the Accounts for the period of 1975 to 1983 which he 'thought' he had. He agreed to 'try and find them'.

I asked him numerous further questions. He took refuge by responding that he was 'unable' to answer them. Of course he was perfectly able to answer them - he was simply lying. But the meeting was worthwhile because it confirmed to me again the lengths to which Brodies and the Estate Manager were prepared to go to stop me seeing those Accounts.

On the 15th January 1996 I again contacted the Accountant of Court's Office to ask when I could expect the Accounts from the beginning of the Curatory in 1983 until 1986. They had already sent me the Accounts from 1986 until 27th December 1995.

Now a Mr Girvan told me that they were battling to find these accounts. He also informed me: 'It was news to us that Mr Ian Carruthers of Brodies was the *Curator-Bonis* from 1983 to 1986. We didn't know about him at all. By pure good fortune we found one Reference Number which led us back to him and we are now desperately trying to find those papers.' He said he would contact me again. And to my amazement, he stuck to his word.

However, when he did contact me he varied his previous statement by saying: 'It was sheer *co-incidence* that we found a couple of old accounts which referred back to that time.' He then suggested that I contact Mrs Hazel Bell of the Court of Session. This I immediately did. She said she would look for them and come back to me. She, too, was as good as her word; another very welcome surprise and she told me that they had been found. I arranged to collect them on 16th January 1996. On that day I collected the Curatory Accounts for period 1983 to 1986 from the Court of Session. Mrs Bell was very helpful indeed. She showed me a document which purported to give Carruthers his Discharge posthumously signed by, of all people his wife, Mrs Carruthers, and others. This Discharge was given again and again; in all fifteen times. I simply could not understand why he had been given so many posthumous Discharges. And why on earth was his wife signing his discharge? She had nothing whatever to do with the Usher business. This remains a mystery to me to this day and one which *must* have been, in some unfathomable way, connected to the overall fraud.

I recalled, clearly, Johnny telling me that he had signed over only Pitheavlis and Norton - but not Wells - to Peter in 1984. I then thought of another possibility: Because Johnny had *not* signed the Wells Estate over to Peter in 1984 Brodies might have decided not to inform the Court of Session that Carruthers had been appointed his *Curator-Bonis* between 1983-1986. This would mean that there were *no* papers or records in connection with Carruthers being Peter's *Curator-Bonis* at the Court of Session.

What then could explain my being allowed to collect those Accounts from the Court of Session on 16th January 1996? One explanation was that when I told Walker of the Accountant of Court of Carruthers Curatorship he had informed the Auditor of the Court. The Auditor of Court had then tackled

Brodies about it and discovered that Carruthers had *indeed* been Peter's Curator and that Brodies had never notified them, as they were legally required to do. The Auditor might then have forced Brodies to provide them with Accounts for the 1983 to 1986 period. This would explain how Girvan had suddenly 'discovered' them. It is important to note that if Brodies had in fact notified the Court, at that time in 1983, as they were required to do by law, Peter would have become a Ward of the Court. But because they had *not* done so Peter was simply a Ward of Brodies. A good example of what lawyers in Scotland do when they get control of the Estate of a mentally incapacitated person. And, for the record, one of the defining reasons which led to the *Adults with Incapacity (Scotland) 2000 Act* was to protect such adults from predatory lawyers (an Act I privately believe was instigated *because* of the colossal fraud perpetrated by Brodies). Too late for the Ushers of Norton and Wells; nevertheless a welcome change in the law.

On the same day, 16th January 1996, that I collected the Curatory Accounts for period 1983 to 1986 from the Court of Session, I asked Stevens again (by phone) for the pre 1983 Accounts as had been agreed with the Estate Manager. His brazen answer now was that there were 'none that I needed to see.' It was not for Brodies to decide what I, acting as an Executor for my brother, Sir John Usher of Norton and Wells, needed or didn't need to see and I told him so. He then informed me, 'The Estate Manager is not obliged to show you *any* accounts.' Of course I immediately told him that of course the Estate Manager was obliged to make available the accounts to the Executor and that he had informed me I should collect them from Brodies. But Stevens still refused to give them to me.

The next day the Estate Manager telephoned me and in rather a frosty voice informed me that the 1994 to 1995 Accounts and Vouchers which, 'You insist upon inspecting,' were ready to pick up from his place. Of course I had insisted on no such thing, because I had already been supplied these Accounts (though minus any vouchers) by Brodies. and told him so. He was simply diverting the discourse and trying to cause confusion. I therefore repeated my demand to see the pre-1983 Accounts, as he had agreed to at our meeting on 10th January. He hesitated before telling me that he was now *not* prepared to let me see those accounts.

I was back to square one.

31

ROCK SOLID DOCUMENTARY EVIDENCE OF FRAUD BY BRODIES

At home I studied the 1983-1986 Curatory accounts which I had collected from the Accountant of Court. I now, at long last, had the Accounts, from the purported inception of Peter's Curatory in 1983 to the death of Robert in 1994. To my delight I discovered that the Accounts were in the name of the *Usher Baronetcy Trust* for the years 1982-1983 but *then,* for the years 1983-1984 and 1984-1985, they were in the name of *Sir Peter's Curatory* and that the Contents of Hallrule House appeared in both these successively named Accounts. However for the year 1985-1986 the Contents suddenly disappeared altogether. This, at long last, was the rock solid documentary evidence that Brodies had been blatantly lying when they said that the Contents had 'belonged' to Gertrude since Stuart's death in 1962. This was also rock solid evidence that Carruther's of Brodies had defrauded Peter of the Contents of Hallrule House in the year 1985-1986. I was delighted to have acquired this evidence in the teeth of the prolonged opposition put up by Brodies, the Accountant of Court, and the Estate Manager.

The Accounts showed that Carruthers had, in his capacity as Peter's Curator simply defrauded Peter of the Contents of Hallrule House but gave no clue as to who now owned them. I therefore deduced that he had placed them in the Trust of his recently deceased client, Gertrude, who had made Carruthers and the Estate Manager the Executors and Trustees of her Will.

I was now more hopeful than I had been for some time that I would bring Brodies and the other parties involved in the fraud to book, despite my ever more rapidly decreasing faith in the Scottish 'Legal' system. In this regard I had been told by well-wishers that if I obtained just one piece of hard documentary evidence of fraud it would be enough to activate a Police enquiry. This would then constitute the legal basis for the Police to investigate all the other frauds.

I also discovered further evidence of fraud. For example all the properties which Uncle Stuart supposedly 'gave' to Clive in 1959 still appeared in the

Usher Baronetcy Trust Accounts of 1982 to 1983 with the Usher Baronetcy Trust still paying the Insurances on them. This meant that the Usher Baronetcy Trust were still the owners of these properties. So Clive, as a Trustee of the UBT, had only posed as being the 'owner' of these properties in the intervening 23 years *despite* the records in the Scottish Records office showing that he *had* purchased them. He never had. That record in the Scottish Records Office had been placed there, along probably with many others, for the express purpose of concealing the fraud. Little wonder that Brodies, the Estate Manager, and others had been so obdurate in their refusal to let Johnny and myself see those Accounts. But I had enough, thanks to Mr Girvan and probably in his error, to prove these frauds. For the record I never *was* and never *have* been allowed to see any Accounts pre 1980. Again confirming Brodies role in a gigantic cover-up

Unsurprisingly I discovered further instances of fraud in these Accounts. For example the Estate Manager and Clive had short-paid the Estate for their share of the maintenance of Buildings and Fencing due under the terms of their leases. The other tenants had also short-paid for their shares but nothing on the scale of the above mentioned two. I supposed that the Estate Manager and Clive somehow felt 'better' about this particular bit of fraud because they allowed the other tenants to benefit in a similar way. Of course the tenants were not to blame for this, although they certainly would have known that they were short-changing what they *thought* was their their 'landlord', the hapless and incapacitated Peter. Yet the reader must bear in mind that Peter was *not* their landlord; the Usher Baronetcy Trust was, and always had been, their landlord since 1927. This was just another large jigsaw piece in the giant fraud puzzle.

When I told Johnny all this he was horrified and expressed his extreme distaste for the 'the whole rotten bunch.' However we decided to keep quiet about these discoveries until we obtained the next payout. Otherwise Brodies would continue to withhold the payment on the pretext that they could not pay out until *both* the Executors accepted the situation, fraudulent as it was, as it stood. Blackmail, pure and simple. I was aware that Brodies would soon be advised of my having acquired the explosive 1982 onwards accounts.

I now realised that it had been non-stop Christmas-time on Wells Estate for everyone living on it, and not just Clive, Gertie and the rest, for decades. This made my blood boil, as you may well imagine. When I told local people what I had discovered they just laughed and said it had been a standing joke, locally, for years. It had been, and still is, a lonely battle. I have long since come to the conclusion that most people will do little or nothing for a just cause for fear of being damaged themselves. In other words I realised that it was still very much a medieval dog-eat-dog world in Scotland and if I were to win this fight I would have to utilise every ounce of courage and determination that I possessed. Would it be enough?

On 20th February 1996 I wrote for the second time asking the Estate Manager if he had received two letters from me dated 6th February and another dated 16th February? These letters were requests for explanations regarding the Accounts that I had at last obtained.

Again no response. Thereafter I sent him further correspondence but received only one response dated 22nd February in which he informed me: 'It is inappropriate for me to answer your various queries and I have accordingly passed all the papers you have sent me to Brodies. I shall be glad if you address any further correspondence to them direct.' The typically evasive answer that crooks utilise to conceal their crimes.

Earlier on 22nd January 1996 I had telephoned Stevens asking him if our continued opposition to his firm on the Contents issue would hold up payments to the beneficiaries of the proceeds from the sale of the Estate which Brodies were now holding and no doubt drawing interest on. He answered 'Yes it would cause a delay of many months because now the situation would have to be gone into all the way back and new negotiations with the Tax authorities would have to be opened.' This was more blackmail to coerce me into signing the Discharge for Houldsworth. It was also an indirect admission that the Contents of Hallrule House being in Gertie's Trust in the first place was a consequence of Brodies own fraud.

On 24th January 1996 Gillian and I had another meeting with Walker of the Accountant of Court in Edinburgh. To our pleasant surprise he greeted us politely and cordially. Obviously we were delighted and responded in kind, although I was on my guard because of his previous *volte-faces.*

He took us to a room in the basement and complained about the cold there saying that the temperature was kept very low to save money and what a bunch of skinflints the government were. What a changed man he was. He straightaway started spilling the beans. Gillian and I listened, hardly able to believe what we were hearing.

He told us that Brodies had tried to double the farm rentals on the Estate during 1992 and 1993 but that the tenants 'would have none of it.' He now accepted the reasons for our outrage and all my questions arising from it over the preceding months and expressed his sympathies to us.

He then proceeded to give us legal advice, to the best of his knowledge. He advised us strongly, whatever we did, *not* to give the *Curator-Bonis,* Houldsworth his Discharge until we had matters sorted out to our satisfaction. I replied that we would be unlikely to withhold his Discharge if this meant that there would be a big delay in the beneficiaries receiving their inheritances as Brodies had told me there would be. And that I regarded this as blackmail by Brodies. He then exhorted us not to 'give in' to Brodies 'blackmail' and that we *must* stand up to them in a powerful way, in the same way that the Court had stood up to them on the issue of the Estate Manager awarding himself large increases in salary year after year. Brodies had fought hard on behalf of the Estate Manager before reluctantly giving way and putting a stop to it. I told him that we were very thankful that the Court had done that, but to remember that I had already stood up to Brodies in as powerful a manner as I was capable of. Also to remember that the Court had the weight and resources of the State behind it while our resources were now drained; not to mention that Johnny's co-Executor (Jacquelin) had suddenly jumped ship to join Brodies and was fighting *for* them *against* the Executry and beneficiaries, one of whom was she *herself!*

I asked his advice on which areas to concentrate. He told us that the areas on which we should concentrate were *Firstly*: All the beneficiaries not being notified by Brodies on the appointment of a *Curator-Bonis* for Peter. He stated that the rules were that all beneficiaries had to be notified. And *Secondly*: Brodies were bound by law to send Johnny, in his capacity as a Trustee of the Usher Baronetcy Trust, the Accounts of the Trust from the time he became a Trustee in 1965 until the (purported but illegal) termination of the Trust in 1983. He emphasised this by stating that it was *totally unacceptable* that he, Johnny, had never been sent those UBT Accounts by Brodies. He also added that it was equally unacceptable for them to now claim that most of the accounts had been destroyed and that was *Brodies problem*, not ours. And *Thirdly*: That we should try and prise open a gap between the Law Agents (Brodies) and the *Curator-Bonis* because if Houldsworth got his Discharge Brodies would simply hide behind the fact that the Curator - who was *their* man - had been discharged by us. He kept re-iterating that we *must* not give in to Brodies and not allow ourselves to continue to be misled by them.

I asked him whether he would stand as a Witness for us when we got to court. He replied that he was sorry but he would *not* and would deny everything he had just told us! That is the way things are in Scotland's legal system these days.

We were both very much encouraged by his welcome change of heart. I deduced the reason for Mr Walker's dramatic change of sides was that he was aware that I had, at last, obtained the Curatory Accounts from 1983 onwards from the Court of Session on the 16th January and that I had discovered the various frauds, as above. He probably thought the game was up for Brodies and his best chance of limiting the fallout to himself was to abandon what he now perceived as the soon-to-be sunk ship of HMS *Brodies* and join us (Johnny and myself).

On 30th January Gillian and I had another meeting with Brodies. At this meeting Stevens told us that 95% of the values had been agreed with the District Valuer. The remaining 5% to be completed were on the Woodlands and Agricultural properties. He also informed us that the Woodlands had been run as a separate business. This was the first we had ever heard about that and wondered why he had not told us before. Again it took me sometime to connect this to my recently receiving the Curatory Accounts. Also that running the Woodlands as a separate business would have made it much easier for Brodies, Clive and the Estate Manager to pillage the Woodlands. Needless to say Brodies never did show me the Accounts of this business.

In answer to a question from me Stevens now informed us that the Contents of Hallrule House issue would now *not* hold up payments to the beneficiaries; the exact opposite of what he had told me just eight days earlier. However he added: 'This now cannot be allowed to go on.' He was far more exercised by this and a whole raft of further issues which I brought up with him than he had ever been. This again appeared to be a consequence of his learning that I had acquired the Accounts from 1983 onwards.

In the afternoon we went to Willis Corroon in Drumsheugh Gardens for a pre-arranged meeting. Willis Corroon were the Insurance Brokers who handled the Estate Insurances. There we met a very helpful clerk called Theresa Clitheroe. She gave us copies of some papers in connection with the insurance of the Contents of Hallrule House and showed us others. One of these related to Willis Corroon threatening to report Brodies to an Ombudsman concerning a letter which Brodies had written to Willis Corroon blaming them for the mess the Insurances were in.

On 6th February 1996, taking Gillian with me again , I had another meeting with Theresa Clitheroe at Willis Coroon to try and trace where the Curatory Insurance policies in connection with the Contents of Hallrule House had disappeared to. She now volunteered that she had always felt that: 'This whole question of the Contents of Hallrule House was going to blow up one day.' Also 'What a tragedy for your family that the Estates had passed to Incapaxes.' We tried to trace the exact date when and by whom the instruction had been given to remove the Contents from Peter's Curatory and where they had gone. She had just given me copies of more correspondence when a middle-aged man entered the office and introduced himself as Mr Mills. He appeared ill at ease and exuded an air of urgency as he told me that he needed to have a word with me in private.

In an office downstairs he told me that I must never tell Brodies what I had seen in the documents that Theresa Clitheroe had already shown us. He was so exercised by this that he asked for my word. I told him that I would give him my word if he, in return, gave me his word that he would not tell Brodies that I had already visited them and would continue to do so as I saw fit. He agreed to this very readily and, his relief now almost palpable, we shook hands on it. Mills then told me, with apparent sincerity, how much he admired me for pursuing my family interest with such vigour. I thanked him for that and was truly grateful for it. However the reason I am able to record this conversation in these pages is because of the subsequent dodging and evasion I was subjected to by Willis Corroon. Mills had told his boss, an evasive twister called Ford Paterson, who in turn spilled the beans to Brodies. A Gentleman's Agreement ceases to apply when one of the 'gentlemen', Mills in this case, has broken it.

When I got back to Gillian, Theresa told me that while I was away with Mills she had been told not to show us any further documents. She was as appalled as we were by this. She remained as helpful as she could be but someone had intervened, significantly in my absence. I could only assume it was her boss, Ford Paterson.

On the 4th February Johnny telephoned with the awful news that our dear Mother had died. She'd had a fall two days previously and hurt her leg. She died peacefully in hospital. She had been a very good Mother to us, cared for and loved us in every possible way in a totally unselfish manner. She always put our and our Father's interests before hers. In this way she built us into a very united family. By word, deed and example she imbued us with the virtues of honesty, loyalty and a sense of duty to family in thought, word and deed above all else. She was also no mean artist, painting in water-colours and oils. She painted some lovely views on Bedrule and our African farms. She made fast friends with many people both in Scotland and Africa, where she was born and where her heart lay. She saw through phoneys like Clive and Gertie rather quickly and avoided them like the plague. She was much interested in Eastern religions and believed in Karma and re-incarnation.

To my dying day I shall regret that I did not show my love for her more than I actually did. But I deeply regret that now. So if any youngster happens to be reading this book: Be warned and show both your parents that you love and cherish them, while they are still alive. I just wish I could pop into heaven and tell both my parents how much I loved them and to apologise for my having been so unappreciative in my younger years. As I now (2019) move into old age I realise more and more the enormous debt I owe my Mother. I would like to tell her of my fight against Brodies and the successes I had already scored. I would then make it crystal clear that she was largely responsible for my fighting in the first place and the successes I have scored are the direct consequence of the values that she had imbued into both Johnny and myself all our lives.

She was cremated in South Africa and I arranged a Memorial Service for her at Bedrule Church at which I gave the eulogy. Valerie slunk in at the back and left without a word of sympathy. I buried my mother's Ashes next to my Father's in our Burial ground at Bedrule. So ended the life of my most noble, talented, worthy and loving mother.

On 5th February 1996, at the suggestion of Mrs Bell at the Accountant of Court I contacted a Mr Fraser at the Court of Session to find out how much the Court of Session would charge for a hearing per hour. Mr Fraser then suggested that I give him the background of the case in writing stating why I was not happy with the situation. He would then peruse this and let me know if he felt I had grounds for registering an official objection to the Discharge of Houldsworth. I therefore faxed him a three-page synopsis from the offices of MacRobert's in Glasgow the next day.

32

BRODIES AND THE WRONG END OF THE STICK

On 7th February 1996. Gillian and I went to have what I intended to be our last meeting with Brodies. I planned to ask the same old awkward questions which they had always evaded answering as well as a lot of new ones, now that they had, at last, recently paid out the bulk of the inheritances to the beneficiaries. However they still withheld £55,000 for blackmail purposes. Their months of delay in paying had also been blackmail. But I felt I had to move now despite their still withholding the £55,000.

Stevens alone had represented Brodies at all the meetings I'd had with them all year. I now realised that this had been by design; to keep Houldsworth out of harm's way in case things became ugly. Houldsworth was senior to Stevens in the Brodies pecking order and, crucially, was Robert's *Curator-Bonis* as well as Peter's sole Executor. Those were the precise reasons for his absence at all my meetings with Stevens. In essence Stevens was Brodies' toe rag. I insisted, therefore, that Houldsworth be present at this last Meeting to make it more difficult for Brodies to shift all the blame onto Stevens alone. I knew, of course, that they would be forced to lie and lie again and in so doing would give us further powerful ammunition with which to further crucify them. I determined to simply ask the questions one after another and note their answers without dispute.

The first thing I asked them was to confirm that they tried to double the Wells Estate rentals in 1992 as we had been informed by Walker of the Accountant of Court's office. Houldsworth answered that this was 'highly unlikely' and said nothing more. This was in total contradiction of Walker's of statement to us on the 24th of January. This particular answer, for example, was sufficient for my purposes because it instead implied that it was *highly likely*.

I then tackled them on why the rentals on the Estate cottages were so low? Houldsworth answered again: 'That was the Rent Officer's fault,' and again went no further. So it was someone elses's fault. But he was Robert's Curator and Peter's Executor and as such it was his function to charge market-related rentals on behalf of the incapacitated landlord Robert and had nothing whatever to do with any 'Rent Officer'. I then asked, 'And who was the Rent Officer and what body did he represent?' Houldsworth told us that the Rent Officer was a local official at the Borders Regional Council who set the rentals on the Wells Estate with the help of a Rent Assessment Committee. I pointed out, as an example, that the *rates* alone amounted to very nearly 50% of the entire annual rental on the cottage that I was renting on the Estate. Houldsworth's only comment was: 'They do appear low.'

I then asked them, with perhaps a trace of sarcasm,: 'Did anyone else, apart from poachers, shoot on the Estate'? He didn't know. That was another lie because one of the documents referred to the Wells Estate Shooting rentals being too low.

I then tackled them about the absurdly low rentals that the grass pastures were let at. The answer was: 'We did not want to incur the difficulty and expense in finding tenants for them.' This was another admission of extreme negligence by both Houldsworth and Stevens in their respective functions as *Curators-Bonis's*. Their 'solution' was to let the Estate Manager have pasture at £10.00 per acre, a neighbouring smallholder at £4.00 per acre and another tenant farmer at about £3.00 per acre, all per annum! From my researches these charges were a small fraction of what they should have been.

I then tackled them about the tenants not paying their half-share of the Building and Fencing accounts. I showed them three examples of this as they appeared in the Usher Baronetcy Trust and Curatory Accounts. Houldsworth's comment was: 'The tenants contribution does appear to be low.' However I pressed them to confirm that there was a gross disparity in the accounts which was to the detriment of the Estate and to the advantage of the tenants, particularly the Mactaggarts, and the Estate Manager. Houldsworth did not even try to justify this gross disparity and responded: 'It would appear that you are correct' and then, as usual, shut up.

I then tackled them about why the Wells Stables Insurance premiums were still being paid by the Usher Baronetcy Trust, 24 years after Clive had purportedly 'acquired' these properties. Their answer: 'We can't understand why Wells Stables appears in the Insurances Account.' Another lie.

I then asked them for an explanation as to why the Contents of Hallrule House appeared in the Curatory accounts until Gertrude's death with the Insurance Premiums covering them being paid by the Curatory, and why all reference to the Insurance Premiums and the Contents disappeared after her death; and could they tell me in which accounts they were now reflected? Answer: 'We don't know what happened here after 1962 - it was thirty four years ago.' So they were charging the Executry £300 per hour to tell us they hardly knew anything. When I pressed them for further explanations their response was, again: 'We don't know.' Of course, they knew because they had admitted in writing that Gertrude had never owned the Contents. In addition to Steven's statement that Dempster had lied about it to the Tax Authorities. The more lies they told, the better for us.

I then tackled them about the heirloom jewellery which had appeared in the Accounts with the insurance premiums being paid by the Usher Baronetcy Trust and then the Curatory Accounts but which they had said belonged to Gertrude. Why had they appeared in these Accounts if they belonged to Gertrude? And how did she acquire them, and from whom? Same answer: 'We don't know.' Same lies.

I then tackled them about the £5,549 of Sir Robert's personal effects which had disappeared from the Accounts in the same way. Yet again : 'We don't know what happened there.'

By now I decided we had enough lies in our armoury so I brought the meeting to a close. Obviously all their denials of knowing anything about the various disappearances of Usher Baronetcy Trust and Curatory assets would never stand up to even the most cursory scrutiny.

As with Walker, Brodies had given up trying to maintain the patent fiction that they had not been defrauding the Estates. This again was another sequel to my obtaining, in the teeth of their opposition, the pre 1990 Accounts. However I did not yet realise that their admissions were a challenge to the Executry to take them to court; a challenge they knew the Scottish Legal system would never allow to come to Court. And how could we take them to court when they had Jacquelin in their back pocket? I also did not realise that Brodies had already planned a campaign to discredit Johnny and myself, which they would soon launch.

However here, and yet again, Brodies were a step ahead of me. They still refused to pay out the last £55,000 to the beneficiaries until Johnny and I bowed to their will and gave Houldsworth his Discharge. This meant allowing them, Clive, Gertrude and the Estate Manager all off with their various frauds. If we did not cease our pursuit of them they would simply consume the £55,000 as 'fees' to cover their own participation in these frauds.

On 14th February 1996 I received a letter from Brodies informing me that they had received official notification from the Accountant of Court that I had formally objected to the Discharge of Houldsworth as Curator. I was outraged because I never had formally objected to his Discharge yet.

I immediately got onto the Accountant of Courts office for an explanation. They told me that Mr Fraser of the Court of Session had forwarded my letter of 6th February 1996 (which Mr Fraser himself had asked me to write to him personally) to the Accountant of Court. The letter was a summary of my reasons for dissatisfaction with Brodies and refusal to give Houldsworth his discharge. His forwarding this letter to the Accountant of Court was inexcusable. I therefore wrote to Fraser by letter dated 14th February expressing my strongest possible objections and asked for an explanation.

His reply on 16th of Febuary stated that he had not even *seen* my letter of the 6th February but that his office had forwarded it to the Accountant of Court who in turn had forwarded it to Brodies. So I telephoned Fraser and asked him why he had not even read my letter to him before forwarding it to the Accountant of Court? That silenced him, but not for long. He apologised for the 'inconvenience' but stated, by way of an excuse, that his department's policy was to deal with mail very quickly. He then went on to waffle about how 'The Court must maintain a totally neutral position,' and such like legal-babble; matters which had nothing whatever to do with his department passing my letter to the Accountant of Court, a letter which he himself had asked me to write to him personally. As far as I was concerned he had lied through his rotten teeth. But the damage had been done, and by design, to place me in an invidious position with the beneficiaries. The Accountant of Court had then been quick to inform and pass on this personal letter to Brodies who then deliberately misconstrued it as my official objection to the Discharge they so desperately wanted for their sly, lying Houldsworth.

I was learning fast that whenever I caught people out in the Scottish Legal system they immediately adopted the tactic of throwing out as many red-herrings as possible, telling lie after lie and so diverting attention away from themselves. Something akin to an octopus squirting ink to conceal its escape from a pursuing predator. With people like Fraser in positions of authority in the Scottish Legal system God help the people of Scotland.

By letter dated 19th February 1996 Mrs A Murray of the Accountant of Court's offices responded as to why they had forwarded my letter to Brodies. Her explanation was: 'I apologise for Mr Walker's *actings* but I believe he acted in good faith, the letter was not, after all, marked as confidential.' She then introduced a red-herring about my consulting a solicitor to represent the Executry against Brodies. This was the definitive red-herring which public servants deploy to extricate themselves from a jam of their own making. As the reader should now be well aware an official objection to Houldsworth's Discharge would have led to the financial ruination of the Executry by means of Brodies charging colossal fees to deal with it. So it *appeared* that Walker had ratted on me. But had he?

I phoned Mrs Murray and asked to be put through to Walker. She now informed me that Walker had been taken off the case and she had taken his place. I suspected that the actual Accountant of Court himself, a sallow, crafty-faced weed called Cockburn had forced Walker to hand over to Mrs Murray who he, Cockburn, believed he could manipulate more easily than Walker. I also suspected that Cockburn knew that forwarding my letter to Brodies would put me in an invidious position with the beneficiaries, which it certainly did. I then surmised that the Auditor of Court, the Accountant of Court, and Brodies were working hand in glove to defeat me and that

Cockburn's office was located in these Scottish 'Legal System Buildings' in Parliament Square, Edinburgh. A facade of 'respectability'.

Walker had told them he would not be party to it anymore; hence his being taken off the case.

As a consequence of all this Brodies immediately attempted to marginalize me with the beneficiaries. Over the next few weeks Brodies promoted the outrageous falsehood that I had laid an *official* objection to the discharge of Houldsworth. Using this as cover they claimed they were not allowed to communicate with me. The same applied to the Estate Manager - he was 'not allowed' to communicate with me either. Of course I made it crystal clear to all the beneficiaries that I had not lodged any objection, let alone an official one, to the Discharge of Houldsworth.

I eventually forced the Accountant of Court's Office to admit that I *never* had lodged any such objection. Giving way, however, they slyly gave me until 22nd March to lay any objection I *did* have. This little episode had been concocted by Brodies and the Accountant of Court to delay matters, damage me, and generally sow confusion, in an attempt to cast me as the villain of the piece.

From Cockburn's perspective this, he thought, was the best way to extricate himself and his despicable department out of the morass into which I had forced him and it. As far as Walker was concerned he had been told to shut up, or else. Their plan now was to squash Johnny and me once and for all.

Constant efforts on my part to contact Stevens by telephone were thwarted by his secretary assuring me he would ring back which he never did.

On 27th February I received an unexpected letter from Mr Walker in which he stated : 'Your comments are noted but as was already explained by the Deputy Accountant, this Department has no longer any jurisdiction over the Curatory.' I was baffled. In the event by the 7th March they had become involved again.

On 7th March 1996 I received a fax from Stevens which was as ambiguous as it was ineloquent. In it he warned me that I would be receiving a letter from the Accountant of Court's Office, a copy of which, he claimed, he had already received. He repudiated what the Accountant of Court stated in that letter (which I was yet to receive) by informing me that the Accountant of Court had 'picked up the wrong end of the stick' in these particular matters.' Gone was Stevens' love of the latin.

Because I distrusted Brodies far more than I distrusted Walker I immediately rang Walker and read Steven's fax out to him. He exploded with fury and for the first time I heard him raise his voice: 'I am *sick and tired* of Brodies' constant lying! I will now report them to the Law Society!' He then said he would write to me straightaway. I told him I would give him a ring on the morrow when I'd received the so-called 'wrong end of the stick' letter. He responded: 'Yes, you give me a wee ring in the morning.'

Sure enough I received the letter from the Accountant of Court's office, written by Walker, dated 6th March 1996 the very next day, the copy of which Brodies claimed that they had already received. 'Hmmmm,' I thought. 'He must have reclaimed his old position back from Mrs Murray.' With great anticipation I gave him the agreed 'wee' ring next morning. To my crushing disappointment I was told that he had been put on 'gardening leave.' Shortly later I discovered that Walker had been taken off the case *again* and replaced by Mrs Murray *again*!

In his letter Mr Walker informed me that Brodies *had arranged* a meeting between me, the Estate Manager, and themselves to finally give me the answers I had long sought. Brodies *must* therefore have told Walker that they had arranged such a meeting. Of course they had never arranged any such meeting with me so were misleading him as usual. Hence Mr Walker's statement about reporting Brodies to the Law Society when he discovered that they had never arranged any such meeting during my phone call to him on 7th March. Brodies of course in a panic when they realised Walker had forwarded this information to me tried to make out that Walker had, 'picked up the wrong end of the stick.'

What had actually happened was that Brodies had written to me on 27th February 1996 saying that they would supply me with answers once *they'd* had a meeting with the Estate Manager at their offices, '. . .at the end of this week'. I'd immediately responded to them by requesting that I also attend the meeting. Brodies had instantly refused my request on the grounds that my attendance would be 'inappropriate.' They had then *misinformed* Mr Walker that they'd arranged a meeting with me and the Estate Manager. With Brodies this lie, and their many other lies, could always be explained away as a misunderstanding. Brodies must have been surprised when they discovered that Mr Walker had written to me to confirm the 'arrangement'. This tactic of feeding different parties, who they believed would not communicate with each other, was, and no doubt still is, classic Brodies. On this occasion and very much thanks to Mr Walker Brodies were hoist on their own petard.

Of course the real purpose of their meeting with the Estate Manager would have been to concoct their answers to my questions.

From all this I deduced that Mr Walker had not gone quietly and had fought for us but had been given no choice but to step aside from the case when Cockburn pulled rank. I was much bucked up that I had found one of the few people in the Scottish Legal System with a modicum of morality.

I have dwelt at some length on this matter because it typifies the very essence of my experience with Brodies. Misinformation, evasion, deceit and deception from the Scottish Legal system, of which Brodies is a part, is standard practice. They utilised every dirty trick in the book, to prevent me from exposing them. An analogy would be that Brodies and I were engaged in a boxing match arranged by the Scottish Legal system in which I was bound to fight by the Queensberry Rules whilst Brodies were not bound by any such rules and had chosen their own crooked Judge, Lord Hamilton, for example, as the referee.

On 21st March 1996, despite Brodies attempts at blackmail, I finalised my list of objections to the Discharge of Houldsworth with Charles Cowie of MacRobert's Edinburgh office. David MacRobert, of Glasgow, had told me that this was the safest way to do it otherwise the Accountant of Court could, and probably would, *misinterpet* my objections. This was an outright admission by a Scottish lawyer that the legal system in Scotland is corrupt. But it did not appear to worry him in the slightest. This apathetic acceptance of corruption in Scotland's legal system has always alarmed me and still does. Why have the Scottish people put up with it for so long? The answer to that, in part at least, is that Scotland's legal system - being separate from the rest of the United Kingdom - has degenerated into a highly sophisticated Crime Protection Syndicate for white collar criminals. This means that the Scottish people have no means other than revolution to do anything about it. Their elected representatives in the Scottish Parliament, many of whom are lawyers themselves, are simply too frightened to do anything about it. They simply take the easy option of drinking tea, eating, and flirting with each other in that new and truly hideous Scottish Parliament Building rather than stand up to this Crime Protection Syndicate.

On 22nd March 1996 Gillian and I went to Edinburgh to hand in my objections to the Discharge of Houldsworth because this was the last day to do so. Mrs Murray met us in the reception area and I handed them to her. I then asked for Mr Walker as I felt he was still an ally of ours, if only morally and covertly. Mrs Murray curtly informed us that Walker was not in. As we turned to leave I heard the unmistakeable cough of Mr Walker himself. I quickly looked round the pillar into the interior of the office and there he was - large as life. I immediately turned and rended Mrs Murray with: 'Why did you lie to us?' She blushed deeply and her eyes shot upwards, searching the ceiling for inspiration, before stuttering, 'He is too busy to see you.' I told her sharply that this did not answer my question as to why she had lied. We wanted an answer to that *right now*! Now that I had her impaled Gillian and I just stood there and waited. She shifted from one foot to the other and back again while her eyes flicked around the place but never once at us. Like everyone working in the Scottish legal system she had been trained to say absolutely nothing when caught lying. Still I stared at her and still we waited. She continued her foot dance and eye flicking. When it became apparent that her 'lie training' would defeat any remnant of morality that she might still have, I glanced at Gillian to signal our departure. We turned on our heels with not so much as a 'good-bye' and forthwith marched out of that particular den of Scottish legal system iniquity.

On 30th March 1996, I received a letter from Cockburn, the actual Accountant of Court, in which he, of course, asked for more details to back up our Objections. I replied to him with nineteen pages of details. Copious correspondence now ensued between us. On 16th April I contacted him by phone as to when I could expect a reply to my fax of 11th April. He told me, 'I cannot understand why you haven't received my letter which I wrote to you on 12th April.' There is always some mystery problem between the Scottish Legal system and the Post Office when the former has been caught with its pants down. In the event when his letter arrived it was post-marked 16th April, the very day he had told me that he could not understand why I had not received his letter of the 12th of April - yet another lie by another senior legal figure in the Scottish Legal system. I challenged him about it. Predictably he did not like being caught out. I got nowhere with him.

In his letter he stated: 'I understand that a receipt for the estate has not been signed by the Executor you represent.' I informed him that this was utter rubbish and that Johnny had signed it in my presence but on condition that other Usher Baronetcy Trust assets could be added to it if found to be missing, which is perfectly reasonable.

Cockburn's stating this in writing was very significant indeed although it took years for me to realise this. Amongst a lot of other things it meant that either: Brodies had withheld Johnny's signed receipt from the Accountant of Court, which was an act of fraud, or that Cockburn had it alright and was lying. In the latter event it meant that he, Cockburn, had known all along that Johnny had *not* accepted that the Accounts reflected all the assets in the Estate. But the matter did not end there either as I was to find out in the coming years. This was just another piece in the giant jig-saw piece in the overall fraud puzzle. But it was a very important piece.

By letter dated the 19th of April 1996 Cockburn responded to my Objections and my nineteen-page substantiation of them. He found no merit in most of my Objections but asked for yet more detail. At the time I was still naïve enough to believe that I might yet persuade him to abandon Brodies and join Johnny and myself. Over the next two months I tried to convince him of the rectitude of my Objections. The upshot of it all was that he repelled eleven out of the twelve Objections on the 15th of July 1996. On the remaining one, concerning the missing items that had not appeared in the Christies sales catalogue, he got Brodies to persuade Christies to produce a list of where these items were. Christies duly sent me this list. Out of the total of 64 missing items which I had listed as missing, Christies list accounted for only two. I had warned him that this would be an exercise in futility and so it had proved to be.

In the event Cockburn did not just reject my Objections out of hand; that would have been a tad dangerous. He therefore had to dress up his rejections a little for confusion and 'placing the onus' purposes. The main reason he proffered for his rejection of the objections was that most of the events to which we objected had taken place in the time of Sir Peter's Curatory (ie 1983-1990) and that our Objections had been lodged against Robert's Curator, Houldsworth. He therefore claimed that the rules precluded him from taking any recognisance of our objections because they occurred in the period of Peter's Curatory as he was only concerned with Robert's Curatory and therefore only Robert's *Curator-Bonis*, Houldsworth.. What he did not say was that Houldsworth was the only person that the system allowed us to object to. I had taken legal advice on this point and was advised that we should *not* give any discharge to Houldsworth precisely because there *was* a connection back to Peter's Curator, Stevens, and if we gave Houldsworth his discharge we could well let Stevens off the hook at the same time. I pointed all this out to Cockburn but he just took refuge in incanting that he was only concerned with Robert's Curator and could not consider any actions by Peter's three Curators. I told him that this was utterly absurd and the implication of these 'rules' was that Peter's Curator could have done anything he wanted to with Peter's Estates. For example he, Stevens of Brodies, could have just sold them and shared the proceeds with Brodies as he saw fit, and not be accountable to anyone. His response to this was to repeat (ie hide behind) his incantation that he was only concerned with Robert's Curator, Houldsworth. Almost certainly Brodies had advised him that this was the best way out for them both.

Stevens and Houldsworth had a huge common interest in protecting each other because if the one was exposed the other would inevitably be exposed as well and, like Jack and Jill, would both come tumbling down the hill, taking Brodies with them on the way. Also that this was the *hidden* imperative which caused Brodies to appoint a *Curator-Bonis* for Peter (Stevens) and another one for Robert (Houldsworth) in 1986. Whoever was the Curator of the survivor of Peter and Robert would then be made the Executor of the deceased Incapax, as was the case here with Houldsworth, Robert's Curator, having been appointed Peter's Executor. This was simply a device whereby the defrauding Curators of Peter (Stevens, Carruthers and Sturrock) could be made immune from pursuit on the grounds of Cockburn's statement that 'I am only concerned with Robert's Curator.' Anyone discovering the fraud and then acting to get matters put right could be put to naught on this single technical 'legal' device. As far as I was concerned the device was simply a Scottish Legal system bad faith mechanism to conceal this, and no doubt many other, decades old frauds which had been executed by crooked lawyers like Brodies on many people in Scotland.

Anyway Cockburn rejected my Objections wholly on this illegal and criminal device. He never once disputed the factual basis on which my Objections were founded. His taking refuge in this purely technical device was a tacit admission that Brodies had indeed been involved in a wide range of criminal activity against my family, through Peter and then Robert, for decades. And he was the Accountant of the Court of Session, the Supreme Court of Scotland. On the basis of my correspondence to him the very first thing he should have done was to have reported Brodies to the Police. My thoughts towards him were most hostile imaginable. He was another example of just another crooked lawyer 'working' in the Scottish Legal system. How these people could live with themselves just beat me.

By late July Johnny and I decided to be guided by what the beneficiaries wanted us to do in connection with the objections. We therefore wrote to them all stating that it appeared the only way they would get what remained of their inheritences was for us to drop our objections to the Discharge of Houldsworth as *Curator-Bonis*. In essence to give way to the blackmail and rubber stamp the fraud. The response from the beneficiaries was that we stood no chance against Brodies and the Accountant of Court and that we should withdraw our objections. We therefore withdrew them in the full knowledge that the Estates had been defrauded by Houldsworth, Stevens and Brodies 'singly, jointly and severally', to use another Clever Dick Scottish legal system phrase which lawyers love. It makes them feel important!

I then faxed Cockburn on 6th August 1996 informing him that Johnny had decided to withdraw the Objections but only on the basis that the beneficiaries were of the opinion that Brodies would never pay them their inheritances until the objections were withdrawn, and nothing else. I then phoned him to see if he had got my fax and to keep him moving. He now could not resist in indulging in a bit of *schadenfreude*: 'You must be absolutely devastated,' he said. I told him I was, but rammed it down his throat that Brodies had defrauded Peter and Robert and that I would get them sooner or later. He continued: 'I never doubted you believed that to be the case. I never doubted your belief that you were acting in the best interests of the Executry.' Criminals usually throw a sop to their victims as an insurance for their own future health and safety. He then became formal again and asked me if I was withdrawing my own objections personally as well. I responded by saying that I would withdraw them if it meant that none of the beneficiaries would be paid their inheritances if I did *not* withdraw them. Cockburn then informed me that if I did *not* withdraw them personally none of the other beneficiaries would be paid their inheritances until I did. I was delighted to have got this statement out of him because it showed how worried he and his deplorable Court were about my continued opposition to them and Brodies. But with the beneficiaries opposing me I felt I had no option but to withdraw my objections. I therefore agreed to withdraw them and informed him that I would write to him confirming this. I did so by Fax straightaway, at the same time outlining our conversation on the phone to him, and asking him to confirm that this was an accurate reflection of our conversation. In this way I hoped to get the paper trail of his statement. I phoned him again to make sure that he had got the fax. He had. I then asked him if my letter was an accurate reflection of our conversation. He acknowledged, without equivocation, that it was. I then asked him to put this in writing and send it to me. Again, without equivocation, he agreed to do so.

The following day (7th August 1996) I got a fax from him in which he acknowledged our withdrawal of the Objections but made no mention of our conversation whatever. I instantly phoned him on receipt of his fax and, after a long wait, got him. He was now evasive. I reminded him forcefully of our conversation and his assurance to me of the day before that he would confirm our conversation in writing as accurate. He then became rattled and said: 'Did I say that? Did I say that'? I told him: 'Yes you did. Yes you did - quite categorically.' Silence, then: 'Is it important to you'? I answered, 'Yes, very important.' Silence for a little. Then he said, more composed now: 'Oh well, I have no problem with it. I am not in the business of letter-writing and have a lot of other work to do.' I kept up the pressure and he agreed to get onto it straightaway.

He faxed me on 9th August. Predictably his fax did *not* reflect our conversation. He had now blithely broken his word, for the second time. I was so furious that I told Gillian about it. She was succinct and to the point: 'They are all liars. You must expect this from everyone who is connected with the Usher family's affairs because they are all in it together.' Episodes like this sent me into the blackest despair. I had not yet learnt how to handle them with the degree of equanimity such despicable conduct warranted.

My health suffered a lot at this time which manifested itself in loss of weight, and, most disturbing of all, my heart started missing beats. I told an old girl-friend of mine who was now a nurse at the Hawick Health Centre about all the trouble I was having with the lawyers and now my health. She now informed me that she likewise had had an awful experience with lawyers in connection with her family farm in the Ettrick valley. She told me that her blood boiled at what had happened and that such a state of mind was dangerous and that I should be alert to the fact that if I let it get to me too much it could kill me and that this was just what Brodies were hoping for. She also told me that lawyers concerned in matters like mine didn't lose a moment's sleep over them and that I wasn't to think that they were unduly worried by my pursuit of them.

I therefore fixed up a meeting with a Doctor in Hawick for a heart test. I was worried stiff about it. A heart specialist from Edinburgh examined me in Hawick. Thankfully he pronounced that my heart was sound, which was such a relief. He put it's missing beats down to stress and told me to try and control it better. I told Johnny and his South African lawyer Ewing about it. They gave me the same advice. I told them that I now realised that health came first and would conduct myself accordingly. They heartily agreed with me.

In the absence of any image of CJ Usher, above is the Merchistonian Club of which he was a member until his death in 2017.

33

TODS MURRAY PARTNERS IN THE FRAUD WITH BRODIES.

On 24th April 1996 I had my second meeting with McLetchie of Tods Murray at their offices in Edinburgh. The purpose of the meeting was to collect Johnny's old correspondence and papers from their offices and see what I could glean. I gave McLetchie a *resume* of what had transpired over the previous 18 months. MacLetchie had the decency to say that he understood our feeling of having been, to use *his* word, 'cheated.' This again was another straight admission that our family had been defrauded because there is little difference between defrauding and cheating as far as I am concerned. Even better it came from a lawyer who worked for the law firm which had been involved in the 'cheating'.

A short while later Mike Simpson, the very man who had misled Johnny suddenly appeared and introduced himself. Concealing my hostility I brought him up to date on what had happened in the Executry, with particular emphasis on the Contents issue. 'Sounds very suspicious to me,' he said portentously, putting on a dark look. I instantly knew that he was putting on an act and that his real purpose in joining us was to assess how much of a danger I was to him and his rotten firm of Tods Murray and to do a spot of fishing, some misleading, and 'cover my back' exercises. McLetchie's statement about our feeling cheated and Simpson making an appearance demonstrated how confident they were that they and their utterly criminal law firm of Tods Murray would never be held to account. But I managed to get the papers from McLetchie which was my main objective and soon made my exit.

When I got home I settled down to go through them and very quickly struck gold! I discovered an Opinion which Tods-Murray had got from a Colin Campbell, an Advocate, in January 1983 in connection with Johnny's objections to Mrs Mactaggart taking over the squattership of Hallrule farm from her squatter father, Clive. Simpson had withheld this Opinion from Johnny, his supposed client, and now I saw why. This Opinion, dated 31st January 1983, stated that the Trustees '*are* the heritable proprietors of the land [and not the current Baronet] but it would be better to keep quiet about this.' I immediately recalled the letter dated 29th November 1982 in which MacLure of Brodies, Johnny's co-Trustee, had written to Johnny. In this letter MacClure wrote: 'My feeling is that the Farm (Hallrule) actually belongs to Sir Peter, the present baronet.' A 'feeling' that was the complete opposite of Campbell's Opinion. And how come MacClure based his statement on a 'feeling'? I've never been able to understand how these lawyers, charging astronomical fees, only ever have 'feelings' or 'instincts', surely they should *know*. As narrated earlier in this book the lawyers had told us in 1962 that Peter had personally inherited the whole Usher Baronetcy Trust Estates and Assets - which included the Estates of Wells and Norton - outright on his father Stuart's death in 1962. MacClure had been one of the those lawyers and an Usher Baronetcy Trustee at the same time and was therefore responsible for informing us thus. So how come 20 years later he only had a 'feeling' that Peter owned the Estates outright? Now here was an Advocate, Campbell, going on record that the Trustees (Johnny and MacClure) were the Heritable Proprietors of the land, not Peter. The opposite of MacClure's 'feeling' in 1982.

No damn wonder Simpson had never let Johnny have a copy of this Opinion. To have done so would have spelt the end of the patent fiction that Peter had owned the Estates since 1962. A patent fiction which MacClure himself had been party to creating and thereafter promoting and which, among many other things, had caused us to uproot ourselves from Bedrule and move to South Africa; the cause of my Father's heart attacks and early death and massive stress to my Mother, Johnny and myself.

The implications of Campbell's Opinion were very serious indeed for both MacClure and Brodies. MacLure's purpose in stating that his 'feeling' that Peter was the landlord was to re-inforce the patent fiction in our minds yet again that Peter was the sole proprietor of the Estates when he knew that this was not, and never had been, the case at all. Hence his use of the word 'feeling', just in case he was caught out. Crooked lawyers *always* leave a little wriggle room.

If Johnny had discovered that he and MacLure were the Usher Baronetcy Trust landlords, and not Peter, as he would undoubtedly have done if Simpson had not withheld this Opinion from him, he would have instantly demanded all the records of the Estates of which he was one of the two landlords, and the infinitely more significant one, and would have never signed the Estates over to Brodies in 1984 and again in 1987. This being the case Brodies would never have been able to get sole control of the Usher Baronetcy Trust Estates by appointing their own lawyer partners to be Peter and Robert's *Curator-Bonis's* and Executors.

Nor would he ever have allowed the Mactaggarts to continue to squat on Hallrule Farm. It would have been impossible for MacLure, his fellow landlord, to oppose him in any way now. MacLure might even have jumped ship to save his own rotten hide by blaming the late unlamented Clive for this now monumental fraud. This was yet another confirmation that MacLure was just another filthy crooked lawyer of which there appeared to be an inexhaustible supply in Scotland. On top of that, this would mean that there never had been any basis for Brodies to have Peter and Robert certified. All Gertrude had to do was to appoint Guardians to look after them in the event of their surviving her.

As things turned out MacLure's own crooked little heart ceased beating in 1988 thereby ending his life of crime and propelling him into Hell to join his late and unlamented partners in crime there, Dempster, Carruthers, Gertrude, and Clive.

Johnny signed the Wells Estate over to Peter's new *Curator-Bonis*, Hugh Stevens in 1987, in the mistaken belief that he was legally obliged to do so; a mistaken belief which was the consequence of the decades of brainwashing that my father, Johnny, and myself had been subjected to by Mackenzie & Black and thereafter Brodies. Johnny's thus signing in 1987 turned out to be the final nail in the coffin for the Usher Baronetcy Trust Estates and led inexorably to their sale in July 1995.

If Johnny had delayed signing, for just another year until the death of the sly, lying fraudster MacClure in 1988, he would then have been the Sole Proprietor of the Trust Estates, without even knowing it. A more farcical situation was, and still is, hard to imagine.

In this event, as the sole surviving Trustee, but still in ignorance that he was also the Sole Proprietor, Johnny would have been in an impregnable position to dictate to Brodies and save the Estates for an Usher posterity. For example, on the grounds that he, as the sole surviving Trustee, did not believe it was at all in the interests of the Trust that he sign the Estates over to Peter whose *Curator-Bonis* was to be a Brodies man. Further he would have insisted that Brodies give him all the Trust records and accounts going back to 1933, the year of the death of old Sir Robert Usher who had set up the Trust. If they still refused to do so he would have simply reported them to the Fraud Squad. Thereafter he would have soon enough discovered that he, and not Peter, had been a third proprietor of the Estates from the 1960s until 1982 and a half proprietor of them from 1982 to 1988 and the sole proprietor thereafter.

Thereafter, with me cheering him on, he would have uncovered the whole fraud and reported Brodies and their surviving fraudster legal mechanics, Stevens, Houldsworth and whoever else and the Estate Manager to the Fraud Squad. He would also have removed Valerie and the Mactaggarts from all the old Wells Estate properties they were squatting on. He would then have slowly resuscitated the Estates by raising the rents to Open Market values for all who lived on them and repaired and rented out the cottages which had stood empty for years. He would have also rescued the forests and shooting and put them onto a commercially viable basis. He would likewise have made it his business to find out exactly what the

Norton and Pitheavlis Estates consisted of and effected the same rescue operations for them as well.

And Peter and Robert? Johnny would have left them to live the rest of their lives in peace and blissful ignorance in Hallrule. He would also have made life more interesting for them; more outings, going to the circus and pantomimes which they always loved, and to the beach for a good paddle in the sea and going to Spain for their usual summer holidays. Gertie had lived like a hermit at Hallrule with Peter and Robert since Stuart's death in 1962 because she had no friends. In essence she had become a prisoner of her own deceit.

The patent fiction that Peter had inherited the Estates in 1962 was a particularly virulent piece of misinformation. It was also a good example of Mackenzie & Black (MacClure and Dempster) and then Brodies, McClure, Dempster, and the successive Brodies Chairman and women, Senior Partners and Managing Partners such as J Ronald Gardiner, William Drummond and Alastair Campbell as well as Carruthers, Stevens and Houldsworth playing the 'Long Game'; decades in our case. There were many more partners going back over the decades, all of whose names I have got.

I also discovered further documentation and correspondence which Simpson had withheld from Johnny. This correspondence showed that yet another lawyer, David Sturrock of the Jedburgh law firm of Turnbull, Simpson and Sturrock *had already been* appointed *Curator-Bonis* to Peter, the purported and now provably bogus landlord, on 27th December 1982 just two days after Christmas. This demonstrated a great and unnatural urgency on Brodies part. But Simpson had studiously avoided telling Johnny that when Johnny was challenging Clives's Will in which he had left his squattership of Hallrule farm to his daughter, Mrs Mactaggart. Sturrock, as Peter's Curator, had then sabotaged Johnny's objections and then immediately resigned his Curatorship. Nor did Simpson's deceit end there. In 1997 I discovered that Sturrock was none other than Mrs Mactaggart's lawyer. So Brodies had sneaked in Mrs Mactaggart's lawyer, to be Peter's Curator, without informing Johnny, in his capacity as a Trustee of the Usher Baronetcy Trust, for the sole purpose of sabotaging Johnny's objections to Mrs Mactaggart's claiming her squattership of Hallrule in the terms of Clive's fraudulent Will. Sturrock had therefore simply perverted the course of justice in favour of his own client thereby allowing Mrs Mactaggart to continue to squat on the farm. She and her dreadful family have squatted on Hallrule Farm and the areas around Wells ever since.

So, Brodies had pulled off another *fait accompli*, with a little help from their crooked lawyer friend in Jedburgh, David Sturrock. For him to have accepted the post of *Curator-Bonis* to deal with Johnny's objections to Mrs Mactaggart while being Mrs Mactaggart's personal law agent was an act of extreme deceit.

David Sturrock known as 'Major' threatened News International with legal action if they featured one of his crooked lawyer colleagues. The *News of the World* was conducting an ongoing investigation into how the Scottish legal profession muscle newspapers away from reporting on scandals involving 'crooked lawyers'. The newspaper was in the process of uncovering a £300,000 swindle of a will

I therefore regarded Sturrock as just another crook in the fraud ring. When I moved to our little house in the country near Jedburgh in November 1996 I heard most uncomplimentary stories about him from people in Jedburgh. And nor did it stop with him. His grandfather had also been a lawyer in Jedburgh. I was told that he (Sturrock's grandfather) had ruined some Jedburgh families in the usual filthy way that crooked lawyers do and that eventually things got so hot for him in Jedburgh that he motored to a spot in England just over the Border on the A68 and shot himself dead. The people of Jedburgh have always been known to take a very hard line against what they regard as really nasty criminals: fraudsters, stealth thieves and the like. This is borne out by the ancient saying: 'Jeddart (Jedburgh) Justice.' Jeddart Justice means: 'Hang them first and Try them later!' In other words 'We don't pussy foot around with nasty criminals.' I assume that Sturrock's grandfather preferred suicide to suffering Jeddart Justice at the hands of the good burghers of Jedburgh. I also assume he committed suicide in England to make it more difficult and expensive for the Jedburgh families he had ruined to get redress.

I then came across the Petition which Brodies had presented to the Court in their and Gertrude's abortive attempt to get the Estate Manager to be Peter's Curator. The Petition was in the name of Lady Sampson, or Usher! After all the damage she had done to our family, and the shame she had brought onto it, now this. As far as I was concerned Brodies had gone along with this falsehood to conceal her true legal status, Lady Usher, for some reason as yet unknown. She and Brodies presenting her as Lady Sampson stuck in my throat very badly indeed, as you can well imagine. Just another sick lie in the overall sick fraud. In Argentina she had been a complete nonentity as far as I was aware and here she was in Scotland parading herself as 'Lady Sampson', with Brodies acquiescing. The sum total of her contribution to our family was to have produced two Down's Syndrome, Mentally Incapacitated sons, cause trouble and then to swindle us for as much as she could and ultimately ruin us by posing as 'Lady Sampson.' Some contribution! Of course that falsehood alone made the Petition illegal.

Significantly again Mike Simpson had also ommitted to inform Johnny that Brodies themselves had accepted that it was 'entirely unacceptable' (Brodies' words, not Johnny's!) for the Estate Manager to be the *Curator-Bonis* because he was also a tenant of Peter's as per Johnny's objections to him, as already narrated in the passage for the 1982/83 period.

So why had Brodies, knowing that it was 'entirely unacceptable', tried to get him made Curator in the first place? The answer is that they thought they would get away with it as another *fait-accomplis*. But when Johnny objected they realised it was too dangerous. After this ploy fell through Brodies simply went ahead and appointed one of their own lawyers, Ian Taylor Carruthers, to be Peter's Curator, again *without* informing Johnny. This was eventually presented to Johnny, yet again, as another *fait accompli* with Carruthers being appointed Peter's *Curator-Bonis* on 26/4/1983. This also confirmed that Sturrock had acted in bad faith in concert with Brodies. If everything had been above board with Sturrock why replace him with Carruthers just a few months later?? On the strength of the fore-going Brodies should change their name to 'Grabbe, Robb and Steele'!

Here I should point out to the reader that an Act of Ommission with the intention of achieving a criminal end is regarded by the laws of most western countries in the same light as an Act of Commission with the same intent. I think this applies, rather surprisingly, even in the 'new, vibrant and modern' Scotland, albeit wholly in the breach of it. An act of Omission with criminal intent is someone knowing about a crime which is to be committed, or is being committed or has been committed and not reporting it to the Authorities. Brodies, in the persons of McLure, Dempster, Carruthers, Stevens and Houldsworth as well as Clive, Gertrude and the Estate Manager and others routinely used this tactic of Omission to conceal their serial criminal activity against the Usher family from my parents and thereafter on Johnny and myself. Those still living today, Stevens, Houldsworth, the Estate Manager, Mrs Mactaggart and many of the past Chairmen of Brodies, such as Alistair Campbell and his predecessors continue to shelter under this 'device' to the present day.

So much for Mike Simpson of Tods Murray. He had acted in bad faith towards Johnny from day one. That explained Johnny's missing and misplaced letters and the like. Just another pack of lies. As luck would have it I managed to get a little revenge on Simpson a few years later much to his fury. You will read it about this when it occurred

34

I REPORT BRODIES TO THE CAPITAL TAXES OFFICE IN EDINBURGH

On 26th April 1996 Gillian and I dropped in at the Capital Taxes Office in Picardy Place, Edinburgh, *unannounced.* I had by now, at last, realised that the unannounced visit offered the best prospect of eliciting information on the 'Catch 'em cold' principle. Another advantage was that this would preclude them from contacting Brodies and concocting some cock and bull story between the two of them to fob me off. My immediate 'on the face of it' objective was to find out why 'the negotiations' between themselves and Brodies were taking so endlessly long thereby causing the huge delay in the beneficiaries getting what remained of their inheritances. However my real objective was to alert the Tax Authorities to the fraud in connection with the Contents of Hallrule House. If I had simply reported Brodies to the Tax Authorities for fraud it would have been much easier for them to just dismiss me. However by leading them into it by this 'on the face of it' objective I banked on catching them out so badly that they would not be able to simply dismiss me as talking nonsense. In essence I was reporting Brodies for Tax evasion.

We announced ourselves. A very polite and correct lady called Miss Patrick attended us quite quickly. I asked her what was causing the delay in the negotiations about the inheritance tax in connection with Robert's estate. She answered: 'The negotiations regarding the chattels of the deceased.' She then shut up. Just like Houldsworth and Stevens had been at my last meeting with them. 'Aha, so you too have been well-trained,' I thought. I then told her that this was very odd indeed because, according to Brodies, Robert owned very few 'chattels' - only two paintings and some silver and that I could not see how three items could cause such an incredible delay. If she was surprised by this she managed to conceal it and stuck to her guns about Robert's chattels. In a matter of fact way I asked her to confirm this in writing to me. She agreed to do so. Having got her agreement I decided against giving her chapter and verse on the Contents issue there and then as I thought this might alert her to the danger of putting her statement to me in writing. We therefore thanked her for attending to us so quickly and made our exit as soon as we politely could. Safely outside the building I expressed my delight to Gillian about Miss Patrick's statement about Robert's chattels and that with a bit of luck she would let out more information of a damning nature for Brodies in her letter to us.

Unlike so many before her Miss Patrick was as good as her word and faxed me later that day. Her fax stated: 'Settlement of the value at the death of the deceased's own *furniture* [italics mine] and effects which is still under negotiation with Messrs Brodies.' *Bingo,* I thought. 'Brodies are still maintaining the patent fiction that all the Hallrule furniture belonged to Robert personally.' She also gave another reason for the delay which she had not mentioned in the morning. This was that negotiations on Gertrude's Trust were still ongoing. *Bingo* again, I thought, with the greatest delight. Why on earth should negotiations on Gertrude's Trust be holding up the final payments to the beneficiaries, more than eleven years after her death? That simply was not tenable. Why then were Brodies and the Capital Tax Office locked in these negotiations?

I waited for the hard copy of her fax which duly arrived on 1st May 1996 and responded to her the next day. In my letter I asked her what furniture Robert owned and explained to her that Brodies had always stoutly maintained that he owned *no* furniture at all and that this had resulted in a huge dispute and correspondence between Brodies and myself, with my insisting that he did own the vast majority of the Contents of Hallrule House.

On 7th May she responded. She now changed her position completely by stating that: 'The deceased did not own furniture, but he did own silver and paintings.' And that was it. Short, sharp and sweet, and in *total* contradiction to her first letter.

On 20th May I faxed her asking her for an explanation for her conflicting statements. I also explained that I was addressing these questions to her as I had never been able to get any credible explanations from Brodies. I also asked her to keep our correspondence confidential from Brodies.

Predictably she now went to ground and a two month silence ensued. Miss Patrick, eventually replied by letter dated 17th July, and apologised for stating that Robert owned furniture in her first letter. Her apology meant absolutely nothing to me because I regarded it as just another damage limitation device. But her effecting a 180 degree turn, this time in our favour for a change, on the matter made me very happy indeed. From this and the near two months delay in replying I deduced that we had set the cat among the pigeons between the CTO and Brodies and that the CTO had caught Brodies out.

Her final letter to me was dated 23rd July 1996 and was a relatively long letter in which she went to some lengths in an attempt to clear the CTO. She now told us that we would be receiving a refund of £41,000 and that this was as a result of an, 'Overpayment in respect of one part being set off against a payment due by another part of Robert's estate.' I did not believe that was the whole story at all because she never mentioned *which* 'parts' of Robert's Estate these were.

On that very same day of 23rd July Brodies suddenly faxed me and all the other beneficiaries stating that they had found an 'error' in their calculations and that this would result in a refund of about £40,000 to the executry. Stevens then further stated: 'I have to admit to an amount of surprise at what they (the CTO) have accepted but there is certainly no intention to look such a gift horse in the mouth.' I did not believe this gift horse twaddle for one second. I then surmised that the CTO had come to some sort of deal with Brodies to get them out of the mess in which Brodies had landed them both. Another clue was the fact that the date on the letter had been typed in the normal fashion and then very thoroughly crossed out and '23' written by hand in its place. This indicated that this letter had been withheld by Brodies until they heard from the CTO that they (the CTO) had written to me. Brodies then quickly got in ahead of them by faxing me so I got the news first from them.

As a consequence of all this I suspect a team of senior CTO inspectors had descended on Brodies and discovered that Peter, as far as they were concerned, had been defrauded of the vast majority of the Contents in the 1985-1986 financial year and therefore that they had never passed to Robert. They would then very likely have gone back to 1963 and discovered that Dempster's return to the Inland Revenue Estate Duty Office was fraudulent and that Gertrude had never owned the contents at all and by progression that Peter likewise had never owned them. They would have arrived at this conclusion when they discovered, as I had done, that the Contents were reflected in the Usher Baronetcy Trust Accounts of the early 1980s and the Insurance for of them had been paid by the Usher Baronetcy Trust. This of course meant that the Inheritance Tax that they had agreed for 'Gertrude's Trust Estate' and the £40,000 it had already paid them was based on a fraud.

But instead of reporting Brodies to the Fraud Squad, as they should have done, the CTO appears to have struck a deal with Brodies whereby the CTO would re-imburse Robert's Estate with the £40,000 which Brodies had already paid to it out of his Estate, not Gertrude's as we had been led to believe, on condition that Gertrude's Trust re-imburse the CTO with the £40,000. Paying Gertrude's Inheritance tax out of her son's putative Estate was just another dirty Brodies fraud. This best explained Steven's fax to me in which he tried to disguise this £40,000 as a 'gift-horse.' Remember they had used this 'disguise' tactic before in connection with Jacquelin's various thefts from the Executry. I had caught them, and the thieving Jacquelin, out then and I had caught them out again now. When were they ever going to learn that someone somewhere usually notices such frauds sooner or later? My oblique 'on the face of it, dropping in' approach to the CTO had worked beautifully.

It has recently occurred to me that when the CTO discovered that no Death Duties, as they were known as in the 1960s, had been paid on the Contents, they might well have charged Brodies for them plus interest at their penal rates for the intervening decades. If so Brodies would have had to pay an enormous sum; the sum they had used to threaten me into silence in 1994. If this had in fact occurred it was the sweetest of poetic justice. I hope like blazes that the CTO had done just that.

However I could not avoid the conclusion that in acquiescing in this arrangement the CTO itself had become party to the fraud. In essence they gave Gertrude's Trust a clean bill of health from the Taxation side of things after it paid the Inheritance Tax for the Contents which it now must have known had been acquired by Gertrude's Trust by a Brodies fraud. This acquiesence also gave Brodies' contention that the Contents belonged to Gertrude's some currency but only from the taxation side of things. I reported the matter to the UK Tax Authorities in London but soon got the message, loud and clear, that I would get nowhere with them.

I was over the moon about this whole episode because it had yielded me a very useful and, as far as Brodies were concerned, an extremely damaging paper trail. And I would never have got it if Gillian and I had not cold called the CTO on that cold and blustery April day. If we had not cold called them on that cold day we would never have got the £40,000 back.

In the event of Ms Patrick reading this book I would say that both Gillian and I realised that she had to keep quiet about the whole matter or lose her job. On top of that I suspect that it was taken out of her hands and dealt with by more senior CTO staff. So please don't feel too bad about it Miss Patrick. At least you had manners and we appreciated that.

On 8th May 1996 I at last discovered a well known firm of Estate and Land-Agents who appeared to be keen to look into the Estate rentals. I met them this day at their offices in Edinburgh. The gentleman I dealt with knew the Wells Estate and told me that he could never understand what had happened on Town O'Rule farm in the mid 80s with the tenant - the Estate Manager - going out of the farm and then re-occupying it a year later. That was, in his opinion, 'an extraordinary business.' We went through the leases together and had a long and fruitful meeting.

We agreed our terms of business, one of which was that I was to never identify him or the firm for which he worked unless and until the case got to Court - indicative of the power of the Edinburgh legal establishment Mafia . He would inspect Town O'Rule farm, incognito, and then do a Report on it. I gave him all the information I had including the leases and rentals going back to only 1974 which was all I had got after months of effort and at enormous expense charged to the Executry by Brodies. I also gave him the rentals and leases of the other farms on the Estate, for comparison purposes.

He eventually produced his report on 22nd of August 1996. His report stated that the rentals were well below what they should have been and that Town O'Rule farm 'received more favourable treatment than other properties on the Estate.' The Report covered many aspects of what appeared to have been the very favourable treatment being enjoyed by the Estate Manager but was not as complete as it might have been due to the lack of information which Brodies and the Estate Manager had conspired to deny me. The Report also stated that the Curator, Carruthers of Brodies, failed to invoke the wide 'irritancy' clauses contained in the lease should the tenant break the lease in the way that the Estate Manager had broken it in 1985. If the Curator had invoked these clauses it was very likely that the landlord (perceived to have been Peter at the time) would have obtained vacant possession of the farm under very favourable circumstances to the Usher Baronetcy Trust. But of course the Curator had *not* invoked these clauses. Further, he allowed the Estate Manager back into the farm a year later; again under very favourable circumstances to him. This piece of chicanery ultimately lost the executry well over half a million pounds in 1995. But remember Johnny had not yet signed Wells Estate over to Peter until 1987. So Carruthers acting in this fraudulent manner was undertaken from within an already existing fraud.

The Report also stated that *all* the Estate rentals were far below what they should have been. For example the rent on Town O'Rule farm in 1979 was less than £1 per acre per annum. Just three years later in 1982 the Report stated that smaller farms than Town O'Rule in the area, but otherwise similar in nature, had attracted bids of £27 per acre per annum. This indicated that the rental which the Estate Manager had been paying was more than a twentieth less than what he should have been paying. Little wonder that Brodies had fought so hard to stop me acquiring a copy of the lease. And again, little wonder Angus Cheape of Langley Taylor on 21st June 1995 stated that the rentals on Wells Estate were 'astonishingly low.'

He warned me that it would be very difficult to win against Brodies because I would keep coming up against a "wall of silence". I told him that I was already well aware of this Wall and had encountered it on numerous occasions. He told me that my main difficulty would be to 'break-through', as he put it. How right he proved to be. His encouragement proved that there were at least some decent professionals in Scotland who backed me, albeit covertly. This encouraged me greatly to fight on.

On 20th June 1996. I contacted Charles Cowie of MacRobert's Edinburgh Offices with whom I was now dealing. I asked him to put the statement which Mr Lake, the Counsel whom MacRobert's had used for an Opinion on the grounds of our suing Brodies and all the others for loss to the Estates into his Opinion which he had made, in writing to me. Lake's statement was:

'It was most unfortunate that Brodies were the Law Agents for the Executry when they were also the Law Agents for the Curatory.'

There again I had it from the horses mouth. It was more than 'unfortunate' of course; it was criminal and had proved catastrophic for our family for decades and would continue to prove catastrophic in the coming years. This was yet another example of a lawyer, Lake, trying to limit the damage to his fellow lawyers, Brodies. He should have described this situation as follows:

'Brodies appointing one of their number to be Peter's Curator and then appointing themselves to be the Law Agents to the consequent Curatory and thereafter Executry, were acts carried out with criminal intent.'

On 24th August 1996 I met an Advocate whose name now evades me in Edinburgh whom I had met briefly once before at a cocktail party and with whom I'd had brief discussions about him taking on the case. I told him that we had dropped our objections because it appeared impossible for us to get anywhere with them. His comment was: 'Yes, that's it, I am afraid.' What a reaction and how illustrative of how confident he was that crooked lawyers would never be brought to book for the crimes they committed against their clients. Also how well stitched-up the legal establishment's safety net was in stopping the few victims who fought back. From that moment I regarded him as yet another crooked lawyer himself.

Jonathan Lake QC.

'. . .most unfortunate that Brodies were the Law Agents for the Executry when they were also the Law Agents for the Curatory.'

35

ANOTHER CROOKED LAWYER CALLED ROBIN FULTON OF THE LAW FIRM SHEPHERD AND WEDDERBURN OF EDINBURGH.

Before and after my meeting with Jacquelin and Brodies on 18th December 1995 I had been engaged in a long running correspondence battle with Brodies trying to have Jacquelin repay the money she had defrauded from the Executry. Brodies had gone to enormous lengths to defend her because they realised the danger posed by their involvement in trying to conceal this particular fraud. I agreed to the matter going to arbitration as my evidence of the fraud was so strong that I thought that any arbiter, even a crooked one, would be bound to find for me or face ridicule.

To this end I received a letter from Stevens of Brodies on 25th September 1996 in which he informed me that a Robin Fulton of Shepherd & Wedderburn had agreed to act as the arbiter on what he called the 'Executors Expenses Dispute.' This was the usual mendacious Brodies. It never was 'expenses dispute' - it was about Jacquelin defrauding the Executry. Stevens then said he would have what he called 'the papers' delivered to Fulton.

I immediately replied to Stevens by fax instructing him not to send *any* papers to Fulton on the grounds that any such action would be prejudicial to the Executry because he did not *act* for Jacquelin but for the Executry and that it was up to Jacquelin alone to convince Fulton that she had *not* defrauded the Executry and for me to justify Johnny's expenses.

By 26th September 1996, I became more and more worried that Brodies would send these 'papers to Fulton' and that the 'papers' would be the usual brainwashing twaddle to put Jacquelin in the clear and Johnny and myself in the mire. I therefore got Fulton on the phone on this day and asked if I could make a submission giving him the real background to the whole business. Fulton told me that he would not accept any submission from me but that I could write to him on the matter - a contradiction in terms. I did so straightaway by fax and warned him that I felt that Brodies 'papers' would not represent the interests of the Executry but would instead represent their own and Jacquelin's interests. I also stated that Brodies should have nothing whatever to do with any arbitration between Executors who were in conflict.

As suspected I then received a fax from Stevens stating that Fulton had already received the papers; Stevens had 'felt obliged' to send them. However Fulton's hostile attitude on the phone had already aroused my suspicions of a cover up. I decided to stay with it as I was still confident that I would catch Jacquelin out so badly that even Fulton would have no option but to side with me.

On 2nd October 1996. I tried to get Fulton on phone because he had not had a replied to my letter of the 26th of September. His secretary assured me that he would ring me back as soon as he finished the call he was on. Three quarters of an hour later she had the decency to ring me back and tell me that he had now gone out and would not be back until the Friday. She assured me that he *would* ring me back on Friday. Friday came and went and no telephone call from Fulton.

On Monday, 7th October 1996, I received a four line reply from him with no reference whatever to my request that I be allowed to put in my submission. In his four lines he stated: 'I have now heard from Brodies and shall be giving this matter my attention.' Having got Brodies 'papers' but none from myself.

On 18th October 1996 I faxed him a short letter enquiring as to what progress he was making. As I'd heard nothing from him by 24th October I phoned him at 11.20am that day. His secretary said he would ring back soon. Fulton did ring back at 4.10. He told me that he would soon be issuing his judgement which would be binding on both parties. I instantly told him that this was not what had been agreed with Brodies when we had accepted arbitration - that we were to have a meeting before he made any determination on the matter at which I would have an opportunity to present my evidence. I told him there was no point in his adjudicating if there was to be no meeting and no submission from me. He then said he would refer to Brodies again. I then immediately faxed him covering our conversation in writing. Also referring him to my fax of 26th September 1996 and the fact that he had never replied as to whether he was prepared to receive a submission from me.

There followed further correspondence between myself, Fulton and Brodies. For example I wrote to Brodies protesting that Fulton could not possibly adjudicate on the basis of receiving a submission from one Executor and refuse to receive one from the other. I also wrote to Fulton again in the same terms. Again I never received a reply.

Brodies now entered the fray by creating as much smoke and confusion as they could. For example Stevens wrote: 'It would be quite wrong in my view as I have already said to try and impose on him the way that he should carry out his adjudication.'

Curious though it may seem I still had hopes that my evidence of Jacquelin's theft was so overwhelming that even Fulton would be deterred from finding *for* her. It all now rather depended on my performance in the meeting which I was still trying to have him agree to. I kept up the pressure by holding the position that there was no point in continuing with the 'arbitration' unless there was a meeting. At last, on 29th October 1996 Fulton gave way and agreed to a meeting and began asking me for information on Johnny's claim for expenses.

The Meeting was fixed for 11am on Friday 8th November 1996. I went to the meeting fully armed, including the lengthy submission which Fulton had previously refused to receive.

The Meeting commenced at the agreed time. He had a list which stated that Johnny had been paid £178.00 in the middle of 1996. This was absolute rubbish and I repudiated it. We spent an inordinate amount of time on this before he and Jacquelin gave way. I later realised that this had been introduced as a red-herring to divert attention away from the real issue which was Jacquelin defrauding the Executry, and to waste time. Jacquelin sat virtually silent - a sure sign that she had been told to keep her mouth shut. I waited for Fulton to ask for my submission but as he never did, I gave it to him. He immediately left the room and came back with it and two further copies of it a short while later. He kept one copy for himself and gave the other to Jacquelin and returned the original to me.

He now stated that he thought £90.00 a month that I had claimed to cover the phone calls between Johnny in South Africa and myself was 'too much.' I expected him to ask for the itemized bills of my calls to Johnny in South Africa but he didn't. Gradually we neared the end of the alloted 'arbitration' time without having discussed anything of substance so I made the move that I had planned carefully. The bulk of Jacquelin's 'expenses claims' were for travelling to Hallrule from Chesters everyday. However in a newspaper interview in which she gave to the *Glasgow Herald* in October 1995 she had informed the reporter that she was living at Hallrule and only returned to Chesters occasionally. I therefore asked Jacquelin to inform us which one of these statements was the the true one. Caught out, yet again, Jacquelin just sat there with a reddening face and then denied she had been staying at Hallrule. Fulton then dashed to her rescue saying: 'Oh, we can quite easily get the Housekeeper to vouch that she did *not* stay at Hallrule.' A rehearsed answer if ever there was one. Fulton then said: 'I understand everything now. I have got everything I need. . . I have got everything I need.' Twice - a sure sign that he intended to do the dirty. He then gathered the papers and rose to signal the end of the meeting. I was now feeling most uncomfortable and could hardly believe that this utter travesty of an 'Adjudication' was happening. And he *still* had not read my submission. Her claim was plainly fraudulent as she, Brodies and Fulton well knew. So the meeting ended.

Robin Fulton of Shepherd and Wedderburn WS - 'Adjudicator' commissioned by fellow-crook Hugh Stevens of Brodies WS. Note the 'oh-so innocent look'.

Jacquelin quickly made herself scarce, as the guilty do on such occasions. Fulton shadowed me to the lift in a show of manners. I felt an impotent rage thinking of the utterly cynical manner in which he had just perverted the course of justice. I refrained from speaking and stared him down in utter disgust. He looked from me to his shoes in silence, his head shaking slightly. I thought that as he moves into old age this, no doubt many of his other similar perversions of justice, will come back to haunt him.

As I went to my car my emotions welled up and I shouted silently to the streets as if in a nightmare, 'This can't be happening to me!' I drove home in Black Despair.

I slowly recovered my senses. I only now realized that Fulton had not given me copies of Brodies and Jacquelin's submissions which he'd had at the meeting. Yet he had been as quick as lightning to give my submission to her. Bad mistake on my part. I was now most apprehensive that he would quickly produce his report before I had even seen those submissions and before I could get him to comment on my submission. If he managed to do this I could be in an invidious position with the beneficiaries. Everything now depended on my moving fast to stop him from producing his report. The minute I got home I phoned him for these submissions. Not available. My heart sank. I therefore faxed him straightaway asking him for the two submissions and instructed him to do nothing further until I had studied these and come back to him. After I faxed it off I rang his office to see if they had got it. They had. By the grace of God I then got Fulton on the line. He was now suddenly available. He had got my fax and immediately disagreed that Brodies communication with him had been a 'submission.' He insisted that it was a 'Statement of Fact.' I insisted that it was a submission. I also told him that I had instructed Brodies to have no communication with him at all and make no submission to him. He again insisted it was not a submission to the point of rudeness. However he reluctantly agreed to send me the two submissions and whatever else he had received from Brodies and Jacquelin. He also agreed to do nothing further until he had heard from me again. I heaved a sigh of relief although his agreeing to do nothing further did not mean that he would break the agreement the minute it suited him to do so. But it was better than nothing.

That evening we went over to Ayrshire to spend the week-end with Rosemary, Johnny's ex-wife, and my niece Caroline. On the way over I could think of nothing but what had occurred that day. I was now worried stiff that he would break his word to me in the way that Cockburn had done and produce his report over the week-end. The first thing I decided to do, irrespective of what Brodies and Jacquelin's submissions contained, was to notify Fulton that his services were no longer required before he produced his report. I did this the next morning, Saturday 9th November, and posted the letter to him by recorded delivery, from Maybole, Ayrshire. Recorded Delivery is a *must* with Scottish lawyers. Had I not posted it Recorded Delivery Fulton almost certainly would simply have binned the letter and then lied that he had not received it.

On Monday 11th November 1996: Serendipity! I received both Mrs Wolfe-Murray's and Brodies submissions to Fulton. And they *were* submissions and not just 'the papers' as Brodies had so misleadingly described them and certainly not 'Statements of Fact' as Fulton had even more misleadingly described them. Brodies submission inevitably heavily favoured Jacquelin and marginalized Johnny and myself. Brodies had also produced Jacquelin's submission *for* her. And Fulton had received Brodies submission on 25th September 1996 the day that Brodies informed me that they *would* send him 'the papers.' Another Stevens lie. As for the Brodies constructed Jacquelin submission Fulton had received that on 16th September, *nine days earlier*. Brodies only moved fast when they were in danger of being exposed as fraudsters and thieves. I therefore immediately faxed Fulton informing him that his conduct of the 'arbitration' had been totally unacceptable and dispensed with his services, yet again. At the same time I told him that I did not want to hear from him again and would not respond if I did.

Despite this he immediately faxed me back on the same day. When white-collar criminals like Fulton spot danger they move fast. No holidays, nor weeks of silence. In his reply Fulton set another trap for me by ending his fax with the words:

> 'I would invite you to consider, upon a without-prejudice basis, giving consideration to my submission upon the issue of expenses because it may well be that it will represent a view which finds acceptance with you. Unless I hear from you to the contrary I shall presume that you are prepared to proceed on that basis.'

He was now hoping like hell that I would stick by my word not to respond and on that basis he would have gone straight ahead and produced his report damning me. Of course I gave him no such chance and immediately turned down his heavily-baited offer in writing. I never heard from him again.

Inevitably he went ahead and produced his Report. But that did not matter so much now because I had already fired him. For the record he, of course, found for Mrs Wolfe-Murray and cut our expenses claim right down on a basis which can only be described as criminal. For so doing he charged the Executry £600 which Brodies settled at our expense without demur.

However I got my own back on Jacquelin and Fulton in 1999 in a rather satisfying manner. I reported Fulton to the Law Society for perverting the course of justice in his so called arbitration. In 1999 the Law Society produced its inevitable whitewash of Fulton. However in this whitewash I discovered a 1996 letter from Brodies which described her fraud as: 'A genuine misunderstanding on her part.' Sometime later, as I kept up the pressure, Brodies graduated to: 'She exceeded her authority and has had the embarrassment of having it shown that she had to repay the executry.' And now the Law Society's report of 1999 referred to her fraud as 'Improper'! It was improper alright but it should have described it for what it really was: Fraudulent. On this basis the law society would describe a lawyer who had murdered someone as having acted 'improperly'!

In the lengthy correspondence in which Brodies tried to get her off the hook they tried to scare me off by telling me that the costs of their correspondence with me on this matter had probably cost the executry more than the amount that she had stolen, which was just short of £2,000. Of course I did not give in to this intimidation and kept the pressure up. At last she and Brodies caved in by agreeing to repay the £2,000. Brodies effected this by deducting it from the final payout of her inheritance. This saved just under £250.00 for every beneficiary.

I then insisted that she pay the executry the same amount again to cover the costs of Brodies correspondence with me. Neither Brodies or she ever responded to this, so I billed her from time to time adding interest as the years passed. But never a peep from her, which was hardly surprising. She had no defence. But the fact remains that she still owes every beneficiary £250 plus interest over the last seventeen years.

And where did her eventual repayment and the Law Society's description of her fraud as 'improper' leave Fulton's 'determination on the Executors' 'expenses dispute' as Brodies and he had so artfully described it? Dead in the water. But he had made a very quick £600 out of his perversion. He was, and almost certainly still is, is just another crime-concealing lawyer who brings shame onto Scotland.

36

FALSE DOCUMENT CERTYFYING SIR PETER USHER AS MENTALLY INCAPACITATED AND THE KANGAROO COURT OF SESSION'.

On 27th September 1996 I wrote to a Dr Cliff Sharp who was a consulting Pyschiatrist at Dingleton Hospital in Melrose in pursuance of my phone call to Dingleton on 10th of that month. Dingleton was a hospital for the mentally handicapped. I wanted to find out who had certified Peter as 'Mentally Incpacitated' and the exact grounds on which he had been so certified. This should establish once and for all whether he was indeed Downs Syndrome or whether he suffered from some other malaise or a combination of both. I had already asked Brodies for the Certifying Document but had got nowhere. Dr Sharp assured me that he would send the documentation on Peter to me very shortly.

Not receiving the papers 'very shortly' I phoned again on 6th November. Dr Sharp now told me that the papers should have been posted out to me the previous week and could not understand why I had not yet received them. In the event they arrived on the following day, under cover of a letter dated 6th November, the very same day that I had phoned him. The now familiar pattern of evasion was already emerging.. I surmised that Dr Sharp had contacted Brodies for 'guidance.'

On going through the papers I discovered a letter dated 14th December 1982 from Brodies to a Dr Garcia at Dingleton Hospital. Brodies' letter consisted of instructions for the *wording* that Dr Garcia was to use to certify Peter as Mentally Incapacitated. As usual Brodies were calling the shots instead of leaving it to those better qualified to diagnose Peter's condition. Brodies' letter also stated that Dr Garcia should contact the Estate Manager in order to make an appointment to examine Peter and that 'Lady Gertrude was extremely upset.' Curious that Brodies now called her Gertrude instead of Lady Sampson. So did Dr Garcia, therefore, compile the certifying document as directed by Brodies but not sign it? A document was signed by a Dr K.E.M Melville of Duns in Berwickshire which was about 40 miles from Hawick. There were a number of statements in this certificate, which certified Peter as Mentally Incapacitated, which were utterly false.

Firstly, the Document replicated Brodies' wording exactly. The relevant part of Brodies' wording was:

> 'In my opinion he is incapable of managing his own affairs or giving instructions for their management. The mental infirmity is permanent and he will never be able to manage his affairs or give instructions for their management *again* [italics mine].

Secondly, the certificate made no mention whatever of Down's Syndrome.

And Thirdly, the certificate was dated 15th December 1982.

With regard to the First point above: Of course Peter had *never* been able to manage his 'affairs', let alone 'give instructions' for the administration of his 'affairs' at any time in his life. Brodies wording was intended to mislead anyone who read the certificate into thinking that Peter must have had some 'permanent' mental breakdown of recent origin, and that he had been managing his 'affairs', as a normal person, all his life until he had this mental breakdown.

With regard to the Second point: To have stated that Peter was Downs Syndrome would have shown the impossibility of his ever having run his own 'affairs'.

And Thirdly: It was very unlikely that Dr Melville had signed the Certifying document on 15th December 1982 because Brodies had posted it to Dr Garcia at Dingleton Hospital in Melrose only the day before on the 14th. If he, Dr Melville, *had* signed it on the 15th he would have had to examine Peter on the same day that Dr Garcia had received the letter if in fact by some miracle he had received it that day. This would have meant that Dr Garcia would have had to contact Dr Melville to drop whatever he was doing at the time and contact the Estate Manager to make an appointment with the upset Gertrude to examine Peter, then contact Gertrude, make the appointment and then leapt into his car and motored to Hallrule and examine and certify Peter all on the same day that Dr Garcia had received that letter from Brodies. I will leave the reader to decide whether this is believable.

On top of that Brodies managed to persuade Dr Melville to accept full legal responsibility for the Certifying Document by getting him to write, underneath their instructions, the words: 'Adopted as Holograph' and then sign it himself; thereby distancing Brodies from the falsehood and shifting the liability largely onto Dr Melville.

This Certifying Document was therefore based on just another Brodies falsehood to enable Brodies to gain complete control of Peter's purported Estates. Note that Brodies did not use the word 'Estates.' Instead they used the word 'affairs.' 'Affairs' was the ultimate 'catch all' word which gave no information away. If Dr Melville had been told that Peter was Downs Syndrome and the sole proprietor of extensive and valuable Estates he

C.S.R. Stroyan, W.S.
E.J. Cuthbertson, W.S.
Iain C. Jackson, W.S.
P.K. Stirling-Aird, W.S.
M.N.C. Gascoigne, W.S.
John A.L. Miller, W.S.
David S. Williamson, W.S.
James F. McLaren, W.S.
Andrew M.C. Dalgleish, W.S.
Hew D.K. Dalrymple, W.S.

J.A. Loudon, C.A., W.S.
J.R. Gardiner, W.S.
T.F.G. Nicol
James G. Clark, W.S.
Iain T. Carruthers, W.S.
James G. Birrell, W.S.
Karen Bruce Lockhart, W.S.
J.E.G. Hendry, W.S.
Alan J. McAndrew, W.S.
Hugh J. Stevens

David H. Houldsworth, W.S.

Ronald K. Watson, W.S. - Consultant

BRODIES W.S.
Solicitors
7 Rothesay Terrace,
Edinburgh EH3 7SD.

Court Dept: 031-226 5391
Answering Service: 031-225 9232
Telex: 727 129

Rutland Exchange Box No. 10 (Edin).
In reply please quote DPS/DSW
Your Ref.
Date: 14th December, 1982

Doctor S. Garcia,
Dingleton Hospital,
Melrose.

Why did they drop Dr Garcia?

Dear Sir,

Sir Peter Usher

We refer to a conversation on the morning of 10th December between our Mr. Sellar and a lady from the department of your Hospital which covers the Roxburgh area. **We are afraid that we** cannot remember the lady's name but she was kind enough to phone back and to confirm that you would oblige us by examining Sir Peter Usher in order to establish that he is legally incapable of managing his own affairs.

As we explained to the lady we spoke to we require to appoint a legal official known as a Curator to Sir Peter in order that this official may make a decision concerning the property of Sir Peter. As we explained the matter is one of considerable urgency as the decision must be made within a very short time. As far as we recall it was agreed that you should contact either the family doctor, Doctor Ross of O'connell Street, Hawick or the Factor to the Estate, Mr C. John Usher at Courthil, Hawick (telephone 0450 2728) in order to make an appointment to see Sir Peter. As we stated on the telephone Sir Peter's mother, Lady Gertrude is extremely upset at the prospect of Sir Peter having to be examined albeit in this case it will be a complete formality and it is necessary therefore to proceed through either of these two gentlemen.

We are sure that you are familiar with the form of certificate which the law requires but to remind you we enclose below a style for such a certificate. We thank you for your co-operation and we look forward to receiving your report as soon as possible, bearing in mind the urgency of the situation. Your Fee for this examination shall of course be paid by us immediately.

Yours faithfully,

Style Medical Certificate

Date /

Left: The letter to Doctor Garcia dated 14th December 1982 - damning evidence. How could Doctor Melville have examined Peter and signed the certifying document only the next day, giving Doctor Garcia little time to even receive the letter? And how would any qualified Doctor explain that Peter must have been managing his own affairs perfectly well until this urgent date? Clearly this is a desperate cover-up.

- 2 -

Doctor S. Garcia 14th December, 1982

Date

I (Full Name, Address & Qualifications) hereby certify on Soul and Conscience that I have this day at (place of examination) seen and examined (Full Name of Incapax, Former Address and Present Address). In my opinion he is incapable of managing his own affairs or giving instructions for their management. The mental infirmity is permanent and he will never be able to manage his affairs or give instructions for their management again.

I further certify that in my opinion a personal service upon the said (Full Name) of a Petition for the appointment of a Curator Bonis would, in his present state of health, be harmful.

"Adopted as Holograph" - in your own handwriting

SIGNATURE

The so-called 'certificate' pre-ordained by Brodies, suggesting Doctor Garcia simply fill it in and sign it. The whole tenor of this certificate and request is questionable in the extreme. And why then, did Doctor Garcia *not* sign it.

would have immediately realised that Peter had never managed them in any way whatever the minute he clapped eyes on him and would have refused to sign the document.

Did Dr Melville know that the Certifying Document was a falsehood? He must have done, *if* he had examined Peter. But then his signing the Certifying Document was a falsehood in itself. On top of that he had signed the Certifying Document on the Doctor's oath of 'Soul and Conscience.' I believe it very unlikely that Dr Melville ever *did* examine Peter.

Of course this Certifying Document would not fool anyone who had ever spoken to Peter. In this regard only Johnny and myself posed a danger because no outsiders would ever dare poke their noses into such a delicate matter. The only people living who ever had regular contact with Peter, other than Johnny and myself and the Hallrule House staff, were Clive, Valerie, the Mactaggarts, Mrs Blamey and cousin Katherine. Brodies no doubt had been banking on my never discovering this bogus Certifying Document.

So why had Dr Melville signed it? To find out I rang Dr Melville's home. His wife answered. To my great disappointment she told me he had passed away some years previously. This was very bad news indeed because, one way or the other, I should have been able to find out much more about the matter. The fact is that by signing that fraudulent Certifying Document Dr Melville had played a vital role in the ruination of my family. Dr Melville's signing it had, and still has, extremely serious implications for Brodies, despite Brodies 'Holograph' trick on him. All I needed was an honest lawyer to pin it onto Brodies.

However the matter did not end there. Brodies must have always feared that the bogus Certificate would one day come back to haunt them because they attempted to have Peter 'certified' again in June 1986. The new Certifying Document now did refer to him being Down's Syndrome and that this was the cause of his being incapable of managing his affairs. That, in itself, was a confirmation that the 1982 Certifying Document was a falsehood and had been drafted by Brodies with criminal intent. This new Certifying document was again designated for Melville to sign. However he never signed it. On top of that, this time Melville was not designated as a Doctor as he had been in the 1982 Certifying Document and which he *had* signed *as a Doctor on his Soul and Conscience.* This new Document referred to him only as KEM Melville. I suspect the reason for Melville's refusal to sign the new certifying document was because it differed so much from the 1982 bogus one which he had signed. The important point is that it was unsigned.

I also discovered that Brodies had Robert certified at the same time, 1986.

Within two weeks of Dr Melville purported signing of the bogus 1982 document certifying Peter as Mentally Incapacitated Mrs Mactaggart's lawyer, the egregious David Sturrock of Turnbull, Simpson & Sturrock of Jedburgh, was appointed Peter's first *Curator-Bonis* on 27th December 1982. His remit was to represent Peter, the unknowing bogus landlord with the bogus Certificate of Incapacity, and to reject Johnny's objections to the squatting Mrs Mactaggart continuing to squat at Hallrule farm under the terms of her father's fraudulent Will. Sturrock was appointed Peter's *Curator-Bonis* by Brodies acting on the 'instructions' of Gertrude. At the same time Brodies stated that they were acting on behalf of the Usher Baronetcy Trust in this process, one of whom was Johnny. This meant that

Brodies had obeyed the 'instructions' of their client, Gertie, but would also act for the Usher Baronetcy Trust as its law agents - despite the fact that the Usher Baronetcy Trust had supposedly (according to Brodies) ceased to exist in 1962.

Of course neither Brodies nor Johnny's pretence lawyer, Simpson of Tods Murray, had informed Johnny of Sturrock's appointment as Peter's Curator, as already narrated. However there was no Petition to the Court to have Sturrock appointed Peter's *Curator-Bonis* amongst the papers. Its absence indicated another act of ommission by Brodies to attain a criminal end with the aim of defeating Johnny's objections to Mrs Mactaggart being allowed to continue to squat at Hallrule farm.

This meant that Peter's status as an Incapax rested only on the 1982 Certificate which, being a falsehood, had no basis in law. The implications of this were colossal. It meant that Brodies appointment of first Sturrock, followed by Carruthers, and then Stevens as Peter's successive Curator-bonis's were all based on the bogus 1982 Certifying Document and then the unsigned 1986 Certifying Document were all fraudulent. That, in turn, meant that every action that Brodies had executed in the name of these three *Curator-Bonis*'s from 1982 onwards were likewise fraudulent. However this was just a small 'fraud enabling device', albeit an absolutely vital one, for the express purposes of enabling an already huge fraud to be further concealed, *and* enabling that concealed fraud to be continued and built upon thus enabling further large frauds to be executed in the future.

The last letter I got from Dr Sharp related the history of the events surrounding Peter and Robert's Certification in a way which did not tie up with what the record showed and in a manner which limited the damage to Brodies and the Medical authorities.

On 14th November 1996 I prepared for my meeting with the Auditor of Court which had been arranged by Brodies for 2.00 pm the following day which was a Friday. The purpose of the meeting was, on the face of it, to give the Executors the opportunity to comment on the level of what Brodies euphemistically called their 'fees' which they had charged the Executry. I did not want the Auditor to allow Brodies *any* of their so called 'fees' because of all their frauds on the Usher Baronetcy Trust in the names of Peter and Robert. As so often before I found myself agonizing as to whether or not I should show the Auditor the evidence of these frauds. I eventually and wisely decided against on the grounds that I did not now trust *anyone* in Edinburgh legal circles, no matter how august their position. In fact the more august their position, the less I trusted them. Notwithstanding this I decided that I would take a large suitcase full of damning papers with me just to send the message that I was well armed and also to see if he would ask me to show him some documentary evidence of the frauds.

Early Friday on the 15th of Nov 1996 saw me lugging this very heavy suitcase from Waverley station up to the Parliament Square Buildings next to St Giles Cathedral which is a long, steep climb and, relatively fit as I was, it took some doing. I found Jacquelin and Stevens waiting for me. Jacqueline, predictably, had no papers at all. She feigned innocence and affected to be reading one of the day's tabloids. We were quickly ushered into the office of the Auditor of the Court of Session.

The Auditor was an elderly man called Haldane-Tait. He was polite and commenced proceedings in a civilised manner.

I informed him in no uncertain terms that Brodies had obstructed me from the outset from carrying out my duties as acting Executor on Johnny's behalf. On this basis I therefore asked him to disallow whatever Brodies claimed as fees for most of their correspondence in connection with the Executry. I also asked him to allow nothing for Brodies' valiant defence of Mrs Wolfe-Murray's Executry Expenses claim. I further asked him to allow them nothing for all the correspondence on the Hallrule Contents and gave him my reasons for doing so. I was careful not to use the words 'stolen' or 'fraud.' In the year 2017 as I edit this book for the umpteenth time I very much regret that I never used those words..

To push the point home I told him that I regretted ever having tried to do my duty as an Executor because of all the obstacles which Brodies had put in my way and the flagrant Conflicts of Interest situations in which which Brodies had placed themselves in and in which they were still operating. With hindsight again I wish I *had* used the words 'fraud and fraudulent' in this connection.

Haldane-Tait became more and more agitated as I told him all this. When I had finished he asked me if I had taken legal advice on the matters I had brought up. He appeared to be anxious to get me to admit that I *had* taken legal advice. So, like an idiot I told him that I *had*. Immediately Haldane Tait then said, 'As you have taken legal advice you had the opportunity to do something about it. Why didn't you do anything?' I responded that I *was* doing something about it and that it was my intention to sue Brodies for damages on behalf of the Executry and that was why I had taken legal advice. I should have refused to answer his question on the grounds that it was none of his business whether I had taken legal advice.

Throughout this exchange Stevens had kept quiet affecting an angelic air but on hearing of my intention to sue Brodies he expressed *grave* disappointment and lied to Haldane-Tait that Jacquelin had already repaid the executry her 'expenses.' She had repaid alright, but they were not 'expenses'; they were a series of thefts. Jacquelin made no contribution whatever to the proceedings. She just sat there in silence as she had done at the meeting with Fulton at Shepherd & Wedderburn's offices.

As a sop I said I was agreeable to Brodies receiving 30% of what they had asked for. Another big mistake on my part: I should have asked him to allow them absolutely nothing. Interestingly it never occurred to me to ask how much Brodies *had* in fact claimed - yet another mistake. Of course

Haldane-Tait never offered me this information, which, if he had been acting in good faith, he would have done. This showed how much I had yet to learn in dealing with the Scottish Legal system. His not informing me of what Brodies were claiming was akin to my bargaining for the purchase of a car the price of which I did not know. How idiotic was that. Despite my rather poor performance at this meeting I was certain I had given Haldane-Tait plenty to think about and hoped that it would have some good effect on him.

After the meeting I got in touch with Haldane-Tait's office. I was never allowed to speak directly to Haldane Tait on the grounds that 'the Auditor does not get involved in conversations with people.' I therefore spoke to the only person I was allowed to speak to: a Mrs Janet Buck, his secretary. I found her to be a thoroughly decent person; a rare creature within the Scottish Legal system. She listened with care, growing concern and ultimately horror to what I told her. She was as shocked as any decent person would be and sincerely sympathized, but told me she was powerless to do anything about it. I also put in three further lengthy submissions detailing all the extra work and cost which Brodies' various frauds had caused to the Executry. She assured me that Haldane-Tait would study them.

In the event Haldane-Tait allowed Brodies £75,000 in fees. For what? Little else than for a pack of crime concealing lies. After he had set the fees Mrs Buck told me that, 'The Auditor had decided not to give you a breakdown at how he arrived at the £75,000 because he felt that this could well be in your favour in the future.' And: 'I am very, very sorry for you', and the like. However, as always, it was more than her job was worth to make a stand. She was far and away the most pleasant and decent person I ever came across in all my efforts for the Executry.

In later correspondence Brodies deplored the fact that Haldane Tait had not allowed for a lot of what they misleadingly described as their 'work' for the Executry. It took me years to realise that Haldane-Tait had read and accepted at least some of my various written evidence of Brodies 'misconduct' and consequently might well have cut Brodies 'fees', possibly by between £40,000 and £70,000. Brodies then tried to explain this away by stating that they accepted this because it went 'it went with the turf.' Was I thankful to Haldane Tait? No, I wasn't. I was certain that the only reason that he had cut Brodies fees was to limit the damage to himself in case the whole stinking mess was publicised and he was called to account to explain why he had rubber stamped the whole amount of the 'fees' they claimed. That would also explain Mrs Buck's statement about his 'thinking long and hard about it.' I suspected that he was thinking long and hard about himself, not the Executry. But I was thankful that I might well have saved the Executry tens of thousands of pounds.

37

BRODIES FALSIFY ACCOUNTS

The 12th December 1996 saw the start of a new saga involving Brodies and Jacquelin. Brodies wrote to me stating that they had sent the second lot of Executry Accounts, for the period 30th November 1995 to 2nd December 1996, to Jacquelin for approval and signature after which they would be sent on to me for my approval. All innocent enough on the surface. However there had been nothing in the slightest innocent in their conduct towards the Executry to date and this letter heralded what was to become another huge dispute between Brodies and myself.

First some background: In mid 1996, very much under duress, I had signed the first set of accounts which covered the period from 26th September 1994 to 30th November 1995. I had signed them *first* as requested by Brodies, Jacquelin therefore signed them second, below my signature. Jacquelin signing this new set of accounts first was at my request, and I did this because I wanted to sign them below her signature as this would give me the space to record the conditions upon which I would sign these accounts. My conditions would be that I signed the Accounts without prejudice to the proceeds of the Contents of Hallrule (and other assets which I now knew were missing from Robert's purported Estate) being recovered and placed in his Executry.

On 14th December I had asked Brodies to send me a copy of the accounts which they had already sent to Jacquelin for signature. I received this copy on 19th. On the 20th Brodies faxed me that Jacquelin, 'is fairly busy over the Christmas and New Year but hopes to be able to deal with the Accounts early in the New Year.' Of course this would hold up the final payments to the beneficiaries.

I therefore contacted Brodies on the same day. Stevens was unavailable so I dealt with his secretary. I objected to Jacquelin's delay in signing the Accounts and only 'hoping' to be able to 'deal' with them in the New Year. I told the secretary that signing the Accounts would only take her a few seconds in view of her having stated all along that she was happy with every aspect of the Accounts and Brodies actions throughout the time of the Usher

Baronetcy Trust, the successive Curatories and the present Executry. And would she therefore please sign them as a matter of urgency to enable the beneficiaries to receive their long overdue money. I also asked her to ask Stevens to immediately fax the Accounts out to Johnny as I was damned if I was going to continue to pay the huge telephone bills that my constant fax communications with Johnny were costing me. Brodies had not paid us any Executor's expenses for over a year. The secretary assured me that she would fax them out to Johnny straightaway.

Two weeks later, Johnny rang me and told me that he still had not received the Accounts. I therefore wrote to Stevens on 9th January 1997 and asked him to see to it that the accounts were faxed out to him straightaway. He replied on 13th assuring me that he would see to it that they were immediately faxed to Johnny. He also said he would contact Jacquelin 'about signing the Accounts,' and come back to me. Stevens then wrote to me on 20th January stating that Jacquelin had been trying to get hold of me but that 'she believes your number is ex-directory.' My telephone number had never been ex-directory. She was, as usual, lying again and I told Stevens so in no uncertain terms. I reiterated that Jacquelin's continued delay in signing the Accounts was seriously prejudicial to the Beneficiaries and totally unacceptable. It was perfectly clear that the usual 'something' was going on in the background.

Lo and behold Jacquelin rang me the next day, Tuesday 21st, at 8.25am. She now apologized for 'misplacing' my telephone number and stated that she was 'anxious to get the Accounts settled.' Note, no mention now of my Tel No being ex-directory. She suggested that we meet at a Public House. By now I held her in such contempt I would not lower myself to have a drink with her, so I turned down her heavily baited offer to meet. Instead I asked why she had delayed signing the accounts for well over a month? She responded by stating that provided I signed them first as I had done with the previous set of Accounts she would then be happy to sign them.

'Aha', I thought. 'Brodies have warned you of the danger in your signing first.' I then told her that as I had signed the previous set of Accounts first it was only fair that she should sign the second set of accounts first. Her reaction could not have been more revealing: She said, 'That is not an option you have' and slammed the phone down on me! That's what crooks do when they are cornered.

This confirmed that Brodies did not want either Johnny or me signing in the second position to obviate our including any conditions below our signatures. Conditions very similar to the ones that Johnny had inserted when signing the Receipt for the Estates in January 1995.

I straightaway faxed Stevens and told him what had happened. I then phoned him and we agreed that Jacquelin and I would sign two sets of the Accounts individually and at the same time in his Office. Stevens claimed he was 'at a loss' as to why Jacquelin refused to sign the Accounts first. Of course he was not 'at a loss' at all. On the same day (21st January 1997) Stevens then faxed me a letter in which he immediately reneged on what we had just agreed to on the phone and came up with another scheme for getting the Accounts signed. I repudiated this scheme by fax to Stevens the next day.

On 27th January I received a letter from Stevens stating that he had now received the Accounts *signed* by Jacquelin and that she had raised no questions. He stated that she had now signed them first. However he did not send me a copy of them. I therefore faxed him back immediately asking him to send me the newly-signed Accounts. Gillian told me that evening: 'I'll bet you there will be some trick in this.' She turned out to be dead right.

The next day Tuesday 28th January 1997 I received the signed Accounts from 'Brodies' (not from Stevens note) as he had now gone on 'gardening leave.' And of course there *was* a trick. Stevens had marked a place for me to sign immediately *above* the place where Jacquelin had signed, leaving me no space to insert my conditions. And that wasn't all. Jacquelin's signature was now three times the size of her signature on the previous set of Accounts, commencing from her area of signature and rising steeply at a thirty degree angle eventually ending well above my area for signing. This of course made it impossible for me to insert my conditions for my signing. Another day, another dirty trick, and another *fait-accompli* in the lives of these fraudsters.

I was livid about it for a start but soon realised the silver linings in this latest deception: Their use of such artifice indicated their extreme concern and the lengths to which they would go to stop me from entering any conditions on my signing. In addition Jacquelin's contrived signature would be good evidence when the Fraud Squad investigated.

I therefore instantly faxed Brodies on the same day repudiating the signed accounts and ask him to get to her to sign another set properly, and as agreed. Brodies faxed me back a short while later on the same day stating that I had agreed to this procedure. I had never done any such thing as the record attests. Brodies now claimed that she *had* signed first in the *chronological* sense, knowing very well that this was not what I had meant. This was another example of the constant deceit that Brodies and Jacquelin used to extricate themselves from the many holes into which I kept forcing them. Lawyers never reply to you on the same day unless you have them worried.

More correspondence followed in which I tried to get Jacquelin to sign the Accounts first and in the top position but to no avail. I then decided to sign the Accounts but only on the condition that the beneficiaries were paid what remained of their inheritances. I therefore asked for a fresh set of the Principal Accounts which I determined I would sign with my conditions on them. My objective in doing this was to see if Brodies would accept them or not.

Stevens then sent me the fresh set of accounts, the same set which Jacquelin had signed with her greatly enlarged and rising signature. On closer inspection I found that one of the beneficiaries was reflected as having received only £5,000 of the £50,000 she was due whereas all the other beneficiaries had received £50,000 each. This beneficiary was none other than Mrs Mactaggart! Knowing her for the money grubber squatter she was she would have squealed like a stuck pig had she been paid £45,000 short. But not a squawk, let alone a squeal. So, on the face of it, she must have received the full £50,000. I also found that Jacquelin had not been charged for various other personal costs she had charged the Executry. So she was still fiddling the Executry. There followed further correspondence to sort these 'mistakes' out and a flurry of exchanges of amended Accounts between Brodies and me.

On 11th February 1997 Stevens wrote that Brodies might have inadvertently sent me an unamended copy to sign and also wrote that he was enclosing an entry from the Estate records which showed Jacquelin repaying a small fraction of her private calls to the Executry. All this twisting and turning and amending of the Accounts clearly demonstrated that the set of Accounts which Jacquelin had signed was manifestly incorrect.

The upshot of all this was that the Accounts were amended; not at all as I wanted them, but an improvement on what they had been These amended Accounts now recorded Mrs Mactaggart's receiving £50,000 instead of the £5,000 as had been recorded in the set of Accounts that Jacquelin had signed. Eventually I signed them, knowing them to be fraudulent on 17th February 1997, but with my conditions in place. My conditions were that I signed them without prejudice to my recovering whatever assets were not reflected in the Accounts and to obtaining redress for the colossal losses caused to the Estates by their being 'mismanaged' (a polite alternative for 'defrauded') and so on.

This must have infuriated Brodies because Stevens responded quickly by letter dated 20th February. In it Stevens stated that my conditions were 'completely unacceptable' and that he would therefore make no further payment to the beneficiaries until I withdrew them. A more blatant example of blackmail it is difficult to imagine. I therefore faxed him on 23rd February stating that I was not prepared for the beneficiaries to be kept waiting any longer for their inheritances and that I would therefore go to Brodies the next day to sign a new amended set of Accounts without my conditions.

I took a friend with me for witness purposes because Gillian was working. Arriving at Brodies with my friend I asked the lady receptionist to let Stevens know of my arrival as he was expecting me. I got the answer I was half expecting: 'Mr Stevens is not working today'. The last thing he wanted was for me to tell him, preferably in front of the receptionist and the other people in the waiting area, that his accounts were fraudulent but that I would nevertheless sign them because of his blackmail. Expecting a similar response I then asked to see Houldsworth. She immediately informed me that he was 'too busy' to see me. Too busy? Too frightened was more like it. For the record I did not for a moment believe that Stevens was absent from work or that Houldsworth was too busy to see me. They had told the lady receptionist fob me off with these lies.

I therefore asked her for the Accounts. When she produced them I told her in a raised voice so that everyone else in the reception area could hear that it was most humiliating for me to sign these Accounts because I knew them to be fraudulent. To ram the point home to her and everyone else in the room I held my nose as I signed them. I hope that this convinced her and everyone else in the room that Brodies were a criminal organisation. Brodies posted off the cheques to the beneficiaries four days later on the 28th.

During those 4 days I repeatedly tried to contact Stevens but without success. His secretary became embarrassed by his constantly assuring her that he would return my call and then not doing so. She told me: 'I don't understand why he does not return your calls as he repeatedly assures me that he will.'

I then asked Brodies to furnish me with the set of amended accounts which I had signed with Mrs Wolfe-Murray's new signature on them. After a certain amount of 'dodging' Brodies sent me, on 1st March 1997, just the one page with Jacquelin's signature on it. This was the same signature as on the original unamended accounts. This was not what I had asked for. At the same time they sent me a separate copy of the full accounts that I had signed but this did not have Jacquelin's signature on it. It was like wrestling with a many-headed snake.

This therefore meant that we had signed two different sets of Accounts. It also meant that Jacquelin had not signed the accounts with the amendments which I had forced Brodies to make. This in turn meant that the Accounts she *had* signed still reflected Mrs Mactaggart receiving only £5,000 instead of £50,000 whereas the set I had signed reflected that Mrs Mactaggart had received £50,000.

So why had Stevens sent me only the one page of the patently 'inaccurate' accounts with only Jacquelin's signature on it? The reason appeared to be that he did not want me to see the amended Accounts which I *had* signed because he had amended them again *after* I had signed them so that they would fit with the original fraudulent accounts which Jacquelin had signed. I would be none the wiser - for the time being. However I became 'much the wiser' in 1998, as follows:

In March 1997 I had reported Brodies to the Law Society of Scotland. During their so-called investigation of Brodies the Law Society asked Brodies for a report on their handling of the Executry's affairs. Brodies then produced a 141 page report and sent it to the Law Society in November 1997. I procured a copy of this report. In it were the accounts that Jacquelin had signed with her steeply rising and contrived signature. But here was the trick: There, sure enough was Mrs Mactaggart's payment still reflected as only £5,000. But not quite. Brodies had inserted an extra skeletal '0', in *longhand ink*, so that it now, with a bit of a crush, read £50,000. This alone took away its basis in law.

Obviously there had to be £45,000 missing somewhere in the Accounts, but I was never able to find it at the time . This again was a relatively straightforward case of a fraud committed to conceal an already existing but by now very complicated and ever growing fraud.

It was sometime again before it dawned on me that this missing £45,000 might well be connected to the £40,000 'gift horse' from the CTO, as already narrated. It therefore appeared that Brodies had somehow hidden the £45,000 in the accounts which I might or might not have seen. But the fact that they included this in their Report to the Law Society indicated that there was a strong imperative driving them. It might have had something to do with their final deal with the CTO, which they now could not change.

The reason why Brodies had singled out Mrs Mactaggart's entry to take the £45,000 from, had two possible explanations: one being she really *had* only been given £5,000 and had agreed to it because she had received so much more elsewhere including the £600,000 she had made on the day that she had 'purchased' Hallrule farm.

The other more likely explanation was that Brodies *had* paid her the full £50,000 but had entered it as £5,000 to make it look like a patent error. In the rather unlikely event of her ever having the 'error' in the accounts pointed out to her she would not have cared less because the cheque she received was for the full £50,000. Of course there are other possibilities but when dealing with lawyers like Brodies the possibilities become endless.

So on the face of it I had been 'had' again. But this dark cloud also had a large silver lining. I now had a further example of Brodies fraudulent activities in my paper trail. This made me feel ever more confident that I now had enough on Brodies to expose them if and when I ever got to Court. That was to prove yet another major saga. However at that time I had no conception whatever of the huge hurdles that the Scottish legal system would place in my way to stop me getting to court..

In early March 1997 I contacted the Hawick Police again and asked them to keep a lookout for the silver and other items that had gone missing from Hallrule. They informed me that a video would be shown at Kelso Police Station on 26th June 1997 of a lot of goods which were suspected stolen, — including a lot of silver. Most of this suspect stuff had been taken from the premises of a dodgy antique dealer in the Newcastle area, only fifty miles from Hallrule. I decided to watch the video to see if any Hallrule stuff showed up. With quite a number of other people I settled down to watch.

Interminable pieces of silver were shown none of which had our crest on as far as I could see, but that of course was not conclusive because there were many pieces in the collection without our crest. I was not at all acquainted with the collection because Gertie always kept it hidden well away for her self appropriation purposes, as we had now discovered.

Suddenly up came a plaque of indeterminate material with the clear inscription on it: 'Sir Robert Usher of Norton and Wells.' 'Gotcha!' I thought to myself, hoping like blazes that other Hallrule items would appear. But I was unable to identify any further items. But, given that I had identified that one item, it was certain that there had been others from Hallrule House which I had not been able to identify. Who then was/were the thief or thieves? With her track record it was almost certainly Jacquelin. She was too stupid to realise the dangers of selling whatever she had stolen to a nearby Antiques Dealer. The Estate Manager? It was very likely that he too had stolen stuff but, being the cunning fellow he was, he would have realised the dangers of selling them to a dodgy Antiques Dealer so close to home. I therefore doubted that any items on the video had been stolen by him.

I was told that the plaque was at the Hawick Police Station. I took the precaution of taking an ex Estate employee with me to Hawick in case he/she (for their security) recognised the plaque. It turned out to be an iron plaque possibly denoting Sir Robert's ownership of a painting or whatever. Not much value to it in itself but enough to be of interest to the dodgy antique dealer. Of course I asked the Police if I could take it for the Executry. Not at all, I was told: 'You have to prove that the Sir Robert (the Incapax) owned it'. More lunacy! The Police were well aware of my position. I deduced that they had already been told not to give it to me if wanted it. For the sake of peace I told them him to just hang onto to it in the meantime because I had more important quarry to hunt down.

However this little episode vindicated my constant claims to Brodies, the Acc of Court and so on, of items missing from Hallrule. I later found out that the Police had informed Jacquelin about this stolen plaque. That must have given her another fright. She had done nothing about it and, of course and very revealingly, never breathed a word of it to anyone. I never did follow this up more which I later regretted.

38

THE MACTAGGART SQUATTERS

I had a Meeting with a lawyer called Currie of the law firm RB Anderson of Jedburgh on Tuesday 21st January 1997 about obtaining the correspondence that my Father had with Anderson in 1962 and 1963 about ways and means of saving the Estates for an Usher future. Currie appeared helpful.

I then told him about my being usurped in Hallrule Farm by Mrs Mactaggart and the filthy role that his fellow Jedburgh lawyer, David Sturrock of Turnbull Simpson and Sturrock, just a few doors away, had played in it. Currie, unusually for a lawyer, now let a very large cat out of the bag. He told me that Sturrock was Mrs Mactaggart's lawyer. So that was why Brodies had got Sturrock to be Peter's secret Curator in December, as already narrated.

On 20th March 1997 I contacted Currie again in connection with a letter which I had drafted for him to write to Mrs Mactaggart on my behalf. This letter formally put Mrs Mactaggart on Notice that her father, Clive, had broken the Gentleman's Agreement he had with my Father under the terms of which he should have got out of the farm in 1973 in my favour and therefore that I would like to meet her, her Mother Valerie, her sons and her lawyer with a view to coming to an amicable settlement on the matter. Mr Currie then informed me that an earlier letter from me to Mrs Mactaggart, 'had probably caused some internal politics to take place, leading them to switch from Sturrock to Purdoms, lawyers of Hawick.' Purdoms had answered on behalf of Mrs Mactaggart to my earlier letter. Of course I now realized why Mrs Mactaggart had not used Sturrock to reply to me: She knew that Sturrock had been Peter's first Curator and that he had done a hatchet-job on us to defeat Johnny's objection to her continuing to squat on Hallrule farm. Hence her using Purdoms to conceal that the egregious Sturrock was her official lawyer.

Having obtained Purdom's letter in reply to Currie's letter I decided that I would handle all the correspondence with Mrs Mactaggart and Purdoms myself from now on. I wrote two further letters to Mrs Mactaggart, neither of which she answered herself, but got Purdoms to do so for her. That in itself told me a lot. Purdoms simply would not give me an unambiguous answer to my request for a meeting. I therefore gave them the deadline of the 3rd of April to respond unambiguously whether they would agree to a meeting or not, failing which I would make public the proofs of the existence of the Gentleman's Agreement and the various correspondence in which Clive had agreed to vacate the farm in 1983 in Johnny's favour.

They did not meet my terms. I therefore sent a 36 page Pack on the subject to 30 families in the Borders who knew both the Mactaggarts and ourselves on the 26th of May 1997. The pack included a letter outlining the history of this particular fraud. I also sent a slightly modified pack to Mrs Mataggart, and to Purdoms. I did not mince my words in informing the 30 families of the fraud and asked for their moral support. In my covering letter to Mrs Mactaggart I asked her to vacate the farm with her family at Michaelmas (November) 1997 and leave it in good order for me to take over. I also wrote a separate letter to her husband at the same time in which I told him that I did not hold him or his sons responsible for their occupying Hallrule farm and to use his influence on his wife to honour the Gentleman's Agreement by vacating the farm in November.

As luck would have it I met the egregious Mrs Mactaggart in the High Street of Jedburgh one day not long after I had sent the letters out. She flashed me her usual insincere smile but said nothing and hurried past me. I turned and shouted after her in a voice loud enough to be heard by the many people in the street that day : 'When are you going to get out of Hallrule farm. You have no rights there or anywhere else in Rulewater', for everyone in the street to hear. She half turned round, face agape, bobbed twice as though someone had hit her in the solar plexus, and then fled up the street without a word! The people who witnessed and heard this 'friendly' episode simply stood there, unsure how to react. But I had made my point in public. Had she been in Hallrule farm lawfully she would have had every right to take legal action against me for that. Such are the tribulations of people who betray their families! I spread this episode far and wide and continue to do so to this day.

On 28th May 1997 Mr Mactaggart phoned me. He asked me 'What are you trying to achieve'? I told him that it was quite evident in my letter to him and the rest of his family: 'You must get out of the farm as per my letter.' He then lied that we had never been interested in the Wells Estate. This was simply standing the truth on its head. I repudiated him and told him that he knew that what he had just said was a lie. He then asked me: 'What are you hankering after'? I told him that I hankered after what was rightfully mine, Hallrule farm, out of which I had been cheated by his father-in-law and further if he had an ounce of decency he would remove himself and his family out of Rulewater forthwith. He responded to this by saying that if I said anything further bad about Clive he would 'run his sword through me,' accompanied by a nervous laugh. I told him he was welcome to try but that he would undoubtedly get the worst of it. He had no immediate answer to this. I then told him that he was fully aware he and his family had no right whatever to be living at Hallrule farm and the same applied to all the other Estate properties that his father-in-law, Clive, had occupied by fraudulent means. His answer to this was very revealing: 'You can't sue a dead man. You should sue the lawyers.' No attempt whatever to refute my charge of Clive's fraud. And no more 'sword talk' either. As far as I was concerned this was a tacit admission by Mactaggart that he and his family had no right to any of the properties they presently occupied in Rulewater. I then told him that I would sue the lawyers and his family as well if they did not get out of the farm. He then hung up on me and that was that.

A few people responded to the packs and gave me their moral support but not on the scale I expected, which I found somewhat disheartening. But I soon got over it and put it down to the same old reasons; fear of getting involved is a natural human trait. Until the crocodile got *them* that is; at which point they would scream for help only to discover, to their horror, that no one would lift a finger to help them escape the terrible beast. For the record, I never received any response from any of the Mactaggarts. That figured alright. In essence the Mactaggarts' blanket refusal to accord me the courtesy of a reply was a convincing admission that they knew that their presence on our beautiful Wells Estate was a consequence of fraud by Clive and Brodies, with Gertrude's acquiesence, and their own refusal to accept that their new-found wealth was based on it

I therefore decided that the best way to get the Mactaggarts out of Hallrule farm and Rulewater was to provoke them into suing me for defamation. To this end I told lots of people that the Mactaggarts were squatters on all the properties they occupied in Rulewater and, as such, should be hounded out of the valley. Also that they were swindlers and so on. I have done this from that time to the present day. Their reactions ranged from a knowing wink to incredulity and shock. I doubt that a single person disbelieved me because almost no one defended them. But ne'er a squawk from the squatting Mactaggarts despite their having ample funds to take legal action. They kept the silence of the guilty.

I therefore ask all the readers of this book who know, however remotely, the Mactaggarts and their offspring to tell them, in no uncertain terms, to immediately remove themselves from all the properties on which they are presently squatting on what used to be the Wells Estate for the benefit of the Usher family of Norton and Wells.

39

I REPORT BRODIES TO THE LAW SOCIETY OF SCOTLAND

In March 1997 I made enquiries about various ways in which I could fund suing Brodies and discovered that the only practical way was going to be if I could find a lawyer to take the case on a No Win No Fee basis. Strange though it may seem to the reader I at the time believed that I would not have much trouble finding one. Ultimately I contacted about forty different firms of Lawyers and to my great chagrin not one of them was prepared to take the case on.

I then contacted the Law Society to inquire how to lay a complaint against Brodies. I dealt with a Mr Philp who appeared to be quite competent and a decent fellow. I faxed my list of complaints about Brodies to the law society on the 18th March 1997.

On 10th June I had a meeting with a retired Army Officer friend who now had a foot in the legal profession. He took great pains to obtain as much of the picture as any person could reasonably have been able to do given the complexity of the whole foul business. He then approached a firm of Glasgow Lawyers called Digby Brown with whom he was associated.

He reported back to me on 18th June, stating that Digby Brown believed there may well be a good case, but that they expected Brodies to admit nothing. However an 'enormous amount of expensive research would have to be done,' and that there would be little prospect of a settlement unless Johnny and I could convince Brodies' Insurers that we were prepared to spend a very large sum of money in bringing the case. To this end Digby Brown wanted £10,000 as a minimum retainer, but that this retainer would not even cover the issuing of proceedings.

This course of action was plainly impossible for Johnny and me and therefore of no use whatever.. We were in danger of being buried alive. I recalled the warning a guest at a wedding had given me in 1996. When he was younger he'd had some sort of *contretemps* over a family farm and, getting nowhere, had given up and decided to become a lawyer himself He entreated me, for the sake of my wellbeing, to give up immediately as the

Scottish Legal system would obstruct me, and ultimately 'crush' me if I persisted in pursuing Brodies. I thanked him for his concern but told him that I was duty- bound to fight on.

At much the same time as this Digby Brown's £10,000 retainer nonsense things had been 'happening' on the Law Society front. No progress of course, just mysterious reactions, misconceptions, misinformation and confusion. Much of which I should have by now expected, but somehow didn't.

For example by letter dated 16th April 1997 a Philip Yelland of the Law Society attributed to me a wish that I wanted to send a letter to Brodies, a wish I had never expressed. This was an early example of the Law Society prescribing and diverting the discourse in an attempt to confuse and discourage me. The rest of it indicated that Yelland had little or no idea of my Complaints. I wrote to Mr Philp, not a lawyer, who was the only chap I could get any sense from at the Law Society on 19th April informing him that Yelland appeared to be confused and would he please now investigate my complaints. Of course Yelland was not a bit confused

I soon realized that the Law Society was not acting in good faith. I therefore wrote a letter dated 21st May stating: 'I do not now hold out much hope that any form of justice will be forthcoming from your Society. I hope that I am proved wrong. Notwithstanding this I still require the Society to carry on with your investigations into Brodies.'

Yelland now withdrew from handling my complaints and a Mrs Birnie replaced him. More correspondence of a confusing, procedural and generally meaningless nature followed over the next month or so. On 3rd July Mrs Birnie informed me that she would be leaving the Society the very next day and that a Mrs Gurney would be taking over from her. I therefore contacted Mrs Gurney straightaway, making it crystal clear that I was most unhappy at the manner in which the Law Society had handled my Complaints against Brodies to date. She quickly moved to mollify me and suggested that we meet. Neither Yelland or Mrs Birnie had ever suggested a meeting so this augured well. I met her on 11th July 1997 at the Law Society offices in Edinburgh. Seeing my extreme displeasure she said, 'This is big, isn't it?' I assured her it was very, very big and the implications were also very, very big. She became animated, showing genuine sympathy and desire to investigate thoroughly. Cheered, I recovered my equilibrium and we had a good productive meeting in which we covered more ground than I could have hoped for. I slowly came to trust Mrs Gurney to the point where on 15th August I gave her confidential documentary evidence of a very damning nature.

By the end of September, however, we had still not agreed what they called the 'Heads of Complaint.' Still I felt that Mrs Gurney meant business, was on my side, and was morally a good person. But law and morals are not compatible - the root cause of the cancer which lies deep within the system of Scottish Law. Morals and the law should be *made* compatible.

On 9th October I faxed Mrs Gurney and re-inforced my earlier requests for confidentiality with regard to the documentary evidence I had handed to her. She replied next day assuring me that all correspondence was safe 'within her file' and only she had the key to the drawer where she kept it.

On 27th November Mrs Gurney informed me in writing that she was leaving the Law Society - and that a Mrs Rhona Bradbury would be taking over.

On 10th December she wrote again and informed me of the very bad news that Yelland would now be taking over my file from her and not, as she had been told, Mrs Bradbury. This was the worst possible news, for obvious reasons. I therefore replied on 13th December1997 that Yelland taking over from her did not fill me with delight at all and that I would only accept his takeover on a 'no prejudice basis.' I also asked her for a list of all the documentary evidence I had sent her and for her to return it all to me because I did not want it to fall into Yelland's leprous hands. For whatever reason she never sent me the list and nor did she return the evidence although I believe she meant to. Most probably she was forbidden from doing so by Yelland. So much for her trusting that it would not fall into his hands.

Had she acted in good faith? I was certain she had. The most likely reason for her departure was that the Law Society fired her when they discovered that she was conducting herself in a *bona-fide* manner in connection with my Complaints. However when I tackled her about her leaving so suddenly she told me that she was leaving for another job of her own free will. I doubted that very much and suspected that she had become aware that the Law Society was not acting in good faith in connection with my and other Complaints and had decided that she wanted no further part of it and had

Phillip Yelland 'leprous hands'. The Executioner-in-Chief for The Law Society of Scotland

therefore resigned, as any decent person would. Sometime later I surmised that a near full page article in the *Sunday Times* of 16th November 1997 on my fight for justice for my family was another likely reason for the big nobs of the Law Society taking the investigation away from her; and that she had objected and then either resigned or had been sacked. If so, thank you Mrs Gurney, you were the only decent person I ever came across at the Law Society and you appear to have paid the price. I have no doubt at all that you had no regrets in leaving that Crime Protection Syndicate.

On 10th January 1998 I asked Yelland for the list by letter. He replied on 28th January acknowledging my letter but did not send me the list. I therefore faxed him the next day stating that I would if necessary come to the Law Society and collect all my documentary evidence. His next letter of 3rd February acknowledged my fax but made no mention of my collecting the documentary evidence. I asked him again on 19th February but received no response. I then realised that all this correspondence was fruitless as Yelland would have made copies of it all and then passed them onto Brodies. I had lost yet again.

On 27th March out of the blue Yelland rang me. Brodies had agreed to make some further paperwork and documents available to him and that he regarded this as a breakthrough. Was I prepared come in and look at them. Also that Brodies would be giving him a further submission on Monday the 30th replying to my rebuttal of their earlier 141 page submission of November 1997 - for which they might well have charged the Executry to produce . I replied that of course I would come in to see them. He then told me that he would fax them to me straightaway and asked me to ring him once I had perused them.

'Curious, he has never contacted me before like this,' I thought. His enthusiasm was somehow hollow. Of course, and as always in such situations, I gave no clue as to my doubts and feigned great enthusiasm myself. He was very much 'Yessir, No Sir, Three bags full Sir', for the first time ever.

By 3rd April 1998 no fax had arrived. I therefore asked him in writing what the delay was. On 9th April, nearly two weeks later, he rang at 3.20pm. He now made no mention at all of the papers and documents that he had said he would fax me 'straightaway' but stated that he had received 'another letter' from Brodies. He then went on to say: 'I understand that a fax has been sent to Sir John for whom you act as Attorney seeking confirmation of certain matters.' He did not state who had sent this fax to Johnny and what the matters were that required confirmation. All very cryptic and indicating, yet again, that something was brewing. When he had finished his crypto-babble and hung up I immediately contacted Johnny by phone to find out what the fax was about. Johnny told me that he had not received any fax from anyone in Scotland. So either Brodies or Yelland or more likely both of them had lied, yet again. I told Johnny that something was brewing and to contact me the minute he heard from either Yelland or Brodies. Of course I faxed Yelland immediately for an explanation as to why Johnny had not received the papers yet as per his statement to me on the phone on the same day. By way of an answer Yelland wrote to me on 17th April that he was going on holiday and would answer me on his return. However later that day Johnny phoned me to say that he had now received a fax from Brodies which he would immediately fax through to me.

In this fax Brodies threatened to remove Johnny as Executor if he did not agree with their way of doing things. Johnny and I were outraged. He, and I as his agent, had done our best to do that which every *bona-fide* Executor was duty-bound to do, namely to ingather the Estate of the Deceased person and act in the interests of the beneficiaries. But Brodies and Jacquelin had stopped us from doing so at every turn. And here Brodies now threatened to deprive Johnny of his Executorship. It was beyond belief and another example of Brodies doing as they pleased using Jacquelin, their 'in our back pocket' thieving executrix, as their rubber stamp.

We realised that this latest ploy meant that Brodies and the Law Society knew that we had them trapped and had decided their best way out was to simply strip Johnny of his Executorship, thereby neutering me. They were also aware that Johnny had been diagnosed as suffering from cancer of the prostate gland some months previously and had been told to avoid all stress by his Doctor. To this end, and at Johnny's request, I had been making inquiries about my replacing him as Executor, although I did not see why this had to be done as I had already been functioning as Executor in his place and stead under a Power of Attorney from him for the last two years. His South African lawyer, Ewing, had written to Brodies for clarification on Johnny resigning and my replacing him as Executor and Brodies had misled him by stating that this was not possible. I had then approached the Sheriff Court in Jedburgh on the matter and they told me that the Law Society was the place to find out about this. I asked the Law Society who in turn told me that the Accountant of Court were the people to consult. I did so. They in turn referred me to the Court of Session. I therefore asked the Court of Session and lo and behold they in turn referred me back to the Jedburgh Sheriff Court; where I had started on the wild goose chase.

Sometime later I became aware that if an Executor fell ill and was unable to act all they had to do was to appoint anyone they wanted to replace them as Executor. The simplest thing in the world. I then realised why Brodies had moved so quickly to strip Johnny of his Executorship: To stop him doing exactly that. I did not realise at the time that of course neither Brodies or Jacqueline, either singly or jointly, had any power to strip Johnny of his executorship. Brodies threat was therefore an empty and illegal one. Of course with Johnny stricken with cancer, I did not want to bother him too much, but I had to because events would not wait. Brodies saw to that.

On 14th April 1998 Yelland answered my earlier faxes in connection with why he had not sent me the new papers and documentation, about which he had put on such a show of contrived excitement, as per our telephone talk of 27th March. He now simply denied that he had ever told me that I could see these papers and documentation. In an attempt to make his totally mendacious denial more plausible he stated that 'one of the partners in Messrs Brodies dealing with this matter was on annual leave and did not wish to dispatch the letter to you until *he* had seen it.' All just a pack of misleading twaddle. In the event neither Yelland or Brodies ever did send me those papers and documents.

It was at this point that I fully realized the potency of the 'holiday' device which Brodies, the Law Society and others in the Scottish legal system had already repeatedly used on me: Whenever I had caught them out lying or had them in a corner, which by now had been quite often, another person would respond stating that Stevens, or Houldsworth or Yelland or whoever else I had caught out 'were now on holiday' and would not be back for X number of days or weeks. This device had the effect of taking the immediate heat out of the situation and gave them time to think out new stratagems to get themselves out of the embarrassing/awkward situations into which I had repeatedly forced them. And the new person would 'accidently/on purpose misunderstand/misinterpret' the situation and so cause further confusion. Time would then pass and, if necessary, some new 'crisis' would be manufactured to deflect attention even further away from the original serious issues on which I had caught them out. Neat and nasty.

It was only much later that I realised I should never have told Brodies about Johnny's cancer. I should have had him move fast to appoint me as Executor in his place on the grounds that his cancer made it impossible for him to carry out his Executorship. If this had been done it would have been a *fait compli* which Brodies had to accept. This would have seen Mrs Wolfe-Murray and myself as Executors instead of the undesirable situation of Mrs Wolfe-Murray remaining as the lone Executor. This situation would have made it much more difficult for Brodies to continue their perverting of the Executry as and when they chose. I would have opposed them all the way, resulting in a 50/50 split with Mrs Wolfe-Murray backing Brodies' position.

There would, besides, have been other advantages for me as an Executor. Firstly, I would have been in a much stronger position to obtain access to the Estate Records at Brodies' and various other places such as Accountants, HM Revenue, the Scottish Courts and so on. Secondly I would have discovered many more document and records than I eventually actually did; and then only years later. All this combined would also have been much to the benefit of the ultimate Beneficiaries of the remains of the Estates. A final advantage of actually being an Executor would have been that I would have had greater credibility with the media at large."

40

A MINE OF INFORMATION

In the Accounts which I'd obtained from the Accountant of Court were various names of Housekeepers and staff who had worked at Hallrule over the decades. I determined to contact one of them in the hope that I might get some useful information. I therefore made inquiry amongst ex-Estate staff and was recommended to consult one particular Housekeeper who had worked at Hallrule as a Housekeeper-cum-Companion for Gertrude from about 1975 to 1984. Her name was Mrs Darnell. I traced her to Portobello, near Edinburgh. She was delighted to meet Gillian and myself for a talk. We had this meeting at her home on 16th October 1997. She was a sprightly lady, 80 plus years young, with a sparkle in her eye. We both took to her straightaway.

She could not have been more helpful and forthcoming. We discovered that she was a qualified Nurse. The first thing she told us was that she had been employed under false pretences by the Estate Manager. That figured alright. He had not told her that Peter and Robert were Downs Syndrome and Mentally Incapacitated. She only discovered this, to her horror, when she arrived at Hallrule. However as she had already given up her previous post there was no turning back.

In 1998 I discovered that this was not the first time that this had occurred: I was told that Gertrude used to advertise for nannies in Britain in the 1930s and 40s to look after 'the children' Peter and Robert, in Argentina. When these nannies arrived in Argentina they were surprised and horrified to discover that 'the children' were hardly children anymore and were Downs Syndrome and Mentally Incapacitated to boot. As an Argentinian, why didn't Gertrude employ Argentinian nannies the reader may well ask? The answer to that was her social climbing proclivities: much more prestigious to have a British nanny in Argentina than an Argentinian one. Johnny and myself always had an African nanny each in Tanganyika as did the vast majority of the Europeans livng there. Gertrude was a good example of the old saying: 'Give a peasant a horse and watch it ridden to hell!' Poor horse.

Mrs Darnell had not taken to the Estate Manager from the moment she met him. Nor had she taken to Gertrude, at the beginning, but in time grew to 'some fondness' of her. She went on to say that Gertrude guarded the Contents of Hallrule very carefully indeed. To this end she taught Peter to snoop on people, including her, Mrs Darnell. Peter often snooped and became something of an expert at it. I also imagine he quite enjoyed it because it gave him something to do. Gertrude did not at all trust her niece, Mrs Blamey, and encouraged Peter to lurk behind the curtains and snoop. One of Mrs Blamey's tasks was to look after Peter: *the watcher being watched by the watched.* This made me smile. But how interesting that Gertrude did not trust her niece, Mrs Blamey. That indicated that her whole family was not to be trusted and not just Mrs Blamey. It takes a thief to know a thief. She also told us that a Hawick Doctor had referred to the Estate Manager as 'the meanest man in the district.'

Mrs Darnell then went on to tell us that whenever our existence in South Africa was mentioned by the few visitors who came to Hallrule we were always marginalized as of no consequence by Gertrude, by Clive, and by Valerie too if all they happened to be present, the subject being quickly changed. She had never understood this and had never accepted it because she had always heard a different story about us from the local people. Also that my Father was easily the most popular and well thought-of between himself, Stuart, and Clive and much-liked by people of all walks of life in the area. She had eventually concluded that jealousy was the cause. She then told us that Gertrude, Clive, Valerie, and the Estate Manager were regarded as twisters and self-seekers by the local people, and certainly by herself. Of course Gillian and I quite agreed with her on that and told her that this was exactly why we were sitting in her room that day.

She then said that it was so sad that *these* 'Ushers' had got control of our family's affairs because she had always heard the most wonderful things about our family in the Edinburgh area.

I was anxious to get things into perspective for her about our family at Wells. To this end I told her that the only Usher of our branch of the family who was an out and out crook was Clive and that his five elder brothers were decent, honourable men. In this regard I explained that John, the eldest, drank too much but was otherwise well intentioned. Ronald, the second son had lived a relatively successful life but died young. Stuart, the third son had the misfortune to marry Gertrude who bore him Peter and Robert and he had become embittered by their condition. Alexander, the fourth son had been killed in the War, but was a highly thought of man. Then my Father, the fifth son whom she had already covered. Then Clive, the crook; the runt of the litter.

I also told her that the Estate Factor was *not* a member of our family of Norton and Wells. She was amazed about this because he had always told her that he was a 'cousin'. I instantly put her right on that by telling her that the only connection he had to our family was an Usher, a distant relative, who was born in 1738. Hardly a cousin.

She had also often thought it odd that the Estates had been allowed to go to Peter in the first place. I explained how that had happened and how my Father had fought it and how it had eventually killed him and how shocked many people in the Borders had been when it happened.

She then let another rather interesting cat out to prowl: one night Gertrude's niece, Alice Blamey and a grand-niece of hers, who was visiting from London, had invited Mrs. Darnell to join them in 'finishing' Gertrude off by giving her an overdose! Mrs. Darnell had been utterly horrified at the invitation and immediately refused to have anything to do with it. Of course Gillian and I were totally flabbergasted at this. It had never occurred to me that Mrs Blamey would ever contemplate murder because she did not appear to be that type at all. The opposite in fact because she was quite shy and retiring and had always appeared, to me at least, a decent person. With Mrs Darnell refusing to join them Mrs Blamey and the grand-niece dropped the plan. Gertrude had a lot to thank Mrs Darnell for scotching what might have been her murder that night. I now wish I had asked her more about it.

I then gave Mrs Darnell more detail of all the crookery that we had discovered in connection with the Estates and Peter and Robert's affairs and that Gertie, Clive, the Estate Manager and Brodies had been up to their eyeballs in defrauding our family for decades. She wasn't a bit surprised, but was dismayed at the extent of the damage already done and now the Estates having been sold. She wished us all the luck in the world in getting matters sorted out.

Gillian and I were over the moon about our meeting with Mrs Darnell. It was also a very pleasant change to have met someone who gave spontaneous answers instead of the all the bum shifting ambiguities, averted eyes and evasions of just about everyone else we had met so far. She was marvellous. The information she gave us that day vindicated our position and would be very useful in the future.

On the way home I thought more about the contemplated murder of Gertrude. There would have been some moral justification for giving Gertrude an overdose if she had been in great pain and suffering and had asked Alice Blamey and the grand niece for the overdose. But Mrs Darnell would have told us if that had been the case, but she hadn't. On top of that Gertrude had been well enough to quarrel with Johnny on his 1982 trip when he had told her that it was her duty to do what she could to secure the Estates for an Usher future. Johnny had made no mention to me of Gertrude being unwell, suffering, being in pain, or anything of that nature. He certainly would have heard of it during the course of his visit if she had been. So why would Mrs Blamey and her grand niece want to do away with Gertrude? There had to be something really powerful motivating them.

One explanation might have been that Gertrude had told them that she had left the Contents to them in some or equal shares? This fitted in nicely with Gertrude's statement in the early 1980s that she had left half the contents to Mrs Blamey, as earlier narrated. And they, Mrs Blamey and the grand-niece, were impatient to get them while we were still in South Africa. At that time Mrs Blamey would have been well aware of Johnny's efforts in 1982 to save the Estates and his intention to return to Scotland and his quarrel with Gertrude.

But why invite Mrs Darnell to join them? They must have known that she would be very unlikely to agree to such a thing and might even spill the beans to Gertrude. This would have been bye-bye to the Contents as far as they were concerned and possibly have landed them in gaol as well. It remains a mystery to me to this day. The only ones who know about this now, I think, are Mrs Darnell, Gillian, myself, Mrs Blamey and the grand-niece whose identity I never discovered.

In November I contacted the media about doing an in depth investigation into the fraud. By now I had realised that the more publicity the fraud got the worse for Brodies and their acolytes and the better for us. The upshot was my being visited by a journalist called Jenny Shields. I filled her in as to what had happened and took her on a tour of what had been the Estate. She was sympathetic to me, and us as a family, at what had happened. The result was a full page article in the Sunday Times of 16th November 1997.

This was the first of many media features and articles on my fight back over the next six years. These included printed media and radio broadcasts. My campaign against Brodies even made it into America with Harpers Magazine publishing a feature on it. Eventually Britain's Channel Four Television made a 'Cutting Edge' Documentary in 2001 on my fight . In some ways Channel Four made me look a bit of an idiot in the Documenntary, but not entirely so. As you can imagine I did not like this but bore it because the core message of Brodies and their pals being fraudsters did go out to some degree at least. I was also confident that the vast majority who read the articles and features and heard and saw the broadcasts would make allowance for me being portrayed as a bit of an idiot by the media as just typical of the media. I cover this Documentary in more detail later in this book.

In January 1998 I reported Brodies to the Police because of the refusal of the legal fraternity to assist me to bring their fellow lawyers Brodies to account. On 15th January 1998 Chief Inspector Downey of the Hawick Police visited me at my home with a Policewoman. I gave them a letter asking them to investigate five different acts of either theft or fraud and the relevant corroborating documentation, to keep things simple for a start. They were both helpful and polite and appeared to accept that there was a case to answer.

On 25th January, they came to my home and, to my extreme disappointment, returned the documentation and informed me that the Police now required me to furnish them with proof that Peter and Robert had in fact *owned* the Estates from which the particular assets were missing. As you can imagine I was dumb-founded. With all the trouble I had already been through with Brodies there was no earthly hope of my being able to convince them of that - for the very straightforward reason that Peter and Robert had never *owned* the Estates. I soon realised that this request was just another device to justify the Police in taking no action. I told Chief Inspector Downey and his assistant that this was absurd. He then told me that he had read all the documentation I had given him and thought it a shocking business, 'Plenty of skullduggery there,' were the words he used. But he re-iterated that the Police could do nothing about the matter unless I proved that Peter and Robert had owned the Estates. Brodies fraud was a piece of genius - their double-dealing and twisting meant that the police believed they were unable even to investigate a few relatively straightforward examples of fraud and straightforward theft *irrespective* of who the real owner was.

In a final effort to get them to do something I warned them that if I could not get anyone to do anything about it I would be obliged to take the Law into my own hands. Chief Inspector Downey just laughed and told me, 'I didn't hear you say that.' And off they went.

Channel Four screened their 'Cutting Edge' documentary 'The Fall of the House of Usher' in 2001

41

I CEASE MY ATTEMPTS TO OBTAIN A LAWYER

For a large part of 1997 and well into 1998 I contacted more than forty law firms all over Scotland to take on the Executry's case or, failing that, to act for me personally on a no win no fee basis. Alas to no avail, as already narrated. I also tried various bodies like the Scottish Consumer Council and the Citizen's Advice Bureau. These bodies were sympathetic, but that is all. 'We can't get involved, you have to find a lawyer yourself,' was the never-ending refrain.

Eventually I was warned by an acquaintance who had operated on the periphery of the legal profession that I should not approach any more lawyers because the more often I was turned down the less chance I had of getting one. My best hope was to get one by word of mouth, through contacts. I thought this sound advice and therefore ceased my lawyer hunting.

Before ceasing my hunt I had however had contact with a David Lyle of David A Lyle and Company of Glasgow, Solicitors in the Supreme Courts. I sent him extensive documentary evidence of the fraud. Lyle was quite helpful in his own way, but declined to act for me on the grounds that the case was 'outwith my league,' as he put it. We met in Edinburgh on 7th May 1998 and visited the National Archives to see if we could find more dispositions of Trust property. As so often in these cases we did not have much success. He advised me in writing that any lawyer I got should have Indemnity Insurance far in excess of the mandatory £1 million due to the potential size and risks of the case.

On 15th April 1998 I succeeded in getting an Advocate to take my case on a no-win no fee basis. I was absolutely delighted and now assumed, because I had an Advocate, getting a lawyer would be a doddle. How wrong my assumption proved to be. Try as I might I simply could not get one. And I was not allowed to meet or even speak to this Advocate myself - this could only be done through an accursed lawyer. Not being allowed to meet and speak with him meant that I could not ascertain the 'cut of his jib'. This was another example of the farce that parades itself as the Scottish Legal system.

On 30th April I wrote to the Police again informing them that I did not accept their previous position and would they now please investigate the various thefts and frauds. On the 5th of May 1998 the Temporary Det Chief Inspector wrote to me stating that a DS Cunningham would deal with the case. By letter dated the 7th of May 1998, a C/I Scott wrote stating that the CID 'considers that this is essentially a civil matter and would strongly advise me to consult a lawyer.' However I only received this letter on the 15th of May 1998 which is what usually happened when I had someone rattled. I therefore immediately and on that same day repudiated his suggestion by letter and explained yet again the impossibility of getting a lawyer and asked him to get on with the investigation. On the 21st of May 1998 I got a letter from someone called Taylor of the Hawick Police who now informed me that Det Chief Insp Mitchell had been put onto the case. I do not know what happened to Cunningham. and never heard of him again.

In the event Deputy Chief Inspector Mitchell arrived at my home with another officer on that same day the 21st of May 1998. Mitchell was also shocked at the evidence and now told me a different story to the one from Scott. He informed me that the case fell in both the criminal and civil fields and, that being the case, the Police could not pursue it unless I had a lawyer with whom the Police could work. I, yet again, told him that I simply could not get a lawyer, try as I might. They sympathised, and genuinely as far as I was concerned, but re-iterated that the Police could do nothing about it unless I got a lawyer and even then there was no guarantee. This however was an entirely different reason to the one that CI Downey had given me in January, namely that I had to prove that Peter and Robert were the successive owners of the Estates. That was something which might prove useful in the future. I then decided on a new course of action and informed the Police to do nothing further on the case until further notice.

On 3rd June 1998 I embarked on my new course of action which entailed my approaching both the Procurator Fiscal for Roxburghshire and the Sheriff's office for the Sheriffdom of the Lothians & Borders in Jedburgh. I thought if I showed this Procurator just some of the most 'open and shut' documentary evidence of the fraud he would be bound to do something about it. I therefore made an appointment to meet him 3.00pm on 3rd June. He turned out to be a Mr Graham Fraser. He took a long statement from me. When I had finished he told me that it certainly appeared to be a most shocking state of affairs and quite understood my concern that something should be done about it. I then gave him hundreds of pages of documentary evidence and correspondence on some aspects of the fraud. He told me that he would peruse them and come back to me as soon as possible. For a moment I thought: 'At last I might be getting somewhere,, as he appeared to be genuinely concerned. But I had been down this road before, so kept my feet firmly on the ground.

He responded on the 17th of June 1998 with a long letter. It was the usual put-down. He declined to ask the Police to prosecute the matter on the grounds of, *inter-alia*, the passage of time and that he,

> '. . .was not persuaded that any of the items can be regarded as criminal by nature. While it may be argued that some of these items displayed a severe degree of mismanagement and that the Estate Manager may well have benefitted from his own mismanagement as a result. . . [and while] the theft of sundry items from Hallrule may well be dishonest the fact that the dates on which the items went missing and the identities of those who took them cannot be ascertained pose fundamental difficulties to any possibility of a criminal prosecution in relation to them.'

This statement alone was just nonsensical. Since when had theft become 'may well be dishonest'? Theft *is* dishonest, full stop. And he was a lawyer! And then his statement about the Estate Manager benefitting from his own mismanagement was simply not credible. In essence that meant one way of making money in Scotland is to steal from someone for whom you are meant to be managing in the knowledge that the Scottish Legal system would class this only as 'mismanagement'. It therefore is a fact that Procurator Fiscal, Graham Fraser, refused to institute a Police investigation based on the perfectly clear documentary evidence of theft and fraud that I gave him.

Of course this worked me up no end. I therefore repudiated his letter and its conclusions on the 21st of June 1998 on the grounds that it was manifestly impossible for him to have come to his conclusions in good faith.

Graham Fraser
Procurator-Fiscal:
'the theft of sundry items from Hallrule may well be dishonest. . .'

Does this mean the theft of sundry items may well be honest?

There then followed more correspondence between us of an unsatisfactory nature which did not bring me any closer to any action being taken on the matter. Again I had come up against a brick wall — the same one that had blocked me all the way thus far.

Concurrent with the wild goose chase which the Procurator Fiscal had led me I was receiving the same treatment from the Sheriff's Office in Jedburgh. This commenced with a letter from myself to the Sheriff Court at Jedburgh on the 14th of May 1998. No reply. I wrote again on the 18th of May asking for a reply to both my letters. I also visited the Sheriff's Offices on that day to find out how to raise a criminal action on behalf of the Executry and myself personally against Brodies and other parties. The Sheriff Clerk, Ian Williamson, informed me that I, by Scots law, would not be allowed to raise a criminal action. I had to get a lawyer to do that for me. I told him that I couldn't get one. He had no answer to that and took refuge in incanting that he could not offer me legal advice. But I had not asked him for *any* legal advice. Williamson eventually wrote to me on the 1st of June 1998 as follows: 'I would strongly advise you to consult a solicitor.' And 'the services of an Edinburgh Solicitor (note the capital S!) and an Advocate would almost certainly be necessary.' And further useless 'advice', all of which, in practice, guaranteed that my case never got to Court.

By this time Johnny had been told to resign as Executor by his doctor on the grounds of his prostate cancer. I therefore tried to find out from the Sheriff Court what the procedure was for me to replace him as Executor by letter dated the 22nd of June 1998. Williamson replied on 24th of June that I should get legal advice on this or just leave the one executor in place to complete the affairs of the executry. This would, of course, not be in the interests of the Executry at all because it would leave the weeding, stealing, crime concealing, Brodies controlled Jacquelin as the sole remaining Executor. I very nearly told Williamson what I thought of him, but something in his manner made me desist; the same feeling I'd had with Walker!

Actually it was Williamson who had set me off on the circular wild goose chase about replacing Johnny as Executor, which I have already narrated. That was just another example of how effective the Scottish Legal system is in protecting crooked lawyers like Brodies.

For a very pleasant change this episode had a feliticious sequel some years later. In 2006 I met Williamson in the Jedburgh pub I often frequented on Sunday afternoons. I had never seen him there before and, remembering the unsatisfactory nature of my dealings with him in 1998, I returned his greeting somewhat coolly. He responded warmly and, without further ado, told me that he absolutely agreed with my views, which by then were widely known in Scotland, on Scottish lawyers and the Scottish legal system in general; that it was utterly corrupt, self serving and stank to high heaven! I was delighted. So my feeling about him had been vindicated and I was glad that I had not gone for him in my earlier dealings with him. He apologised for the way he had treated me but said he was forced to do so, and had not liked it at all. I then said I regarded the Scottish legal system as infested with vermin and God help anyone who went to it for justice. He again agreed whole-heartedly and told me that he'd suffered a nervous breakdown because of the stress of working in such a dishonest system and how glad he was now to be out of it. A decent man, but one who had paid the price for being decent in a thoroughly indecent system.

So I was snookered again. There seemed to be absolutely no way to prosecute Brodies and their associates for the fraud. Ultimately the Crown Office in Edinburgh was responsible for this. This was hardly surprising because it also was *infested* with crooked lawyers. What else could I do?

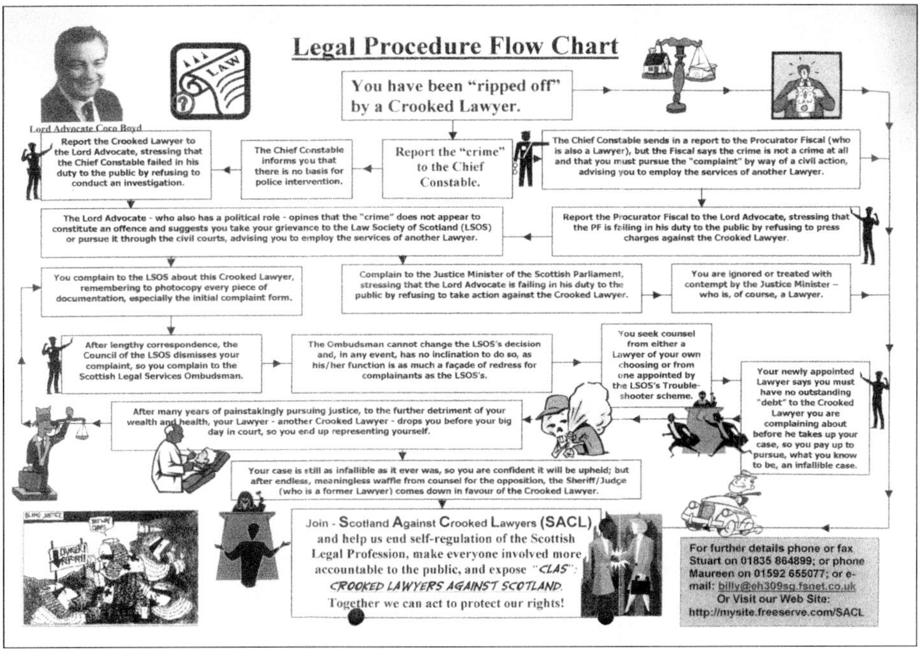

Legal Procedure Flow Chart constructed by 'Scotland Against Crooked Lawyers'

42

THE DEATH OF JOHNNY

On 24th June 1998 I decided to do some more research on Stuart's Will - the Will which the lawyers had informed us 'could not be found' after Uncle Stuart's death in 1962 but which now had, according to Brodies all of a sudden made an appearance in support of their claims in connection with Gertrude's 'ownership' of them.

I rang the National Archives of Scotland on this day and was put through to a Mr Shaw who was in a senior position in connection with Wills and an expert in the historical section. Mr Shaw was very helpful. I told him that Stuart's Will was not signed and that I had the copies of Sir John Usher's Will (d 1951) and of Clive's Will (d 1982) both of which *were* signed. Could he give an explanation as to how an unsigned Will could have been accepted for registration at the National Archives? He could not and told me that Wills kept at the NAS had to be properly signed *and* witnessed before they were accepted for registration. He then told me that he would consult a colleague on this and ring me back. He was as good as his word and told me that the colleague agreed with his views on the matter and that Stuart's Will not being signed was a mystery.

At this time I was also in communication with a Mr Macnamara from Glasgow. I had congratulated Mr Macnamara for getting the Courts to order his lawyers, Tods Murray - the law firm which had misled Johnny - to abate their bill of £382,000 by £94,000. Mr Macnamara and I became friendly and after an exchange of documents he offered to provide the financial assistance to fund my case against Brodies.

However on 25th July 1998 Johnny's younger son, Michael, rang me from South Africa at 7.00 am BST with the devastating news of Johnny's sudden death. I was utterly bowled over. By the Grace of God I had spoken to Johnny the previous evening for about seven minutes or so and he had sounded in perfectly good form. His new wife, Georgina told me that he had got up in the very early hours of Saturday morning to watch the Springboks play the All Blacks in New Zealand in the Tri-Nations Rugby. Johnny was an avid Springbok supporter and would have been very happy

Brother takes up fight to restore the house of Usher

WILLIAM CHISHOLM

MEMBER of a dynasty that as once one of the wealthiest nd most powerful in Scotland to take up his late brother's ght to recover millions of unds which he claims have en lost to the estate.

ir John Usher, 58, the sev- th Baronet of Norton and lls, died suddenly in South ica last weekend as he tched a rugby match on vision.

Sir John's efforts to restore the family's prosperity did not succeed, but now the fight to win back the missing Usher fortune is to be taken up by his brother, Stuart Usher, who lives with his wife and two children near Jedburgh.

He is talking to his lawyers about the possibilities of raising court actions for compensation for the lost money.

The family, which gifted the Usher Hall to Edinburgh with a £100,000 bequest in 1896, made their money from whisky. At the height of their prosperity, the family owned thousands of acres of land across Scotland, country houses in the Borders and a castle in Perthshire.

However, according to Mr Usher, who worked for a time as a minicab driver to make ends meet after returning from South Africa in 1995, the great wealth of his family has been unacceptably diminished.

For 30 years before 1994 the estate was owned by two brothers, Peter and Robert, who both had Down's syndrome. This meant that they were legally incapax – unable to manage their own affairs. A number of lawyers and others were appointed to run the estates on their behalf.

Mr Usher said: "I am continuing to investigate events and transactions which took place during that period and will be lodging a multi-million pound claim for damages."

It is claimed by Mr Usher that assets which belonged to the incapax landlords have either gone to outsiders or dramatically diminished.

A Law Society of Scotland inquiry, which is still going on after 14 months, began after Mr Usher lodged complaints against Brodie's, an Edinburgh law firm, which acted on behalf of the incapaxes between 1962 and 1994.

"My brother and I have done our best to gather in what is due to the executry," Mr Usher said. "I intend to carry on the fight until matters are put right on his, the executry and the Usher family's behalf."

Sir John Usher: Fought to reclaim family's wealth

Fall of the house of Usher, Page 3

No 48,272

News report after the death of Johnny

that the Springboks won that match. Georgina woke up at seven in the morning and was surprised that Johnny had not come back from the sitting room as the match was now long over. She went through to the sitting room and found him dead in his chair, as though he had fallen asleep and just never woke up.

Generally speaking we had always got on very well. I deferred to him because he was older than me and also far more competent in the ways of life. When we left for South Africa in 1968 we both realized that we had to get on together if we were to make our fortunes and purchase our family properties back in Scotland. It was an unwritten and unspoken compact between us. Of course we quarrelled from time to time, but we always made it our business to make up quickly. We both knew that should we have a serious rift our aims in Scotland would be jeopardized, if not put to naught. When he was in difficulties I rallied to him and when I was in difficulties he rallied to me. In this we did not count the cost to ourselves.

Soon after arriving in South Africa in 1968 with his then wife, Rosemary, and their three toddlers, Andrew, Caroline and Michael he purchased a six hundred acre mixed dairy, orange and crop farm in the Natal Midlands just north of Pietermaritzburg. The farm included a thirty acre orange orchard and a forty acre plantation of mature pine. The farm was called Khayalami which means 'My Home' in Zulu. Before the arrival of the White man in the 1800s this was all Zulu country. In 1970 the South African government expropriated about 100 acres of the low lying land on the farm which was to be inundated by water from a new dam it planned to build on the Umgeni river downstream from the farm They paid him open market price for this land. He then subdivided the remainder of the farm into fifty acre smallholdings and sold them. He did very well out of them and then invested in property in Pietermaritzburg on a rising property market. Again he did very well. At the same time he continued farming but on a much smaller scale, mainly oranges and tomatoes. This kept some of his original labour force in work. His Headman was called Begsisa who lived on the farm with his large family. Begsisa was a wonderful man. Always willing and cheerful. Another notable person on the farm was Elizabeth, the Housekeeper. She could prepare for a large dinner party at short notice with seemingly no fuss at all.

With hindsight Johnny should have stuck with his property investing. However on the advice of a friend he purchased an electronics business. The problem was that neither Johnny nor his friend knew anything about electronics. So the business went downhill and ultimately went bankrupt in 1994, taking Johnny with it. I had always warned Johnny not to go into any business of the trading variety, because I was already in such a business myself and knew some of the pitfalls first hand, and realised that Johnny and that type of business would not work. For that matter I was no good at that type of business myself. Farming and Property Investment suited Johnny well and he had proved himself in them. He was quite sharp and prescient in those fields.

But it was not all work by any means. He joined the local Polo Club called Otto's Bluff and became a very handy No. Four (rear position) player. The No. Four in polo rather dictates the play. A rotten No. Four will ruin any game of polo. A few years after joining he was appointed Captain of the club. By then I had also taken up polo, playing in the No. One position, who was meant to be the main goal scorer. We had great matches against each other over the weekends. These matches were keenly contested between our two teams which were called the Whites and the Blacks and were enormous fun.. The club shirt was black. Once a year we staged a polo tourney to which many other clubs came. These likewise were enormous fun and took place over two or three days with much socialising and endless beer.

Johnny loved nothing better than taking his family on holiday to the big Game Parks such as the Kruger National Park or to one of the Drakensburg Mountain resorts such as Sani Pass. He also became a keen golfer and birdwatcher as he grew older.

I arranged a Memorial Service and Wake for him at Bedrule and had half of his Ashes interred at our Burial ground there. The other half of his Ashes were scattered in a very pretty place in the southern part of the Kruger National Park in South Africa. Before the Memorial Service Gillian and I decided to bar the Mactaggarts if they appeared. However we agreed that we would not bar Valerie if she came, largely because I wanted to gauge her reaction to the eulogy I planned to give. In the event the Mactaggarts did not appear. However Valerie did turn up. Not daring to sit in the front pews, as she was entitled to as 'family' - although by now I did not regard her as family - she hid herself away towards the back of the Church and hard up against the wall.

In my eulogy to Johnny I related how he had always abhorred all forms of dishonesty and things like cheating and swindling in particular. I then enlarged on this by stating that he had spent many years of his life fighting to keep the Wells Estate in our family but his efforts had been put to naught by the knavery of the people who had gained control of it, some of whom were still living on the Estate. As I spoke I glanced at Valerie briefly from time to time. She just sat there, stony faced. I went on to say that I would continue the fight in memory of Johnny and would call these knaves to account. Just after finishing my eulogy and as I stepped down from the lectern I gave Val a last look. She was by now crouched low, what little I could see of her face a crease of misery.

So ended the life of my brother, Johnny. A life that had been grievously and wickedly blighted ever since the death of Robin in 1947 by dishonest lawyers in collusion with a dishonest element of our family. Johnny was everything that any family could wish for in an heir: Tall, slim, handsome, elegant, fair minded and competent.

What if Peter and Robert *had* been by-passed in favour of my Father as was the general expectation at the time of Uncle Stuart's death in 1962? Johnny would have succeeded to the Title and the Estates on the death of my Father in 1969. There can be little doubt that Johnny would have turned the Estates from decades of loss-making into profitable enterprises. He would have also discovered the full extent of the Trust assets in the Edinburgh area and Perth and put them to work. More than likely he would have gone into Housing and Commercial development schemes in Edinburgh and Perth and wherever else the Trust had land and property, as he had successfully done in South Africa. He almost certainly would have lived in Bedrule House until the survivor of Peter and Robert had passed away at which time he would have moved into Hallrule House. With the profits he would have undoubtedly extended the Wells, Norton and Pitheavlis Estates by purchasing neighbouring farms, houses and properties as and when they came on the market.

Since my homecoming I had kept Johnny as fully informed as possible as to what was going on and the like. He always cautioned me from taking the stronger stance which I wanted to take against Brodies and their allies. He was even slower than I was in realizing and accepting the extent of Brodies deceit over the years. Like me he was also slow to accept the systemic corruption of the various arms of the Scottish legal system. Notwithstanding this he was outraged at my discoveries and gave me his full backing to try and have have matters put right. However he sometimes told me that he felt we had no chance of succeeding because Brodies and their despicable allies were just too powerful and that the other beneficiaries would just want their money out quickly and would fail to make a fight of it. Why should they? None of them were Ushers. They simply would not have the motivation that we had. I have no doubt whatever that Johnny's death, just like my Father's death, was hastened by Brodies and their treacherous allies in the fraud.

Of course I felt much bereft and alone now in the fight. It was now borne in on me that only I stood in the way of Brodies and the other fraudsters getting off Scot-free. If I did not succeed, our branch of the Usher family would be totally extinguished in the geographical and social sense. I was the only person living with first-hand knowledge of many of the events I have so far described in this book. I also took, and still do take, strength from this because my fraudster opponents know, as long as I live, they can never rest easy. This in turn made me realize that I should take even more care of my health. I am happy to say that I feel I have been successful in this, to a degree at least, and am improving all the time.

I notified the media of Johnny's death. Broadsheets and tabloids carried it widely and also my intention to fight on alone. *The Scotsman* of 31st July 1998 made it front page news with an article and picture of Johnny and a further large article on page three of the newspaper which was headlined: 'How the real House of Usher fell from Glory.' These reports were sympathetic to us as a family and also my fight to get things put right. How Brodies and their associates in crime, Jacquelin, the Mactaggarts, and Valerie must have hated that. For the record I never received one word of regret or sympathy from any of them at Johnny's passing. That also told me a lot.

Though I was delighted with the most unexpected and very generous offer of financial help from Mr Macnamara I came to realise this was not a healthy situation and that Johnny would have cautioned against it. Mr Macnamara had stoutly refused to take any portion of compensation which might accrue to me as payment. I therefore wrote to him in January 1999 informing him that I would henceforth handle my own affairs and thanked him very much indeed for his unselfish assistance and support to date. He was very understanding about it and we parted on good terms.

43

THE LAW SOCIETY WHITEWASHES BRODIES WS, SHEPHERD AND WEDDERBURN WS, AND ROSS HARPER WS AND BLACKWASHES ME

Throughout this period I was in heavy communication with the Law Society in connection with my Complaints. I shall give just one example of its attempts to confound me:

In connection with my Complaints against Fulton of Shepherd and Wedderburn WS, Yelland of the Law Society wrote me by letter dated 6th October 1998 giving me seven days to respond with any comments I wanted to make on the 'Facts and Circumstances Report' which he had sent me in September. As always when dealing with organisations such as the Law Society I had come to realise that I should always check the date on the letter and *compare* it with the date of its posting. The date of posting was the *13th* October 1998. Yelland, the filthy dog, had therefore waited the seven days before actually posting his letter. The day of his posting was of course the very day when the opportunity to respond expired. I received his letter on the 14th, one day *after* the expiration of the deadline. Of course I immediately faxed him for an explanation of the seven-day delay in posting his letter. This put him on the back foot and true to form he went to ground. By letter dated 21st October he responded by stating that he was, 'not in a position to explain the apparent delay in the letter being sent out to you. I have to say that I am aware that there was a difficulty in our Dispatch Department at one stage and this may be the reason for the difficulty.' This 'I have to say' and 'difficulty' is typical of the legal-babble deployed by the vermin who infest the Scottish legal system. I didn't believe a word of it. I therefore *immediately* contacted the Law Society's Dispatch department. They told me categorically that there had been no problems at all with the dispatch of their post. To reinforce this I rang them again some hours later and was again told the same thing. The very next day Yelland wrote to me again blaming the Dispatch Department which indicated that he had, too late, told the Dispatch department to corroborate his story.

In the event however I had already faxed my comments on the 'Facts and Circumstances Report' to the Law Society on Friday 9th October, well within Yelland's time limit

When dealing with lawyers, readers be warned: Always compare the dates on lawyers' letters with the dates of posting on the envelopes and keep the envelope if there has been a delay in posting. This is a tactic crooked lawyers commonly use if they think they can achieve some advantage from it. Most people simply tear up the envelopes of mail they receive without checking the post mark. Without the envelope such people have no documentary defence of when the letter was posted. On occasion Brodies used a variation of this tactic: They simply left their letter undated and in the place where the date should have been they inserted the words 'Date as Postmark.' No record again as to when the letter was *actually* written. Neat and despicable.

As far as the 'Facts and Circumstances' report itself was concerned it, inevitably, reflected neither the facts nor the circumstances on which my Complaints had been based. It was therefore irrelevant. I made this and a lot else crystal clear to Yelland and the Law Society. The purpose of the Law Society in producing this 'Facts and Circumstances' report was simply to cause confusion and divert attention away from the real issues contained in my complaints.

On the same day, Friday the 9th October, that I faxed my comments to the Law Society, I also notified the Scottish Legal Services Ombudsman in a detailed three page submission that the Law Society was acting in bad faith in connection with my Complaints. I warned the Ombudsman that the Facts and Circumstances Reports in connection with both Brodies and Shepherd and Wedderburn were so 'glaringly off the mark that it is certain that the Law Society will find for Brodies and Shepherd & Wedderburn and against me.'

In response to my comments on the 'Facts and Circumstances Report' Yelland stated that the Reporter stood by his 'F&C Report.' This was an example of the Law Society using the 'Big Bluff' to overcome dangerous situations for its lawyer members and its whitewashing Reporters. However Big Bluffs become successful only when the person being Big Bluffed either believes it or runs away from it. I had absolutely no intention of doing either.

By letter dated 18th December 1998 Yelland informed me that the Law Society had 'upheld your complaint' against Ross Harper but 'determined that no sanction was appropriate.' Typical Law Society. With his letter he enclosed a 'Heads of Complaint' and the 'Facts and Circumstances Report' schedules neither of which I had seen. The Law Society had sent me their 'Facts and Circumstances' reports in connection with Brodies and Shepherd and Wedderburn only for my comments before issuing their determinations so why not in connection with Ross Harper? Good question and one which only the Law Society can answer. Will they ever answer? No chance.

However when I read these documents I discovered that the Law Society had *not* 'upheld' my complaint against Ross Harper as Yelland's letter dated the 18th of December had misleadingly stated. What it had done was to add two further Complaints of its own to the three that I had laid. It then rejected all three of *my* Complaints and one of its own Complaints but found for the remaining one of its own. In essence it had laid two complaints against one of its own members on my behalf *without* informing me and then finding for me on only one of them. Of course I realized that all this was a ploy to justify their dismissal of my own three Complaints which were of a far more serious nature than their two added Complaints. 'When in trouble always divert the discourse' is the golden rule routinely deployed by Law Society, Brodies and the Scottish Legal system in general.

As if that were not bad enough I then discovered that the 'Reporter' was not an 'independent lay person' as the Law Society had always loudly proclaimed their Reporters to be. In this case it was, hang onto your hats for you would never guess it: none other than Yelland *himself!* Can you beat it? Their whole 'investigation' had been their usual nasty farce to whitewash their usual nasty crooked lawyers.

Despite finding against Ross Harper on its own Complaint it did not propose to issue any sanction against Ross Harper. Another farce. I did however manage to extract an apology from Ross Harper. That of course vindicated my *own* complaints against them.

I suspected the Law Society found 'for' me in this patently spurious manner as justification for their intended dismissal of my Complaints against Brodies and Shepherd & Wedderburn, which were, and still remain, of a far greater magnitude than the ones against Ross Harper. After all they could then contrive to argue: 'We found for him once and against him twice. We are utterly impartial.'

However that was not the last of Ross Harper. I crossed swords with them again in the years 2008 and 2009. By then they had changed their name to Harper Mcleod. Law firms often change their names to make themselves more remote from prosecution, lose their rotten reputations, and the like. At about this time an English lady called Mrs Durrant approached me for assistance related to a case of medical negligence which had taken place in Scotland where she and her husband were then living. Her medical negligence claim arose from her husband dying an agonising death as a consequence of NHS negligence. She had appointed Harper McLeod to pursue the case on her behalf. In the usual Ross Harper/Harper McLeod manner they misled her into paying them good money in advance; then misled her further; and then dropped her. Needless to say, they kept her money. She emerged from this, her first and only experience of the Scottish 'legal system', a much wiser but poorer lady. To her great credit she never gave up and lives in hope to this day that she will eventually get the justice she so richly deserves.

Nor was even that the end of Ross Harper McLeod's shenanigans: In 2012 the Law Society closed them down on the grounds of 'poor accounting practices' and the 'extremely challenging financial circumstances' it faced. At the end of the Report (by BBC News for Glasgow and West of Scotland on 30th April 2012) there was a very telling statement by the Law Society. Here is part of it:

> '. . .because the accounting records are so poor we cannot tell if client's money is missing.'

This makes it certain that Ross Harper had stolen their clients' monies and then, not surprisingly, had not recorded these thefts in their accounts. This Law Society statement had the added advantage for them of making it very difficult for those clients who had been robbed by Ross Harper to claim against the Law Society. In essence the closing down of Ross Harper was just another crime-concealing and damage-limitation device by the Law Society of Scotland on behalf of the Scottish 'Legal system.' For the record and for posterity the lawyer Donald Dewar, Scotland's first 'First Minister' in 1997, worked for Ross Harper before he became a Labour Party politician. He died on the 11th of October 2000, a multi-millionaire. I suspect the foundation of his fortune was made while he was a Ross Harper lawyer.

By letter dated 22nd December 1998 Yelland informed me that all my Complaints against Brodies and Shepherd & Wedderburn (Fulton) had been dismissed by the Law Society as having no merit and that he was now closing his file on them. This was exactly what I had expected and about which I had, very importantly and thank God, already warned the Ombudsman.

In connection with my Complaints against Brodies the author of the Report described me as 'paranoid', 'ranting', 'niggling' and that he had read my correspondence 'with great tedium' and so on. I took this as a further manifestation of Brodies' and now the Law Society's campaign to discredit me. Of course, initially, I was somewhat incensed but soon realised that the Law Society had scored yet another own goal by doing that. Finding the correspondence regarding my family's estates being plundered 'tedious' is irrelevant to his function. His function is to make recommendations on the basis of the evidence before him. He had not done so. My evidence was more than compelling; it was irrefutable. But only irrefutable in a *Bona-Fide* arena.

On this basis the 'Reporter' ('Liar' actually) recommended that the Law Society dismiss all my Complaints. This they had done now without further ado. After discovering that Yelland had been the Reporter in connection with my Complaints against Ross Harper, then for all I knew the Reporter may well have been a Brodies lawyer, or even Stevens or Houldsworth themselves . And why do they call these mystery people 'Reporters'? People lodge Complaints with the Law Society in the expectation that their Complaints will be investigated. Calling the unknown person a 'Reporter' instead of an 'Investigator' tells a story in itself.

Of course I was not going allow them to simply bury me in this deceitful manner. It simply strengthened my resolve to expose them and Brodies, Shepherd & Wedderburn and Ross Harper, for exactly what they are – gangs of criminals in pin stripe suits.

I therefore contacted *The Scotsman* newspaper and sent them the Law Society's Reports, as well as some of my documentation which flatly contradicted the Law Society's determinations in vivid and unmistakeable ways. They published quite a lengthy article on it on 5th January 1999. This in turn generated letters to *The Scotsman* all of which supported me, with one exception. The exception was from a Member of the Scottish Parliament at Holyrood - a lawyer needles to say.

One of the letter writers later telephoned me and told me of an event which confirmed that Brodies had been defrauding the Wells Estate for years: Her ex-husband was an Edinburgh Sheriff called Andrew Lothian and he had told her in the early 1990s:

> 'I have heard that there is something radically wrong with the way the Usher estates have been administered for many years. We could easily buy a lovely house near Jedburgh for virtually nothing from the Usher Estate.'

She also informed me that Lothian and his fellow Sheriffs used to tell each other at cocktail parties how they enjoyed catching a plaintiff out on a legal technicality and then watching him or her squirm before dismissing their case and how she had hated that type of sadistic behaviour. Mrs Lothian and I became friendly and on 13th April 2003 she gave me a written statement on what her husband, Sheriff Andrew Lothian had told her. Here it is, verbatim:

> 'I recall during renovations and conversion work to the above property [the house they were converting near Lauder] in the early months of the summer of 1992 my then husband, Sheriff Andrew Lothian, suggested that we abandon the project due to various difficulties with the building work. He proposed that we could easily buy a lovely house near Jedburgh for virtually nothing. When I questioned him of the propriety of such a purchase he went on to state that the houses available were part of the Usher Estates and that the Estate was held in trust by Brodies for two Downs Syndrome brothers.
>
> Andrew Lothian then stated that in legal terms the Downs Syndrome brothers were incompetent and he and his associates were 'untouchable', there would be no legal repercussions if we were to buy property at under market value from Brodies.

I rigorously declined this offer, it was morally offensive to me to take advanatage of the two brothers because of their misfortune and horrified that Brodies would.

It has now become public knowledge that Stuart Usher is legally challenging Brodies regarding maladministration of the Usher Estates at that time.

From what Andrew Lothian told me in 1992 and subsequently I presently believe that through his association with members of the Speculative Society [of Edinburgh] or a similar society, property belonging to the Usher Estate was offered to him and others at considerably under value.'

That said it all. The Scottish Legal Establishment were quite aware, and had been for decades, of Brodies defrauding our family, through Peter and Robert, and had done absolutely nothing about it.

FAX FROM : 01578722740 13/04/03 21:55 PG: 1
14-APR-03 13:03 HARRIET LOTHIAN 01578722740 PAGE: 1

TO WHOM IT MAY CONCERN.

This statement is made by Harriet Jane McEwan or Lothian on the 14th April 2003.

Residing at;

Hurcheon Cottage,
Boon,
Lauder,
Berwickshire,
TD2 6SB.

I recall during renovations and conversion work to the above property in the early months of the summer 1992 my then husband, Sherrif Andrew Lothian, suggested that we abandon the project due to various difficulties with the building work. He proposed that we could easily buy a lovely house near Jedburgh for virtually nothing. When I questioned him regarding the propriety of such a purchase he went on to state that the houses available were part of the Usher Estates and that the estate was held in trust by Brodies for two Downs Syndrome brothers.

Andrew Lothian also stated that in legal terms the Downs Syndrome brothers were incompetant and he and his associates were "untouchable", there would be no legal repercussions if we were to buy property at under market value from Brodies.

I rigorously declined this offer, it was morally offensive to me to take advantage of the two brothers because of their misfortune, and horrified at the suggestion that Brodies would. At that time the scheme seemed far-fetched, possibly illegal under the circumstances described by Andrew Lothian and I wanted no part in it if it were all true.

It has now become public knowledge that Stuart Usher is legally challenging Brodies regarding the maladministration of the Usher Estates at that time. It has also come to light Sherrif Lothian, members of Brodies and a relative of Stuart Usher are members of The Speculative Society of Edinburgh.

From what Andrew Lothian told me in 1992 and subsequently, I presently believe that through his association with members of the Speculative Society, or a similar society, property belonging to the Usher Estate was offered to him and others, at considerably under the market value.

This statement is true and as I recollect events at the time and subsequently.

Harriet Jane McEwan or Lothian.

The original letter from Harriet Lothian

As fate would have it Mrs Lothian eventually obtained a position working as a gardener on one of the Wells Estate properties which had been sold.

In 2007 the paths of Sheriff Lothian and myself were to cross once more. 'Scotland Against Crooked Lawyers' for the first time put up candidates in the Scottish elections contesting the Edinburgh and Lothians, and the Glasgow Regions.

Will the real Sheriff Lothian please stand up? Sleazy Sheriff Andrew Lothian is a wife-beating drunk who's obsessed with prostitutes, it was reported in a National Newspaper. The shamed 66-year-old was forced to quit the bench in 2009 after claims of spanking and whipping sessions with an Edinburgh hooker. It is understood he was allowed to keep his £84,000-a-year pension.

In the event we achieved approximately three hundred votes in each Region which we thought was quite good given the very little canvassing we did. However the election was adjudged to have been a farce by various international electoral observers. This resulted in an enquiry by the Electoral Commission and part of the report by the Department of Government at Strathclyde University stated:

> Although there were a number of other administrative problems, the unusually large number of ballots rejected in the 2007 Scottish Parliament elections attracted considerable media interest and comment and provoked a special enquiry by the Electoral Commission. It is generally accepted that the new design of the ballot paper was the major factor in causing problems and that these problems were greatest in less well-off areas. So far, however, little attention has been paid to the views and perceptions of electors, especially with reference to the question of the legitimacy of elections. Analysis of specially collected survey data shows that the voters recognised that there were serious problems in the elections and, although offering a variety of explanations, tended to blame the authorities. Trust in the fairness of the electoral process has been reduced by the experience and this may result in reduced voter participation in future elections.

The Ballot papers had been designed in a way that confused the voting public and secondly the counting machines had malfunctioned, resulting in about 140,000 ballot papers votes being voided. In view of this we lodged a claim in the Small Claims Court in Edinburgh to have our Deposits amounting to £1,000 returned. We depended upon the statements of various international observers to support our case. One of our members the redoubtable Billy Burns represented us in Court. At the third and final

Hearing, who should appear as the judge - none other than the lamentable Sheriff Lothian himself. Inevitably and without further ado he simply dismissed our Appeal. In doing so, however, he adopted a bullying and insulting manner towards Billy Burns.

Neither does the distasteful tale of Sheriff Lothian end there: In December 2008, he hit the headlines when he was publicly exposed as a serial frequenter of brothels within which he practiced an 'addiction for deviant sex with vulnerable women'. Needless to say Sheriff Lothian resigned in disgrace but was allowed to do so on full pension. Such is the 'punishment' meted out to wrongdoers in the Scottish Legal Establishment by the Scottish Legal Establishment.

I shall now return to Law Society's despicable rejection of my Complaints. I also received phone calls of support. The recurrent theme of these calls was that I should stand my ground and not let the Law Society bury me. Some of these callers told me that these tactics of character assassination were routinely deployed by the Law Society against those who posed a threat to them, their members and licensees.

Some years later, and in this regard, I got the Police to visit me at my home in an effort to get them to prosecute the Law Society. The Police Officer told me that they were not *allowed* to prosecute the Law Society because it was an *Institution!* Again that said it all and no wonder that the whole Scottish Legal system sustains itself from the proceeds of institutionalised crime.

In January and February 1999 I spent many days in composing detailed Rebuttals of the Law Society's Facts and Circumstances Reports, Opinions and Determinations on all three cases. I repudiated the whole Law Society findings on a paragraph by paragraph basis. By now I realised that it would be very foolish indeed to let the Law Society have copies of my rebuttals as this would simply forewarn them of the extent of my ammunition. This would, in turn, result in their warning Brodies, Shepherd & Wedderburn and Ross Harper, thereby allowing them all to get rid of incriminating evidence and sanitise their records as best they could. However I got them posted on the Internet Website of an indigenous Scottish Pressure and Lobby group called 'Injured by the Law', based in Perth.

Nearly two years had passed since I had first reported Brodies, Shepherd & Wedderburn and Ross Harper to the Law Society. I had expended an enormous amount of time and effort in corresponding with them and therefore had built a long and detailed paper trail. It stands, at present, as mute testament to the Law Society's bad faith dealings with me. This book should go some way to 'un-muting' it and in doing so, I very much hope, will go a long way to awakening the general public to the damage the Law Society does to them and the country in general year in year out. On the basis of my paper trail I have no hesitation whatever in stating that Yelland, the head of the euphemistically named 'Client's Relations Department' of the Law Society and many of the unknown lawyer 'reporters' working there as well as the vast majority of the lawyers in positions of authority there, including successive Presidents of the Law Society, were, and still are, out and out criminals. They all should have been arrested, charged, tried and imprisoned for long sojourns many years ago. That they are still free wreaking havoc and misery on the victims of their own members and licensees and not in gaol is a National Disgrace.

For the sake of balance what about the Law Society of England and Wales? The *Daily Telegraph* of the 5th of April 2001, under the headline of 'LEGAL MAFIA IS FAILING PUBLIC', carried a report on the Law Society of England in which it quoted the views of some English MPs on it and lawyers:

George Stevenson (Labour, Stoke-on-Trent, S): 'Do they (lawyers) have to be murderers before the Law Society will take action?' This was in connection with someone who had fallen foul of 'his' lawyers and had complained to the Law Society of England and the English Ombudsman, in vain.

Austin Mitchell (Labour, Great Grimsby) said that Self-Regulation was failing consumers: 'In Law, the practice of the Mafia regulating the Mafia has failed, is failing, and needs to be abolished.' He then went on to state that, 'The Lord Chancellor's department had taken on the role of protecting vested interests and was in collusion with the Law Society.'

Quite so, and well said Messrs Stevenson and Mitchell.

One final referral back to Ross Harper and Yelland the Law Society 'Reporter' claiming he found my complaints 'tedious'. An unwritten law among the wig lice of Edinburgh states they must never steal from *within* the profession. It seems Ross Harper did just that. Presumably Yelland did not find *this* 'tedious'. In such cases a police probe will be deemed essential. According to news report in the *Daily Record* dated 17th September 2017 Ross Harper and Co, who had offices across Scotland, were shut down in 2012 after more than 50 years in practice. It emerged that public cash claimed in Legal Aid fees was not paid to suppliers and experts hired by the Glasgow firm. A lengthy probe by the Law Society of Scotland led to four partners being struck off.

Price : Struck off

Susskind : Struck off

Fyfe : Struck off

44

I REPORT THE LAW SOCIETY TO THE SCOTTISH LEGAL SERVICES OMBUDSMAN, GARRY WATSON.

On 2nd January 1999 I reported the Law Society to the Scottish Legal Services Ombudsman in Edinburgh in connection with its determination on my Complaints against Brodies. By letter dated 6th January the Ombudsman, Garry Watson, replied by stating that he would not be examining my Complaints for 'some months' due to the number of cases ahead of mine. Charming, but hardly surprising. He also enclosed a copy of a SLSO leaflet which stated that he and his office was not a 'Consumer Champion.' On reading this twaddle I thought 'The brainwashing to do the dirty has already started'. Despite this on the 7th January 1999 I reported the Law Society to the Scottish Legal Services Ombudsman again for their so called 'investigations and determinations' in connection with my complaints against Shepherd & Wedderburn. The Ombudsman informed me that I could expect to wait for six to eight months before he issued his determinations. However at the same time he also enclosed another SLSO leaflet which stated that the determinations would be completed in 'not less than two months and not more than four months'. Obviously his office was falling behind because of the sheer scale of Complaints about the Sottish Legal Services. On 22nd January 1999 I complained again; this time in connection with Ross Harper.

To better inform the reader I here reproduce my letter of Complaint to the Ombusman in connection with the Law Society's handling of my complaints against Brodies:

'Dear Sir.

THE LAW SOCIETY OF SCOTLAND'S HANDLING OF THE COMPLAINTS AGAINST BRODIES WS.

I have very recently been notified by the Law Society of Scotland that they have rejected all the Complaints which I laid against Brodies WS of Atholl

Crescent, Edinburgh on 1st April 1997 on behalf of the executry of the late Sir Robert Usher, Incapax, who died in 1994.

For the record I would state that I do not accept that the Law Society acted in good faith in connection with these Complaints. I make this statement for the following reasons, *inter-alia:*

1) The Law Society appears not to have to carried out any meaningful investigation of the Complaints. It appears, rather, that the Law Society set out with the intention of whitewashing Brodies from the beginning.

2) The Law Society took very little cognisance of my assertions but took full cognisance of Brodies assertions which go against the record which back up my assertions.

3) The Law Society producing a 'Facts & Circumstances Report' which accuses me of ranting, paranoia, niggling and the like. I repudiate all these accusations with contempt.

4) The Law Society failing to produce a Facts & Circumstances Report in their normal format, — an example of which I have seen. The 'F&CR' they did produce does not reflect either the facts or the circumstances which led me to lodging my Complaints in the first place. It therefore follows that the Law Society rejected all my Complaints on the basis of a highly inaccurate, abnormal and misnamed 'F&C Report.' I objected when I first saw it but the Law Society declined to do anything about it as suggested by myself. I would state that an infinitely more accurate description of this Report would be: 'A Myth and Conjecture Report.'

I enclose herewith the 'Facts & Circumstances Report' and my reply to it to the law society entitled: 'Comments on F&C Report' and the covering letter which went with it.

In conclusion I would state again that I am quite convinced that the Law Society acted in bad faith towards myself and the executry of the late Sir Robert Usher in the handling of the Complaints.

I also feel that the law society had to find against us because it would have been just too embarrassing for it to find against such a large and well-known 'Edinburgh legal establishment' firm like Brodies. Particularly in view of the fact that it licences Brodies to conduct its business. This in itself is Conflict of Interest and is a prime example of self regulation which never has, does not, and never will work in the interests of either Complainants or the legal profession itself.

I did write to you on 8th October 1998. That letter also sums up my feelings very well, - and the Law Society finding against me and for Brodies merely confirms my forecast as correct. The finding was NOT on the merits of the Complaints but, it appears, largely for reasons of expediency. I feel very strongly that they must not be allowed to get away with such cynical behaviour.

I therefore require you to investigate the Law Society's handling of the Complaints and, should you find that they did act in bad faith, as recorded above, as well as in other respects which I have not yet included in this letter but which should be apparent to you from the correspondence

> between the Law Society and myself, to take the necessary action to ensure that the Law Society does not abuse its functions again in the future.
>
> For the record I would state that I feel totally outraged at the Law Society and the Legal profession in general, — very, very deeply so. I look to you, more in despair than in hope I regret to say, that your offices will at least try and do something about the Law Society. Further I am not the only one who has suffered at the hands of the Law Society as I have received letters from many people who have gone through a similar charade. It is therefore very much in the public interest as well that something is done about the matter.
>
> I look forward to hearing from you'.

I had been warned by friends and well-wishers, who had already been through the 'Ombudsman Charade', that he and his office would do everything possible to limit the damage to Brodies and the other law firms and, like them, try to figuratively 'bury' me once and for all. So my reason for reporting Brodies, Shepherd and Wedderburn and Ross Harper to the Ombudsman was also for paper trail and catching him out purposes. At some future date I intended to hoist him on his own petard if he behaved in that manner.

Anyway I let him have six months to get on with the job. I wrote to him on 8th July 1999 enquiring as to when I could expect his investigations to be completed, as it was now two months beyond his leaflet-stated maximum of four months . He replied on 13th July 1999 stating that his backlog had increased and that I would now have to wait to 'the end of the year' for my first Opinion only. So the backlog had increased from two to four months to twelve months. Just like that. Obviously I was one of a rapidly increasing number of Complainants.

I publicised this dramatic increase in his backlog to *The Scotsman* newspaper. This led to a further exchange of letters in *The Scotsman* and eventually resulted in the Ombudsman issuing me a public apology. The Scottish Legal system's *modus operandi,* when caught procrastinating and lying was to apologise but at the same time to infer: 'Of course our apology carries no liability.'

To force the Ombudsman's hand I arranged a meeting with him on 4th August 1999 at 3.30pm. Gillian, standing foursquare, came with me. The first thing Watson told us was it was very unusual for him to meet with Complainants, which indicated that he recognised the great danger our case posed to the Scottish legal system. He had recently employed a second member of staff, a Miss Millan; no doubt to try and catch up on the burgeoning backlog. Watson exhibited social grace and conducted himself with civility - a rare occurrence within the Scottish Legal system. However, I had already experienced such behaviour from Haldane-Tait, the Auditor of Court and I was reminded of Hamlet:

O villain, villain, smiling, damnèd villain!
My tables—meet it is I set it down
That one may smile, and smile, and be a villain—

Watson agreed with me that the Scottish Solicitors Disciplinary Tribunal's punishments for 'errant' [his word] lawyers were far too weak. Also that lawyers who were fraudsters and practised deceit on their clients should be struck off and never allowed to practise again. 'Bully for you,' I thought, 'but I won't believe you until you prove yourself.' In my mind I considered that his ideas for 'errant' lawyers, if carried out, would result in 99% of all legal practitioners in Scotland being immediately struck off. How would the country function in such circumstances? Much better say I that lawyers should be barred from becoming Members of the Scottish Parliament. The reality of course is that the whole Scottish Legal System needs to be scrapped *in toto* and replaced with one founded on moral and ethical principles.

One day I was in their Office for the purpose of checking whether the Law Society had in fact supplied the Ombudsman with all the correct papers connected with my Complaints. During this process I was forbidden to even *see* the papers in question. In a surreal way the whole operation had to be conducted verbally with me sitting at one end of a long table and the Ombudsman's new clerk, Miss Millan, at the other end. I had to raise my voice unnaturally to ask her questions regarding what papers she had or did not have and strain to hear her answers.

After some 15 minutes of this farce I needed to visit the Gents and was suprised to find Miss Millan in tow. Before entering the Gents I asked her why she was following me. Miss Millan answered: 'It is standard practice in this office.' She was still waiting at the toilet door when I emerged and then followed close behind me back to her office. This episode is a vivid example of how the Scottish Legal system treats those who lodge complaints against it. In essence complainants are treated as potential criminals rather than law-abiding citizens blowing the whistle on criminals. Miss Millan gave me every impression that she did not regard her following me to the Gents and back to her office as in the slightest bit out of the ordinary. This showed how thoroughly brainwashed she had been. For the record she refused to either confirm nor deny that she had *any* file in connection with my complaint against Shepherd & Wedderburn. I was baffled.

At the beginning of January 2000 I received the Ombudsman's 'Opinion' on my Complaints against the Law Society in connection with their so called investigation of Brodies; exactly one year after lodging them. To use the Ombudsman's exact words: 'This Opinion is designated as satisfactory.' In layman's language this meant that Watson exonerated the Law Society of all wrong-doing and dismissed my Complaints against it.

'. . .one may smile, and smile, and be a villain.'

Garry Watson, so-called 'Legal Ombudsman'. Without blushing he dismissed my complaint against the Law Society. A cynical whitewash.

The Ombudsman commenced his 'Opinion' by stating:

> 'I am not required to assess the merits of the particular complaint against the solicitor.'

Quite how anyone could produce a credible Opinion on whether or not the Law Society had handled my complaints against Brodies without assessing the merits was impossible to conceive. I therefore regarded his Opening Statement as a 'catch all' device with which to dismiss my complaint - and the vast majority of other complaints - against the Law Society.

The Ombudsman had, though, put in a lot of blood, sweat, and tears into his Opinion because it consisted of twenty nine pages. Unfortunately it was twenty nine pages of crime- concealing twaddle.

Of course my opinion of the Ombudsman sank to rock bottom. I informed him so in writing and made it very clear to him that he was shirking his duty to himself and society at large by whitewashing the Law Society in this case. He never replied.

The Ombudsman's other two Opinions on the Law Society's handling of my complaints against Shepherd & Wedderburn WS and Ross Harper WS came through in February and March respectively. He gave the Law Society a clean bill of health in respect of its handling of my complaints against Ross Harper but designated the one in respect of Shepherd & Wedderburn as 'critical'. However on reading his 'Opinion' I discovered that he had been 'critical' on only one of ten aspects; all ten of which were of *his* invention and not based on my complaints. The aspect he *was* 'critical' of was that the

Law Society had produced its report on my Complaints *without* having even obtained the files from Shepherd and Wedderburn. That of course explained why Miss Millan had refused to answer my questions in connection with the Shepherd and Wedderburn files. She simply did not have them. But she never told me that, the evasive brainwashed vixen..

Even this was a hollow victory as the Ombudsman imposed no sanctions whatsoever on the Law Society. *None*! The reason for this was because he had absolutely no powers of sanction over the Law Society. It appeared that he was an irrelevancy designed and set up to deceive Complainants into thinking that there *was* a point to his existence! This was yet another example of the criminal pantomime that is the Scottish Legal system.

I had been warned to expect a whitewash, but the cynical manner by which it had been executed was still a shock. Still, I had achieved my objective of creating a long and incontrovertible paper trail which demonstrated that the Ombudsman's and his Opinions were unsustainable

Strange to say the Ombudsman resigned shortly after issuing his bogus opinions on my complaints against the Law Society.

45

A CROOKED LAWYER CALLED T.H. MURRAY, OF STIRLING.

In late 1998 a lawyer called Tom Murray who practised in Stirling had been recommended to me by a gentleman called Stewart Mackenzie of Pitlochry. I therefore contacted Murray and he came down to my place for a meeting on 28th January 1999. For a start he appeared to be alright but as the meeting progressed he managed to arouse some misgivings in me. However I was now so utterly desperate to get to Court that I would have accepted the Devil himself as my lawyer. Time Bars were approaching. In Scotland if you do not raise an action within three years, or in some cases five years, you are barred from ever doing so. This, in itself, is a massive encouragement to lawyers to defraud clients, talk mumbo-jumbo, and employ delaying tactics. Brodies had kept me at bay for years, followed by the Law Society for almost two years and then the Ombudsman for another year. By design, then, I was already out of time. This therefore was yet another device by which the Scottish legal system squashes the victims of crooked lawyers.

I gave Murray hard documentary evidence of fraud by Brodies and after a general discussion he agreed to take the case on. He informed me it would be no longer than a month before we got to Court. He then stated that he needed £3,500 in advance to commence work on the case. About a year later I discovered that asking for money upfront is a flagrant breach of the Law Society's own Rules.

He wrote to me by letter dated 2nd February 1999. The content of this letter was materially different to what we had agreed at our meeting. For example it was full of warnings about Time Bars and all rather gloomy. As if it was all my fault, which it never had been.

I therefore telephoned him on 3rd February 1999 to pin him down as to what exactly my £3,500 would achieve. He responded that the £3,500 would cover the necessary research, perusal of documents, a Deeds Office search, the production of a 'Memorial' [mumbo-jumbo] for an Advocate, the cost of the Advocate's resulting Opinion and the invoking of the 1981

Administration of Justice Act for the purpose of forcing Brodies to make available all the Usher Baronetcy Trust records and the subsequent records of the Estates of the two successive Incapax purported Landlords. By invoking 'Time Bars' and the imminent danger of my case *prescribing* he managed to obtain the £3,500 which I sent to him on 19th February. Readers will probably be shaking their heads about how this was a very foolish thing to have done. Never, ever, *ever* pay a lawyer in advance no matter how desperate you are.

Having cashed my cheque Murray went to ground. I did not hear from him for over a month and not again until 20th May 1999 by letter in which he stated that the matter was taking slightly more time than he'd anticipated. This was in reply to numerous letters from myself imploring him to proceed on the terms we had agreed. After all he was the one who had kept warning and worrying me about 'Time Bars.' Once my cheque had been safely cashed it seems that 'Time Bars' were of no further consequence. In addition it was virtually impossible to reach him by telephone.

On 15th June, however, I did get him on the phone, four months after paying him the cheque. He told me that he had now 'perused all the material' and stated that he would contact me before the end of that week. He failed to do so. I desperately told myself not to become paranoid, but not until 28th August 1998 did I at last received his 'Memorial.' In the dreamlike world of the Scottish Legal system a 'Memorial' means a document which a lawyer prepares for an Advocate. Murray's Memorial was factually inaccurate and more than six months late (despite the worries about my case *prescribing*). I quickly amended the Memorial to make it more factually accurate. Murray then produced a revised Memorial based on my amendments which he sent to me on 7th September. I improved on that and the result was the final Memorial which I received from Murray on 21st September. I still regarded it as a poor effort but agreed to it because of my fear of 'Time Bars.' I asked him to forward it with the corroborating documentation to the Advocate, Mayer, as a matter of the greatest urgency.

The swindling Thomas Hugh Murray, of Stirling

Murray agreed to do so. Mayer was the Advocate who had said he was willing to represent me a year and a half earlier.

At this point everything went dead. I wrote to Murray 27th October asking if he had heard anything from Mayer. That same day I received information from a renegade lawyer called Thomson that Mayer had never received the Memorial at all. Of course I immediately wrote to Murray asking for an explanation. On 15th November Murray left a message on my answering machine that 'Mr Mayer had received the papers.' The next day I checked with Mr Mayer's clerk, Barney McKinnon. He stated that no papers of any sort had come in from Murray. So Murray had lied. Thomson, the renegade lawyer, told me that Murray *had* been lying but put this down to his incompetence and advised me to stay with him as I would never get another lawyer. Lying should never be described as 'incompetence' but I went along with his advice because: 1) I had already paid Murray and 2) Thompson was right; I would never get another lawyer.

On 23rd November 1999 Murray informed me by telephone that Mayer agreed that Brodies and the other parties involved had a case to answer and that he, Mayer, would take the case on a no-win no fee basis. I was delighted. We agreed to a meeting before Christmas. In the event this did not happen until 21st January 2000. My previous many rotten experiences with everyone involved in the defrauding of my family again caused me to again take my long suffering wife Gillian with me to this meeting.

Murray introduced me to Mayer. My first reaction to him was as positive as one might expect in those circumstances. However when I told him that Gillian would be present at the meeting his demeanour immediately changed . He straightaway informed me that he would not allow her to attend the Meeting because she had 'no interest' in the matter. I disputed this with him and after a quarter of an hour he backed down and agreed that she be present, although it was very apparent that her presence disquieted him no end.

The meeting commenced with a 20 minute discourse by Mayer on the problems of having Gill present at the meeting. According to him one of these problems was that she could well be a liability as a witness. I did not understand this reasoning and became even more baffled when he insisted that she would have to absent herself when I gave him my verbal statement of the various frauds and wrong-doings. Objectively I knew it was part of an elaborate act but subjectively I was so desperate for action that I deluded myself that everything was 'alright'. Deep down, I knew it wasn't.

Mayer now launched into a long and complicated monologue in which he stated that he had not come across any hard evidence of wrong-doing by Brodies in my documentation and ended by saying that, actually, we should drop the case.

When he'd exhausted his repertoire of brainwashing fabrication, I piped up. Mayer instantly stopped me and asked Gillian to remove herself. I remonstrated, but eventually and reluctantly gave way. Gillian was then escorted out of the room by Murray. The minute Gillian and Murray had left the room Mayer grabbed my left arm above the elbow and told me: 'I am your *man*, believe me. I am your *man*,' with great earnestness. I felt disorientated.

Murray then returned leaving Gillian standing alone outside. In answer to their questions I gave them examples of fraud by Brodies. I noted that both Murray and Mayer made copious notes of everything I said. My discourse, with many interruptions from Mayer, lasted only twenty minutes. At its conclusion Mayer informed me that my performance had, in his 'mind and view,' resurrected my case from 'near dead' and he now recommended that we pursue the matter further. Also that I had shown that I had 'the balls' for the case. The word 'balls' resonated and deep down I knew I was being set up.

Mayer then warned me, with all the gravitas he could muster, that I was not to tell Gillian *anything* of what I had told them in her absence. He further warned me that if I did tell her anything I would most definitely be 'found out.' I played along with this. As we were leaving Mayer again informed me in front of Gillian that if I breathed a word of what I had told him and Murray we would be 'found out.' At the time I regarded all these warnings as utter rubbish but decided to continue with Mayer and Murray because of my desperation to get to Court.

As soon as we were out of the building I told Gillian *everything* that had been said while she was out of the room. With hindsight I wished I had called Mayer's bluff and told her everything in front of him and Murray the minute we emerged from the room; and then fired them both on the spot.

Mayer had asked me to produce what he termed a 'Black Chain' document. This was to be a narrative of the misdeeds linking one to another and so on, in chronological order. I decided to give him this despite my near certainty that he was not acting in good faith. This turned out to be another very stupid thing to have done. I completed this 16 page narrative on 28th January after days of work on it. The black chain contained thirty links which connected one misdeed to the next and so on. I posted it to Murray the same day so he, 'could forward it to Mayer' because I was, 'not *allowed* to post it to Mayer direct'.

On Saturday 5th February I received a call from Stewart Mackenzie, the man who had recommended Murray to me. He now warned me to watch out for Murray and to 'keep my back covered,' and so on. Despite all this I determined to keep going with Murray largely because I had already paid him the £3,500.

On 12th May I received a fax from Murray which was a copy of a letter dated 8th May from Mayer to him. In this letter Mayer stated that there were now *no* grounds for any action, that I would not impress the judge,

John Mayer, Advocate. Ironically, now a well known author of legal fiction.

that I had made extremely serious allegations against very respectable lawyers without *anything* to support them. Here is part of his letter:

> Mr Usher boldly asserts that all of these parties (Brodies and others) and perhaps people in the Department of the Auditor of the Court of Session committed fraud upon him, on a grand scale over many years. If proved this would send reverberations such as have never been seen before through the College of Justice and much wider afield. I should think the Justice Minister himself would wish to chair any following investigations.

Mayer's final paragraph contained the very revealing sentence:

> I realise that Mr Usher will forever have many unanswered questions.

This letter caused me to fully and finally accept that Mayer had been acting in bad faith from the very outset. Also that his sole purpose from the very beginning had been to extract as much information as he could for the purpose of showing it to Brodies; thus enhancing his career prospects. He now had my Black Chain of the various frauds over the decades. And so, of course, did Brodies. This was a very credible and cogent record in a very readable, logical and easily transferable form from the only man who knew the whole story. Not to mention all my other papers and documents which he had got from Murray. Sometime later I had the satisfaction of reading that Mayer only narrowly escaped gaol on another matter.

While all this was going on I had been in contact with a London firm of Private Investigators with a view to their assisting me to unmask Brodies and the other parties involved in the fraud. I chose a London firm because I did not now trust *any* Scottish firm in that line of business. This London firm were interested alright and to this end sent up their Managing Director to meet with Murray and myself on 2nd June 2000 at Norton. I won't name either the company or the Private Investigator because all their correspondence to me was marked 'Private and Confidential.'

I opened this meeting by asking Murray to inform the Private Investigator of Mayer's new attitude and change of mind. Murray did so by informing us that the most likely reason for Mayer stating there was no case to answer was that he feared for his future career. So there I had it from the horse's mouth.

On hearing this I thought: 'Why the hell are we even *having* this meeting: whatever further frauds the Private Investigator uncovers will go the same way as the frauds I have already uncovered. Nowhere!'

Murray then proposed a scheme which entailed me raising money by selling the exclusive rights to the 'story' to the media. Murray told us that he had been approached by the *Sunday Times* about this on more than one occasion. I was rather taken aback by this and asked which *Sunday Times* reporter had contacted him. He said it was Jenny Shields, who had already done a big report on my fight on 16th November 1997, as already narrated. Murray then advised with all the gravitas he could muster that I hand over whatever money 'the story' raised to him. He justified this by assuring me that this would stop Brodies getting the money off me which they could claim as a deposit to cover their costs in the event of my losing the case. This is yet another monstrous device routinely deployed by Scottish lawyers and the Scottish Legal system to rob and prevent people from gaining access to the Courts. Murray assured me that Brodies could never get the money off him on the grounds of 'client confidentiality.' He would then settle all *his* fees, the Private Investigator's fees and my costs with this money. Note the order in which he put these proposed settlements; quite revealing. Also note that I was to get only my costs. He estimated that the exclusive rights to the story would fetch between £50,000 and £200,000.

The Private Investigator then stated that he had met Max Clifford the publicist and suggested that he approach him on our behalf. We agreed to that in principle and decided to have another Meeting on 19th June 2000 to finalise our terms of business. This next Meeting would be interesting and the last one I would have with Murray, after which I planned to fire him.

In the meantime Murray informed me that he was trying to get pre-cognitive statements from people who had helped me in the past. Again I was slow in realising that the sole reason for his doing so was to 'get at' them. An example of one person whom he did get at was Theresa Clitheroe of Willis Corroon, the insurance brokers. She was the lady who had been so helpful to Gillian and I, as already narrated. I soon discovered that she 'no longer' worked there. The usual story of decent people 'moving on'.

When I eventually traced her she went cold on me very quickly indeed. Murray and/or the Scottish Legal Mafia had done a good job on her.

In the days before my final meeting with Murray and the Private Investigater at Norton I prepared myself very carefully. The morning of 19th June dawned and off I motored to Norton not exactly with a song in my heart but in keen anticipation that I would glean further useful information. Arriving at Norton on time I found both the Private Investigator and Murray already waiting for me.

Murray reiterated that any money realised from the sale of the story must be held by him because it could never be traced to him, whereas it could be traced to me or any of my friends. He also stated that the Court would insist on me dropping some aspects of the case on the grounds that if I did not drop them the Court would arrange matters in a way that would leave my case 'dead in the water.' He then stated that I had to be 'very careful' not to upset Court officials, Judges and the like because, if I did, they would make things much more difficult for me. He warned me that the Judge in the case would hold it against me that I had not employed the services of an Advocate as he (the Judge) himself would have been an Advocate before he became a Judge. He further stated that I must do everything that he, Murray, told me and trust him implicitly. I was no longer surprised at anything Murray said and realised his sole object in telling us all this nonsense was for the express purpose of enriching himself at my expense. And so the Meeting drew to a close without any commitment from me.

Now we come to something *very* interesting indeed but of which I knew nothing at the time. On 13th June 2000, just six days prior to the Meeting at Norton with Murray and the Private Investigator, a Decree had been issued by the Stirling Sheriff Court against Murray for the payment of £14,261.96 to a company called DLL Technology based in London. No wonder Murray had been so keen that I sell the exclusive rights to the story and give him the money. I did not find out about this until 2005, nor was I to know that Murray would be sequestrated in less than a year's time.

I fired Murray by letter dated 27th June 2000. At the same time I notified him that I would collect my papers from his office on Thursday the 29th. When I, accompanied by my son Richard, arrived at his office on that day Murray pleaded with me to change my mind. I refused and collected my papers. After we left Richard and I agreed we were uneasy in firing Murray as we where back where I had been for years; without a lawyer.

To ease these doubts I decided to check out his story about the *Sunday Times* reporter, Jenny Shields, approaching him with a view to her writing more articles on the matter. I therefore rang her on 1st July 2000 and asked her if she had approached Murray. She responded with some heat that she had never approached anyone about doing another article, let alone Murray, of whom she had never heard. She then expressed her outrage at his claim. So Murray had lied. Of course I let the Private Investigator know that I had fired Murray and that his being approached by Jenny Shields was just another Murray lie.

When I checked the correspondence I had collected from Murray's office against the copies in my files, I discovered that well over half were missing, particularly those with the most damning allegations of fraud against Brodies. Also missing were the *resumes* of my two Meetings with Murray and the Private Investigator, at Norton.

On 9th May 2001 I received information that Murray had closed his Practice and left the country and was setting up in 'business' in Italy. This was stated in Court 3 of the Dundee Sheriff Court. I decided on a plan of action to get my missing correspondence back and cover this later when I put it into action.

As a postscript to this chapter the reader will be interested to know of an article in the *Daily Record* dated 3rd July 2012 which tells of a Lawyer named Tom Murray (yes, it's the same T.H. Murray) who was accused of embezzling a client (Neil McKechnie) out of £18,000 and who dodged paying compensation by holing up in the town of Lucca, in Tuscany. Murray had been arrested by fraud squad detectives in 2007. Weeks later he was arrested again trying to flee the country. At the time of the article Murray had been found guilty three times of professional misconduct: concealing his own bankruptcy in 2001, acting dishonestly and deceiving myself; and then in 2009 guilty of ignoring a court order to repay his embezzlement victim fees and compensation. According to the report, the Scottish Solicitors Discipline Tribunal 'took six years to rule that Murray was guilty of dishonesty and deception' in my case. Yet he was never struck off. On the embezzlement charge first the Crown Court decided that the Law Society needed to deal with it and later (yes, you've guessed it) Phillip Yelland of the Law Society announced they were abandoning the case because of,

> 'The challenge around the question of enforcement arises because Mr Murray is now resident in Italy'.

The injured party Mr Neil McKetchnie is quoted as saying, 'Anyone with the misfortune of being the victim of a lawyer should realise that [their] self-regulation is [their] self-protection'.

PPS. In an article in *The Times* of August 30th 2003 Mr John Mayer, advocate, was found guilty of contempt of court for failing to appear in court to defend a client. *The Times* claims 'this is the first ruling of its kind in Scotland'. Lord Hardie summoned Mayer for an explanation and discovered not only was the advocate meant to be at the Sheriff court but was also due to be at another High Court trial at the same time.

46

SCOTLAND AGAINST CROOKED LAWYERS

I was now back to Square One. I had given it my best shot and had achieved little in the five preceding years other than acquiring a ton of documentary evidence. It had consumed my meagre resources to the extent that we were forced to sell a lot of our furniture to just keep our heads above water, consumed an enormous amount of time and energy, and caused my family great anguish and stress. So was it game, set and match to Brodies and their associates in crime? Over my dead body.

Brodies had defrauded my family on a gargantuan scale. The Accountant of Court had not spotted this *inter-alia* it was largely staffed by lazy and incompetent people who were far more interested in drawing their inflated salaries and safeguarding their pensions. The Law Society of Scotland had concealed the fraud, and the Scottish Legal Services Ombudsman had whitewashed the Law Society, thereby further concealing the fraud. The Police had declined to do anything about it, despite admitting that there was a lot of *skullduggery* in the evidence I had given them. And no lawyer would help me bring Brodies to book, except in bad faith as demonstrated by both Murray and Mayer. What on earth was I to do? The solution came to me very quickly: I would provoke Brodies into suing me and get to Court that way.

Friends and allies had already told me that it was much easier being the Defendant than the Pursuer in the Scottish Courts, because the onus of proof was on the Pursuer. All the Defendant need do was tell the truth. Simplicity itself. My best hope was that the case would be widely reported in the media and that the media would side with me. In that context the Judges would have to decide which was the least damaging to the Scottish Legal system: To pervert the course of justice and find for Brodies and face a media outcry or to find for me which would certainly mean the end of Brodies and, hopefully, the end of the Scottish Legal system in its present utterly corrupt form. I suspected that the judges would take the former course as the lesser of the two evils and brazen it out. However if they did this there would be a price to pay.

MAKING A STAND: Stuart Usher didn't mince his words during his one-man protest outside the legal firm Brodies in the city's Atholl Crescent

House of Usher on streets

A MEMBER of the family which gave Edinburgh the Usher Hall has taken to the streets to protest against a legal firm he claims owes his family millions of pounds.

Stuart Usher carried out a one-man protest outside Brodies and the Law Society of Scotland.

His extravagant claims against Brodies included statements that they are "crooks and fraudsters who, with others, ruined my family".

But the firm and the Law Society of Scotland said that despite years of protest, none of his accusations had ever been proved.

The protest is the latest move in the bizarre legal wrangle Mr Usher has waged since the death of his brother, Sir John, and centres on the fact that Brodies administered the family estate between 1962 and 1994.

Mr Usher, from Jedburgh, claims the estate is owed millions because assets have gone to outsiders or been reduced. A Law Society of Scotland inquiry concluded his complaints were unfounded.

The *Evening News*, carrying the story of my protest outside Brodies' offices.

I therefore commenced a Direct Action Campaign against Brodies to provoke them into suing me for 'Defamation'. To this end I arrived outside Brodies offices at 8.45am on Tuesday 25th July 2000 with two large posters which could be easily read from fifty yards away. I also had 200 flyers with the same comments on them and, in addition, warnings to people not to engage Brodies under any circumstances on the grounds that Brodies were crooks and fraudsters.

I greeted everyone entering the building very cheerfully indeed and handed them my flyers. And I was feeling very cheerful because this was action at last, after years of playing by their Rules and getting absolutely nowhere.

Brodies clerical staff, though somewhat astonished, were surprisingly friendly. One even gave me a covert thumbs up. The lawyers, of course, had faces like thunder which did not stop me telling passers-by in a raised voice, so that these lawyers could hear, that Brodies were fraudsters and thieves whom they should avoid like the plague.

Shortly after nine, to my delight, I espied none other than James Carnegie-Arbuthnott mincing his way towards me. He was the Brodies creep who had done the so-called 'surveying' of the Wells Estate. He read the posters, looked unhappy, and squeaked: 'You had better watch out.' I responded by telling him that he had it the wrong way around and that it was Brodies who had better watch out. He stood there for a moment looking uncomfortable before shuffling off into the building without another word.

Next came two real life lawyers affecting the inevitable umbrellas, approached, stopped and read my posters, but said nothing. I therefore asked them: 'Bad day for Brodies?' The younger of the two, Drummond, who was a Senior Partner, feigned mystification and asked 'Who are you?' I laughed because of course he was well aware who I was. I loudly *enlightened* him. He drew upon his years of training in the black arts: 'Oh, I thought that matter had all been sorted out.' I told him that it had never been sorted out as he well knew. He slunk off, leaving me with the other lawyer, a sallow-faced, small man called Taylor who piped up: 'You know, this could damage us.' No attempt at denial or threatening me with court action. Nothing. I corrected him by telling him that it *would* rather than *could* damage them. Taylor then added: 'But it could also damage *you*.' I looked him squarely in the eye: 'This *will* cause Brodies great damage and do my family a great deal of good.' He turned, and said, with a vicarious smile: 'Ahh, but will anyone believe you?' He then slouched off into the building.

At 9.30am the *Scotsman* and the *Evening News* arrived to cover my one man *exposé* of Brodies. They both published reports on the event. The *Evening News* also published a fair sized picture of me with the posters.

Surely Brodies would now be bound to sue. At 11.30am I packed it up at Brodies and went round to the Law Society of Scotland with the Posters and Flyers and gave them the same treatment.

I gave Brodies a repeat dose in August. Very shortly after arriving and setting up my posters a pleasant-looking young man emerged from Brodies offices and introduced himself to me as Ed Emerson of Brodies Marketing Division. He was American and naturally I inquired if he was a connection of the famous Ralph Waldo Emerson of whom I was a fan. He *was* related, but only distantly. I recalled a pretty piece of Emerson poetry:

> 'Men who for truth and honour's sake
> Stand fast and suffer long.
> Brave men who work while others sleep,
> Who dare with others to fly. . .
> They build a nation's pillars deep
> And lift them to the sky.'

I asked him did he really think he ought to be working for such a dishonest, disreputable, and disgraceful outfit such as Brodies.

Shortly thereafter *Scottish Television* arrived in the person of the effervescent Martin Geissler and a most pleasant and excellent cameraman called Steven. While they were filming Emerson asked me quietly and out of earshot: 'I have to *ask* what you want?'

My answer was: 'I would like Brodies to sue me.'

He asked: '*Other* than wanting Brodies to sue you, what else?'

My reply was, 'Ed, I want justice for my family.' He then whispered: 'I'm sorry, but I have to repeat how *much* do you want?'

I told him that I required damages from Brodies equal to the damages they had inflicted on my family. Ed sighed and stated: 'I have to be clear. How *much* damages do you want?'

I told him that because Brodies had refused to give me access to all my family records I was not in a position to quantify the damages. Only when I had seen all the records would I be in that position.

He persisted and asked me how much damages I would require from the records that I had already acquired. I told him that this figure already amounted to many millions of pounds. At this he looked thoughtful, excused himself, went back into the building; and sent out tea and biscuits. A civilised man at least.

I told Geissler that Brodies had just asked me to name a figure but that I was apprehensive of doing so. Geissler then interviewed me 'live.' I did not mince my words and accused Brodies, Clive, Gertrude and the Estate Manager of fraud and re-iterated my challenge to Brodies to take legal action against me. I then prevailed on Geissler to go into Brodies' offices and issue the challenge on my behalf. To my surprise he did so. When he re-emerged he informed me that 'Brodies have no intention of suing you at this stage.' I was disappointed but a little encouraged by the 'at this stage' bit.

In the afternoon I went over to the Law Society Offices and gave them a repeat dose of the same medicine. Not a peep from them other than the odd shifty face watching from the windows.

The newspaper *Scotland on Sunday* contacted me asking if I would agree to a major feature in its Magazine section. I was delighted and their very pleasant Jackie McGlone came to my home to interview me. The result was a five page main feature spread in the magazine section of the newspaper, with numerous family photos and illustrations of Wells House and Usher Hall. The front cover featured a full page photograph of me on my wife's horse, Royal Choir. I was certain that this major feature would cause enormous damage to Brodies and that they would have no option but to sue. Thank you *Scotland on Sunday* and to Jackie McGlone for restoring some measure of my faith in humanity.

I kept up the pressure on Brodies by picketing their offices. Emerson came out again one day in September, but fearing a trap I declined to give him a figure. I never saw him again. I like to think he realised that Brodies were crooks and fraudsters and had left them forthwith.

The following month a Brodies goon, who never introduced himself but sported a livid scar on his cheek, emerged. He was humourless, thuggish and surly, the very antithesis of Emerson. But like Emerson he asked me how much I wanted. By this time I had decided I *would* name a figure so I told him that I would cease hostilities if Brodies paid me £30 million. He stood there looking uncomfortable, bit his bottom lip, but said nothing. After an uncomfortable silence I decided to test him: I asked him if someone at Brodies had slashed him on his cheek? He neither denied nor confirmed this but looked from side to side as if checking for spies. He eventually mumbled something I couldn't hear and shuffled off into the building. I never saw him again and this time there were to be no tea and biscuits.

An unexpected off-shoot of the publicity generated caused other people who had been swindled by lawyers to pluck up the courage to contact me. This gave me the idea that I should gather as many people as possible to demonstrate outside the Law Society Offices. At that time I was part of a small campaign group called Injustice by the Law which had been founded by a Scot called Anne McKinnon and was being run by an American called Ray Keddie from his home in Perth. I contacted Ray and put forward my idea. He thought it an excellent plan and quickly agreed. The result was that we held our first demonstration outside the Law Society of Scotland.

We decided to build on this success and another demonstration was organised for 1st October 2000 at the same venue. This went off so well, with increasing numbers attending, that I determined to start a brand new Group for the sole purpose of harrying and exposing crooked law firms and lawyers.

So came into being 'Scotland Against Crooked Lawyers.' In the coming years SACL became widely known in Scotland and regarded as a credible champion for the consumers of legal services. It also attracted a following in the rest of the UK.

Scotland Against Crooked Lawyers in action, Edinburgh

47

THE ONSET OF FROST

As this book is primarily about the fraud executed on my own family it is with a heavy heart that I have decided *not* to deviate by describing the many successful activities and achievements of *Scotland Against Crooked Lawyers* here. I will say, however, that these were exciting and uplifting times. The interested reader will still find some SACL activities on the internet.

In early October 2000 I commenced drafting a Writ on behalf of Johnny in my capacity as one of his Executors and another one on behalf of myself for the damages done to ourselves personally. I did this largely 'for the record' purposes because by now I knew I would never be allowed to succeed with them until the whole Scottish Legal system had been either drastically reformed or abolished altogether and replaced by a system which would serve the public interest instead of the lawyers. The existence of the writs I was preparing would also be proof in the future that I had tried to gain personal access to the Courts for Johnny and myself but had been denied access, overcoming any arguments about the passage of time and Time Bars precluding our successors resurrecting these claims at some future date. In the words of the English Judge, Lord Denning: 'Crime overcomes all Time Bars. . . it unravels everything.'

On 11th October 2000 I went to lodge these writs in the Edinburgh Sheriff Court, with Gillian agreeing, as always, to accompany me. On arrival the lady receptionist, Karen Stewart, told us that she was expecting me. How on earth she knew we were coming I do not know because I had never told anyone. Anyway she took the Writs and left the reception area. Shortly thereafter she reappeared accompanied by a man. He informed me that the Writs were not correct, in rather a dictatorial manner. On my asking him what was wrong with them he told me: 'The word *condescendence* is spelt wrongly.' Big Deal! I thanked him and told him that I would put that right in a jiffy. Once I had done so he then upped the ante by informing me I must set out the *Grounds of Jurisdiction* and that the *Pleas in Law* must directly and not *indirectly* back up the *Craves*. He then slouched off leaving me none the wiser.

I then asked Karen Stewart for assistance. She informed us that she was not allowed to give 'legal advice' and that we should consult a lawyer. 'Over my dead body,' I told her. 'We've had *them* in chunks.' She eventually suggested that we consult the Citizens Advice lawyer, downstairs, who would be delighted to help us.

Cheered, we headed downstairs, but the Citizens Advice offices were empty. On knocking on an internal door a woman from somewhere deep within shouted bad-temperedly, 'I'm busy on the phone!' She eventually emerged and having established that she was Susan Downs we asked her if she could explain what was wrong with our Writs. She took a perfunctory look at them before declaring: 'I can't help you. You must consult a lawyer.' We patiently explained that the Court Clerk had sent us downstairs to see her, the Citizen's Advice Bureau lawyer, in order for her to amend the Writs into the required forms. She reluctantly conceded, that she *was* indeed a lawyer but that her working for the Citizens Advice precluded her from giving us any advice - it was against the rules.

We then politely asked what exactly her function was, as a lawyer, in that office if she was not allowed to give the general public advice? She took refuge in the usual lawyer's ploy of answering our question with a question of her own: 'Would you like to see my line manager?'

'Yes we would,' I said. 'About your refusal to assist us.' She didn't like this at all but went off to fetch her 'line manager.'

A short while later the line manager, a Mrs Cameron, entered the room from another door and proceeded to give us another reason altogether as to why Susan Downs couldn't help us: 'Her case load is too heavy,' she gravely intoned.

'Can *you* help us?' we asked.

She told us she could not help with our Writs as it was against the rules. 'Why then are the Citizens Advice offices situated in the Sheriff Court building?' I asked her. Evading my question she then said, with apparent sincerity, that she deplored the Citizens Advice Bureau not being allowed to help members of the public with their Writs and that both she and the CAB had fought this for many years, but with no success at all. She appeared to be genuinely concerned as she told us this. In view of her concern and apparent sympathy for our predicament I invited her to join Scotland Against Crooked Lawyers. As expected she immediately declined the offer. I left it at that other than to tell her that I would write to her to confirm our conversation and her views. She did not like this either but said I could do so if I wanted. We thanked her and left.

At this time I'd also warned Brodies to expect the Writs, and that they were not, under any circumstances, to sell any remaining Trust property. Over the next three months I tried hard to have the Writs accepted by the Sheriff Court but to no avail.

In November 2000 I met a man called Martin Frost in Kelso. He had teamed up with Andrew McNamara of Glasgow, forming a partnership which they called Frost and McNamara. Frost told me he was pursuing many crooked lawyers and law firms on behalf of their victims and claimed to have already notched up notable victories. He certainly seemed to know what he was talking about and I quickly decided that I would let Frost and McNamara represent me. We therefore agreed our terms of business which were that Frost and McNamara would take 20% of whatever the Courts awarded me. Frost then asked me for copies of all the correspondence and documents I had. I, yet again, and as I had done with Murray made copies of them all. This was a monumental task which took me many days. I gave him about 3000 sheets of papers substantiating the various frauds Brodies and their predecessors had perpetrated over the decades.

Frost then calculated that, with competent management the Usher whisky wealth alone including properties should have grown to £365 million. He based his calculation on the whisky-based wealth of our family in 1900 and the increase of property-values since. He also told me that the higher the figure was, the more it would worry Brodies. Eventually I gave him the go ahead to intimate the Writ for £365 million to Brodies mainly because I did not want to cramp his style. He was, after all, the legal expert as far as I was then concerned.

The resulting Writ was described by a Glasgow lawyer in the media as: 'The greatest writ ever raised in this country.' This also resulted in more publicity all over Britain with Brodies being named more and more. Of course these media organisations gave Brodies the opportunity to comment on my fight against them. Brodies simply denied any wrong-doing and sheltered behind the Law Society's findings that they were innocent of any wrongdoing; their *only* comment, courtesy of the Law Society's whitewash.

So by early 2001, I was on the offensive in three different ways: the 'legal' way, the SACL way, and the media way. I was now conducting an unconventional campaign against Brodies. One which they, and the Scottish Legal system, had never before encountered. People on the periphery of the legal milieu told me that the legal establishment now regarded me as a loose cannon rolling around the deck. A cannon they did not have the means to bring under control and one which threatened to sink one of their flagship law firms: 'HMS *Brodies*.' If they lost HMS *Brodies*, who was to say that the rest of the rotten fleet would not go the same way. After all they had humiliated, robbed, and ruined my family. I would continue being the loose cannon.

In early 2002 Frost lodged a new writ (aside from the £365 million writ citing Brodies). However this writ was for only £46.5 million because this represented only my own one eighth share of the £365 million.

An Intimation [a notification to a party that a legal proceeding will be taken] was then issued to each party involved, or suspected of being involved, in the fraud - whether dead or alive. I delivered one of these Intimations to Taits offices, Kelso where the late JGG Leadbetter had spent most of his 'working' sinecured life as a lawyer. I also delivered one, again by hand, to the egregious David Sturrock WS at his office on 15th July 2002. To my great annoyance he refused to sign a receipt for it, twister that he was. One was also sent by registered post to Jacquelin in Hampshire, where she had fled with her new husband, a man called Faulkner, poor devil.

I also gave the Estate Manager his Intimation personally on 12th July 2002, my 61st birthday with Gillian accompanying me for the usual witness purposes. He answered my knock and I wished him 'Good Day' handing him the sealed envelope. 'What is it?' he asked, with some discomfit. 'An intimation requiring you to provide a detailed account of your role in the management of the UBT Estates and later in the affairs of the late Sir Peter and the late Sir Robert Usher, Incapaxes.' He hesitated briefly and then said, 'I don't have to accept this from you.' I responded, 'I am quite aware of that. If you accept it I require you to sign a receipt for it.' He weighed the envelope in his hands, looking thoughtful. Eventually he said, 'I don't think I will accept it.' Note that crooks like the Estate Manager invariably indulge in half-statements which invite reactions from which they hope to gain some advantage. I was in no mood for evasive games and simply demanded, 'Will you or will you not accept it?' This did not allow him any wriggle room. To bring the matter to a close I pulled out my prepared receipt and asked him to sign it. After further cogitations on his part he eventually told me that he would not accept it and handed the envelope back to me. I then said, 'You have declined to accept the envelope. You won't get a second chance.' And turned to leave. He then started to remonstrate. 'Too late, you've had your chance,' said I and off we went leaving him looking somewhat forlorn on his doorstep. We immediately went to Hawick and posted it to him by registered mail.

The Proof hearing of my case for £45 million was set for Monday the 14th of April 2003 at 10am. This was the moment for which I'd waited years. A 'Proof' in Scottish Law is a watershed hearing when, for the first time, hard evidence is provided. In my case I had proof of fraud, theft and a whole host of other criminal activities by Brodies, Clive, the Estate Manager, McClure, Dempster, Carruthers, Houldsworth, Stevens and Jacquelin. On the day before the case Frost told me that it wouldn't actually commence until, at the earliest, 10.30 - so I needn't come at 10.00. I duly arrived at 10.20 and ran into the Court clerk on the stairs. I asked him if Frost had arrived and was everything ready to commence. He just looked at me and said, 'It's all over. Everyone has gone.' Well, you could have knocked me over with a feather. 'Now what?' I thought, and went off to find Frost, fearing the worst. I soon located him in a nearby cafe. Much to my relief he told me that he had changed his mind and had 'sisted' the case because he wanted more time. 'Sisted' is another Scottish legal system mumbo-jumbo word not to be found in English dictionaries and therefore much used by Scottish lawyers to confound lay men and women. It means 'freezed'. He then assured me that the case would be heard in the next month or two. I was only partially satisfied with this explanation but gave him no clue of that.

The next morning Borders TV rang me from Carlisle and expressed their disappointment at my 'giving up'. I soon put them right on that and asked them to arrange an interview with Frost and myself at Frost's house so that they could broadcast it on their Evening News. I was very anxious to stop any notion getting about that I had given up the fight before it gained currency. Borders TV instantly agreed and we did the interview at Frost's house that day. They then broadcast it in their Evening News. Of course I was very thankful indeed to Borders TV. Their boss man, Mr Halliday, had always backed me, no doubt to the fury of Brodies. If you happen to be reading this book Mr Halliday thank you very much for your support; it meant a lot to me and I deeply regret that I never showed my appreciation to you more at the time. In my defence I was constantly in a state of discombobulation with my mind forever in a whirl of disbelief and confusion. Sorry, Mr Halliday. You are welcome to contact me at any time and I will make amends.

A month passed and still no date for my case to be heard. Another month passed with the same result. I therefore decided to have a look at the Court records of my case on the day the 'Proof' was heard. I was aghast to find that there it was in black and white: My case had been abandoned.

Martin Frost - faux lawyer and serial criminal.

Shortly thereafter I, at last, admitted to myself and to my family that Frost had conned us from the word go. It was a retired Lancashire Policewoman and her lady friend who finally convinced me to ditch him. She told us that he was a conman *par excellence* with a long history of conmanship behind him. In the two and a half years I was associated with him he did my family and myself a great deal of damage in terms of material cost and pyschological stress. For example he swindled me out of my beloved Gypsy Queen, Nellie Faa Blyth who featured earlier in this book.

Of course I reported Frost to the Police but they, as usual, declined to do anything about it. One of the Policemen had the decency to tell me that they wouldn't do anything about Frost because he was 'very clever with the law' leaving me in no doubt whatever that many people had reported him to the Police in the past and that they had done absolutely nothing about him.

Frost was the most evil and disgusting person I ever met in my life - and as the reader by now knows, I have met quite a few. He was eventually sequestrated on 27th February 2004 by the Unity Bank and declared a vexatious litigant by the Scottish legal system at about the same time. Thereafter he removed himself to England, thank God.

My only excuse for trusting him was that he was a good actor and an even better liar. He must have made a long study of the art of conmanship. In our case it now quickly became apparent that his aim right from the start had been to make as much money out of the fraud on my family as quickly as possible and to blazes with Macnamara and myself. This would necessitate him scaring Brodies into paying him to abandon the proceedings against them. Many other things now dawned on me. Amongst them was his constant encouragement to me to exaggerate our family wealth. His claim about Professor Green in his 'History of Empire' stating that Andrew II and Sir John being amongst the wealthiest men in the British Empire sprang to mind. I therefore checked out Professor Green's 'statement' and found it did not exist. It was just another lie in Frost's extensive portfolio.

In essence his *modus operandi* was to find indigent victims of professional crime and pose as a White Knight. He would then pretend to help them and when he had got all the information out of them, and what little money they still had, he would threaten the professional criminals with exposure unless they too paid him. In this disgusting process he would spin the same old lies to his victims, for example, 'You know I have just been diagnosed with leukaemia and given only two years to live,' and then put on the look of a Saint who had been unjustly punished by the Almighty. He forged signatures as and when it suited him and utilised every filthy device imaginable to deceive his victims and scare the lawyers into paying him off. On top of that he was a sadist. One of the two ladies who warned me about him said he referred to my family and myself as his ' prey.'

And how did the Trustee of Frost's sequestrated estate fare? The Trustee was an RS MacGregor of the Accountancy firm of MacGregors of Edinburgh.

As soon as I heard he had been appointed the Trustee of Frost's estate I contacted him and warned him about Frost. He was at first sceptical but then began to take some heed as he became inundated with complaints about Frost from a host of other creditors. I told MacGregor that he would get nowhere with Frost and that 'his' assets were non existent but his liabilities were rock solid and growing fast all the time and therefore he should warn the creditors straightaway that they would get nothing.

I rang MacGregor in December of 2011 (eight years later) to find out how he had got on. By good fortune I got a lady who was actually *still* working on Frost's sequestration when I rang. She informed me that they still had not produced a final set of Accounts on the sequestration. She also informed me that she was still waiting for a response to her last letter to MacGregor's own solicitors, which had been sent in July 2010 - a delay in replying of one year and five months. She also told me that MacGregor had received less than one thousand pounds for all his work in the multi million pound sequestration. But that all the lawyers 'involved' and the Accountant in Bankruptcy had run up costs in excess of £200,000, payable by the Taxpayer, on a sequestration that had achieved next to nothing. Also that the Accountant in Bankruptcy refused to communicate any more with Mr MacGregor. And yet the man who precipitated all this misery, Frost, was allowed to walk Scot-free. Sound familiar?

For the record I never spoke to Frost again until 12th July 2012, my 70th birthday. I was talking to a friend in Jedburgh Town Square when I saw him walking towards us. When he was close to us I demanded, 'What the hell are you doing in Jedburgh?' He mumbled inaudibly. I then asked him, 'Are you still conning people, you bastard?' He responded: 'Of course.' And then shuffled off.

48

I PUT THE BANKS ON NOTICE AND CHANNEL 4 TELEVISION ENTERS THE FRAY

Towards the end of 2000 the man, Nigel Percy-Davies, who had purchased Hallrule House and a lot of the forestry from Reddihough in 1995 went bankrupt. He was caught in the Stockmarket crash in the Far East at that time. He had spent a great deal of money on Hallrule House and the Stable block. He also had a collection of vintage cars stored there. When he purchased Hallrule House he was reputed to be awfully rich. However he now suddenly disappeared, losing Hallrule House, the woodlands, his vintage cars and his Swiss wife into the bargain. He also left the Hallrule House staff unpaid. Of all the newcomers to Rulewater he was the most pleasant to me, so I did have a little sympathy for him despite his evicting us from our little cottage near Wells in the winter of 1995.

As soon as the Percy Davies' properties were advertised for sale I wrote, by recorded delivery as always, on the 7th November 2000 to all the major British Banks and Building Societies, putting them on notice not to lend money to any aspirant purchasers of these properties on the grounds that Court action was planned to have them returned to their rightful owners - my family of Usher of Norton and Wells. In the same letter I also informed all these Banks and Building Societies that the occupation of properties in Rulewater by the Mactaggarts was the consequence of another huge fraud and should the Mactaggarts attempt to use the Title Deeds of these properties as security for trying to purchase any of the Percy-Davies' properties to have nothing whatever to do with them. This, equally, would be an act of fraud. Amongst the Banks I put On Notice, both to their Head Offices and their branches in the Borders of Scotland, were the Royal Bank of Scotland, the Bank of Scotland and the Clydesdale Bank. In like manner I also notified the leading Estate Agencies in the Borders such as John Sale and Company in connection with the sale of these properties. I received a brief response from most of them acknowledging receipt but from the Mactaggarts, to whom I also had sent copies of the Notices, not a squeak. Not a squawk.

In the first week of April 2001, I received a telephone call from a David Nath of London Weekend Television. He specialised in producing Documentaries for Channel Four. He had been following my fight against Brodies in the media and asked me if I was agreeable to a Documentary being made on it. I told him I was.

I gave Nath an outline of Brodies' role in the pillaging of our family and he told me he would put it to the Documentaries Department of Channel Four and revert to me quite soon. About three weeks later he contacted me and told me that he had the go-ahead. He informed me that the filming would take many months and would be broadcast as one of Channel Four's 'Cutting Edge' series in the late Autumn. I was delighted. Actually this was the third approach I'd had from Television firms.

Channel Four were keen to have Brodies participate. To this end they repeatedly invited them to give their side of the story. Not surprisingly Brodies steadfastly refused to do so. They were, as usual, playing possum. However their not participating began to make even the sceptical Television people wonder: 'If Usher is a lying toad this would be a wonderful opportunity for Brodies to expose him as just that. How come they refuse to give their side of the story. Is it possible Brodies are a group of saints who have done nothing wrong? Unlikely.'

Nath and his capable cameraman, Paul, arrived at my home to commence filming in May. By the Grace of God our first day of filming couldn't have been nicer - splendid sunshine, the trees clothed in spring glory, lambs gambolling in the fields and the whole Border country looking its pristine best. I took them on a tour of what had been our beautiful Wells Estate. Nath told me that the documentary would focus on me and my long and lonely fight, first and foremost and would not get involved in the legalities of the situation. I was rather disappointed at this as I had envisaged the documentary delving into specific instances of fraud by Brodies; but it was much better than nothing. I felt that people would draw the inevitable conclusion when they saw my passion and integrity.

In the ensuing months we did a great deal of filming on the Estate, at my home near Jedburgh and in Jedburgh itself. We also did some filming of the locals and myself in action in the Cannon pub in Jedburgh one Friday night. I warned the publican, Vincent Mortimer, of our coming and suggested that we play our normal Friday evening games of chess. Vince and I adore the game and are about the same strength. Vince was perfectly amenable to this but told me that he would play badly on purpose as it wouldn't do for the viewers to see me lose the game. A very sporting gesture and the measure of the man. Getting beaten would not have worried me at all, but I concurred with his plan. So the evening commenced with introductions all round.

I soon espied a potential spy amongst the company in the pub who I knew to be friendly with the Mactaggarts. I had never seen him in the pub before.

After about a quarter of an hour he left, seemingly in a hurry. Well wishers in the pub told me that this fellow had spoken badly of me and that this had annoyed them so much that they told him to get out, fast. I immediately suspected that he was a Mactaggart plant.

Vince and I commenced our game. Vince soon gave me the chance of capturing one of his knights in a shallow combination which I would normally have seen straightaway. However, looking this gift horse in the mouth, I missed it and soon thereafter blundered badly myself by leaving one of my own pieces *en prise*. Vince had to take it. He then gave me a nudge with his foot under the table to tell me to: 'Wake up!' Anyway I played like a fowl that evening and only 'won' by default, courtesy of Vince!

Meanwhile the film crew interviewed various pub worthies for their views on my struggle with Brodies. They all did me proud as I discovered when the documentary was first broadcast.

We also filmed two Scotland Against Crooked Lawyers demonstrations in Edinburgh. One on the south side of Princes Street, Edinburgh and the other outside the Scottish Parliament buildings. We also did some filming both inside and outside the Usher Hall where we received every possible co-operation from the management. We did two stints of filming outside Brodies' Offices with a bagpiper friend of mine, Davie Wood, playing stirring Scottish marches and the odd lament and myself with posters and the like. Nath had asked me to make new, less offensive posters to protect London Weekend Television and Channel Four from any Brodies litigation so these were rather tame in comparison to my usual "smack 'em in the eyes" posters. I took my wife's Shetland pony, Briar Heather, alternatively known as 'Fatty', to the second of these demonstrations to add a spot of colour. I informed the Brodies staff, and members of the public as they entered the building, that I was there to collect a £365 million cheque from Brodies, to the accompaniment of Davie Wood playing a stirring rendition of 'Scotland the Brave'. Needless to say Fatty proved a great hit with passers-by.

In contrast the Brodies lawyers regarded Fatty and the rest of us with icy, reptilian eyes. They were obviously under the strictest orders from the big guns at Brodies not to react in any way. At the appointed time of 11.00am I entered Brodies Offices to collect the cheque. It was not ready. I therefore asked to see the egregious Drummond, the senior partner of Brodies. A large, gravelly-voiced woman who I took to be his secretary then appeared and repeatedly told me that he was on his way down to meet me. After 20 minutes, however, he had still not appeared so I told the woman that Drummond had lied to her. He never did appear.

So the summer passed with filming taking place for two or three days every fortnight or so. Luckily the weather was invariably good. We received exceptional co-operation and support from the locals with the exception of the people whom I regarded as usurpers, now living on the Wells estate as 'owner occupiers'. They just looked 'uncomfortable.' Those who had purchased land with timber on it were not slow in cutting it down, ready to fell or not. A good example of this were the Mactaggarts cutting down the avenue of trees leading to Hallrule House. This was a typical example of their lack of appreciation of the finer things in life, not to mention her usual avatism for money. One of the last bits of filming was of Fatty and myself climbing Ruberslaw and looking out over Bedrule and what had been the Wells Estate.

There was however one discordant note in this period - Frost. Nath asked him repeatedly for sight of the £365 million Writ. Frost always assured him that he would let him see it, but never did. In the end Nath expressed his doubts about its existence to me. I assured Nath that it had been served alright because Frost had repeatedly assured me he had done so. But still Frost would not let Nath have sight of it. I therefore tackled Frost about it. As usual he assured me that it *had* been served. 'Why then haven't you shown it to Nath?' I asked him. He just stood there, shrugged his shoulders . . . and changed the subject. I told Nath I could not understand it but to my great later regret did not insist on seeing the Writ myself. The trouble was, to my shame, that I did not want to offend Frost by inferring that I did not believe him. This was the age old story of what happens when a victim of fraud becomes desperate to avoid further bad news. I therefore buried my disquiet, even overlooking other dubious behaviour by Frost.

In August Nath wrote to Mrs Mactaggart asking her if she would like to take part in the Documentary. It took her three weeks to reply. She flatly refused to participate, saying she did not want to get involved with, 'Stuart Usher's fight with Brodie.' Sly, but clever. Of course my fight was as much with *her* as it was with Brodies. After all it was Mrs Mactaggart who was squatting on Hallrule Farm.

Our last stint of filming was in late September. There now ensued months of waiting for the documentary to be broadcast, but it kept being delayed. First there was the Sept 11th attack on the World Trade Centre in New York. Then some other big news items. 2002 came. Then the Queen Mother died. It was to be broadcast in March, then April, then May. Eventually Nath told me that Brodies were applying enormous pressure to have it cancelled. This in itself was a good measure of how worried they were. I did my best to counteract this pressure from Brodies. Channel Four did some editing to make it more palatable to Brodies who had, I later discovered, seen the documentary sometime in mid-summer 2002. Of course I thought this most inequitable because I had never seen it because Channel Four had never told me that they had shown it to Brodies. If I had known that I would have objected. As always Brodies seemed to be one step ahead of me. Then Nath told me that Channel Four had agreed to blot out the text of my already much toned-down posters and to put in a statement by Brodies at the conclusion of the documentary. Brodies intimidation seemed endless and this worried me no end. I reminded Channel Four that Brodies had not had the courage to sue me in the past, despite my accusing them of being Crooks and Fraudsters on my posters in the most public way imaginable. Also that Brodies had refused to take part in the Documentary when asked to do so when it was filmed. So how come they were now letting Brodies edit the documentary? At last in early September Channel Four took the plunge and decided to broadcast, despite all Brodies' intimidation and bluster. I heaved a sigh of relief.

Predictably they entitled the documentary 'The Fall of the House of Usher' and it was extensively trailed to be broadcast on 12th September 2002. I sat down to watch it and actually missed the beginning as Richard battled to set up the recorder. I was a little apprehensive in case Channel Four, under sustained pressure from Brodies, had turned the whole thing against me. Some people had warned me that this had sometimes happened. So it was with some reservations that we, Gillian, Richard and myself sat down to watch it. My daughter Katherine was away at the time. Quite quickly, and with much relief, I knew that my worst fears would not be borne out. Yes, some clever camera angles, mischievous editing and equally mischevious choice of accompanying music conspired to make me look a bit of an idiot but overall and despite Brodies best efforts to sabotage the production, I felt the viewing public would side with me.

And mercifully this proved to be the case. the phone started ringing even before the programme ended. All the callers, the majority from strangers, damned Brodies and the Scottish legal system in general and encouraged me to fight on. I was touched and very much heartened.

In the days following the broadcast I received countless messages by letter, e-mail and via Channel Four from people who had watched the programme. Every one of those people supportive in the extreme and encouraged me to soldier on. I was enormously grateful and tried to contact as many as possible. If I missed anyone who is reading this book please accept my most sincere apologies and you are welcome to contact me at any time. Here is an extract from one such letter, from a Scottish medical doctor:

> 'It may be of interest to you that I have spent many years of research into Scottish Law, taking Legal Seminars etc, for my book on Scottish Law. Perhaps you could advise me on a good title for it. My preference is for: *Scots Law, Satanic Law.* My wife thinks : *'Scots Law, Rotten to the Core'* might be better. . . Everything breaks down in Scotland from the complete disaster which is Scottish Law.'

For the record I suggested that his wife's idea was the better. This title is certainly true because Scots Law has now evolved into a sophisticated and refined system for the enrichment of its practitioners only and to blazes with such naive concepts as justice for the victims of injustice. Originally Scots Law was rooted in Roman and Germanic customary law. In the normal course of events it would have evolved into a decent legal system which delivered justice to the Scottish people. However, probably commencing in the 1500s, it started being perverted by Scottish lawyers into a weapon to be used for their own benefits rather than for the Scottish people. Over the ensuing centuries this perverting process continued unabated turning it into, in the words of the good doctor, the present 'Satanic Law' now pertaining in Scotland. I suspect this process of corruption accelerated rapidly after World War Two with the establishment of the Law Society of Scotland at that time. Much the same applied to English Law since the end of World War Two.

Unfortunately the good doctor's book has never, to my knowledge, been published and I have lost contact with him

Here is another extract from a letter from an Edinburgh resident:

> 'I am usually indifferent to anything televised. However I felt compelled to contact you to make known my own feelings with regard to your plight. You have no chance of receiving recompense because the structure is specifically in place to prevent such, and has been established for many, many years and, at this moment in time, is inviolable. In other words, even when you have undeniable evidence to support your claim, the corrupt system is so well organised that protection of the club members is never breached (except when a scapegoat is necessary).'

This precisely reflected my opinion and experience. However nothing lasts forever and surely it is only a question of time before the anger in Scotland reaches a level which demands that this abomination is replaced it with something worthy of the country.

stuart usher

From: <SSSSHH20202@aol.com>
To: <stuart@the-house-of-usher.co.uk>
Sent: 28 January 2003 12:56
Subject: Concerned 22 year old Student from Kenley in Surrey-

Dear Mr Usher,

It is Tuesday 28th January 2003, I saw a documentary about your fight for your family's heritage and rightful wealth. I was disgusted by what I saw. I cannot believe you and your family were forced from your magnificent estate and livelyhood. It is blatently obvious to me that the company which handled the estate after the death of your uncle was only looking out for their own corrupt interests!! I would like to know how you have got on in your fight against them? I would also like to know if there is any petition people can sign or any help that can be given to your cause?
I have always been very interested in history and am very proud to be British! I therefore am outraged by the demise of your family's estate and way of life which was unique. This also has an affect on the continuation of the historical traditions in British society.

Just a few of parts from emails which I received in the days and weeks following the Channel Four broadcast

ushers@freenetname.co.uk

From: <FOXINA2@aol.com>
To: <stuart@the-house-of-
Sent: 12 September 2002 22:22
Subject: Stuart I am with you

Dear Stuart and Family

I am absolutely with you but please do not lose the plot. I am from England I understand completely the systems used by lawyers. I am also a woman and have had to fight myself..in England they are no different although my situation was very different from yours. I did an MBA and studied some law...unbelievable tricks used and therefore believe you and think you are absolutely right...I have no doubts. but please maintain your sanity....you need an analytical approach...you are thrashing about dear. Keep gong you lot....and if I can help, I can analyse and I think that is what you need.

Love Christinexx

My main purpose in contacting you is in the hope that the many who have suffered similar fates as ourselves will also contact you and we may, through the sheer volume of victims, be in a position just even to instigate the exposure of the corrupt system. If this forlorn hope looks like it may have the beginnings of a foundation I would be pleased to discuss any way forward. It is twenty years since my problem. I stopped taking direct action about six years ago. Your attitude portrayed on television is exactly the same as my own and I would consider restarting concerted efforts. I agree with you that, whilst others imply the methods involved are bizarre, the brain is not clouded and right should always take precedence.

Within a week of the documentary being broadcast Valerie, who the reader will remember was Clive's wife and Mrs MacTaggart's mother, passed away after a short illness. Also within that week, on 17th September 2002 the police arrived at my home. Brodies had taken the gloves off.

The two policeman were courtesy personified but appeared to be somewhat embarrassed. They informed me that 'someone' had made a complaint about a comment I had made in the documentary.

'Really,' I answered, wracking my brains. 'And what was the comment?'

They told me the comment was that I had threatened to, 'Nail a few lawyers in Edinburgh.' Now the penny dropped: Nath had asked me on camera, if I sometimes got frustrated in my fight against Brodies. I had responded by telling him that indeed I did, and that I sometimes felt like borrowing a gun and going to Edinburgh to 'nail a few lawyers', but had made no mention of Brodies by name. The two policemen seemed more amused than anything else about this and tipped me the wink that regarding the crookedness of lawyers they couldn't agree more. Of course I asked them who had laid the complaint but they apologised and told me they were not allowed to tell me who it was. I then said I had no option but to conclude that it was Brodies. They allowed a silence to hang in the air. They then questioned me at length on my comments, giving me an opportunity to retract what I had said. I declined to do so. When pressed on whether I *would* ever carry out my feelings I informed them that I would *not* because any action of that sort would be detrimental to my case. Still, rather apologetically, they told me they had no option but to ask me for my shotgun and shotgun certificate. I considered refusing because they had no warrant but eventually I agreed to do so, purely as the lesser of two evils. However I agreed to do so on the express condition that they sign a document of my making which was to the effect that I handed my shotgun over on a 'without prejudice' basis and that I expected it to be returned soon. They were thankful for this and signed the document without demur. We then parted on excellent terms.

Naively I believed I would have my shotgun back within a few weeks after all the fuss had abated. Of course, this had been another ploy by Brodies to discredit me. The media interviewed me on the matter and published reports on it.. Likewise the radio broadcast an interview with me on the matter.

49

I CHALLENGE ALISTAIR CAMPBELL, THE CHAIRMAN OF BRODIES, TO A TRIAL BY COMBAT

The more I thought about the confiscation of my shotgun the more incensed I became. By now I had discovered that Trial by Combat had never been repealed in Scotland. This gave me an idea. What about my challenging Brodies to a Trial by Combat? After all the Scottish Legal system had denied me the right to hold Brodies to account by trial in the Courts. Brodies had then refused to sue me for 'defamation' despite my having given them ample opportunity to do so. That being the case I decided that I challenge them to a Trial by Combat as the only means of obtaining some form of justice.

But who would I challenge? Houldsworth the snake? Stevens the lying toad? Alistair Campbell, the Chairman of Brodies and therefore Chief reptile? I decided on Campbell because I thought, as the man ultimately responsible at Brodies, he was the most likely person to have got the Police to confiscate my gun. I therefore faxed Alistair Campbell on the 23rd September 2002 challenging him to a Trial by Combat in the arena of my choice: Princes Street Gardens - The Field of Combat.

This *must* have exercised Brodies - Campbell in particular and yet I waited for a response in vain. I therefore faxed him again on 5th October and warned him of the consequences of his continued refusal to reply to my challenge. This had the required effect. I received a reply on Brodies letter-headed and water-marked writing paper dated 8th October 2002, but not signed by Campbell nor any other partner of Brodies. The letter was however signed by a person called 'Brodie'. The letter stated that no one would turn up from their office for the Trial by Combat. I did not accept this on the grounds firstly, that there is no person called 'Brodie' listed as a partner at Brodies, secondly that I had not challenged anyone called 'Brodie' to the Trial by Combat, thirdly I had not challenged the firm of Brodies to the Trial by Combat, and fourthly my challenge was to Campbell and Campbell alone. Readers please note: When a lawyer does not sign letters emanating from his office, or signs them under a *nom de plum*, you can be sure you have him worried. I therefore notified Campbell on 19th October 2002 of my choice of weapons, venue, date, time and prizes as he had not availed himself of the opportunities I had given him to reply. I reproduce this letter below:

'Alistair Campbell (Chairman of Brodies WS)
c/o Brodies WS
15 Atholl Crescent
Edinburgh

19/10/2002

Sir

TRIAL BY COMBAT.

I refer to my letter dated 5/10/2002 and faxed to you on that date.

You have not responded to my challenge to Trial by Combat within the fourteen days stipulated in my letter to you dated 5/10/2002.

I therefore regard you as a coward and shall publicise this fact to all I meet, as per that letter.

I also re-issue my challenge to you to meet me in Trial by Combat on the following conditions:

1 WEAPONS: Fists (Bare).

2 MODE: Boxing (Queensberry Rules) and Wrestling.

3 VENUE: Princes Street Gardens (opposite the New Club)

4 TIME: Trial by Combat to commence on the firing of the one o'clock gun on Edinburgh Castle

5 DATE: Saturday 16th November 2002.

6 PRIZES:

6.1 My shot-gun.

6.2 One million pounds sterling.

These prizes to go to the winner of the Trial by Combat. As I am not worth more than a few pounds (largely thanks to the firm of which you are the Chairman, Brodies WS) I shall pay you (personally) out of the sum on which my court case is based (£365 million), now in the Scottish Courts, in the unlikely event of your prevailing against me. If the Police have not returned my shot-gun at the time of the Trial by Combat you will have to collect it from them in the (again) unlikely event of your prevailing against me.

In the likely event of my prevailing against you I require you to pay me the £1 (one) million pounds sterling within one month of my victory over you. My information is that you are, not surprisingly, a very wealthy man and well able to pay the £1 (one) million pounds. Should my information be incorrect I expect you to liquidate all your personal assets (with the exception of the clothes and shoes you stand in) and pay the proceeds to me. If you do this in good faith I shall let you off whatever the shortfall might be. You will then get a taste of the poverty which my family and I have had to endure these past few years and have plenty of time to rue the day you commenced your career with Brodies of Edinburgh WS.

In case you did not know (and for the record) I did receive a very brief letter on Brodies letter-headed and water-marked paper (dated 8/10/2002) signed by someone called *Brodie*. This *Brodie* chap does not appear among the list of the people associated with Brodies WS and printed on that letter. Please inform me who he is, why he wrote to me and what function he carries out for Brodies WS.

Finally I would be obliged if you would confirm or deny (unequivocally) that the firm of which you are the Chairman (Brodies WS) was founded by the successor(s) of the infamous Deacon Brodie, the robber and murderer who was hung in Edinburgh in 1788. I was informed by an Edinburgh resident that the firm of which you are the Chairman (Brodies WS) was founded by a successor of the infamous Deacon Brodie, — hence my inquiry.

Yours with sincerity and contempt

Stuart Usher.'

Still no response.

With the help of friends and allies in Edinburgh who disliked crooked lawyers as much as I did we enlisted the help of an enthusiast of medieval modes of battle in Scotland and the music played before battle who agreed to attend the Trial by Combat to make it more authentic. He also brought along a bagpiper, drummer and other musicians to aid authenticity. They all agreed to provide their services free of charge because they were aware I had no money to pay them and because, like me, they also held the legal profession in contempt. I was most heartened and thankful for this support. I then notified SACL members of the imminent Trial by Combat and one of them, Billy Burns, consented to be my second.

The day of the Trial by Combat dawned rather dull as I left home for Edinburgh. Gillian came under her own steam. I think she thought I might be arrested or make a fool of myself. Thankfully the weather cheered up as I approached Edinburgh. I decamped at the Usher Hall, suitably armed with Flyers, the Scottish Battle flag, Scotland Against Crooked Lawyer Banners and the Poster referring to Campbell as a Coward in the event of his not turning up. Billy Burns, my Second, arrived soon after with more banners. The Pipe and Drum Band then arrived and we introduced ourselves. The band then struck up ancient pre-battle preparation pieces. These, as one would expect, were very stirring indeed. It was a tremendous and most stirring sound and spectacle. The band were replete with a bagpiper, clad in 14th century battle dress; a brownish plaid with buckles and wound ribbon socks and rough footwear. All this gave the proceedings

My Medieval Battle Band, outside the Usher Hall, are ready to set off for the Field of Combat

a dramatic and authentic air - and of course this resulted in a crowd gathering to watch. I handed out flyers to them which invited them to join us in the Princes Street Gardens to watch a crooked lawyer receive the thrashing of his life. Not surprisingly some people were incredulous that it was not against the law for me to give this lawyer a thrashing. On my telling them it was quite lawful in Scotland, they wished me well saying that the lawyers and the legal profession in general 'stank' and could do with a good thrashing. A member of a singing group called the Hothouse Flowers, who were to perform at the Usher Hall that evening took quite an interest in the proceedings and posed for a photograph with me. I hope he got some musical ideas from the medieval band.

At 12.45 we formed ourselves into a column and, with banners flying we marched down to the venue in Princes Street Gardens. The band then struck up ancient pre-battle preparation pieces. These, as one would expect, made for a most most stirring sound and spectacle. We arrived at the venue in good time, shortly before one o'clock. Off went the Edinburgh *One O'Clock Gun*, bang on time, as it had done since 1859, with an ear splitting crack! One of the women in the crowd, probably a tourist, nearly passed out with

Alistair Campbell, the Chairman of Brodies, fails to show up for the ancient and honourable Scottish tradition of settling disputes: Trial by Combat

fright. She might well have thought the gun going off was Campbell taking a cowardly potshot at me from a safe distance

We planted a claymore in the middle of the ring we had marked out and awaited the arrival of Alistair Campbell. Whilst thus waiting I looked up at the New Club which was opposite us on the other side of Princes Street and thought to myself: 'I hope you filthy lawyers in there are watching this.' The New Club in Edinburgh is infested with lawyers. In the duplicitous world of Edinburgh lawyers any lawyer who does not belong to the New Club is regarded as a complete non-entity by the lawyers who do belong to it. Much the same applies to the Muirfield Golf Club in East Lothian.

I allowed Campbell of Brodies fifteen minutes in which to show. To my profound disappointment he funked it. This led to my second, Billy Burns, a man steeped in Scottish History and the best type of patriotic Scot saying of Alistair Campbell, the Chairman of Brodies WS: 'He must be of *the Campbells are coming, ye ken by the smell* lineage.' I then planted my board accusing Alistair Campbell of Brodies WS of being a Coward in the middle of the ring facing Princes Street and the New Club. This could be read by the people who had gathered in Princes Street to watch. We then removed ourselves, packed everything away, and had a few pints at the Shakespeare pub next to the Usher Hall.

The media covered this event. The drip drip of media stories did not do Brodies any good at all. Various reporters told me of Brodies contacting

Alistair Campbell (note the eyes).

'It is not what a lawyer tells me I may do; but what humanity, reason, and justice tell me I ought to do.'

Edmund Burke

them and complaining bitterly about their reporting on my campaign against them. A short while later *Harpers Magazine* of New York rang me and asked me for a copy of my letter challenge to Alistair Campbell of Brodies. I gave it to them and they published it in full in an article on the Trial by Combat in their 1st of March 2003 edition under the heading: 'A Thane in the Ass.'

Here I have a correction to make! In my challenge to Campbell the Coward I referred to the notorious Deacon Brodie as a murderer and grave robber. I had always thought this was the case but have recently discovered that this is not true. I apologise for the misapprehension. Brodie was, rather, a serial burglar by night as well as a wealthy and respected Deacon by day. It is generally accepted that Robert Louis Stevenson's world famous novel 'The Strange Case of Dr Jekyll and Mr Hyde' was based on the life of Deacon Brodie. Here is part of an article on Deacon Brodie:

> 'In 18th Century Edinburgh, a city famous for more than its fair share of scoundrels [no change there] Deacon William Brodie stands out. Brodie was the son of a well known cabinet maker and inherited a great sum of money on the death of his father, as well as the business. However he could not keep the dark side of his nature from rearing its dissolute head.
>
> He roamed the dark and dangerous streets of Edinburgh by night and frequented the most disreputable and hellish whorehouses, gambling dens and pubs. His companions were of the worst sort; drunkards, whore-masters, burglars and worse. But none of this activity was known to the City Elders and other pillars of society with whom he often mixed by virtue of his being a Deacon (a Head of a Guild). His talents as a cabinet maker were sought after by the wealthy. With regular access to the large houses of the wealthy Brodie secretly made wax impressions of their door keys. With these and inside knowledge of the comings and goings of his wealthy

patrons Brodie and his gang of burglars robbed them time and again. During the day he mixed with the gentry and at night he robbed them!

He became richer and richer and his gang larger and larger. He took two mistresses and sired many illegitimate children with them. He went on robbing undetected for many years. He hobnobbed with Robert Burns, Scotland's National Poet and Scotland's most famous painter, Sir Henry Raeburn.

He eventually over reached himself by robbing the Edinburgh Excise Office in 1788 and fell under heavy suspicion when one of his fellow burglars spilt the beans on him to get the reward which had been offered by the government. He was arrested as he tried to board a boat for Amsterdam. He was quickly found guilty and sentenced to hang in October 1788. A crowd of many thousands watched his hanging, amazingly on gallows that he himself had designed."

But the story of Brodie did not end there. Reports soon started coming in that he had been repeatedly seen in Amsterdam. These reports caused the masses in Edinburgh to think that the Auhorities had hung someone who looked like him and that Brodie had escaped or was even being protected by them. Accusations of a cover-up then started. To scotch these stories once and for all the Authorities had his coffin dug up to show his body to the people. However when they opened his coffin it was, hang onto your hats, empty! Stories then circulated that he'd had a steel collar and other apparatus made in his workshop which he fitted to his neck and body on the day of his hanging to stop the rope breaking his neck; and that he'd

Deacon Brodie as portrayed by an American drama series (note the wig)

bribed the Hangman to put the rope around the steel collar. So it appears that Brodie, resourceful as ever, had survived his hanging., and thereafter escaped. He was never seen in Edinburgh again. Rumour has it that he left Amsterdam and went to America, no doubt to continue his life of crime in that country.

If Brodies the lawyers had in fact been founded by a descendant of the infamous Deacon this would be an explanation - though no excuse for the many people it has damaged and in some cases, like my family, ruined. Brodie the robber in the eighteenth century and Brodies still robbing in the twentieth and twenty first century, nothing has changed except the *modus operandi*.

In fact the only marked difference between the present day Brodies, the lawyers, and William Brodie of the eighteenth century is that the present day Brodies commit their crimes mostly by day whereas William Brodie committed his at night. However the present day Brodies occasionally show their true colours at night as well as the following episode attests:

On the evening of 12th June 2005 Brodies held a party for its staff at the five star Sheraton Hotel in Edinburgh. According to one media report the party descended into 'complete mayhem' with 'fists flying everywhere' and 'it got pretty nasty.' Another report stated that, 'All hell broke loose with the five star hotel resembling something out of the Wild West.' The Police were called but nothing ever came of it, of course. That was vintage Brodies.

The Guardian

Then there was the party last week at a five-star Edinburgh hotel [The Sheraton Grand] given by one of Scotland's leading law firms, Brodies. 'The fists were flying everywhere' according to one witness. Unfortunately involved in the fracas was Alistair Orr, a partner in the firm. But no longer. Brodies has confirmed that Orr has resigned as a partner, with immediate effect.

Visit Scotland

All is Forgiven

Brodies Champions of Tennis is delighted to announce the Sheraton Grand Hotel & Spa as their official hotel partner for the inaugural Brodies Champions of Tennis tournament due to be held in Edinburgh between 20 and 23 June, 2013. This unique offer is available for accommodation on the 19th or 20th June, with tennis tickets available on the 20th or 21st June. The cost is £370 per room, based on two sharing, including a hearty breakfast.

Throughout the month of June, the Sheraton Grand will be celebrating this unique partnership by hosting "Tennis Month".

To book the Brodies Champions of Tennis package, please reserve online

50

WAS MY CAMPAIGN HURTING BRODIES?

The reader could be forgiven for concluding that my own immediate family and I were the only ones who suffered in this imbroglio. This was not the case at all; Brodies also suffered. In war you do not tell your enemy how you are faring. Instead you try and ascertain how your enemy is faring. So I kept my ears open as to the damage my campaign was inflicting on Brodies. And I was damaging them alright, as the following attests.

In 1999, as a consequence of a report in the *The Scotsman* newspaper about my campaign against Brodies, an Edinburgh lady went public about her own rotten experiences with Brodies. She had fired Brodies in 1998 and asked for her papers to be returned to her. Brodies had sent what she thought were her papers to her by taxi. Other peoples' money is no object at Brodies. On opening the parcel she was horrified to discover the Wills and Last Testaments of the Earl of Seafield and Ross, the Brodie of Brodies Castle and Sir George Tennant, all significant landowners The lady immediately asked Brodies to uplift the Wills. Brodies failed to do so for a whole *year*! This showed how little Brodies cared about the Wills of their clients. Reading about my fight against Brodies the lady then decided, very wisely, that she would also land Brodies in the mire! She informed *The Scotsman* about their failure to collect these very confidential and sensitive documents. *The Scotsman*, to its credit, immediately published the episode. The effect on Brodies was immediate: They sent another taxi forthwith to her home to collect the Wills; but the damage had been done.

At about the same time a Scotland Against Crooked Lawyers supporter who lived in Edinburgh informed me that the Brodies partners were taking out individual insurance policies to protect themselves against my claim, as opposed to relying only on the Law Society's 'Master Policy' to protect them and that this had never happened before in the murky, criminal world of Edinburgh law practices.

Towards the end of 2001 I was told that Brodies had lost three seriously wealthy clients as a consequence of my campaign against them.

In an effort to repair the damage Brodies placed a large advertisement in *The Scotsman* of 12th December 2002. This advertisement opened by stating: 'Brodies: not only performance enhancing, but entirely legal.' And went on to state that they had 'never failed in random testing.' With the Law Society doing the 'testing' *of course* they had never failed. The advertisement ended with an appeal to contact Alastair Campbell, the Chairman of Brodies [the crook who had funked a public thrashing from me in Princes Street Gardens] to find out how Brodies could help. For a law firm to be reduced to placing advertisements in the media which claimed that they were 'entirely legal' was a dead giveaway. It was also a bald lie.

I also heard from another acquaintance in a very senior position in a large organisation that the organisation had received an appeal from Brodies to place their business with them. Naturally I advised him against it doing so. He instantly re-assured me that his organisation would not have anything to do with Brodies in view of all the adverse Press about them in connection with myself and others.

Also in December 2002 another friend told me that he had been informed that someone who had applied for a job at Brodies had been warned by them that they had a most determined enemy in me who was pursuing them for £365 million.

In January 2003 someone phoned me, incognito, and informed me that my campaign was definitely causing Brodies concern as they had just introduced new security measures to monitor clients entering their offices.

Over the next few years I received telephone calls from a succession of people who had been defrauded by Brodies. They all became supporters of Scotland Against Crooked Lawyers. Each heart breaking story revealed individuals and families mercilessly swindled by these professional criminals.

Sometime in mid-2002 Brodies appointed a Public Relations firm to try and improve its now frightful image and reputation.

In a desperate attempt to improve their now frightful image they changed their advertising colours and the format of their letter-headed paper. With regard to their letters they dispensed with the interminable list of the names of all the Brodies Partners. They thought it wiser to keep the names of the Partners anonymous, almost certainly as a consequence of pressure from the Partners themselves.

They also binned their old bold brass door plate with its large inscription 'BRODIES' and replaced it with another plate with a very diminutive, tiny 'brodies' on the extreme bottom right hand corner.

At the time I declared war on them Brodies used to place full page adverts in the leading Scottish newspapers and journals advertising the properties they had for sale. These properties were often top end of the market properties and sometimes large Estates like the Wells Estate. Since I commenced my campaign against them however there had been a steady decline of these Brodies adverts. For example in *The Scotsman* Property Guide of 18th December 2003 Brodies had just one singularly undistinguished flat advertised for sale in Edinburgh. Other Estate Agencies who used to advertise on a far smaller scale had by now comprehensively outstripped Brodies and were taking full page adverts themselves.

'Usual suspects' take stage

Executive hearings into profession and legal aid bill may miss some crucial voices

PAUL ROGERSON
paul.rogerson@theherald.co.uk

COMMITTEE hearings begin next week which will decide the fate of the controversial Legal Profession and Legal Aid (Scotland) Bill.

A slew of interested organisations has been invited to appear, comprising what might be dubbed the "usual suspects". However, fears are growing that not one single consumer who has allegedly suffered poor service from their lawyers or seen their complaints mishandled or ignored will get the chance to tell MSPs their story.

"People have lost houses, homes and families through dealing with incompetent or corrupt solicitors. The politicians should listen to them," said one reformer who did not wish to be named.

An overwhelming majority of respondents to the Scottish Executive's consultation on legal complaints-handling want to see the nation's 10,000 lawyers stripped of rights to police themselves. But not all are happy that "direct action" lobby group Scotland Against Crooked Lawyers has apparently been selected as a proxy for reformist public opinion.

This is the body whose website Justice Minister Cathy Jamieson moved to shut down last year because it contained "potentially defamatory" material.

Prominent reformers unaffiliated with SACL fear the body is an easy target for opponents of change because of the allegedly extremist bent of some of its members. Four years ago, society figurehead Stuart Usher had to hand over his shotgun and firearms licence to the police after telling Channel 4 that he sometimes felt like taking his gun into Edinburgh and "nailing" a few lawyers.

Such bellicosity would be seriously counterproductive in the wake of January's stabbing of law society chief accountant Leslie Cumming by an as-yet unidentified assailant.

There is no evidence that SACL or any of its members had anything to do with that attack.

Committee members looking for advice as to whom they might talk to could also consider contacting Gail McEwan, the Renfrewshire woman who has mounted a nationwide campaign for justice on behalf of hundreds of Scots allegedly missold mortgage endowments by solicitors.

She was awarded £700 in compensation by the legal services ombudsman after the Law Society of Scotland bungled her own complaints about a policy she was sold by a Glasgow firm of lawyers.

Another individual who has certainly earned the right to appear is Stewart Mackenzie of Perthshire. He was the subject of the leaked law society internal memo sent by chief executive Douglas Mill back in 2001 which observed: "There is no doubt Mr Mackenzie is (an) intelligent and well-organised individual (sic) who could, unlike some of the other thorns in our flesh, come over very well at (an) investigation."

Mackenzie was denied the chance to appear before Justice 1.

His MSP, former SNP leader John Swinney, is pressuring Justice 2 to hear what he has to say.

Other omissions from the parties giving oral evidence are the key bodies which favour extending paid advocacy rights to people who are not members of the Law Society of Scotland or Faculty of Advocates. The Office of Fair Trading, the Association of Commercial Attorneys – which first raised the matter as a body in 2002 – and the Chartered Institute of Patent Agents all want an end to the "lawyers monopoly".

The OFT, Britain's premier trading watchdog, has cited evidence that "some potential clients have experienced difficulty finding a solicitor to represent them".

In a statement, a spokesman for Justice 2 said the body may decide to take additional oral evidence after it has considered the full range of written submissions to the bill.

The deadline for submissions is Friday.

From the 'Herald' 17th April 2006

51

THE BEDRULE WAR MEMORIAL

Towards the end of 2001 a retired local farmer called Charles Douglas urged me to do something about getting my Uncle Sandy's name up on the Bedrule Parish War Memorial. Uncle Sandy, Major Alexander Balmer Usher of the First Lothian and Border Horse, had been killed in France in June 1940, as narrated earlier in the book. I had never noticed this ommission as a young man but I had noticed it when I was over on my 1973 holiday and had since often wondered about it. When I came home for good in 1995 I determined I would get Uncle Sandy's name put on the War Memorial. But what with all the drama of having to contend with Brodies and all the other crooks I had never got round to doing so. So I was pleased with this timely reminder. On 21st February 2002 I contacted the Scottish Borders Council and got them going on it.

At this point I should state that Uncle Sandy and my father had always been close and regarded each other as favourite brothers. Only two years separated them. Uncle Sandy had been given Bedrule, which adjoined the Wells estate and was very close to Wells House. As he was not married he continued to live in Wells House with his mother, Katherine, Lady Usher. This was company for her as all her other sons had flown the nest. Anyway when the war broke out in earnest in 1940 away went Uncle Sandy, with his regiment, to France. His death came as a terrible blow to his mother. At this point an Edinburgh 'clairvoyant' happened upon the scene and assured her that Sandy was not dead and would come home one day. It appears that Katherine believed this quack and to her dying day in 1948 believed that Sandy would come home one day. I was told that this charlatan 'clairvoyant' had charged her a pretty penny for his 'services' — — a pack of lying twaddle was more like it.

Anyway the Borders Council moved fast and got a suitable plaque engraved which commemorated Uncle Sandy and affixed it to the Bedrule

War Memorial just in time for Remembrance day 2002. In the presence of a small group of local people and the Hawick Scout Cadet Pipe band I unveiled the plaque in the course of the Remembrance day Memorial Service, sixty three years after Uncle Sandy had made the supreme sacrifice.

The reader may well ask: 'Why did no one do anything about it before?' Good question. One explanation would be out of respect to Lady Usher's belief that Sandy would come home one day. But that argument would have become more and more unrealistic ten years or so after the war ended when Sandy would have been in his fifties. So why hadn't my father arranged for Sandy to be remembered on the War Memorial? A possible explanation is that he meant to get it done but kept postponing it as people sometimes do with things like that. Another explanation was that a plaque had been installed in Bedrule Church which commemorated Uncle Sandy. Also why had Stuart and Clive done nothing about it? After we went to South Africa in 1968 Clive had another fourteen years to get it done. So why hadn't he done anything about it. They had, after all, been fellow soldiers and fellow soldiers usually honour each other. Clive had retired from the army with the rank of Brigadier and as such was in the ideal position to honour Sandy's memory by getting a plaque put up for him. But in all those years he had not lifted a finger? Whatever the reason for Uncle Sandy being forgotten in this manner, it was despicable. Well, he was now honoured and remembered, and every time I drive past the War Memorial at Bedrule, usually on my way to Church there, and see Uncle Sandy's plaque, my heart lifts.

They shall grow not old, as we that are left grow old:
Age shall not weary them, nor the years condemn.
At the going down of the sun and in the morning,
We will remember them.

52

USHER AND LEADBETTER WILLS MYSTERY

I now come back to JGG Leadbetter. Did he get something for agreeing to the Trust Deed being amended to enable Stuart to resettle the Estates onto my father? I never thought so until I examined the Will of Great Aunt May, his mother, who had always been so pleasant and who had died on the 11th November 1955. She was the last of Sir Robert's generation and his youngest sister. As such she was a champion of his interests. I obtained a copy of the Sheriff Court recording of her Will in January 2003. It had been drafted in April 1951 and was unsigned. The Will stated that her son, JGG Leadbetter and his sister, Mary, were to be her Executors and her only beneficiaries. However this Will had a major alteration in it. The alteration was a clause which had been inserted into it between the regular lines of the original text. This inserted clause added her youngest daughter, Jean Leadbetter (Bailey on her marriage and the mother of the Alan Bailey already mentioned in this book) to also be a beneficiary and therefore must have been inserted after the Will had been drafted and typed. In December 2004 I got a copy of Aunt May's Will from the National Archives to check it against the Sheriff Court copy. This National Archives Register of Deeds copy had no insertion and did include Jean as a residual beneficiary and was signed by Great Aunt May and witnessed. To the best of my knowledge the Sheriff Court is the body that gives Confirmation (Probate) to the Executors of the deceased person.

On this basis therefore the Executors of Great Aunt May appear to have had themselves confirmed as Executors on the basis of the unsigned and altered Will. When I tackled the National Archives about the difference they stated it must have been an 'innocent mistake.' Given all the fraud surrounding Stuart and Gertie's Wills and 'the lawyers bogged up on the Usher Wills' according to Valerie, I did not, and still do not accept such trite 'innocent mistake' explanations.

However there was something else that added to my suspicions. This was that her Executors delayed for *two years and three months* before presenting Great Aunt May's Will to the Sheriff Court to get Confirmation (Probate) to her Estate. Confirmation was only granted by the Sheriff Court in February

1958. Only then did JGG Leadbetter and his sister, Mary, get the authority to wind up her Estate. Normally Confirmation is applied for and given within a month or two of the Deceased's death. JGG Leadbetter, being a lawyer and one of her two Executors, would have presented this to the Sheriff Court. So the question was: What had stopped him getting Confirmation to his Mother's Estate for well over two years? Getting confirmation would have been routine for him with the deceased clients of the law firm for which he 'worked.'

I smelt another rat here alright, but what was it? A possible explanation was that 'the rat' had something to do with Leadbetter getting something in return for his agreement that Sir Robert's Trust Deed be amended. But I do know that a lawyer would not have delayed for two years and three months before getting confirmation to his Mother's Estate unless he had a compelling reason to do so. What was it? I still have not discovered it for certain but suspect that it was something to do with Leadbetter agreeing to the Trust Deed being being changed to preclude Peter and Robert from succeeding to the Trust Estates.

I must make it clear that his sister Mary (my cousin) would never, ever have knowingly been part of anything untoward or dishonest. She was a paragon of virtue and would have never tolerated any form of underhand dealing. Of course her brother would have fobbed her off with some, to her, plausible excuse.

Nor was that the last 'Will Mystery' in connection with Great Aunt May's family. There was something decidedly fishy about her daughter Mary's Will as well. She died in September 1975. My suspicions aroused by Great Aunt May's Will, I got a copy of Mary's Will from the National Archives. It was signed by her alright but, again, there had been two major alterations in it neither of which had been signed and endorsed by her. This meant, again, that the alterations had been effected *after* her death. The first alteration was that five lines had been scored out and replaced by another five lines. The second alteration was that the signature of one of her Witnesses, one of her house staff, had been scored out and replaced by the signature of another Witness, a lawyer or clerk of Tait's lawyer offices in Kelso where her brother, JGG Leadbetter 'worked'. On this basis therefore Confirmation should never have been given to Mary's Executors. And who were Mary's Executors? Inevitably two lawyers working at the law firm of Taits.

These unwarranted alterations should have rendered Mary Intestate. She had done her bit alright but her will being tampered with after her death should have resulted in it being rejected. So who had tampered with it? By far the most likely suspects were the two lawyer Executors. And there must have been compelling reasons of a bad nature for them (and whoever else) to have done so. Of course I smelt another rat here and a large one at that. Time for the cat again!

Apart from these Leadbetter Wills there was something very interesting indeed in the Inventories of JGG Leadbetter himself and his sister Mary. Leadbetter died in 1965 and his Inventory showed that Clive, alone of the Usher brothers, owed him money, £5,000, at the time of his death. Then Mary died in 1975 and her confirmation showed that Clive owed *her* £5,000 as well. That, at the very least, showed that neither had been repaid at the time of their deaths. As we have seen this was typical Clive. Did Clive ever repay either debt? Knowing Clive I doubt it very much.

> 'Oh, what a tangled web we weave, when first we practice to deceive!'
> (Sir Walter Scott, 1808).

Another Usher Will event occurred in 2002. I popped into an Antiques Show and Sale which takes place regularly in the Jedburgh Town Hall in the summer. A lady called Shirley Storar approached me and told me that her maiden name was Usher and that she came from Liverpool. She stated that her father was called Robert Edward Usher, exactly the same names as our Robert at Hallrule. This indicated a distant branch of our family. She stated that her grandfather, George Edward Usher - also much-used names in our family - who was born in Newcastle, only fifty miles from Jedburgh, had been approached in the street outside his parents' house in Liverpool when still a young boy by two Edinburgh lawyers, probably in the 1910s. He had taken them into the house to meet his parents where the two lawyers informed the family that he, George Edward Usher, had been left money by an Edinburgh Usher. They gave him five shillings and told him they would be in touch about the rest of his inheritance shortly - he never heard from them again. The family never saw hide nor hair of the two lawyers ever again. With my knowledge of Edinburgh lawyers I deduced that these two lawyers had classed this family as easy prey and simply robbed George Edward Usher of his inheritance. This was exactly what Brodies had done to our family a century later, using Peter and Robert as the 'easy prey'.

Taken cumulatively all these Wills with their various scoring outs, insertions, non registrations, 'not being found' and so on demonstrates, at the very least, that the usual 'something' had been going on behind the scenes for decades.

In view of what happened with the Usher and Leadbetter Wills, and with Stuart's Will in particular, in addition to other reports I have been sent about Will fraud and various newspaper reports about lawyers 'losing' Wills I am now certain that Will Fraud is practised on a much larger scale than is generally realised in Scotland.

53

BRODIES DIG THEMSELVES INTO A HOLE

By letter dated 30th April 2004 Brodies wrote to all the beneficiaries informing them that they were the 'owners of the assets in the Executry'. However in the same letter they then referred to these assets as 'Estate Assets'. Brodies constant use of such contradictory language was an attempt to conceal something by a subtle use of contradictions of which this is an example. The assets were either *Executry Assets* or *Estate Assets*. They could never be both. I had difficulty in getting the other beneficiaries to accept that such subtle differences of description were there by *design*, rather than by mistake. At this stage the other beneficiaries had already reached the stage of distrusting Brodies but either could not, or would not accept, that Brodies were as bad as I made them out to be. Likewise they were now beginning to distrust the executrix, Jacquelin Wolfe-Murray. They were to slowly learn, the hard way, just how badly she had betrayed them.

Interestingly Brodies put me at the head of this list of the beneficiaries and Johnny last. In family pecking order this was way off beam. Johnny should have headed the list, followed by myself (as the only Ushers) and then the others. Again this was by design to promote the notion that family names, pecking orders, generational differences, age and the like were meaningless in the brave new world of Brodies Fraud. In essence it was an attempt by Brodies to demean Johnny's position. In the normal course of events, he would have inherited the Estates in 1969 on our Father's death.

The only asset remaining of which I was fully aware was a field to the rear of the Norton Hotel and two Baronies, those of Wells and Hallrule. We had owned the Baronies of Norton, and possibly Hatton, near Norton, and Bedrule as well. These latter two appeared to have been furtively disposed of by Brodies and Jacquelin. What happened to the proceeds I do not know.

The Norton field was variously described as either eight or twelve acres. Brodies put a value of £25,000 on it until it was included in the Rural West Edinburgh Local Plan in December 2003. On the strength of this Brodies then put a value of £750,000 on it. When the required planning was granted

Brodies estimated its value would increase to about £3 million. They gave us a time frame for the required planning permission to be granted and the land being sold and estimated that this would occur in the Spring of 2006.

Brodies then went onto state that:

> 'It is possible that there remain small unidentified plots still within the ownership of the Executry. Our recommendation is that there is no further costs incurred in seeking to identify any such areas now.'

What a statement to come from them at this stage, nearly ten years after the inception of the Executry.

Given all Brodies' past deceptions and frauds against our family their recommendation that no 'further costs' should be incurred in trying to locate these possible remaining plots was rich to say the least. I reason to believe that Brodies were fully aware of the wherebouts of these plots. Their airing the possibility of their existence only now was an exercise in evading the consequences of someone discovering these plots at a later stage. I suspected that their plan was to wait until all the beneficiaries were dead and then claim them for themselves; at which time it would be highly unlikely that anyone would be any the wiser and even more unlikely that anyone who, by some miracle, had discovered them would do anything to recover them from Brodies. These small plots of ground can be extremely valuable.

Here are some examples of evasive Brodies' responses and letters to the beneficiaries in this period. On 30th January 2004 I requested that they send me the latest Executry Balance Sheet. They responded by letter dated 17th February 2004 stating:

> 'We are not sure what you mean by a Balance Sheet.'

And yet they had had an in-house Accountancy practice called 'Brodies Accountancy Services' for many years. Clearly this was another lie.

Some letters from Brodies gave no clue as to who had written them and were only signed with an indecipherable scrawl; a straight line with a couple of kinks in it. Crooked lawyers do this type of thing when they do not want to be identified as the letter writer.

By letter dated 9th June 2004 Brodies referred to the beneficiaries as

> 'beneficiaries of any land comprised within the Executry Estates.'

Yet in a letter dated 30th April 2004 Brodies had stated that the beneficiaries were the

> 'beneficial proprietors of the land.'

Which is it? Again it cannot be both.

By letter dated 17th May 2006 Brodies informed us that the Edinburgh City Council had published its Report in October 2005 in which it recommended that our land should *not* be zoned for development after all, despite all their earlier assurances that the chances for it being so zoned were excellent. Why the delay of seven months before informing us? And why hadn't Jacquelin informed the beneficiaries of this very important development straightaway? This came as a most unpleasant surprise to us all. Never slow to hit a man when he is down, Brodies now put the boot in further by claiming that we now owed them an additional £40,000 in fees and there was no money left in the Executry to settle the account. And yet there had been very little correspondence with Brodies and they had made no mention before that the Executry was insolvent. Also they had not bothered to attend various Edinburgh City Council Meetings to promote the land for zoning. And never a word from Jacquelin to the beneficiaries for eight years as to what had been going on and how this new £40,000 debt had been incurred.

Brodies then went on to inform us that in place of our site another site nearby, which had *not* been included in the original West Edinburgh Plan as our land had been had now been unexpectedly chosen as suitable for development. In connection with the choice of this site Brodies introduced another of their 'catch me if you can' ambiguous statements:

> 'Although not directly linking this to our site it seemed that this might have been done'.

What the hell is that supposed to mean? Particularly so because this site adjoined a road on the other side of which was land that had been part of the Norton Estate. This site was a long way from our field. This was another example of Brodies protecting themselves from future discovery. Had they been bribed to sabotage our land? If I was asked to give a Yes or No answer to that question my answer would be an emphatic 'Yes'.

Another of Brodies' proposals was that we simply sell the land as it stood for £250,000; no doubt so that they could settle their bogus accounts from the proceeds and then walk away with a laugh, 'Cheerio, you idiots, we caught you nicely there, yet again'. In that event it would have been more than likely that they were in cahoots with potential purchasers to then have it zoned and thereafter sell it for the millions we should have received.

In view of this most unwelcome news the beneficiaries tried ever harder to arrange a meeting with Jacquelin. She had repeatedly agreed to meet with us over the previous eight months but always avoided setting a date for it, almost certainly on Brodies' instructions.

At last Brodies instructed her to have a meeting with us. The first inkling I had of it was an approach from Alan Bailey at Bedrule Church on 28th May 2006 where he informed me that he wanted 'a chat' with me. We agreed to meet at my place at 10.00am on Tuesday 30th May. Arriving at my home he spoke about wind farms and the like, but nothing could disguise the fact that he had not come to discuss windfarms. So I waited patiently. After about twenty minutes of windfarms he said he had some business to discuss with me. As soon as he said that I was certain that it had to do with Jacquelin with whom he was on friendly terms and had often had her stay with him. Sure enough that was the reason. He asked me if I had any objection to his chairing a meeting which was to include only three of the beneficiaries: Jacquelin, Mrs Mactaggart and myself.

I immediately turned his proposal down on the grounds that 1) he had no interest in the Executry and 2) I would only attend a meeting to which *all* the beneficiaries were invited. Bailey accepted my refusal with grace by telling me that he would therefore not chair any meeting which I did not attend and that was that.

I subsequently discovered that this 'three only' meeting of the beneficiaries, had been suggested by Brodies. I assume they had chosen Bailey to chair it because he was a fellow 'professional' and would therefore be some counterweight to me. Of course Jacquelin being the Executrix, should have chaired it herself, but evidently Brodies thought that altogether too dangerous on the grounds that she would bungle it.

The very next day I received a letter from Jacquelin inviting me to the meeting at Bailey's place at 10.30am on Friday 2nd June 2006. The envelope was postmarked 30th May 2006, the very day Bailey had come to my place. I immediately tackled Bailey about this and he told me that he was now 'seriously annoyed' with Jacquelin for having gone ahead with organising a meeting at his place when he had told her that he would not chair it unless he could convince me to attend. But that now he felt obliged to chair it with only Jacquelin and Mrs Mactaggart present.

Towards the end of the year I asked Bailey, at Church again, if the meeting with Jacquelin and Mrs Mactaggart had actually taken place. He now told me 'I can't remember.' I didn't believe that at all. In the meanwhile I had informed the other beneficiaries of this approach to Mrs Mactaggart and myself. Predictably they did not like that one little bit.

So why had Brodies attempted to get me to attend this meeting chaired by Bailey with only Jacquelin, Mrs Mactaggart and myself present? The only plausible explanation was that Brodies wanted Jacquelin, under the chairmanship and guidance of Bailey, to inform only Mrs Mactaggart and myself of something which they did not want the other beneficiaries to hear. Divide and rule. And what was this 'something'? I do not know so I can only speculate. One possibility is that Brodies wanted to make some deal with me. But why then include Mrs Mactaggart? A possible explanation was her squattership in Rulewater: she was therefore vulnerable. They also knew that I was the only person still alive, other than themselves, who knew that and, much more importantly, that I had no intention of letting the matter rest. I therefore suspect that the purpose of the Meeting was to broker some deal whereby I would agree to shut up.

In retrospect I came to think that my refusal to attend this meeting was another big mistake on my part. The more I thought about it the more I thought what an idiot I had been, yet again. In mitigation all I can say is that when the proposition was put to me I instantly suspected that it would be bad for all the other beneficiaries, with the exception of Jacquelin and Mrs Mactaggart. For that reason alone I immediately turned it down, without thinking further.

I now decided to keep my communications with Brodies to a minimum and arranged for another beneficiary called Elizabeth Richards in Wales to correspond with Brodies, ask questions and so on. She was the only beneficiary who had by now fully accepted that Brodies and Jacquelin were not to be trusted under any circumstances. This was the same Elizabeth who had arrived at Bedrule as a baby in 1948. Thankfully she had long ceased the bawling which she had subjected us so mercilessly to at Bedrule! Brodies and Jacquelin would be much less on guard with her than with me.

This paid off. For example on 10th June 2006 Jacquelin told Elizabeth, 'Stuart has caused a great deal of trouble,'. She also told her, 'Someone [presumably an Edinburgh City Council official] has taken a back-hander to exclude our land.' Sad to say, that is typical Edinburgh. And no wonder given the huge number of lawyers infesting it.

By letter dated 16th June 2006, after years of evasion, Jacquelin actually contacted all the beneficiaries by circular letter and enclosures for the first time ever in the more than ten years she had been an Executrix. She'd had this letter and enclosures written and typed by a third party who lived near her hideaway in Hampshire whither she'd fled. I instantly knew she was utterly incapable of writing a letter of that grammatical standard. In it she complained that Brodies had been 'disregarding' her instructions and that Brodies actions must have given us all 'the notion that I must be completely incompetent.' The other beneficiaries had by now long regarded her as incompetent, but still did not fully accept how dishonest she had been and still was.

We kept the pressure on both her and Brodies to produce an Itemised Account detailing how the new £40,000 Bill had been arrived at and what it represented. By letter dated 26th June 2006 Brodies sent us a series of 'Interim Accounts' amounting to just over £22,000 but made no mention of what this figure represented other than it was 'in respect of certain matters post executry.' And that was it.

Of course I had a pretty good idea of what the 'certain matters post executry' represented: The time that Brodies had spent on concealing their past frauds and something which was somehow connected with our land and the other 'missing' Usher plots.

And the balance of £18,000? The vast majority of it appeared to be fraudulent. One example: £4,280 was spent on the Pitheavlis and Norton

'Notices of Title'. One of these 'Notices of Title' I later discovered was to correct a fraudulent 1998 'Notice of Title'.

Our keeping the pressure on Jacquelin eventually resulted in her telling Elizabeth that she would pay the £40,000 bill herself rather than go into what the Bill represented. This made it certain that the Bill was bogus and was a further manifestation of a continuing fraud. However we were delighted that she would pay it.

Shortly thereafter, to get herself out of the hole into which she had dug herself, she now recommended that we take out a £40,000 loan from the Royal Bank of Scotland and give her a Power of Attorney to control this money and everything else in connection with the Executry assets. No doubt so that she could pay Brodies' bogus bill with it thereby saving herself from doing so. I warned all the beneficiaries of the catastrophic consequences, in addition to our losing the £40,000, that would arise were we to agree to her proposal. Thankfully they agreed with me and turned her proposal down.

Another interesting statement in her 16th June letter was: 'With the help of Mr Forbes-Mar, a Planning Consultant, we have succeeded in getting the Field zoned'. How crazy was that? Brodies had just informed us, not a month before, that the Field had been excluded from being zoned.

By letter dated 16th June 2006 (coincidentally the same date of the letter Jacquelin sent to all the beneficiaries) Edinburgh City Council wrote an interesting letter to Brodies. Interesting because it was addressed to:

> 'Robert E Usher (Sir) Trust c/o Brodies.'

Obviously Robert, an Incapax, had never created any Trust so such a body had never existed. So why this appellation? The only possible explanation was that Edinburgh City Council had used that appellation because Brodies had used it in their correspondence to them in the first place. But why should Brodies do that? What advantage could they gain by doing so? I was non-plussed until it struck me that Brodies would do so if Edinburgh City Council had our field listed as belonging to the Usher Baronetcy Trust. Remember that this land had been put into the Usher Baronetcy Trust by the original Sir Robert Usher in 1927. Brodies could not deal with the Council on the basis that it was *other* than UBT land. Brodies rather ingenious way out of this was to head their letters to the Council 'The Robert E Usher (Sir) Trust' to mislead the City Council into thinking that this was the original UBT set up by Sir Robert Usher in 1911 when in fact it referred to the Down''s Syndrome and Mentally Incapacitated Robert Edward Usher. This would also dovetail with Brodies' patent fiction that Robert the Incapax had 'inherited' the land from his brother Peter the Incapax.

This started me thinking about a man I met in Hawick in the Borders at about this time who told me that he had heard from a local 'professional' that a lot of Usher money had been laundered through Coutts Bank. Why should this man, a stranger to me, volunteer this information. He was a patently honest and decent man as far as I was concerned. He also told me that he had heard of the loss of the Contents of Hallrule House to our family and how he deplored 'that sort of stinking behaviour.'

Self on left with other victims of Scottish Lawyers outside the Law Society's offices in Edinburgh

54

JACQUELIN WOLFE-MURRAY, NOW MRS FAULKNER, CAUGHT OUT 'HOOK, LINE AND SINKER'

After much twisting and turning by Brodies, and after more broken promises of a general meeting to which all the beneficiaries would be invited, a meeting, at last, was arranged for the 15th of August 2006 at the Norton Hotel.

The question now was: 'Would she cancel at the last minute?' I had been in touch with my niece's husband, Digby Guy, who was a Land Agent in Argyllshire. He knew Brodies well and knew its Chairman, the infamous Alistair Campbell, very well because he did business with them. I thought bringing him in might help to break the log-jam. I agreed that he chair the first part of the meeting. Taking Richard with me we arrived at Norton and went into the conference room, with my large tape-recorder.

All the UK-based beneficiaries were there. On top of that the egregious double crossing Jacquelin had taken the precaution of having Forbes-Marr, a Surveyor and Planning Consultant and her daughter, Dorinda, attend. She immediately came over to me with an extended hand of feigned welcome and a hopeful smile. I declined her hand and did not smile back. Why on earth should I shake hands with the traitor who had cost the Executry years of wasted time and an unknown vast amount of money? She walked away rather dejected. I think she thought, in her upside down, convoluted way that I would be nice to her if she was nice to me. It was far too late for that. The South African and Australian-based beneficiaries failed to show.

I then noted that Jacquelin had suddenly become very nervous indeed; hands trembling, and flushed face. I felt great satisfaction at this. How the wheel of fortune had turned! My thoughts were:

> *'For eleven long years ago you have betrayed all the beneficiaries, and your own family, by making common cause with Brodies who you yourself had already told me were crooks in 1994. When I finally came home in 1995 you had done some deal with Brodies and immediately put the boot into me, confident that you, with Brodies, the Estate Manager, Valerie and the Mactaggarts backing you, would be*

Jacquelin Wolfe-Murray at meeting in Norton Hotel, 2006

The word 'shifty' comes to mind, as do the words 'hot water' prophetically in the background.

able to squash Johnny and me. But you didn't manage to squash us then nor ever since. On the contrary I squashed you by exposing you as a thief and Brodies and many others as crooks. Millions of people all over Britain have become aware of my long and lonely fight against Brodies and the vast majority of the people of this country who are aware of this fraud back me; not you nor your friends and partners in crime, Brodies and the others. Your duty was to fight with us and for our family, but instead you betrayed us and your own family and joined Brodies and fought against us. Very few people know of your betrayal yet, but, by the time I have finished with you, many will. At this Meeting I intend to show you up for the Traitor and Thief you really are.'

Before the Meeting commenced I heard her incanting: 'No tape-recorders; no tape recorders.' No doubt at all that it was my tape recorder that worried her stiff. Digby Guy commented that Jacquelin was, 'a very nervous lady'.

Guy eventually called the Meeting to order. Dorinda, was to be the Minute taker. I immediately realised that this was a further attempt by Jacquelin to limit the damage to herself. What better way than to have your own daughter take the Minutes. But she had not reckoned on my Tape-recorder. That had thrown Dorinda's planned creative 'Minute taking' into disarray. Also her purpose in having Forbes-Marr there was to let him do all the talking and thereby divert attention from herself. When we were all seated and as Guy opened the meeting, I quickly jumped up and asked if anyone had any objections to my taping the meeting. This was greeted by a deathly hush before Guy, trying and not succeeding to disguise his displeasure, asked if anyone objected. No one did. Jacquelin just sat there, trembling. Dorinda likewise did not look at all happy. The rest of the beneficiaries gave no indication one way or the other. This was the best thing they could have done - let the tape-recorder do its business. In the event taping that Meeting turned out to be an absolute God-send.

So the Meeting began. Again I jumped in first because I wanted to catch Jacquelin while she was still in disarray and before the 'professionals' took the meeting over. I asked her what had happened to our 220 plus remaining Feus in Perth and the 22 in Ratho. A Feu is the giving of a tenure of land in perpetuity in return for a continuing annual payment of a fixed sum of money to the owner of the land

Jacquelin responded that the Feus had been sold 'for what they were worth', but said she had no idea what the sale price had been. How then could she know if they had been sold 'for what they were worth?' I took this to be another lie. She then well and truly let the cat out of the bag by stating that the proceeds had been used to pay the costs of the Usher Baronetcy Trust . If Brodies had been present I suspect they would have brained her there and then, in her chair. They had always maintained, and still were maintaining, that the Usher Baronetcy Trust had terminated on Stuart's death in 1962. Her statement now tied in with my theory that Brodies were still using the Usher Baronetcy Trust, by the 'Robert E Usher (Sir) Trust' device, as the vehicle to defraud it. This was just another vintage Brodies' deception and therefore another Brodies crime.

So the Meeting went on, with Jacquelin being asked for explanations on the various matters which she had evaded answering for years. She either could not or would not give any remotely plausible answers. For example she was asked what the terms 'Matters Post Executry' in the Accounts signified. She put that down to 'lawyer-speak.' Stupid as she was even she knew that it was not just 'lawyer speak'. Some time later I repeated the question. She now changed her answer to: 'It has changed, hasn't it? This thing has been going on for such a long time now, that's why. . .' and petered out. All just lying twaddle. It was then pointed out to her that we could never agree to pay Brodies Bill without being told what we were paying for. She then informed us that Brodies' Bill had now risen to £48,000. But that was not what we had asked. The question was therefore repeated: 'Ok. What is the *£48,000* for?' Desperate now, she said: 'Oh, it's for running *bits and pieces*.' What a sick joke. As if running bits and pieces could possibly justify £48,000. She was then asked what had happened to the £20,000 plus that had been in the account until quite recently. Her answer to this was another crass lie: 'Oh that. It has been used for running the Account. . . that sort of thing.' Pressed yet again, and now at last cornered, she said: 'I do not honestly know where the money has gone.' Her performance was so truly abject that the beneficiaries now, at long last, realised just what a lying toad she always had been and how badly she had betrayed them.

She then piped up again about our giving her a Power of Attorney to enable her to make final decisions on Executry matters. Obviously the beneficiaries now unanimously refused.

It was now obvious to everyone present, including her daughter Dorinda, that on top of being a liar, she had never carried out her function as Executrix in good faith from the outset. Her performance had confirmed what I was already pretty sure about: That she was well aware of where the £20,000 had gone and also what the £48,000 represented. Also that she was aware of a whole host of other Brodies' frauds of relatively recent origin. Brodies might even have included her in some of these frauds. If so this this alone made it impossible for her to betray Brodies to the beneficiaries.

So what *had* happend to the £20,000? I don't know but I suspect one, or a combination of, the following:

1) Brodies had used it to fill some other hole in their fraudulent accounting.
2) Brodies had used it to pay for the costs arising from their continuing fraud against the Executry.
3) Brodies had shared it with Jacquelin to keep her on side.

Other than the above there was a lot of discussion about the Norton Field and how we should progress the matter. Plans of action and promises Assurances were given by Jacquelin *and* Guy, not a single one of which they kept.

But the Meeting had been well worth it if only because it had finally convinced all the other beneficiaries present that both Brodies and Jacquelin were dishonest shysters who had hidden a whole host of things from us. This made me feel less alone - an assurance I badly needed at the time. Nevertheless I dared not tell them how bad I believed things *really* were.

Another significant thing about the Meeting was that I detected a hostility towards me from Guy and, for the first time in both our lives, from my niece, Caroline, his wife. This should have warned me more than it did. With the passing of time I came to the conclusion that Guy, being so friendly with Brodies and particularly its lying and cowardly Chairman, Alastair Campbell, had been 'leaned on' to protect them and Jacquelin. Of course I realised that he made his bread and butter out of dealing with criminals like Brodies and that he would rather have his bread and butter than make a stand on what could be regarded as an unprofitable principle.

Elizabeth transcribed the tape recording of the whole Meeting and produced a transcript within a few days. However she, wisely, did not send it to the beneficiaries, including Jacquelin, until we received the Minutes of the meeting from Dorinda the 'official' Minute taker. We wanted to see first how Dorinda would manipulate the Minutes to conceal Jacquelin being repeatedly caught out. Predictably Dorinda went to ground. She no doubt was waiting to see *our* transcript before she produced *her* Minutes. It was a Mexican stand-off.

In early September we contacted Jacquelin as to what was causing the delay of Dorinda's Minutes. On 9th September 2006 she wrote a curt note to Elizabeth stating that she had been waiting for the draft of the Minutes to be approved by Guy, the Chairman, and that he had now returned them to Dorinda 'for her to produce the final Minutes.' Guy, as Chairman, of course, had no right whatever to amend Dorinda's Minutes. The Minutes should have been sent to all the beneficiaries by Dorinda, the *official* Minute taker, as they stood, without sending them to Guy for approval.

The Minutes were obviously exercising Dorinda no end, as I knew they would. The bugbear as far as she, Jacquelin and Guy, were concerned was our tape recording. Having enrolled Guy as the damage-limitation Chairman, Forbes Marr to do the talking and Dorinda to take the Minutes, Jacquelin no doubt thought she had the meeting well and truly stitched up. The tape-recorder had put an end to that ploy. So Dorinda was faced with the unenviable task of producing a set of Minutes which reflected positively on Jacquelin as well as recording what had actually been said; an impossible task. No doubt after much agonising, and with the help of Guy, Dorinda eventually produced some Minutes one whole month after the meeting. Elizabeth then sent her transcript based on my tape-recording to every beneficiary.

Dorinda's Minutes were, as I fully expected, misleading and factually and purposely incomplete. For example they studiously avoided all reference to the many questions on which Jacquelin had been so spectacularly caught out. By comparison the transcribed Minutes produced by Elizabeth were an accurate and faithful reflection of everything that had been said at the meeting. Tape recorders do not lie. They just record - everything. That is why the Scottish Courts have never tolerated them.

The one thing that everyone had agreed at the Meeting was that Jacquelin would keep in regular contact with the beneficiaries henceforward. In the ensuing months Jacquelin broke this agreement in the same way that she had broken every other agreement she had ever made with us. She simply went to ground and would not respond. We did however get misleading responses from Brodies, usually Houldsworth. Most of this correspondence was conducted through Elizabeth Richards.

We kept the pressure on as best we could. Eventually Jacquelin and Guy organised a Meeting at the offices of James Barr, Planning Consultants, in George Street, Glasgow on 17th November 2006. Elizabeth could not attend this Meeting largely because of the extremely short notice which Jacquelin had, purposely, given us to attend. I attended with the three Kirkpatrick beneficiaries. Jacquelin and her minder Guy also attended. This Meeting was chaired by Stuart Macgarvie of Barrs.

Macgarvie gave an outline of what was required for the field to get Planning permission. One of the requirements was that we would have to offer the Council an inducement. As an example he suggested that we should agree to refurbish Ratho Station to make it more user friendly to the local people. Guy said this was bribery. I was glad that he said that and voiced my agreement with him. Macgarvie also agreed it was bribery but informed us that bribery had become the norm in Scotland and we should all just accept it without demur, otherwise we would get nowhere. Another key requirement was knowing the Planning Officers. It appeared that the merits and demerits of the suitability of the Field for development were of no consequence whatever. It all depended on bribery and knowing the relevant apparatchicks working in the Public Sector. I did not like this at all and made my feelings known. This was another example of Scotland descending into a northern hemisphere Zimbabwe, Somalia *et al.*

Towards the end of the Meeting Jacquelin stated that she 'had fought hard to get access to the Field.' This made me prick up my ears! Brodies had told us that they had organised the access to the field and this therefore had never been regarded as a problem by the beneficiaries. So *why* on earth was Jacquelin, at this late stage, making this statement? I asked her who she had been fighting *against* to obtain the access. She just gave me one of her 'rabbit caught in the headlights' looks and clammed up. Eventually Guy, making an art form of it, again came to her rescue; by changing the subject.

She then came out with another startling bit of news: 'All the mature trees (hardwoods) on the south side of the Field have been stolen.' And clammed up. Again why had she suddenly brought this up at this Meeting, which was purely about getting Planning Permission? I asked her if she had reported the theft to the Police. Her non-response to this was: 'The timber was stolen about five years ago and is now in Germany and nothing can be done about it,' and clammed up. I therefore took it that she had *not* reported the theft to the Police. I asked her why she had just told us that the trees had been stolen when the site plan showed that we no longer *owned* the ground on which they had stood? There was no credible way out of this one. Silence! I could almost hear her brain ticking away feverishly as she thought up another lie to get out this jam. Eventually she answered, 'We owned the trees but not the ground.' Another bald and utterly absurd lie which no one in the room believed. I tried to pursue the matter but was asked by Guy to drop it, because it was not 'relevant'. Of course it was *highly* relevant but I agreed to drop it - for now. To this day I still do not know the true situation of the ground where the trees stood although I knew that the Usher Baronetcy Trust had owned the land *and* the trees since 1928 when old Sir Robert had placed it into the Trust. So who had stolen the trees? I don't know, but would not be a bit surprised to discover that it was Jacquelin herself.

But she was not finished yet. Shortly before the end of the Meeting she piped up with yet another thunderbolt: 'Sir Robert Usher donated the Field to the Edinburgh City Council.' This beggared belief. Of course I immediately asked her: 'Why then are we sitting around the table here today discussing the only matter which is deemed by the Chairman to be 'relevant'; getting planning permission for the land to be developed if Sir Robert had already given it away?' She then answered 'Sir Robert did not give it away at all.' I persisted; 'Why then did you just now tell the meeting that old Sir Robert had donated it to Edinburgh City Council'. She sat there in stony silence staring at the floor. Guy had to come to her rescue yet again.

Jacquelin suddenly looked up and loudly informed us in her usual attention seeking way that, 'Houldsworth no longer worked for Brodies.' Followed again by silence. In fact Houldsworth continued to communicate with the beneficiaries for years on Brodies letterheaded paper and never informed anyone that he had left Brodies, nor did Jacquelin ever offer an explanation for this further bizarre statement.

However her bringing up these matters at the meeting immediately demonstrated, to me at least, that there was something seriously amiss with the Field and that she knew what it was. In case we discovered what exactly *was* amiss she was evidently banking on her sliding out of it by claiming she had already informed us of it by her gobbledgooky statements at the meeting. In essence she was *half* telling us, in a riddle, that there was indeed something wrong with the Field

In response to my sending Guy an e-mail in connection with my discovering further evidence of fraud by Brodies he responded by e-mail on 3rd December 2006. He stated that my e-mail made him 'nervous' and that the only way to sort out 'incorrect or even illegal behaviour' by Brodies was by taking advice from 'skilled and professional lawyers.' I had wasted many years and a lot of money trying to do exactly that to no avail as he well knew, so his writing to me in those terms was very unhelpful indeed. He was well aware that if I followed his advice I would simply end up being robbed by the lawyers, yet again.

So the months passed with no progress being made. We never even received the Report that Macgarvie said he would produce. This made us think that he had never produced it. Many months later we discovered that he *had* produced it and had sent it to Guy who in turn had sent it on to Jacquelin. She however had refused to forward it to us. This of course made the beneficiaries dislike her even more.

In view of this the beneficiaries decided to use Morton Fraser, solicitors, of Edinburgh to try and break the log jam. Morton Fraser were a well known and large Edinburgh law firm who had been the late Lady Stodart's lawyers and were now, by succession, Elizabeth's lawyers. Every bone in my body screamed 'No!' because I regarded them as crooks having heard complaints about them via Scotland Against Crooked Lawyers. Not in the same league in the Crooked Stakes as Brodies, but crooks all the same. Despite this, I had to go along with the other beneficiaries because they outnumbered me. However I warned Elizabeth of my distrust of Morton Fraser. Understandably Elizabeth said *some* action was better than *no* action because we had to do *something*. The lawyer we elected to deal with at Morton Fraser's was called Scott Rae, a senior Partner.

Throughout this period Elizabeth was in correspondence with Brodies seeking answers to all the mysteries in the same way that I had done for years. Ultimately she fared not a whit better than I had, Brodies responding from time to time with lengthy, ambiguous brainwashing letters from Houldsworth. They all had three elements in common: They were all written in rank bad faith; all with the intent to mislead; and all at enormous expense. But Elizabeth kept doggedly at it and I thanked God for her lone support.

55

JOHNNY'S SON DUCKS HIS FILIAL DUTY.

I'd been in long and largely futile correspondence with Johnny's South African lawyer, Andrew Ewing, and Johnny's younger son, Michael, both of whom were, along with me, the Executors of Johnny's Will. Ewing and Michael were generally sceptical of my allegations against Brodies and did not give me the level of support that I needed from them at the time.

Shortly before he died I asked Johnny to make a new Will with only myself to be his Executor because I did not want to have to refer to any South African based co-executors. I knew that this would cause needless delay and confusion in fighting for his interests. Johnny straightaway agreed and told me that he would immediately make the new Will with only me as his Executor. However he had suddenly and unexpectedly died before his lawyer, Ewing, had drawn it up for him. I knew that Johnny had asked Ewing to draft the new Will because he told me that he had. Guy also told me, after Johnny's death, that he knew that Johnny had asked Ewing to draft the new Will with only me as his executor because Johnny had told him so.

We, the British-based beneficiaries, repeatedly asked the South African based beneficiaries, Andrew and Michael Usher, to our various meetings in Scotland because this was the only way for them to acquaint themselves with what had really been going on over the previous thirteen years and also to witness for themselves Jacquelin's twisting, turning and squirming. Regrettably they never came to a meeting despite being in Scotland at the time of some were convened. Of course I had written to them at length explaining the situation as best I could.

In a final effort to try and win them round I determined to catch them on one of their several holiday breaks in Scotland and present my strongest evidence to them. Their next holiday in Britain and Scotland was to be in August 2007. I spent several days creating a document which would give them a clear chronological account of Brodies criminal activity towards

Johnny and all the other beneficiaries since the purported inception of the Executry of the late Sir Robert Usher (Incapax) in 1995. By way of corroborating this narrative document I produced the supporting documentation which I numbered to match the different paragraphs in my narrative document, so that reference could be easily made.

I then tried to arrange a meeting with Andrew and Michael at Guy's place near Dunoon, Argyllshire on Tuesday 21st August 2007. I told Michael Usher that we would need at least four hours, but he sounded anything but enthusiastic. He eventually informed me that he and his brother Andrew would meet me only in the presence of Guy and Guy's Edinburgh lawyers, Gillespie and McAndrew in Edinburgh and for *one* hour only. This was like the kiss of death because I was pretty sure that any lawyer who saw my evidence would report back to Brodies through the lawyer's criminal old-boy network. I was also aware that Guy's lawyer was called Scott Dempster who worked for the law firm Gillespie & McAndrew, just a few doors away from Brodies. Of course the surname 'Dempster' immediately aroused my suspicion, as it would the reader of this book. I reluctantly agreed to this meeting but only because I felt duty-bound to do so, as Johnny's Executor, to enlighten Michael (my co-Executor) and Andrew, and Caroline, their sister, of the true state of affairs in the executry. Having agreed to the meeting I thought further on the matter and very nearly cancelled it so worried was I that Dempster would spill the beans to Brodies. But my duty to keep my co-executor, Michael Usher, informed eventually overcame my reservations. In retrospect I have no doubt whatever that I should never had agreed to that meeting in the presence of Guy's lawyer in Edinburgh.

The Meeting commenced at 11.10 at the offices of Gillespie & McAndrew in Atholl Crescent and was scheduled to last one hour only. Present were Michael Usher, Andrew Usher, Guy, myself and Scott Dempster, the lawyer. Guy suggested that I take the floor and inform all present of the wrong-doing of Brodies.

The first thing I did was ask Scott Dempster if he was any relation to TG Dempster, originally of Mackenzie & Black and then of Brodies (the Deathbed Thief). Scott Dempster told me that TG Dempster was, indeed, his great uncle. I then informed him that his great uncle was one of the key figures in the fraud against the Usher family from the late 1940s until his retirement in the 1980s. Was he still comfortable to be involved in the meeting? Scott Dempster responded by stating that he felt no ties to his great uncle, owed him nothing, and therefore it would make no difference to his chairing the meeting. Interesting that he never defended his great uncle in any way, no protestations to my accusations against him. . . nothing. Again in retrospect I should have ended the meeting there and then. But I didn't.

I then handed everyone present a pack of the narrative document and the supporting documentary evidence and led them through each page explaining in detail and referring them to the corresponding documentary evidence. I reproduce this narrative document below:

SITUATION AT PRESENT [August 2007]:

Taking the period from the death of the late Sir Robert Usher (Incapax) on the 26th of September 1994 to the present.

INFORMATION FOR THE EXECUTORS RESIDENT IN SOUTH AFRICA:

Brodies informed all the ultimate beneficiaries that they were the beneficiaries of the late Sir Robert Usher (Incapax). I, like all the other beneficiaries, believed this to be the case until late 2006. I believed this because all correspondence, yearly accounts and general communications from Brodies to me, both while I was acting under Power of Attorney as one of the Executors for Johnny and personally as an Executor after Johnny's death in 1998. All these communications from Brodies to me were headed 'Sir Robert Usher's Executry.'

However this was *not* the case at all. The beneficiaries were in fact the beneficiaries of the late Sir Peter Usher (Incapax). This had certain profound implications, as follows:

PROFOUND IMPLICATIONS: [for every implication I referred to and made evidence available which I numbered Exhibit 1, 2, 3, etc)

To make sense of this I have to draw attention to various developments, in chronological order, over the last three years [prior to and including 2007] which enabled me to establish the current situation:

1 By letter dated 30th April 2004 from Brodies, headed 'Sir Robert Usher's Executry' (undesignated, unsigned, and author unknown) to me. I checked with Elizabeth Richards if she had received the same letter. She had. In this letter Brodies notified us that we were all now the 'Beneficial Proprietors' of the Executry assets - one of which was the field at Norton, last page (not numbered). Brodies stated: 'It is possible that there remain small un-identified plots still within the ownership of the executry.' And: 'Our recommendation is that there is no further cost incurred in seeking to identify any such areas now.'

2 I immediately suspected that something was up on the grounds that Brodies had always previously referred to us only as 'the beneficiaries'. I was also worried about their reference to the 'lost' plots.

3 I had Elizabeth Richards respond to Brodies' letter because I knew Brodies would be much more on guard with me than with her. Brodies' David Houldsworth replied to her by letter dated 21st May 2004 in a manner

in which they would never have replied to me. Houldsworth made the following statement: 'It is not reasonably possible to map all the disposals of the estate in the past, and it is only if that exercise was capable of being undertaken that any small unidentified plots remaining in the ownership could be found.' And, '. . .where we have been asked to grant title confirming that the estate no longer has any interest in the particular plot concerned but is not guaranteeing that they have title to it.'

4 By letter to me dated 17th May 2006 Brodies' Houldsworth informed the beneficiaries that the Report of the Inquiry into the development of West Edinburgh area recommended that the Field should *not* be included in the Development Plan, against all their confident predictions in 2004 (ie its inclusion by the Council in its RWELP Plan). Houldsworth informed us: 'Another site that previously was *not* proposed for zoning in the areas of Ratho village (Freeland Road) and although not directly linking this to our site it seemed that this might have been done.' [sic] Within a month this Freeland Road site was accepted.

5 I then acquired a document from the Sasines Office which stated that a farm called Rathobyres, originally within the Usher Baronetcy Trust, had been transferred into the name of Jacquelin Wolfe Murray 2004, along with other original Usher Baronetcy Trust lands and houses in the Norton area. Jacquelin had spent the summer of 2006 informing myself and the other beneficiaries that there were no other properties vested in her other than the Field remaining within the executry.

6 I therefore made an on site inspection of the whole Norton area and discovered that Rathobyres - lo and behold - *bordered* Freeland Road! The site chosen by the Council to be included in the local plan also bordered Freeland Road.

7 I procured further documents. One of these was Jacquelin's issuing a Minute of Waiver for £1,350 as the Executor of the late Sir Robert (incapax) Usher's Father (Sir Stuart Usher) in 1999 who died intestate in 1962.

8 Another profound implication was Jacquelin selling a cottage in the Norton areas for £1,000 in 1998 only three months after Johnny's death.

9 In late 2006 I then got the actual Deed referred to in the Document transferring the various Norton properties to Jacquelin in 1998. You will see that this Deed refers to a Notice of Title (*per Incuriam*) in favour of Jacquelin which was registered in September 1998, just two months after Johnny, the other executor, died. *Per Incuriam* is an admission that the person holding the Title in 1998 did not have title to the assets of the late Sir Robert Usher. *Per Incuriam* is used to purportedly fix such illegal states of affairs and seeks to *give* titles to the person(s) who *do* have the right to those titles. The Deed then, goes on to state that the *Per Incuriam* Notice of Title of 1998 only 'purported to complete the title of the said Jacqueline Wolfe-Murray as *Executor Dative* [where there is no Will, or a nominated executor is deceased, then an application is be made to the Sheriff Court for the appointment of

an executor, known as an Executor-Dative, an administrator] and that this *Notice of Title* had been called into question.' So the purported *Per Incuriam* had not worked (ie it had cured nothing). In layman's terms this means that Jacquelin still did *not* have title under that purported Notice of Title. To *fix this,* the executry assets were then transferred into Jacquelin's name in 2004 - *after* she had already sold property at Norton and Pitheavlis.

APPARENT STATE OF AFFAIRS AT PRESENT TIME [August 2007] ARISING FROM THIS DEED.

Jacquelin, as Executor-Dative, has only had the assets vested in her since late 2004, possibly including the Field at Norton but not for certain. Please compare this with the written statement by David Houldsworth on page 2 of his letter to me dated 25th June 2007. Here he states that the Title still stands in the name of Sir Peter Usher. This despite his having transferred the Title to Jacquelin from himself by the 2004 Deed. Both statements cannot be true. It has to be one or the other.

IMPLICATIONS

1 Given that this 2004 Deed states that the 1998 Notice of Title only '*purported* to complete the title' and that this 'Notice of Title has been called into question' and that it was '*per Incuriam*' it becomes apparent that Jacquelin as Executor Dative never had title to sell anything pre-1998 *either*. Yet she had done so at Norton. Nor post 1998 because this Notice of Title was successfully challenged causing the transfer of the assets into Jacquelin's name as executive dative as per this Deed. Yet she *had* sold further property post 1998.

2 Most of the assets of which we were aware had already been sold, mostly before Johnny's death in 1998. By whom?

3 The only persons who have the legal title to sell assets of deceased persons are their Executors.

4 The above Deed (EXHIBIT SEVEN) demonstrates very clearly that Jacquelin and Johnny never acquired the title to Sir Robert's (incapax) assets when they were Confirmed as Sir Robert's executors in 1995. As such they could not sell any assets. Only Jacquelin acquired this title and then only in late 2004 as per this Deed.

5 By letter dated 13th September 2006 from Brodies to Elizabeth, Houldsworth stated that 'when Sir Robert Usher died he owned very little in the way of assets personally,' (page 1, 2nd para - See EXHIBIT NINE). Yet Brodies sent Johnny an Inventory, in Febuary 1995, for the Inland Revenue which valued Sir Robert's estate at £2.242 million. (See EXHIBIT

TEN). These assets included the whole of the Wells, Norton (tiny amount) and Pitheavlis (tiny amount) estates.

6 So the question rises: Did Sir Robert own these assets or not? If he *did* all the dispositions should have been executed by Johnny and Jacquelin. However all the dispositions pre Johnny's death in 1998 (the vast majority) were executed by David Houldsworth with the consent of Sir Robert's executors. Johnny never signed any dispostions. (See EXHIBIT ELEVEN). This is borne out by most of the dispositions (sale deeds) of Wells, Norton and Pitheavlis being executed 'by the Executor(s) of the *Curator-Bonis* of Sir Robert Edward Usher with the consent of the Executors of Sir Robert Edward Usher' (See EXHIBIT ELEVEN).

7 Who were these 'Executors of the *Curator-Bonis* of Sir Robert Edward Usher?' They were David Houldsworth and some other person unknown. (See EXHIBIT ELEVEN)

8 Who was the *Curator-Bonis* of Sir Robert Edward Usher? It was David Houldsworth again.

9 On the face of it, it therefore David Houldsworth appointed *himself* to be the Executor of Sir Robert Edward Usher's estate. But Johnny and Jacquelin were appointed Sir Robert Edward Usher's executors according to Brodies and according to the documentation. So there were *two* sets of executors. Johnny and Jacquelin being one set and David Houldsworth with an accomplice being the other.

10 It therefore appears that David Houldsworth sold most, but not all, of the assets in his capacity as the Executor to Sir Peter L Usher (incapax) and concealed this as best he could by referring to himself as 'the executor of the *Curator-Bonis* of Sir Robert Edward Usher' an obvious play on words with the intention to mislead. Apart from anything else a *Curator Bonis* does not have the right to appoint himself the executor of an estate of which he *is* the *Curator Bonis*, for obvious reasons.

11 And nor was David Houldsworth 'The Executor of the *Curator Bonis* of Sir Robert Edward Usher (incapax).' He was appointed the Executor of Sir Peter Usher (incapax) by his own colleague, Sir Peter Usher's *Curator Bonis* Hugh Stevens. This in itself is highly dubious.

12 Who then disposed of properties that were not disposed of by David Houldsworth. Jacquelin did so at both Norton and Pitheavlis in her own right before her Title to do so was challenged (See EXHIBIT SIX). And Sir Peter himself, *after* he was registered Incapax, at Wells and Pitheavlis. (See

EXHIBIT ELEVEN (page 29- 194, Wells) and EXHIBIT THIRTEEN (page 53-7, Pitheavlis).

13 If Sir Peter was capable of disposing of his own purported property, after he was registered Incapax, what stopped him making a Will?

14 Reverting to Point 6 above. If Sir Robert did not own anything or as Houldsworth put it in EXHIBIT TEN, 'he owned very little in the way of assets personally,' then Sir Robert's Inventory is a fabrication.

15 To me it seems very likely that Sir Robert did not own anything other than his personal effects. This is borne out by the fact that David Houldsworth was the seller of the assets. In fact he had to be the seller as otherwise nothing could have been sold on the grounds that Sir Robert (incapax) did not have title to the assets reflected in his purported Inventory. Houldsworth himself was the sole titleholder. Hence his selling the assets under the guise of 'The Executor of the *Curator-Bonis* of Sir Robert Usher.' He was no such thing. He was the Executor of Sir Peter Usher (incapax). But of course he studiously avoided stating that. All with the deliberate intention to mislead, illegally. It seems certain that Sir Robert was *not* the owner. If this is correct then Brodies have submitted false Inheritance Tax forms to the Inheritance Tax Authorities.

16 So the Executors of Sir Robert (incapax): Johnny and Jacquelin, were Executors only with the right sell his personal effects (ie his clothes). They were not the Executors of any assets in Sir Peter Usher's estate. But their Executorships were used by Brodies to rubber stamp what can only be described as a major fraud.

17 Of course Johnny and I had no idea of this at the time. I doubt that Jacquelin did, either, as her one aim was to get away with her various thieving from the executry without being prosecuted. Her aim was: 'See no evil, hear no evil and let's be done with it, cost what it may.' She must have known that she had been gulled in some way but was too frightened to go into it. Hence her total refusal to answer the simplest of questions and her studious avoidance of the beneficiaries until she had a Chairperson to protect her.

18 So we now have the situation where the Estates were illegally sold by a person (Houldsworth) who had no right to sell them and in the name of an Incapax - Sir Robert E Usher - who never owned them with the consent of only one of the Executors of Sir Robert. And in some cases not guaranteeing any Title to the purchasers (see EXHIBIT TWO).

IMPLICATIONS OF THE ABOVE ON THE NORTON FIELD.
I have in my possession a letter from the Edinburgh City Council to Brodies. This letter is addressed to 'Robert E Usher (Sir) Trust c/o Brodies Solicitors.' (See EXHIBIT FOURTEEN). This means that Brodies must have written to them under this highly inaccurate and misleading heading. Why? One reason was to get round the conveyancing conundrum posed by the false Title. Another could be that this is a variation to the Usher Baronetcy Trust set up by Sir Robert Usher in 1911 and Brodies had to conceal the Usher Baronetcy bit and add the 'E' in the hope that Ediburgh City Council would believe this was the original Trust.

It could well be that Edinburgh City Council conveyancers checked on the Title of the Field and concluded that that Houldsworth holding the Title was illegal. That could be another reason why Brodies transferred all the assets to Jacquelin. It could also be that it was Edinburgh City Council who challenged the purported NOTICE OF TITLE dated 1998.

I suspect the above, collectively, was the real reason for Edinburgh City Council not accepting the Field into its development plan. This does not bode well for the Field ever getting the required zoning.

THE LOST AREAS OF LAND AND PROPERTY LAUNDERING.
Brodies have 'covered' themselves by drawing attention to this 'possibility'. I suspect very strongly that Brodies are aware of the locations and extent of the 'missing' areas of land. If nothing is done about it before the executry ends they will have got away with it. I also suspect that they have already sold some. I suspect this could have been one of the reasons for Brodies allowing Houldsworth to retain control of the assets under his various guises.

The Brodies fraud in this respect could have worked along these lines:

1 Brodies knew that Johnny and Jacquelin were the executors of an assetless Incapax. Despite this they managed to persuade Jacquelin to change from great hostility to them in 1994 to bosom pals by early 1995.

2 Brodies, through Houldsworth, retained control of the remaining assets of the Usher Baronetcy Trust which had putatively gone to Sir Peter Usher (incapax). Brodies could have had two Inventories of these assets: An Inventory which reflected all the assets and a false one which reflected only some of the assets. They showed the false one to Johnny, myself, Jacquelin and the Inheritance Tax Offices.

3 The assets in the false Inventory were sold by Houldsworth on a false pretence, with the exception of the Field at Norton

4 Brodies then transferred the Field to Jacquelin for her to 'hold' for the beneficiaries as putative 'Executor Dative' (despite Brodies sending us

accounts marked "post executry"?) to enable them to "close" Sir PLU'S executry. Stevens of Brodies probably gave Houldsworth of Brodies his discharge. Sir Peter Usher's executry would then appear to be closed, to the layman at any rate.

5 The Norton Field would then be sold with JWM signing the disposal as she has claimed in writing to ER. Quite how this squares with Brodies statement in EXHIBIT EIGHT where DH states that he will have to sign I don't know!

What about the remaining assets in the 'true' Inventory. These could have already been sold by David Houldsworth under his guise. Or they could be still there with Brodies waiting until things calm down. Or some of each.

The end result of this would be that Brodies would have successfully effected a colossal fraud. In this regard even tiny, plots can be very valuable. One, the size of a snooker table went for £1 million, not far from Norton. (See EXHIBIT FIFTEEN)

This fraud could only have been effected with one of their number (David Houldsworth) retaining control over the assets. The fraud would have almost certainly been discovered - had Brodies transferred the assets to Sir Robert Edward Usher (Incapax) on the death of Sir Peter Usher, as they should have done - by the Executors of Sir Robert Edward Usher on his death. That alone was one very big reason for Brodies to leave their man (David Houldsworth) holding the assets.

CONCLUSION

I therefore recommend that the exact status of the field be determined before any further effort and expense is put into promoting it, as a matter of the greatest urgency.

I further recommend that serious thought be given by Johnny's executry as to what steps it should take with regard to the manifest deceits, as above, carried out by Brodies against it, all the other beneficiaries as well as the Executries of the late Sir REU and Sir PLU and the UBT which preceded them.

I would also point out that it was deceit by Brodies which caused Johnny to sign over the estates in 1987 to Sir Peter Usher (and therefore his *Curator-Bonis,* Stevens) which was the main cause of us finding ourselves in this debacle with Brodies and others benefiting greatly at our expense.

ADDENDUM

Brodies went to great lengths to conceal Houldsworth's holding the title and that it was only in 2004 that he transferred the title to Jacquelin. Here are some examples:

1 By letter dated 14/12/2006 to Elizabeth Richards Brodies (Robin Mcpherson) stated (Para 2 under No 2, page 1): 'Sir Robert (Usher) was the last owner of the Field at Ratho— — — —-'. This is just misinformation intended to mislead. See (EXHIBIT SIXTEEN).

2 By letter dated 13th September 2006 to Elizabeth Richards (designated as by Houldsworth, but unsigned) Brodies now state that: 'his (Sir REU's) estate was entitled to all of the assets of Sir Robert Usher's Curatory.' We know that Sir REU's Curatory never had any assets. This is more misleading information with the intention to conceal the true state of affairs. See page One, para 2 (EXHIBIT NINE). And at the end of the same para: 'I was Sir Robert's *Curator-Bonis* appointed by the Court and my duties terminated with Sir Robert's death'. So what is he doing selling off assets that do not belong to Sir REU, over the last twelve years?"

ENDS

During my talking them through the narrative Scott Dempster made the occasional comment: 'This is unusual,' and 'I do not understand why they did things like this,' and 'If this is true and Brodies are successfully sued it will put them out of business,' and 'They will fight this all the way as they will know they will be fighting for their continued existence,' and 'This is huge.' When I had finished he also stated: 'Some of your Exhibits could have an innocent explanation but I cannot guarantee that until my contacts have studied them further.'

The reactions of my nephews and Guy? I was not really surprised at their disinterest. 'Oh, well, Ho-Hum,' was the extent of their reaction to my revelations. I thought they would at least express some dismay - but they didn't. Despite this I was sure that privately they accepted that something was seriously amiss but that they had long ago decided to simply walk away from it all and justified their doing so with: 'Stuart must be exaggerating. The Law Society and the Scottish legal authorities would never let Brodies get away with fraud on that scale. It is all just too preposterous. Besides it would cost us a bomb.' It would *not* cost them a bomb, as I had repeatedly told them, because I would continue to do all the fighting myself, at no cost to them, as I had done to date. Ultimately their attitude boiled down to one thing: They would not fight for their family. The reasons for that were: self preservation, laziness, apathy and the advice of their South African lawyer - and Guy - not to get involved.

Guy then piped up and proposed that Dempster study the narrative and corroborating evidence and then have a Meeting with me in a fortnight or so to give his opinion on whether or not wrong-doing by Brodies had taken place and what should be done about it. I agreed to this, although I already thought very little, if anything, would come of it.

The Meeting concluded at 13.45 instead of midday as had been arranged. I was quite chuffed about that.

Once safely outside the building Michael Usher made no comment whatever on the Meeting but felt sufficiently exercised to tell me that he would not stand for any more 'bullying' from Elizabeth Richards. Bullying? Of course Elizabeth had never bullied him or anyone else in her various communications on his behalf and the behalfs of all the other beneficiaries. Instead she had spent an enormous amount of time and effort to inform him of the true situation in the Executry. Michael then informed me that his main worry was that Jacquelin would simply sell the Field at its present low value if she continued to receive 'negative' letters from Elizabeth. These reactions were further indications that he was following the advice of Guy and the South African lawyer, Ewing, not to oppose Brodies in any way. And was there any comment from Andrew Usher? Absolutely none. And Guy? His only comment was that I should trust Dempster. I told him I would do so largely because Dempster had not yet given me any overt reason why I shouldn't trust him, although privately I didn't trust him at all.

Three weeks came and went with not a peep from Scott-Dempster. I therefore phoned him on 10th September 2007. He now informed me that he was awaiting 'instructions' from Guy. In the event I never heard from him again. So much for the fortnight or so.

I was however forwarded, indirectly, a short e-mail from Guy to Michael Usher eight weeks later dated 11th October 2007 in which Guy stated: 'Regarding Stuart's allegations, Robert Scott-Dempster's view is that while there might be something, there is inadequate substance to justify the cost of preparing a case.' The usual crooked lawyer twaddle to stop the fraud from being exposed. Scott-Dempster had done his lying Death Bed Thief great uncle, Thomas Dempster, proud.

Robert Scott-Dempster, a Gateley & Wareing Lawyer. See page 362

'His great-uncle would be proud.'

56

BRODIES CODE AND A LEONARDO DA VINCI PAINTING

During 2007 there was endless correspondence between the lawyer of the British beneficiaries, Morton Fraser of Edinburgh, Johnny's lawyers in South Africa, Ewing & Co, and the beneficiaries themselves. All of which was extremely expensive and achieved very little. According to Brodies moral code they felt it their duty to enter the fray with misleading letters, the intention of which was to prolong the confusion, and generate even more letters which were costing us a fortune and making a fortune for Brodies. Predictably the crime-concealing Jacquelin took the line of least resistance by going to ground.

In this maelstrom there arose a question which generated another huge round of correspondence: 'Did the Executry still exist'. No one seemed to know and Brodies, having created the confusion, then refused to give a clear answer. No one seemed to know who or what body could make decisions. Brodies had us all trapped in a legal-babble machine of its own making.

Another subject was whether we should sell an Option to a developer or appoint a professional consultancy to have the land zoned before putting it on the market. But Jacquelin, unilaterally, had already employed a professional consultant, Forbes Marr and had spent over £4,000 of beneficiaries money on him to no palpable useful effect before, predictably, he vanished from the scene.

All this correspondence grew into a mountain of paper which filled to overflowing three large lever-arch files and cost the beneficiaries more than £25,000 with neither our lawyers, Morton Fraser, nor anyone else any the wiser.

A rift now developed between the British beneficiaries on the one hand and the South African ones, with Guy backing them on the other hand which made things even more difficult. Brodies must have been delighted at this.

However by Febuary 2008 Guy was, at long last, waking up. I discovered this from a lady secretary who worked for Johnny's South African lawyer, Ewing. I think she had come to realise that Brodies were a bunch of crooks and backed me. She therefore sent me copies of some e-mails which Guy had sent to the South African lawyer and Michael in connection with his (Guy's) correspondence with Brodies, leaving me, as one of Johnny's three Executors, out of the loop. This demonstrated that Guy didn't want me to see these emails; and no wonder. These emails showed that Guy now accepted that Brodies had a lot to answer for. Curiously this still did not stop him from attacking all the British-based beneficiaries, with the exception of Jacquelin. For example by e-mail dated 11th February 2008 to Houldsworth of Brodies, Guy wrote:

> '. . .Brodies advice has rendered Jackie impotent to fulfill her duties as sole executor.'

He followed this up with another dated 24th February:

> 'I hadn't appreciated how complicated this situation is. It's a pity that no one explained this before. . . Poor Jackie has been battered by the dysfunctional beneficiaries for far too long and got nowhere but of course you know this. It strikes me that Brodies have not done a very good job in advising Jackie or the beneficiaries. For as long as I have been aware of this mess, for that's what it is, Brodies have failed to issue sound clear advice (or if they have I haven't seen it) and certainly at the last formal meeting of the beneficiaries no one knew who had what authority and we still don't. . .'

Let us take just one of Guy's statements from this e-mail: 'I hadn't appreciated how complicated this situation is. It is a pity that no one explained this before.' This was just a bald lie because I had gone to enormous lengths, backed by documentary evidence to show him, Michael Usher and Andrew Usher, just how 'complicated' the whole situation was at our Meeting with *his* lawyer, Dempster, in the August of the previous year.

According to Guy all the British based beneficiaries were dysfunctional with the exception of Jacquelin and, presumably, his wife Caroline. This was simply not credible.

Brodies had immediately spotted the danger of this sort of criticism coming from a fellow 'professional' as opposed to the laymen beneficiaries. To this end Brodies responded by e-mail dated 29th February 2008 from Stevens (note, not Houldsworth):

> 'I strongly disagree that no sound clear advice had been given to Jackie in her capacity as Executor. I also completely refute your suggestion that Jackie has been left by us to struggle. We have always done what we can to assist and indeed support her.'

Guy had now, at last, found that he himself could not get any meaningful answers from Brodies, just like Johnny and myself for decades before him.

In September 2008 Jacquelin secretly tried to get my niece, Caroline appointed as Executor alongside her, almost certainly at the suggestion of her husband Guy. Doing this was a further manifestation of Jacquelin's desperation never to appoint any of the other British-based beneficiaries as Executor who she knew now had her well and truly rumbled. What better person than the shy and retiring Caroline, whom she had only very recently met, and who knew very little about the history of the Executry. Caroline would be a pushover as far as Jacquelin, Brodies and Guy were concerned. These three would simply use Caroline as a rubber stamp to let Brodies and Jacquelin off with their various frauds and thefts over the decades.

We discovered this 'Caroline to be Executor' proposal from our lawyers, Morton and Fraser. Of course we, all the remaining British based beneficiaries, were vehemently opposed so Jacquelin and Guy backed off. However if we had not discovered it Jacquelin would have presented it to us as another yet another of her *fait accomplis.*

After this repudiation one would have thought that Jacquelin, having been caught red-handed once, would have given up all thoughts of appointing anyone else as an Executor without consulting us. But not a bit of it. She now quickly and secretly moved to have Stuart McGarvie of Barrs in Glasgow appointed Executor instead of Caroline. Here is how I discovered this latest act of betrayal by Jacquelin, in cahoots with Guy, and both under Brodies' control.

Under cover of a letter dated 29th September 2008 which I received on 6th October 2008 from the honest and sympathetic Ewing's secretary in South Africa was a copy of another e-mail which Ewing had sent to Guy. In this e-mail Ewing asked Guy to confirm that 'Stuart McGarvie of Barr's is to be nominated as a co-trustee along with Mrs Jacquelin Wolfe-Murray.' Again Guy had never copied me into his email to Ewing which included this outrageous proposal. Of course I immediately e-mailed Ewing for an explanation. Unsurprisingly I never received a reply. Thankfully this further attempt by Jacquelin to save her and Brodies skins also came to nothing, almost certainly due to my e-mail to Ewing. Jacquelin, Guy, Ewing and Michael Usher must have realised that they could not go ahead with this outrageous proposal now that I was aware of it.

I took a very dim view of Guy going behind my back on behalf of Jacquelin on these three occasions for the irrefutable reason that I also was an Executor of Johnny's Will, in addition to Ewing and Michael Usher, and therefore had every right to be kept informed on everything that could impact on Johnny's Estate. I am so grateful to Ewing's very principled lady secretary who appears to have recognised this deceit - she, at this time, was one of the very few who helped me keep my faith in humanity.

However there could have been more to these secret attempts to have Caroline and MacGarvie appointed Executors. If Jacquelin had succeeded in having Caroline appointed alongside her there was nothing stopping her from then resigning as Executor. In this event she might well have believed that her resignation would free her from the liability of her thirteen year collusion in the fraud with Brodies. Of course Caroline would have no inkling whatever that this might have been one of the reasons for Jacquelin wanting her to be her co-executor. Exactly the same would apply to MacGarvie if she had succeeded in getting him made the Executor.

The above are just some of the many of examples of Brodies' and Jacquelin's twisting and turning and her desperate attempts to avoid the flack to which she was now increasingly being subjected to by all the Britain based beneficiaries - with the exception of Caroline of course who was very much under Guy's thumb. For that matter so were her two brothers, Andrew and Michael. This was, and still remains, a tragedy for our family.

We, the Britain based beneficiaries, kept up the pressure on Jacquelin to have another meeting with us and this eventually bore partial fruit. On 8th September 2008 we all received a letter signed by Jacquelin which invited us to a Meeting at the offices of HBJ Gateley-Wareing solicitors in Edinburgh. It now appeared that Brodies had 'withdrawn' from acting as law agents to the Executry. This was a clever move on their part and a continuation of their plan to shift the liability of their past frauds onto Jacquelin. However it was blindingly obvious that Jacquelin was *not* the author of the letter because she herself was barely capable of stringing two sentences together.

I therefore replied to the letter and asked Jacquelin *who* had actually written it and was she paying the writer out of the Executry. The answer came quickly but not from Jacquelin. It was from Serena, another of Jacquelin's daughters, and sent to all the beneficiaries. In her letter Serena stated that she had decided to help Jacquelin because she did not like to see her being 'hassled' by the beneficiaries. This 'hassling' was causing her mother to have 'sleepless nights.' I will leave the reader to decide what was actually causing Jacquelin to have 'sleepless nights'.

So much for Jacquelin's statement to Elizabeth of the previous year that she 'thoroughly enjoyed' being the sole Executor. Serena went on to state that she would help her mother to 'try and sort out the muddle of the Baronies, the Norton Field, the Executry and *Brodies*.' (Italics mine).

Well, well, well. . . what an admission. But it was not a 'muddle'. It was a deep laid Fraud of long-standing in which her mother had become a willing participant.

This letter made me think that Jacquelin had spilt the beans on Brodies to Serena but still refused to do so to the beneficiaries to whom she owed the fiduciary duty to do so.

Another reason for Jacquelin's sleepless nights might have been a sudden realisation that Brodies were shifting the liability of their greater crimes onto her. Thieves very often behave in this manner after a robbery when discovery threatens. Jacquelin might well have felt that Brodies were throwing her to the wolves. She could have, and should have, at least tried to save herself by throwing Brodies to the wolves first; by spilling the beans to us and making common cause with us. The only plausible explanation for her not doing so was that she was too terrified of our discovering her own involvements with Brodies in their various frauds and thefts. In essence she had become a prisoner of her own deceit.

So off we all went to this Meeting which had been arranged for 2.30pm on Monday 6th November 2008 at the offices of HBJ Gateley & Waring in Edinburgh. I looked forward to Jacquelin's answers to the awkward questions the beneficiaries would now undoubtedly ask her. She had by that stage cost the beneficiaries roughly £350,000 by her lying, dodging, fraud, stealing and collusion with Brodies, not to mention the enormous stress she had caused my family. And yet today I entered the very non-descript building in which Gateley & Waring were located with a spring in my step. I looked very much forward to her being repeatedly caught out yet again as she had been at the 2006 meeting at Norton and the Glasgow meeting at Macgarvie's.

Present at the Meeting, in no particular order, were Elizabeth Richards, Ronald Kirkpatrick, Susan Hobday, Anne Scott, David Richards (Elizabeth's ex-husband) and myself, all equally decent people. These people were all Britain based beneficiaries. Then came Serena Humphries about whom I knew nothing but suspected the worst, being Jacquelin's daughter Then came Scott Rae of Morton Fraser, the lawyer representing the beneficiaries, who I did not at all trust, and the Gateley & Waring lawyer called Alastair Shepherd whose reason for attending was as unclear as the reason why we were meeting in his office. Mrs Mactaggart, the crime concealing Wells Estate squatter, was also in attendance, as was the lying, defrauding and decidedly uncomfortable, Jacquelin. I was certain that this meeting was a set-up, so I kept my eyes and ears open and mouth shut.

The Meeting commenced badly with Serena taking the chair instead of Jacquelin. Shepherd introduced himself as a *conveyancing* lawyer. I'd decided to allow the other beneficiaries to ask the questions for a start because she would be less on guard with them than with me. As they went through the items on the Agenda various beneficiaries asked Jacquelin some awkward questions:

'What caused the delay in having this Meeting which you agreed to have in November 2007, almost a year ago?' Jacquelin gave an excuse which none of the beneficiaries believed and then just sat there unable to conceal her discomfit.

Alastair Shepherd - Yet another Writer to the Signet; yet another crooked lawyer. Shepherd had signed as a Witness for Brodies on the documents which Brodies had deceived Johnny into signing in 1984 and 1987. Now, 20 years later he re-appears representing Jacqueline Wolfe-Murray.

'Have you signed off the Accounts of the Executry (now standing at over £76,000)?' Her answer was: 'I have signed nothing for the last two years.' Note, never a straightforward answer to a straightforward question.

'Has Forbes-Marr been paid?' Her response was: 'I paid off Forbes-Marr in full on the 15th of August 2006.' She then leant back triumphantly in her chair as though that answer would silence us. The 15th August 2006 was the day of our Meeting at Norton with Guy in the chair; so most likely Forbes-Marr had told her that he would not attend that meeting to protect her unless she paid him on that day. However her triumphal behaviour did not last long because David Richards produced a copy of a document signed by her which had been created by Forbes-Marr on 20th February 2007, six months *after* Jacquelin claimed she had paid him off in full. Skewered, her smug look instantly vanished and was quickly replaced by the usual blush and stubborn silence. When pressed and seeing no way out she then admitted that she had no explanation.

'Are Brodies, or are they not, still the Executry law agents.' She evaded that one by stating that Brodies had withdrawn from acting as they had, 'conceded they were holding up the administration of the Executry.' I had not said a word so far but I could not let this one pass without comment and piped up: 'In that event Brodies have sacked themselves. Is this correct?' Jacquelin blushed and remained silent, looking to Serena for help. So I turned to Serena and asked her to confirm that Brodies had sacked themselves. After some hesitation Serena responded very quietly and very unconvincingly: 'Yes, that is correct.'

During this exchange I watched the two lawyers for their reactions. I noted Shepherd was somewhat discomfited by Serena's answer and eventually he piped up and contradicted both Jacquelin *and* Serena by stating that Brodies had *not* withdrawn from acting and were therefore still the solicitors to the Executry. So who was lying here? I suspected they all were. But *had* Brodies in fact withdrawn? It looked very much like it because otherwise why on earth were we having this meeting at the offices of Gateley & Waring.

Ronald Kirkpatrick then asked her about the other Executry assets to which Brodies had alluded from time to time. Jacquelin gave no remotely coherent, let alone credible answers, on this very important and material matter.

The lawyers, Scott Rae and Shepherd, then advised us that the Executry was 'functus'. When asked what this meant they informed us that it meant that the Executry 'had come to an end'. By now I had learnt that lawyers always resorted to some fancy Latin word or phrase when they wanted to mislead their 'clients'. I therefore did not at all believe that 'functus' meant that the Executry had in fact come to an end as they claimed it had.

Scott Rae then stated that the Norton Field and the Barony Titles should be conveyed into the names of the individual beneficiaries. We were all delighted at this because it meant that Jacquelin would no longer be in a position to sell them for next to nothing in a desperate attempt to escape the responsibility for the crimes she had already committed in her post of executor. In fact I was pretty sure she would have sold them all for next to nothing years ago had it not been for my warning her not to do so.

However she was not a bit delighted at the prospect of the Field and whatever other assets that remained being taken away from her. She tried, unsuccessfully, to conceal this. She evidently realised that she would lose her only blackmailing lever over us. When it came to the vote she gave her assent to the Field being conveyed to us only by a very slight nod of the head. When the vote was carried she protested and tried to wriggle out of it by saying: 'But I said nothing!' As if that would somehow negate her vote - she was twisting and turning to the last. Of course it would not have mattered if she had voted 'No' because everyone else present who had a vote, voted 'Yes'.

Agreement was also reached that she would do nothing further in connection with the Executry without consulting a Steering Group of the beneficiaires who were nominated and agreed at the Meeting. This group was made up of four beneficiaries, one of whom was myself, and Serena. Jacquelin declined to be on it. She was, no doubt, delighted for Serena to take her place as this would make her more remote and less accountable. We made it crystal clear to her that she was not to sign any further documents of any nature *whatever,* that Brodies might ask her to sign, nor to pay Brodies any money *whatever* before consulting the Steering Group, which would make the final decisions. She solemnly assured us that she would *do* nothing, *sign* nothing and, least of all, pay Brodies *anything* without consulting us. I did not believe her assurances at all and I doubted that any of the other beneficiaries did either but it was the best we could do in the circumstances..

We were pleased at getting an agreement that the land be registered in our names and so, it appeared, was 'our' lawyer, Scott Rae. We were also pleased that Serena, like Dorinda before her, could not have possibly witnessed her mother's performance without cringing. She had on occasion tried come to her rescue, but with little success. Despite the relative success of the Meeting I was certain that some ambush awaited us

There now followed months of further correspondence and Meetings from time to time. Serena did all the correspondence and attending of Meetings on behalf of Jacquelin, who kept well away. Her only function was to sign the letters which Serena wrote for her. Some of this correspondence was in connection with the setting up of a formal Committee which would be the decision-making body of the beneficiaries. In the normal course of events this would have been easy and fast. But it took months and God knows how many letters. Other correspondence was in connection with the sale of the Baronies of Wells and Hallrule. The Wells Barony was sold in December 2008 for £50,000 and negotiations between Shepherd and the selling agent were taking place in connection with the Hallrule Barony . Brodies insisted, of course, that the proceeds from the sales of these Baronies be forwarded to them; no doubt with the intention of stealing them to settle their fraudulent "for certain matters post executry", bogus accounts which they still had not even tried to justify. We wanted the proceeds to be held by Morton Fraser, "our" lawyers so that we would have at least some control over them as had been agreed at the Meeting. An *impasse* arose, as always. More letters and more confusion. As a consequence one of the purchasers claimed his deposit back. The man who sold the Baronies threatened to return the proceeds to another Purchaser who had paid in good faith. Eventually the two Barony Titles were sold for £50,000 each.

No sooner was the sale completed than the ambush was sprung. And it was sprung by Shepherd. He now stated that he had been representing Jacquelin, since the Meeting, only in her capacity as the Executrix. It mattered not, it seemed, the Executry was 'Functus'. In complete contradiction to the advice, agreement and assurances he gave us at that Meeting he now claimed the Executry *did* still exist and therefore Jacquelin could do anything she liked and was under no obligation to consult us on *anything at all*. The snake went on to say that he had advised her to pay the £54,000 plus the extra £22,000 that Brodies were now demanding with the proceeds from the sale of the Baronies. Of course this breached all the solemn undertakings the beneficiaries had been given at the Meeting. We objected vehemently, the only way we could, through 'our' lawyer, Scott Rae, at enormous expense to ourselves.

Despite our objections Jacquelin then obeyed Brodies' orders again by paying them off in full. Shepherd and Jacquelin had therefore both flagrantly broken their solemn assurances to us.

Shepherd then hit us with another thunderbolt: he presented his own account, just short of £4,000, to the executry for payment.

The Brodies accounts which Jacquelin settled included the one for £40,000 which she had told us that she would pay personally. On top of it all we had to pay Morton Fraser's Account of about £25,000 for the few months they had acted 'for' us. So Jacquelin's slithering had cost us an additional and completely unnecessary £100,000. Brodies, Morton Fraser and Gateley-Wareing must have laughed all the way to their respective banks. This £100,000 plus payment therefore totally absorbed the £100,000 the executry had got for the Baronies. Any honest executor who was not happy with Brodies would have joined us in using Morton Fraser to represent the interests of the Executry instead of selecting another law firm like Gateley Wareing. As things stood the Britain based beneficiaries were paying three sets of lawyers to 'represent' their interests: Brodies, who had never done any such thing, Morton Fraser, who had done a dishonest job at enormous expense, and Gateley Wareing the hiring of whom in which we had no say and whose only function had been to act for Jacquelin in protecting her and Brodies from us.

If Johnny's elder son Andrew had displayed a proper and natural loyalty to his family I might have have been able to persuade the beneficiaries to hand over one of the Baronies to him. As already mentioned I never received any support from him in my fight against Brodies. He moved to South Africa at the height of my campaign against Brodies, when it looked as though I might defeat them and worked as a joiner there. He left South Africa in 2017 and now lives in France, of all places. Why not Scotland? He is now in his early fifties and as he gets older I very much hope he will come to realise that filial duty is sacrosanct and cannot be evaded without losing one's self respect. If and when he realises that I very much hope he will do his duty for our family, for a very pleasant, welcome and long overdue change.

Back to the present: I could not get the name Shepherd out of my head. Elizabeth enlightened me sometime later when, in passing, she informed me that Shepherd had once been a Brodies lawyer. I now recalled, vividly, that Shepherd had signed as a Witness for Brodies on the documents which Brodies had deceived Johnny into signing in 1984 and 1987 in South Africa which purportedly conveyed the Estates from Johnny and McLure, to Peter. I instantly deduced that Brodies had simply told Jacquelin to go to Gateley & Waring as part of their 'withdrawal' strategy knowing that Shepherd would ensure Brodies were paid their unjustifiable Account from the proceeds of the sale of the Baronies; and that he would protect both Brodies and Jacquelin to the detriment of all the beneficiaries

Here is another example of Jacquelin's shocking behaviour according to the Brodies Criminal Code: We needed the agreement of the two Australian beneficiaries to progress sale of the Norton Field. However both Brodies *and* Jacquelin refused to let us have their contact details. This, as intended, brought everything to a stop for months. This was extremely frustrating and prejudicial to the interests of all the beneficiaries. It suited Brodies because at the time they were acting as a conduit for communications between the British and Australian beneficiaries which enabled them to play both parties like puppets on strings, charging a packet for the pleasure of doing so.

The beneficiaries became so fed up with the insane expense and delay, that we asked Jacquelin: 'Who instructed Brodies not to disclose the Australian addresses?' Her stunning response was: "It was my instruction at Brodies' request.' So Brodies simply requested her to give them instructions which suited *them*. Her obeying Brodies' fraudulent requests had been, in a nutshell, the problem from the very outset of the Executry.

Nor was that all by a long chalk as far as Gateley & Wareing were concerned: The Dumfries and Galloway Police, the Strathclyde Police, the Serious and Organised Crime Agency (SOCA), and the Scottish Crime and Drugs Enforcement Agency raided the Gateley Waring offices in Glasgow in October 2007 where they recovered a painting known as '*The Madonna of the Yarnwinder*', by the great Italian Master Leonardo da Vinci. This celebrated painting, valued at between £25 and £30 million, had been stolen from the Duke of Buccleuch's Drumlanrig Castle in Dumfriesshire in August 2003. They arrested two senior Gateley & Wareing lawyers, Calum Jones and David Boyce, and charged them with conspiracy to extort money, along with Marshall Ronald from England, another lawyer. Detective Superintendent Brian Anderson said the arrests were the result of 'a prolonged and thorough investigation' involving 60 Police Officers over the previous four years. This investigation must have cost the taxpayer an enormous amount of money. I took solace that the considerable negative publicity this episode generated had seriously damaged Gateley & Wareing.

Only after Jacquelin had paid Brodies off in full did they, at long last and after years of being asked to do so, give our lawyer, Scott Rae, a record to justify their 'Accounts' in early February 2009. This was, of course, closing the door after the horse had bolted (with the money).

The record they supplied was a ghoulash of what the Executry had already paid and what remained outstanding. It comprised of 82 sheets of paper with approx 1500 separate and numbered charges recorded in print so small as to be almost illegible. Practically speaking it was impossible to ascertain whether these charges actually represented the 'work' they claimed they had done. Almost certainly many of them were either fabrications or gross exaggerations. Scott Rae 'our' lawyer commented to one of the beneficiaries that the Accounts were 'probably bogus.' That was his lawyerly, ambiguous way of saying that they *were* bogus.

In the circumstances there was absolutely nothing that we could do about these bogus accounts. If we had been stupid enough to try Brodies would simply, and very happily, have driven us all into bankruptcy by charging us at their absurdly exhorbitant rate of £5.41 per minute or nearly 10 pence per second for yet another pack of crime concealing lies. So we took it on the chin and kept quiet.

In addition to charging the £325.00 per hour Brodies also charged travelling time at £115 per hour for their crime concealing activities : In 2002, for example, they sent a non-lawyer member of its staff to shoot around Edinburgh on 'Usher business.' Here are further examples of this money burning frenzy: Houldsworth leaving a message on someone's phone cost us £27.50. And on 29th July 2008 a telephone call to Shepherd at Gateley & Wareing cost us a cool £97.50. Here is another one: Meeting Shepherd in the street and 'discussing the hand over generally,' cost us another £32.50. Nice way to make money; bump into an acquaintance in the street and be paid for talking to him about deceiving your respective clients. Another nice way to make money: Meetings with Bill Drummond, Brodies Managing Partner, about getting us to pay their thoroughly bogus bill of £76,000 were charged for. I know of no other business which charges its clients for discussions on how to get them to pay for defrauding them.

Amongst this sea of paper was a letter dated 22nd August 2007, written by Brodies and addressed to themselves, which was signed by Jacquelin as coming from her. This letter stated that she agreed to the Auditor of Court carrying out a 'diet of taxation' on Brodies fees'. The use of this phrase in this context was another example of the Scottish legal system employing gobbleydegook to conceal its real intentions from the general public. It's use in our case was to authorise the Auditor of Court, yet another crooked lawyer called Crichton, to rubber stamp Brodies utterly fraudulent fees, in the full knowledge that they were fraudulent. The letter also agreed to the supposedly non existent executry paying the Auditor of Court for carrying out this 'diet of taxation'. This letter demonstrated that her statement at the meeting in Gateley-Waring's office on 6th November 2008 that, 'I have signed nothing in the last two years,' had been yet another of her brazen lies. Her signing that letter of course locked her into using whatever money still remained in the Executry to pay Brodies fraudulent accounts in full. The day she paid Brodies off in full was the day that she assumed the sole liability, under Scots Law before it was perverted, for her own *and* Brodies frauds over the preceding fifty or more years.

That was the imperative behind Brodies 'withdrawal' strategy. It would have been easy for them to gull Jacquelin into thinking that this strategy would save her bacon as well, when in fact the opposite was their intention. So they approached their ex-employee, Shepherd now of Gateley Wareing and witness to another, earlier aspect of the fraud to 'advise' Jacquelin' from then on. Brodies then instructed Jacquelin to engage him to represent her against us beneficiaries and our lawyer, Scott Rae of Morton Fraser. Jacquelin, as usual, then obeyed Brodies instructions, largely because by now she was terrified of them. So Shepherd had sat there throughout the meeting smug in the knowledge that our passing resolutions and organising committees were about as meaningless as the word of Edinburgh Lawyer. The trap was set and like dutiful lambs to the slaughter we had obliged. The only benefit for us, and only because it suited Brodies and Gateley & Wareing, was that Brodies ordered Jacquelin to hand over the Norton Field to the beneficiaries. The last thing Brodies needed was for her to keep the Field for herself as this was certain to cause me to take to the warpath, putting them in the crime limelight again. At the risk of sounding vain I knew that Brodies regarded me with trepidation and would go some way to avoid antagonising me further.

Most of the rest of 2009 was taken up with further correspondence between Morton Fraser, Brodies, Gateley Wareing, the Chairman of our Committee, Ronald Kirkpatrick, and Serena, acting for Jacquelin. The first objective of all this correspondence was to draft an Agreement formalising the powers of the Committee and its modus-operandi which was acceptable to all the beneficiaries. The second objective was to transfer the remaining assets out of JWM's name into the names of every beneficiary in the requisite shares. Both these objectives were finally achieved in November 2009.

57

FINAL MEETINGS

We had an interesting meeting on 22nd September 2009 at Chapelhill Farm, the home of Ronald Kirkpatrick, near Hawick. Jacquelin turned up, no doubt to try and worm her way into our good books. Very shortly after the meeting commenced she piped up: 'A line should be drawn under all past events and we should be starting afresh.' We politely disagreed by stating that what had happened in the past would inevitably have a bearing on developments in the future. But her making this statement was an obtuse attempt at brainwashing the beneficiaries into accepting all her past betrayals of them.

The reader may be wondering what had happened to her erstwhile protectors: her daughter Dorinda, and then her daughter Serena, and perhaps more curiously my own niece's husband, Guy? The answer is, I believe, that they had all realised that it was too risky for them to continue defending her. Guy, perhaps worrying he was being enmeshed in her vile relationship with Brodies had now himself gone to ground.

Having realised that her twisting and pleading was getting her nowhere with the rest of the beneficiaries she suddenly blurted out that Brodies had twenty-seven large steel boxes of Usher papers. After a stunned silence I jumped in and said we should pick up these boxes for historical and other reasons as soon as possible before Brodies destroyed the papers. I was certain they would destroy them as soon as they felt it safe to do so. The Committee agreed with me. Predictably Jacquelin did not like this and countered with the statement: 'Although Brodies are no longer acting for the Executry they are not requesting the removal of the Usher documents.' But of course *Brodies* were not asking for their removal. They needed that like they needed a hole in the head. I reiterated that we wanted the Usher boxes, and fast. She then assured the beneficiaries that she would arrange for the boxes to be collected by one of our number. Despite further efforts on the part of the beneficiaries by Febuary 2012, two and a half years later, all we had managed to obtain from Brodies, via Morton Fraser, was *one* of these boxes which on opening was *empty!*

I asked for and received the blessing of the Committee to approach Brodies personally to ask for the boxes. On 7th February 2012 I wrote to the Chairman of Brodies, by recorded delivery, asking for the boxes of Usher papers and requesting a convenient time for me to collect them. I gave the Chairman of Brodies the deadline of 21st February 2012 to respond. On 22nd February I received a short letter from Joyce Cullen of Brodies which stated that Brodies no longer acted for the Executry and I should ask Jacquelin Wolfe Murray to instruct them, Brodies, to 'respond to me'.

So I wrote to Jacquelin, by recorded delivery as always, on 24th February asking her to 'instruct' Brodies to let us have the now twenty-six steel boxes of Usher papers. She refused to instruct them and that remains the position to this day with the result that we have never obtained these papers which belong to us. A more blatant example of concealing evidence of fraud is hard to conceive.

Having got control of the Norton Field a year or so earlier we resurrected our negotiations with the Housing Development Company who were still very interested. Of course they had long realised that there was some desperate problem between the beneficiaries, Jacquelin, and Brodies.

To this end we had a meeting with the Housing Development Company at Bedrule Village Hall in 2010. To our surprise Jacquelin pitched up. The others present were Ronald Kirkpatrick, his two sisters Susan Hobday and Anne Scott, and Elizabeth and David Richards, her ex-husband who, with Elizabeth, knew more about the Norton Field saga than anyone else. Mrs Mactaggart sent her apologies, despite living less than a mile away. Yet Elizabeth and David attended from 330 miles away. The South African and Australian contingents failed to turn up, as usual.

Quite shortly after the meeting commenced Jacquelin gave Ronald Kirkpatrick, the Chairman of the Managing Committee, the two proxies which Michael Usher in South Africa and the Australian beneficiaries had given her. Michael had specifically asked that I was not to have Johnny's executry proxy vote and that Jacquelin was to have it, despite my being one of Johnny's executors. Guy had done a good job on him. Jacquelin immediately disregarded the wishes of these beneficiaries by handing them over to Ronald Kirkpatrick to act as proxy for them - par for the course for her.

The meeting then heard presentations from the Housing development company and another firm who were both interested in purchasing the Norton Field. Jacquelin made no contribution to the meeting and, as always, took no notes; she just sat there looking queasy and uneasy. I suspected that she would let some cat out of the bag sooner or later, so kept rather quiet and waited patiently.

When the presenting Developers left we all talked amongst each other, with the exception of Jacquelin who was, not surprisinngly, rather ignored. I could see that she was becoming more and more desperate for attention and my hopes rose that this would cause her to make another of her attention seeking dramatic statements. I was not disappointed.

She suddenly informed Elizabeth, as the latter emerged from the hall kitchen, that she was in contact with her late father, Robin! This was her and my cousin Robin who had died of cancer in 1947, as already narrated. Jacquelin then went on to say that Robin had asked her to tell Elizabeth that he was fine, and she was not to worry about him. She then went on to say that Robin had asked her, Jacquelin, to tell Elizabeth that she should 'relax a bit more and not take things so seriously.' On top of everything else that this poisonously dishonest woman had done to her, and all the other beneficiaries, this was too much for Elizabeth. She exploded by telling her that she did not believe a word of it and to mind her own business. Thus rebuffed a chastened Jacquelin muttered: 'I just thought you would like to know that he is alright.'

The meeting then ended with her hobbling out of the Hall due to a bad leg - a sad, lonely, broken old woman of 79.

The Meeting decided we would deal with one of the potential purchasers and gave them the go ahead. The very first thing they would do would be to check that we had proper Title and Access to the Norton land. Brodies had already spent approx £6,000 of Executry money on upgrading the existing 'very short access.' in addition to an indeterminate amount 'managing' it since 1998. Actually there was nothing to manage except to pay the annual third party Insurance.

We and the Developers were happy that, at last, after years of being obstructed by Brodies and Jacquelin we could now make some progress. The Developers assured us that they would let us know the outcome of their investigations in a few weeks' time.

This they did by e-mail to Elizabeth on 17th May 2010 and it was, inevitably, bad news. Their lawyers could not establish that the Field had *any* access and nor could they rely on the extent of the Field as per the Title Deeds they had been supplied by Shepherd, the Gateley-Wareing in-house crook. Brodies had simply refused to communicate with them, as they had always done in previous years. I had warned Elizabeth and David, and Ewing and Michael Usher in South Africa that I had long suspected that Brodies and Jacquelin were hiding *something* in connection with the Field. We now knew why. Why hadn't Brodies and Jacquelin informed us of this? That alone would be just another another reason for Brodies 'withdrawing' as the Executry's lawyers. It also fitted in with Jacquelin's bizarre, terrified behaviour at the various abortive meetings we'd had in connection with the Norton Field.

The Developers being unable to verify our Title and access, at great expense to themselves, was further confirmation that Brodies charge of £6,000 in upgrading what they had called the 'existing access' to the Field was fraudulent. In essence they had spent a lot of money to leave us with a landlocked piece of ground of indeterminate size. This made the Field virtually worthless because we would be at the mercy of whoever owned the access, the famed 'ransome strip.' I was frankly furious, as were the other beneficiaries. As for Jacquelin, not a word from her. She had gone to ground again as criminals do.

However being furious was not going to get us anywhere. I cooled down and got my thinking cap on. That whole area had been on the Norton Estate, all our land, so how was it that there appeared to be no record of who owned the access? Surely there *had* to be a record of it having been sold sometime in the past. The potential purchasers had looked but could not find any reference to it in any sale. They had then done an on-the-spot, covert enquiry to see if they could find anything out about it from the local people. But that had yielded nothing either. They had even been in contact with the Keeper of Records at the Registrars of Scotland. He likewise could throw no light on the matter. But he advised that the beneficiaries could make an application to register title to the access. This would entail our hiring professional searchers to try and find out who owned this land and if they failed we could then make the application. The Building Development Company advised us that this would cost between £4,000 and £8,000; money the Executry did not have, thanks to Brodies 'management' on the 'instructions' of Jacquelin. On top of that there was no guarantee that the Keeper of Records would find in our favour. So we could spend £8,000 of our own personal monies for no certain return. So what now? I was loath that any of us should expend any more money on the Norton Field because the Executry had already expended thousands on it only to find that it was landlocked and that its size could not be verified. Brodies had known this all along but preferred to keep taking our money.

I therefore went to the Scottish Records Office in Edinburgh to check for myself. A very helpful person there, try as he might, could not throw any light on the matter. This person did, however, say that all the Usher dispositions in the area always reserved the underlying minerals and ground to the Usher family and that this would stand us in good stead in any application to register title to it. I had often wondered how, for example, a house and garden could be sold to someone but that we still owned the ground and minerals underneath it. I had put it down to another example of the lunacy of 'Scots law'.

All sorts of possibilities leapt into my mind as to who might own this tiny piece of ground. I recalled Brodies' recommendation that no effort be made to locate other Usher plots which might exist and which they had recommended should not be searched for. Had Brodies simply conveyed this access to themselves? Had they included Jacquelin in the fraud? Had they registered the conveyance in a way that made it virtually impossible to find? Had they left the conveyance to mature, like good whisky? Then when the time arrived and the owners of the Field wanted to develop it Brodies would simply hold the owners of the Field to ransome. Only a very determined person who was prepared to devote a great deal of time, energy and money would have any chance of uncovering such a fraud.

These were a few fraudulent ways that Brodies might have effected the acquiring of the access. I had no proof but I did have some clues. One of them was Jacquelin's 'informing' us at our Glasgow meeting that we 'owned the trees but not the ground'. A very strange thing to say. Another was that old Sir Robert had already given the Field away. On the surface this was all complete balderdash. But was it?

It is now 2020 as I add this final text to the book. In the intervening ten years myslef and the remaining Beneficiaries have had numerous Meetings about selling the Norton land and still have not managed to sell it. It was always the same old story of potential Purchasers showing great interest at the outset and then backing out 'unexpectedly'.

Of course this greatly aroused my suspicions as to whether we were in fact the owners of the Norton Land. This despite my acquiring a Document from the Registers of Scotland on the 3rd of September 2010 which records the names of all the Beneficiaries, including mine, as being the owners 'of lands and estate of NORTON, & C., in Parishes of RATHO and KIRKLISTON' [this is an exact replication of the wording Brodies used] and that was it. No mention whatever of which land specifically and, most ominously, no indication of where it was situated and no diagram of it.

It appeared to be the same old story of 'something going on in the background' to sabotage our selling the land.

58

SUMMARY AND QUANTIFYING OF THE FRAUD

When the Wells Estate was sold in 1995 the fraudsters would have heaved a collective sigh of relief, believing they were almost home and dry, with only Johnny and myself standing between them and ultimate success. They undoubtedly thought they would overcome Johnny and myself, quite easily. When Johnny died so conveniently in 1998 they would have been delighted and thought: 'Well that's him out of the way. That's Stuart stuffed now. Game Set and Match to us.' Unfortunately for Brodies I wasn't stuffed in 1998 and it is now 2020 and I am still not stuffed. In the intervening years I, with the help of many others, have raised public awareness of just how crooked Brodies and the Scottish Legal system in general were and still are.

I also uncovered further aspects of the fraud. For example in 2004 I discovered that it was actually Houldsworth of Brodies who had sold the Wells Estate and not Johnny and Mrs Wolfe-Murray who were the registered Executors of Robert Usher (Incapax). Houldsworth had executed this particular fraud by, wait for it, simply *posing* as the executor of Robert the Incapax. He had therefore deceived Johnny, myself and Mrs Wolfe-Murray. The reader could be forgiven for thinking that I must have been a total idiot for not noticing this at the time. Well, I can assure any reader who might think along those lines that he/she would also have fallen for Houldsworth and Brodies' deception: hook, line and sinker, because it had been concealed so cleverly. The actual method of concealment was a lot of legal mumbo jumbo with some handy Latin in it for misleading purposes. It simply never occured to me that Brodies would do something like this and the same would apply to any reader of this book had they been in my position. I uncovered this particular fraud by finding a document in the National Archives of Scotland which stated that Houldsworth's of Brodies 'Notice of Title' in favour of Mrs Wolfe-Murray in 1998 had been called into question. This calling the 'Notice of Title' into question had then forced Houldsworth to convey what remained of the Estates from himself to Mrs Wolfe-Murray in September 2004.

What were the consequences of this deception? One consequence of it was that the sale of what remained of the Wells Estate after it had been sold in 1995 was null and void because it had been sold by Houldsworth of Brodies *posing* as the Executor and not by the *real* Executors, Johnny and Mrs Wolfe-Murray. This in turn means that all those who purchased the various properties on the Wells Estate in 1995 have no legal nor lawful Title to the properties they 'purchased' that day. These various purchasers remain blissfully unaware that they have no Title to 'their' properties to this day (June 1919) as I write. In essence what happened was that they purchased properties from a person (Houldsworth of Brodies) who had no right to sell them. Their occupancy of the various properties they purchased is therefore based on a typical Brodies falsehood. In fact these purchasers paid money for something in good faith and got nothing in return.

What therefore should be done about this now? To be plain about it the forces of Law and Order should be activated to remove all these new putative 'owners' from the various properties they presently occupy on what used to be the Wells Estate and these properties should be made immediately available to the Usher family of Norton and Wells. Thereafter Brodies should be forced to apologise and recompense those purchasers it had deceived into purchasing property on the Estate and also recompense my family for the inconvenience of unlawfully being stripped of our lands and possessions. There were many other examples of Brodies executed fraud which I also discovered, after the Wells Estate had been sold in 1995, in the early years of this 21st century.
It is quite apparent from this book that Brodies lied, bluffed and denied their way out of everything, which Johnny, myself and latterly the other British based beneficiaries threw at them. Other law firms involved in, or party to concealing, the fraud include Tods Murray, Shepherd and Wedderburn - and likely many others in Edinburgh - as well as Turnbull Simpson and Sturrock of Jedburgh. The Insurance Brokers Willis Corroon were also involved. The Stockbrokers, Lawrie & Bell of Edinburgh, through their in-house crook, Nicholson, were also part of the fraud. The Borders Accountancy firm of John Welch and Company knew of the fraud but did nothing about it. The Law Society of Scotland, the Scottish Legal Services Ombudsman, and the Faculty of Advocates became accessories to the fraud by concealing it. The same applies to the Court of Session in Edinburgh, the Crown Office and finally the Police. I do not hold the Police directly culpable because they were forbidden from doing anything about it by the Crown Office.

The Contents of Hallrule House

The Property of THE LADY GERTRUDE USHER'S TRUST,
Sold by Instruction of The Trustees, and
The Property of SIR ROBERT USHER, BT., deceased,
Sold by Instruction of The Executors

Objects of Art, Furniture, Porcelain, Oriental Works of Art, Books, Pictures and Silver

At The Assembly Rooms, George Street, Edinburgh

Tuesday 24 October 1995 at 10.30 a.m. precisely

Left and right: A pair of paintings (sized for illustration only) being sold as as a tiny fraction of the contents of Hallrule House in 1995; note the contents are listed as the property of 'The Lady Gertrude Usher's Trust' AND 'The property of Sir Robert Usher BT [Incapax] deceased'. The contents belonged to neither as all property was part of the 'Usher Baronetcy Trust' set up for all time in 1911 (see page 13)

I have now narrated the salient points of the events which led to the plundering of my family, resulting in our losing just about everything. What the causes were, how it was done and, thereafter how it was concealed. I have recorded this as a narrative of the events as they happened as far as practically possible. At the beginning I was too young; as I matured I was naive; in law I was ignorant and I failed to grasp the implications and significance of the various events as they unfolded. However from my researches and the records which I did manage to acquire, despite being obstructed all the way, I have been able to connect the various disparate and seemingly unconnected pieces of the jigsaw together into something resembling a coherent whole. It's not a pretty sight.

I have written at length on the fraud but have not to date tried to quantify it. The reason for this was that Brodies always denied first Johnny and then myself the Usher Baronetcy Trust records; for example Brodies refusal to let us have the 27 steel boxes of Usher records already alluded to. Only the police, in the form of the Fraud Squad, have the powers and resources to force Brodies to hand over the records and thus fully uncover a fraud as large and long-standing as this. Still, it would be an enormous task and take years. It would also be costly, perhaps millions of pounds and would require the assistance of forensic accountants versed in such fraud.

In these circumstances there is no alternative but for me to quantify the fraud as best I can from the records I have managed to acquire and from information about my family I have either been told or read about. In doing this I am aware that my calculations are bound to be inaccurate in some aspects.

So what *was* the wealth of the whisky side of the Usher family a century ago? According to Patrick Murray, the lawyer alluded to earlier in the book, the whisky business was sold for £7 million in 1918. In addition we owned the Norton, Wells, Pitheavlis and Pulteney Town Estates. I conservatively estimate that these Estates would have been worth about half a million pounds in 1918. This figure represents the wealth of the Norton and Wells branch of the family only and does not include the wealth of the Beer Ushers as represented by Thomas Usher & Company of Edinburgh. Nor does it include the wealth of Andrew Usher II which included the Estates of Johnstounburn; Northfield, St Abbs; Bielside, West Barns, East Lothian; Hall Manor, Peebles and finally Blackford House, Blackford, Edinburgh. Nor does it include any of the other properties and assets of Andrew Usher II as he had already passed away in 1898 leaving all these estates, properties, assets and money to his daughters. As an aside, I would confidently assert that the lawyers 'advising' his daughters swindled them to the uttermost.

I am fully aware that my estimate largely relies on the lawyer Patrick Murray's statement that the Usher whisky business was sold for £7 million in 1918. I doubt very much that he had just invented that figure. On top of that he had volunteered it and not in response to any question from me. It was unlikely in the extreme that he, being a lawyer, would volunteer such information unless he was sure of it.

Sir Robert did not realise the whole proceeds of the sale of the business as these were shared between him and his partners. I do not know what Sir Robert's shareholding in the business was. His partners in the business were his brother Frank and Sir Oliver Riddell and two others. I therefore have to make an guesstimate as to what Sir Robert's share was. Being the senior Usher and eldest son I shall suggest that he had a 45% shareholding. On this basis he therefore should have received £3,150,000 in 1918.

When Sir Robert died in 1933 the lawyers showed only £269,058 in the Inventory of his Estate. This was mainly cash and investments. Here remember that this Inventory did not include the Estates of Norton and Wells which he had already conveyed into the Usher Baronetcy Trust in 1927. In 1933 the Wells Estate would have been worth about £150,000 and the Norton Estate about £100,000 and the Pitheavlis Estate perhaps £70,000 (the Pitheavlis Estate consisted of a small castle, the Town Muir and hundreds, maybe thousands, of feus within the City of Perth). The combined total of all these figures comes to £320,000 at his death in 1933. This figure of £320,000 should therefore be added to the estimated £3,150,000 that he received for his share from the sale of the business, which would raise his worth to £3,470,000 by 1933, the year of his death. In today's terms (2015) this figure approximates to between three and four hundred million pounds.

On this basis let us look at the wealth of our family in the year 2000. The wealth of the Usher family of Norton and Wells in the year 2000 amounted only to what Johnny and I inherited in 1995 and 1996 and any appreciation in value in the remaining years to 2000. We inherited about £220,000 each, giving a total figure of £440,000. On top of that must be added the value of the Field at Norton which was £20,000 and the value of the moveables we inherited. I estimate this figure to be about £130,000. The total of these figures is £590,000.

On this basis therefore our family were, in today's values, worth £300 to 400 million in 1933 yet only £590,000 in the year 2000. What therefore caused this enormous erosion of wealth in only sixty seven years ? The following is my theory and the theory which most closely accords with the criteria set at the beginning of this Chapter

After Sir Robert's death in 1933 his Executor's and Trustees, of whom there were no less than seven, would have 'instructed' the family lawyers at the time, MacKenzie and Black, to draw up an Inventory of the Estate. But here was the rub: Two of these Executors and Trustees were MacKenzie and Black lawyers: Adam West Gifford and John Renshaw Gifford. Another Executor was Harry Lawrence Usher, a Chartered Accountant and a Beer Usher. The other Executors were Sir Robert's widow, Katherine Lady Usher, and his two eldest Sons, John Turnbull Usher and Ronald James Usher, and his brother Frank James Usher of Dunglass. The make up of this executorship meant that his wife and two sons were outnumbered four to three by non-members of his immediate family, with three of the non members being, significantly, two lawyers and an accountant. With hindsight not a healthy situation at all.

In fact it is extremely unlikely that the members of Sir Robert's immediate family who were his Executors and Trustees would have 'instructed' anything. They would have left that to the lawyers who they trusted, because, firstly, that was the way things were done in those days, and, secondly, that type of thing fell within their fields of - on the face of it - competence. These lawyer Executors would then instruct the law firm, Mackenzie & Black, in which they were senior Partners, to produce an Inventory of Sir Robert's Estate. If Sir Robert's immediate family had no knowledge of the full extent of Sir Robert's Estate they would accept any Inventory drawn up by their lawyer co-Executors, as long as it appeared plausible. This being the case what would stop the lawyers and the accountant from leaving the proceeds of Sir Robert's share from the sale of the business *out* of the Inventory of his Estate altogether?

Absolutely nothing, other than a fear of being caught or a moral objection to dishonesty by one of their number. My researches and experiences have proved that the vast majority of lawyers in Scotland have no moral objection whatever to lying, cheating and so on in their pursuit of money at the expense of their 'clients' (*prey* would be an infinitely more accurate term). In the unlikely event of their being caught out by one or more of the other executors they would simply feign an apology and claim an error. That would have been the end of the matter. If, however, all the non-lawyer executors accepted that the Inventory was complete and correct these crooked lawyers and accountants would have simply given each other a knowing wink, keep quiet and 'await developments.'

This same theory could be applied to Sir John's Inventory of 1904 in connection with the hiding of some of his assets. For the present we shall stick with Sir Robert's Inventory.

But surely Sir Robert would have told his immediate family or, at the very least, his wife Katherine, what he had sold the business for and, on top of that, the full extent of his own and Usher Baronetcy Trust assets in the Scottish Borders, Edinburgh, Ratho, Perth and Wick. One would have thought so, but that does not mean that he actually did so. In those days it was not at uncommon for wealthy men not to tell their wives and sons about their business affairs and least of all how much they were worth. Remember that Sir Robert lived the greater part of his life in the reign of Queen Victoria. I have already narrated the example when Andrew Usher II objected even to being spoken to by Sir Robert when the latter was a young man.

If this had indeed been the case the only people who would have known the full extent of his Estate would have been his lawyers and accountants. However there was an additional reason which indicated that Sir Robert had not informed his immediate family about what he had sold the business for.

All my life I had been told that the business had been sold for a 'large undisclosed sum.' At first I accepted this without a thought but as I grew older, I wondered more and more why the amount had been kept secret. Now that I had hard evidence of Brodies' fraud since at the very least 1962, and circumstantial evidence of the same since 1948, it slowly dawned on me that there had to be a compelling reason for this secrecy. After all, many large businesses have been sold or merged with each other over the last century and the details of the financial arrangements widely published. Why then not in our case? Something did not add up. What was it? One possibility was that Sir Robert and his Partners had been 'advised' by the lawyers that it was not in his or his Partners' interests to let it be known what the business had been sold for. Now, why would the lawyers advise that? There are a number of possible explanations: One of them might have been for tax evasion purposes. Another could have been simply 'play your cards close to your chest'. The latter is an innocent explanation, but the former decidedly not. Yet there could have been another reason, also far from innocent: the lawyers did not want the public to know what the business had been sold for because they planned to appropriate that money, or part of it, to themselves.

If this was indeed the case what better way of convincing Sir Robert and his Partners that they should not make the amount they received for the business known because of 'tax reasons' and in particular the 'death duties'. No one likes the idea of a large part of one's Estate being snaffled by the government at one's death and Sir Robert would have been no exception.

And he would have believed, as people did in those days, that the lawyers would ensure the money went to his heirs when it became expeditious to do so. If this had indeed been the case it appears that Sir Robert failed to realise that it would be nigh impossible for any of his heirs to inherit such a vast amount of money without the Tax Authorities noticing. But the lawyers would have known that and reckoned that they could steal the money and hide it for many years and then money-launder it decades later and over many years.

There was another advantage in this Tax Evasion scheme for the lawyers of which Sir Robert would have been totally unaware. In the event of the fraud being discovered at some future date the lawyers would be in a very powerful position to tell the discoverer that it had all been a 'mistake', and that it would now be catastrophic to report the evasion to the Tax Authorities. Catastrophic because the Tax Authorities would charge their punitive rate of interest on the original figure, which had not been declared for all the years that the 'mistake' had remained 'undiscovered.' In this event there was also the possibility that Sir Robert's executors would be prosecuted for tax evasion. This of course would include the Katherine Lady Usher, Sir John and Uncle Ronald none of whom would have known anything about it. All this would certainly shut the discoverer of the tax evasion up very quickly. Do I have any examples of this foul trickery.

The simple answer is that this was *exactly* what Brodies had done to Johnny and me in 1994 when I discovered that the lawyers had left the Contents of Hallrule House out of the Usher Baronetcy Trust Accounts on Stuart's death in 1962 after Dempster had lied to the Tax Authorities. This was their 'in error' first defence. They had then warned of the 'very serious' financial repercussions for the yet to be formed executry were the Tax Authorities to be made aware of the 'mistake.' This was their 'intimidation' second rank defence whereby they sought to unload the liability onto the executry of the dead Sir Robert Usher (Incapax) who had been their client and a Ward of Court. At the time I had acquiesced in the fraud because I did not fully realise that it *was* fraud. However by the time the beneficiaries had been paid most of their inheritances, I realised that it was fraud and stopped acquiescing in it by reporting it to Miss Patrick at the Capital Taxes Office on that April day in 1996, as already narrated.

Leaving out the bulk of Sir Robert's Estate in this manner would go a long way to explaining why our wealth had shrunk to a little over half a million pounds by 2000.

And what did the lawyers do with the Sir Robert's share of the sale proceeds after his death? I presume they left it in secret Accounts for many years. If so, they got their opportunity to money launder it when Peter the Incapax 'reigned' from 1962 until his death in 1990. The same applied to Robert the Incapax until his death in 1994, a period of thirty-two years in all. Brodies expanded dramatically after taking over Mackenzie & Black in

Above: Old Bonded Warehouse - Andrew Usher & Co. Edinburgh. Storage capacity 5,000 casks.

Below: Floor of the New Bonded Warehouse - Andrew vUsher & Co. Edinburgh. Storage capacity 6,000 casks.

Once one of the largest buildings for the storage of whisky in the world: The St. Leonards Warehouse of Mssrs Usher, 1911

1972 by establishing the following different in-house businesses: Brodies Insurances Services, Brodies Accountancy Services and Brodies Estate Agency. These were the ideal structures through which to launder money and property. The more I thought about it the more likely it appeared that Brodies had set up these in-house businesses for the singular purpose of effecting this money and property laundering of Usher assets in the least traceable way. When I came home in 1995 they had very recently closed down these businesses, with the exception of the Estate Agency which they used, of course, to sell the Wells Estate and charge their commission. The reason for their closing the other two businesses was most likely because they had finished, or nearly finished, their filthy money laundering over the preceding thirty-two years. That also could well have been the imperative for Mackenzie & Black allowing themselves to be taken over by Brodies in 1973. Far safer for all the money laundering to be done by Brodies in the manner described above than they themselves doing it. Besides that the Mackenzie & Black crooks, like McClure and Dempster, would not have the skills for money laundering. Their speciality was misleading 'clients' with the most vile of intent, then robbing them on their death beds, and then robbing their Estates when their clients were safely underground.

All the above is predicated on Sir Robert selling the business for £7 million in 1918 and his share of the £7 million being left out of his Inventory. Did that cover everything? Not necessarily.

In 2001 I met someone who told me he used to work in the Vaux Brewery in Sunderland as a youngster in the early 1970s. Vaux had taken over Usher's Brewery in 1959. My informant told me that big tanker trucks of whisky arrived at the Vaux Brewery two or three times a week for three or four years in the early to mid 1970s. My informant's job was in the bottling plant bottling this whisky. That got me thinking.

I had seen many of these large red Usher Vaux tankers (red was the Usher brewery colour) on the A 68 road we used to Edinburgh from Bedrule in the 1960s. I had never thought much of it then and nor had my parents. But now nearly fifty years later and enlightened to the all encompassing fraud of Brodies I immediately became suspicious. Why on earth was beer being transported from one brewery to another over a hundred miles away by tanker? Surely each brewery would sell its output in the areas in which it had always sold them: Ushers all over Scotland where it had about three hundred tied public houses, and Vaux in the north east of England. I then thought of the logistics of it. Tankers of Vaux branded beer from Sunderland to Ushers in Edinburgh to be sold in Scotland made little economic sense if the tanker then returned to Sunderland empty. And the same vice-versa. So did it return with Usher beer brands to be sold in the North-east of England? Possible, but it seems unlikely. Could it then be that Vaux beer was being transported to Ushers in Edinburgh from Sunderland and the tankers then returning with whisky from Edinburgh? That would make great economic sense. The St Leonards whisky warehouses of Andrew Usher & Co, the largest whisky warehouses in the world in their time, lay adjacent to Usher's Brewery. What other whisky producer would use a brewery, especially a brewery in England, to bottle its whisky? None, on the grounds of basic economics alone.

The only remotely plausible explanation as to where the whisky had come from was a whisky hoard that had been built up over the decades in the late 1800s by Andrew II and Sir John as a 'liquid reserve' which was still lying untouched in the St Leonards warehouses. And that Sir Robert had 'inherited' this hoard and possibly added to it in his own lifetime and that this also had been left out of his Inventory for the same reasons recorded above.

The size of the hoard? Given that these tankers transported it for three or four years in the 70s and the tankers that I had seen in the 60s I estimate that it would have consisted of millions of gallons of whisky. In this regard the excellent book 'The Whiskies of Scotland' by RJS McDowall, published in 1971, stated that Andrew Usher and Co had a stock of four million of gallons of whisky in bond when the business was sold in 1918 to Scottish Malt Distillers.

The only people who knew its true status as an undeclared hoard were Sir Robert's accountants and lawyers and the Scottish Malt Distiller's management. This could also be an explanation for the business being sold for an 'undisclosed sum'.

And the value of the hoard? Four million gallons equates to about 20 million bottles of whisky. Taking a retail price of £10 per bottle in 2000 this asset alone had a retail value of approximtely £200 million.

I know this appears to be fanciful but it is the only explanation that I can think of which explained those Usher Vaux tankers plying the road between Edinburgh and Sunderland in the 1960s and 1970s. If any readers can enlighten me further I would be delighted to hear from them.

Sir Robert's big mistake appears to have been to trust his lawyer Executors and their successors to pass on the proceeds of the sales of this whisky to his heir or heirs at some opportune time in the future. This arrangement might even have been made on a 'Gentleman's Agreement' shake of the hand basis. Of course the lawyers realised that the hoard was hot merchandise and could never be passed to Sir Robert's heirs for that very reason. The only way to cash in on it would be to 'whisky launder' it over many years and then money launder the proceeds through their Brodies Accountancy Services and other similar crooked Accountancy firms.

I never made any further inquiry into this mystery for the same old reason that if I had done so the shutters would have gone up quicker than Brodies could rob an Incapax! If in fact this was whisky from an Usher hoard anyone still alive who knew anything about it would certainly not tell me, of all people, about it. Besides that, I soon came to the conclusion that if I did make inquiry about it, all I would achieve would be to alert the any old malefactors and their successors that I was onto to them. This would have bad implications for a proper Fraud Squad investigation because it would give such malefactors the time to further conceal their fraud.

The withholding of the amount for which the business had been sold and the whisky being transported to England for bottling in a brewery are two examples of unusual, in those particular circumstances, events which lend weight to my supposition that very large assets in which Sir Robert had either an interest or owned outright had been purposely left out of his Inventory. If this had indeed occurred it would probably rank as one of the great frauds to have been carried out in Scotland in the Twentieth Century and, quite likely, the boldest!

I realise that the reader might well think: 'This is all preposterous. No one would ever get away with fraud on that scale in a modern and advanced democracy like Britain.' My answer to that is: I would have wholeheartedly agreed with you until I discovered all the other frauds over the decades from 1962 onwards as already narrated. So my answer is: 'I agree with you it sounds preposterous, but is it so preposterous? The bigger and more outrageous the fraud the greater the likelihood of it remaining undetected on the grounds that hardly anyone would believe that a fraud of that magnitude would ever be conceived, let alone put into action and brought to a successful conclusion.'

In this regard just look at some recent major frauds: Bernard Madoff, ex Chairman of the New York Stock Exchange, a lion of New York society and respectability personified, somewhat like Brodies in Edinburgh until one dug a little deeper. Madoff appropriated £30 billion of other peoples' money to himself. This was the greatest fraud in history. The Enron fraud? Also billions. Anderson International, the Accountants with whom the Edinburgh law firm of Dundas and Wilson were associated were fined £125 million for fraudulent accounting. The Banks themselves indulge in fraudulent practices which have cost the general public and taxpayers further billions of pounds. Anyone who doubts this should look to the recent (2015) investigation of HSBC and its banking practices in Switzerland. And the consequences of this tidal wave of fraud? Hundreds of thousands of people in our own country alone thrown out of work and many into poverty. Millions worldwide. I could go on *ad infinitum*. All this makes the likelihood of the fraud against my family, as outlined above, all the more believable.

With few exceptions MPs and MSPs have shown little moral fibre and will, given the opportunity, cheat the taxpayer without turning a hair; for example their claiming bogus expenses in both the UK parliament and the Edinburgh parliament. Likewise the legal system in Scotland is irretrievably corrupt and manned by people who range from mildly immoral to utterly immoral. Much the same goes for the legal systems in the rest of the UK. The evidence is before our eyes, day in and day out. But 'none dare speak the truth', as the old saying goes. It's the same old syndrome of 'The Emperor has no clothes.'

If my suppositions above are correct the situation now is that these lawyers had successfully defrauded old Sir Robert's Estate of by far the greater part of its wealth leaving only a small amount of cash and the Estates of Pitheavlis and Pulteney Town as his 'shown' assets as recorded in his Inventory.

His other legacy was the Usher Baronetcy Trust into which he had placed the Estates of Norton and Wells. These Estates were therefore also 'shown' assets. However, as always with Brodies, there was a difficulty with these 'shown' assets. Assets can only be accepted as 'shown' if there is a complete inventory of them and maps showing where they are situated. Johnny and I had asked repeatedly for these inventories and Brodies had repeatedly refused to supply them. Therefore we were never able to establish what these 'shown' assets were at the time of Sir Robert's death in 1933, let alone establish where they were all situated. All that the lawyers had 'shown' were the names of the Estates of Norton, Wells, Pitheavlis and Pulteney Town but no inventory of what they consisted of in 1933. The withholding of these inventories by Brodies was *per se* an indication that the lawyers had already commenced defrauding Sir Robert's legacies in the 1930s. If Brodies had nothing to hide why had they withheld these inventories?

But surely Uncle John would have checked out what the Estates consisted of on his succeeding Sir Robert? These days most people inheriting the *usufruct* (a legal term) in which the holder of a usufruct has the right to use the property and enjoy its fruits for his lifetime. In essence *Fructus* means the profit the holder of the right of Usufruct makes from the leasing out of houses and land belonging to the Trust in which that person has the right of Usufruct. Most people in that position nowadays would make it their business find out the full extent of the assets within the Trust and particularly so if that person was also a Trustee of that Trust, as Uncle John had been.

However it seems that Uncle John did not make it his business to acquaint himself with *all* the assets contained in the Usher Baronetcy Trust probably because in those days most people trusted their lawyers. Everything was left to their 'professional' advisers and the only function of people like Uncle John appears to have been to sign the documents they were asked to sign. Even if he *had* made some effort to establish exactly what the Trust consisted of the lawyers could have very easily misled him. His being a *bon vivant* weakling would also make him easy prey in this regard. I presume that he had a fair idea of what the Norton and Wells Estates consisted if only because he grew up on these Estates but never to their full extent. In these circumstances he would have known very little about the Pitheavlis Estate. When he was succeeded by Uncle Stuart in 1951 the lawyers would treat Stuart with even more disdain than they had treated Uncle John, not least because of his circumstances upon returning from Argentina.

Pulteney Town and Wick in Caithness? This Estate was *not* in the Trust and was left to Uncle Ronald, Sir Robert's second Son. Like Pitheavlis this Estate consisted mainly of Feus. I think we owned most of Pulteney town in Feu form.

Interestingly when Andrew Carnegie, the great Scottish-American Steel King made his enormous donation for a library to be built in every Scottish town of note, Wick was one of the towns on his list. Wick lay adjacent to Pulteney Town. The most suitable site for the proposed Wick library was on some land in Wick which belonged to Sir John Usher, the Father of Sir Robert. The Wick Council approached Sir John to see if he would sell them the site. To their surprise and delight John told them he would donate them the site but on the condition that he had some say in the design and decoration of the proposed library and that his son-in-law, Thomas Leadbetter, be appointed the Architect. His proposal was accepted. The result was the present large, imposing and richly adorned Wick library which opened in 1898. A bust of Sir John stands there to this day.

Uncle Ronald was much more competent than Uncle John and this makes it likely that he would have at least tried to establish the full extent of his inheritance. Whether or not he actually did establish its full extent rather depended on what the lawyers told him about the Estate. However he died, quickly and unexpectedly, in 1948 at the very young age of fifty six as already narrated. His only Son, Robin, predeceased him by a year which left him with only his two daughters, Hazel and Daphne. Having spoken with Daphne at length in 1995 it became apparent that she knew very little about the Wick and Pulteney Town Estate. This indicated that the lawyers had told both Hazel and Daphne little, if anything, about their Father's Estate. This of course left it wide upon for the lawyers, McLure and Dempster the sly Deathbed Thief and Company to pillage it at will.

The only thing that was certain in this scenario was that only the lawyers knew the full extent of the 'shown' assets - the ideal position from which to continue to defraud these Estates.

When no one challenged Sir Robert's Inventory the lawyers might have commenced cashing in on the hidden assets and the hidden part of the 'shown' assets. Or they might have waited a bit to be on the safe side. The more time passed with the fraud remaining undiscovered the greater the chances of it never being discovered.

By the end of the Second World War many of the original malefactors were either dead or getting very old, but they would have told their partners in crime and their sons and daughters, also lawyers or accountants, about the hidden assets before their deaths. This incestuous fraud-encouraging practice of Trusteeships passing from father to son has been practised by the Legal Profession in Scotland for hundreds of years. For example I was told that the egregious McClure's son was earmarked to take over as an Usher Baronetcy Trustee from McClure when he died. In the event this son passed away sometime in the 1980s before McClure himself died in 1988.

By 1947 two of these lawyer criminals had wormed their ways into positions of great influence in my family. One of them was the egregious McClure who by now had become a Trustee of the Usher Baronetcy Trust and the other one was the equally egregious Death Bed Thief Thomas Dempster who was acting, as the personal 'legal adviser' to Lady Usher, Sir John Usher, Ronald Usher, Stuart Usher, my father, William Usher *and* Clive Usher. As such he was in the perfect position to mislead and generally cause confusion and ill feeling within our extended family with the intention of gaining ever greater control. In essence Dempster's role was to soften us up by giving us totally misleading and contradictory advice to the various different parties and thereafter, with McClure, await the developments which would inevitably arise from this misleading 'advice.'

Lady Usher was nearing eighty and her son Sir John was an alcoholic. As far as the lawyers were concerned neither would live very long. Somewhat akin to a lion waiting patiently at the base of a tree for its intended prey to fall. The lawyers would scarcely have been able to conceal their joy at the early death of Robin in 1947. But such joy would have been nothing compared to the news they received in 1948 that both of Uncle Stuart's sons were Downs Syndrome. If they could steer the inheritance of the Estates to Uncle Stuart their long terms prospects would be boundless. The lawyers hardly had need even of a meeting - so developed were their skills - to map out a detailed strategy of how best to turn these family tragedies to their advantage.

Uncle Stuart had the almost heaven-sent qualifications for these frauds to be progressed and brought to a successful conclusion: First and foremost by far, his two Downs Syndrome Mentally Incapacitated sons. On top of that he had been bankrupted, rescued by his Father once and then been bankrupted again. He was therefore vulnerable. He was also much embittered, utterly incompetent, and therefore thoroughly 'qualified' in the eyes of the legal crooks to succeed to the Estates on the death of Sir John. Thereafter he would bow to their agenda. They would then make sure that Uncle Stuart died Intestate and then make sure that he was succeeded by his sons, Peter and Robert, both of whom they would also ensure died Intestate.

In 1948 all they had to do was to await the deaths of Lady Usher and Sir John and it was not long before she began to fail. The stressful discovery that she had two Downs Syndrome grandsons, one of whom might succeed Stuart if he was not by-passed, probably hastened her death on the 2nd June 1948. These criminals now had another almost incredible stroke of luck. Uncle Ronald died from cancer on 29th September 1948 in the same year. As far as the legal crooks were concerned that was another very important nuisance out of the way.

On cue, Uncle Stuart now arrived home, bankrupt, from the Argentine with Gertrude and his two Downs Syndrome Incapax sons. The lawyers made a huge fuss of him and prevailed on Sir John to assume Uncle Stuart and another lawyer, the old bachelor, JGG Leadbetter, as Usher Baronetcy Trustees. The nods and winks McClure and Dempster needed to exchange were few for such Past Masters of Writers to the Signet.

Thereafter the lawyers, with Uncle Stuart beholden to them, had little difficulty in putting to naught any attempts to have Stuart by-passed in favour of my Father. With Stuart they out-numbered the failing Sir John three to one. In this regard my Father told us that Sir John had tried his best for the Estates as described earlier in the book. The lawyers knew that any resettlement onto my Father instead of Stuart, or on his death, would spell the end of their defrauding of my family. Even worse it might well have led to the discovery of the hidden assets which had been left out of old Sir Robert's Inventory.

After the death of Katherine Lady Usher and Ronald, Sir John was therefore isolated and this in turn meant that he could not resettle the Estates in his own Will in a manner which would ensure their remaining within our family, in keeping with the purposes of the 1911 Trust Deed. All this must have worried Sir John greatly and this manifested itself in his taking to the bottle more than ever, thus hastening his death. He died in 1951 aged 59.

The discovery of the Downs Syndrome condition of Peter and Robert and then the deaths of Lady Usher, Ronald and Sir John in that four year period and the order in which they occurred were all bonuses which the crooked

lawyers could never have dreamt of. The odds of such a train of misfortune hitting our family in the order that they did were extremely long:
1 Uncle John, the heir, fathering two daughters only.
2 Ronald then fathering two daughters and one son, Robin, who was the heir. Of these three children it was Robin who died unexpectedly at the age of twenty three in 1947.
3 Stuart & Gertrude having two Downs Syndrome and Mentally Incapacitated sons in Argentina where the fact could be concealed. The odds of having two such sons in succession were, on their own, thousands to one.
4 The deaths of Katherine Lady Usher *and* Uncle Ronald so close together in 1948.
5 The second bankruptcy of Stuart happening in 1948 pushing him into an even more parlous situation then he was already in.
6 Sir John being the only alcoholic of the six brothers and his being the heir.
7 The odds of both Clive and Stuart's widow Gertrude Sampson being intrinsically dishonest were also very long.

Taken cumulatively the odds of these events coinciding and dovetailing so conveniently for the lawyers in the order that they did must be many thousands to one. All it took was the addition of one more ingredient to this deadly brew; the absolutely corrupt nature of the lawyers in control of all this wealth.

Uncle Stuart duly succeeded to the title in 1951, as planned. All the crooked lawyers now had to do was to simply wait for Stuart's death; no great hardship - remember they were being paid handsomely during the waiting. The only person who posed any threat to them all was my Father at this time.

Stuart did not last long and, as planned, the lawyers made it appear that he had died Intestate. They then ensured that his elder son, Peter the Incapax, succeeded him by misinforming everyone that the Usher Baronetcy Trust had automatically come to an end by the 'Stuart's Will could not be found' device and therefore that he had died Intestate. This meant that the Estates, according to the lawyers, now belonged to Peter personally. This was probably the biggest and most damaging lie of all because it was the foundation on which the lawyers based the completion of their fraud and our ruination.

All my Father's objections to Peter succeeding were slickly overcome by the lawyers as already narrated and once the furore had died down and with my Parents and Johnny and myself safely out of the country they must have felt very happy indeed. They now had complete control of both the shown assets and the hidden assets.

Peter the Incapax in his own impenetrable world, did not the faintest idea that he was now the (purported only) landed proprietor of many properties in Scotland. On the Wells Estate Brodies gave Clive and the Estate Manager a free hand to steal and defraud as they pleased. At Norton, Pitheavlis, Edinburgh, Wick and Pulteney town in Caithness, and wherever else, Brodies went ahead unhindered with their filthy work. Of course my Father had tried to find out the full extent of the assets in the Usher Baronetcy Trust but was himself fobbed off by the same pack of lies to which Johnny and I were later subjected.

On Robert the Incapax succeeding Peter he, Robert, likewise did not have the faintest idea of what was going on. Like Peter he lived in great comfort and security at Hallrule.

Having sniffed the air relatively soon after Stuart's death in 1962, and finding it sweet with the promise of plenty of money the lawyers and their accomplices gave each other their usual imperceptible nods and winks and decided the time had come to begin cashing in on the now 70 year old whisky hoard.

Was this the only part of the Usher fortune which was 'Not shown.' No, not necessarily: As a young man I recall the area in Edinburgh where Andrew Usher & Co had their warehouses. It consisted of old Victorian buildings and the like. At that time Usher's brewery was still functioning there as well. This whole area was suddenly developed in the late 1970s and 1980s. One of the new structures is a large black glass-clad building which is the Head Office of Scottish Widows, the Lloyds Bank-owned Insurance Company. And block after block of expensive apartments. The same goes for the area where the Edinburgh Distillery, also ours, stood. Demolished in the 1980s, having stood empty for sixty years; this whole area now consists, again, of expensive apartments.

All the land on which these developments took place had belonged to Andrew Usher & Co from about 1860 onwards to the best of my admittedly rather limited knowledge, thanks to Brodies. I therefore suspect that the lawyers also appropriated this extremely valuable land to themselves. A pointer in the wind to back up this hypothesis is the timing. These demolitions and building developments took place during the period of the serious pillaging 1962 to 1994; the very years in which Brodies were 'untouchable' in the words of the egregious brothel creeping Sheriff Lothian. Here also remember the statement by the crooked Advocate John Mayer in a letter to the equally crooked Tom Murray: 'I realise that Mr Usher will forever have many unanswered questions.' So Mayer knew something but would not tell me what it was. He was however quite happy to condemn me to spend the rest of my life wondering what he knew. In view of Brodies, and the Scottish Legal Establishment's refusal to supply me with answers to these questions all I can do is to answer the questions as best I can myself.

The value of the developments on these sites today? Many millions.

But hang on a minute, the reader might well ask and understandably so:

'Earlier on you wrote that these buildings and ground were included in the sale price of £7 million in 1918. How can you now claim that they might have been sold again?' I have no ready answer to that. 'So why include these assets twice?' The answer to that is that I find it suspicious that all these developments took place when Peter (the Incapax) 'reigned' supreme. I agree that it could be just a co-incidence, but on the other hand it might not have been, and that is why I include it. Another possibility is that all that industrial land was sold in 1918 and Sir Robert had nominally received his share of the proceeds but which the lawyers had then left out of his Inventory, as outlined above. The lawyers had then just sat on these and cashed in on them in the nineteen seventies and eighties, thereby enabling all these developments to take place. I really don't know, but I am still suspicious about those large areas of housing being developed in Peter's time. The ways of fraud are labyrinthine and multifarious and are difficult to detect. My function is to cover *all* the possibilities on which I harbour suspicions, no matter how unlikely they might appear. Brodies have themselves to blame for this. Just remember the twenty seven large steel boxes of Usher papers which we never got as just one example.

To sum up: I suspect that lots of Usher assets all over Scotland were simply appropriated by the 'family lawyers' over the last 80 years, or possibly even since the death of Sir John Usher in 1904.

What about the State? As already narrated the State was up to its eyeballs in the fraud. Not for executing it, but for opposing me all the way to have it rectified when I blew the whistle on it. The organs of State involved in this were: The Scottish Courts, the Scottish Crown Office, the Scottish Legal Services Ombudsman, the Capital Taxes Office, the Accountant in Bankruptcy, and the Police. I do not blame the Police too much because they were ordered to do nothing about the fraud by the Crown Office.

When we left Bedrule for South Africa in 1968 the lawyers would have been absolutely over the moon; another unforeseen bonus. They and Clive now had full control of the 'shown assets.' Yet there remained the problem of Johnny being an Usher Baronetcy Trustee. They overcame that by their usual means: lying, smoke and mirrors, and keeping Johnny in the dark.

If Brodies had either lost or burnt, as they themselves told me, some or all of the pertinent records, then the conclusion has to be that they were getting rid of incriminating evidence. It also means that they will find it difficult to demonstrate the areas in which my hypothesis is incorrect. It is simply not acceptable for lawyers who commit crimes against their clients to be allowed to get away with them simply by burning or losing the files of the clients they have defrauded. This practice appears to be widespread and to have been going on for decades in Scotland.

After Johnny's death in 1998 I publicly accused Brodies of being Crooks and Fraudsters. Despite this Brodies refused to take any legal action against me.

What conclusion can I, or anyone else for that matter, draw from that other than that my accusations were well-founded? On that basis alone, the Fraud Squad is morally obliged to devote its infinitely greater powers and resources to confirm my accusations based on my evidence. It is not the fraud that is in question - it is obvious to anyone and everyone that fraud has been committed; it is the size and longevity of the fraud which remains to be fully uncovered and thereafter quantified.

Do I think that my family were the only ones to have been dispossessed and destroyed in this filthy manner. No, I do not. Here is another recent example, among others, of Brodies destroying an old family in the Highlands of Scotland:

One of their clients was (no relation) Brodie of Brodies Castle, Morayshire. Brodies smashed the inheritances of the rightful heirs to this Estate by alienating the contents of the Castle to outsiders (like Hallrule) and selling the castle to the National Trust of Scotland, all in what appears to have been a fraudulent manner. Of course the present Brodie of Brodies Castle and his brother and sister have fought Brodies (the lawyers) for years on this but, alas, to no avail. Like myself they adopted active measures to publicise Brodies' fraud. In 2001 they camped in the graveyard of previous generations of Brodies near Brodies Castle to express their outrage at Brodies the lawyers defrauding their family. This was widely publicised in the media much to Brodies (the lawyers) fury. People do not go to such lengths unless they have good reason and are absolutely sure of their ground. I received some correspondence from the Brodies of Brodies Castle heir, Alexander Brodie, in 2001 and met him and his charming brother and sister in Edinburgh in 2002. Regrettably these Brodie heirs lived in France and had some residual faith in the Scottish legal system and therefore thought that their best bet was to work within the system. They were to be as disappointed as I was.

I would not have objected if my family had lost everything because of bad investments made in good faith. But I could never tolerate the Will and Stealth fraud which has been practised on us by 'our' so called 'legal advisers'. Losing wealth by one's own incompetence *et al* is one thing, but loss of hearth, home, and land by fraud executed by one's own lawyers is quite another.

Needless to say that Brodies have continued their fraudulent activities unabated. Crimes by lawyers pay very well in Scotland and regrettably successive Scottish governments have done next to nothing about them. For example between 2000 and the present 2017 Brodies have established other offices in various cities around Britain and Europe. Among them are Glasgow, Aberdeen, London and Brussels. This huge expansion can only have been financed by the proceeds of crime; a lot of which I suspect emanated from the the fraud which Brodies perpetrated on my family as recorded in this book.

59

THE EFFECT ON MY IMMEDIATE FAMILY AND MYSELF OF THIS FAILURE OF THE SCOTTISH LEGAL SYSTEM

I have often been asked; 'What effect has this disaster had on your immediate family and on you personally'? It goes without saying that this disaster had a profound effect on my whole being and became the dominant theme of my life. It started with Uncle Stuart's lawyer-manufactured 'Intestacy' in 1962 and the grief it caused my Father, his heart attacks, and his early death in 1968. Since then and up to the present time (50 years) it became the dominating factor in my life - and will always be, until I exeat this world. It was like a monster in my mind every day, year in and year out. A monster which would destroy me one way or another unless I fought back.

My main reaction - when in 1994 Brodies became obliged to actually engage with me - was outrage. As I discovered more and more, in the following years, my outrage grew and grew concomitantly. In fact it was sheer outrage which kept my determination so high. Never for a second could I seriously contemplate giving up my pursuit of Brodies and walking away. And I was uneasily aware of the emotional and material cost to my immediate family, my wife and my children; yet their resolve was unfailing - without it I should have gone mad. Apart from anything else I knew that surrender would result in my loss of self-respect which in turn would end in my early death. I am now 78 years of age; the most long-lived male Usher of my (whisky) branch of the family for centuries. I am certain that I would never have reached this age had I not fought so hard and so long. Fighting for a just cause keeps you young. I suspect that people who give up on life, by walking away from their responsibilities become negative, which in turn has an effect on how long they live.

Thankfully I never became depressed. I was lucky in this because many people have suffered depression, and worse, as a result of the crimes commited against them by Crooked Lawyers and the Scottish Legal system.

Was there a plus side to my campaign? Yes there was. I can safely say that it has made me more aware and a better man that I would have been otherwise. If disaster had not struck I should have ultimately spent my life as a farmer at Bedrule and Hallrule leading the life of a countryman. In this form of life I could never have developed into the person I am today. In the period 1998 to 2010 I kept up a sustained campaign against Brodies and the Scottish 'Legal' system in general, as already narrated. These activities, including my part time work when and wherever I could get it, have given me an insight into the way of the world which I would and could never have had if I had spent most of my life farming Bedrule and Hallrule farms. In short I have now seen and experienced life from both the top and the bottom and the areas in between them as well. This has enabled me to make useful contributions to Society at large which I would never have been able to make had this disaster never struck.

Do I feel vindicated in fighting Brodies and the Scottish 'Legal' system? Yes I most certainly do. I have without a shadow of doubt won the battle against them morally. Materially it appears that Brodies and the Scottish 'Legal' system have defeated me because I never recovered any of our lands and assets to date. However that might be rectified sometime in the future before or after my death. With the unstinting moral and material help of my own immediate family and the many other victims of Brodies *et al* I think it is now only a question of time before the lid is blown off the Scottish Legal system in general. And thereafter it being forced to repay the thousands of victims and their families of their collective frauds over the decades. I very much hope that this book and the one to follow it will hasten that glorious day to dawn.

As far as my death is concerned I want to live as long as I possibly can. To this end I have instituted a healthier life style; ie cutting down on the drink and smoking. It would be marvellous to see Brodies and all the other Criminals working in and for our Legal system being exposed as Criminals in the reformed Scottish Courts. In the happy event of crooks like Alistair Campbell and David Houldsworth of Brodies and many others of their ilk being imprisoned nothing would give me greater pleasure than visiting them. I would even give them tea and scones as they did to me outside their offices. The same would apply to all the other Lawyer Crooks I have named in this book.

My closing words in this book are: Never ever trust any lawyer practising in Scotland, irrespective of Race, Nationality, Country of Origin or whatever else. They are a National Disgrace to both Scotland and the United Kingdom as a whole.

28th November 1990

I, DAVID HENRY HOULDSWORTH, Writer to the Signet, of Fifteen Atholl Crescent, Edinburgh, Executor Dative of the late Sir Peter Lionel Usher *qua* Curator Bonis to the late Sir Robert Edward Usher, brother of the said the late Sir Peter Lionel Usher, conform to Confirmation in my favour issued by the Sheriff of Lothian and Borders at Jedburgh on the Twenty-eighth day of November Nineteen hundred and ninety and, as such Executor Dative, uninfeft proprietor of the subjects hereinafter disponed CONSIDERING THAT the said the late Sir Peter Lionel Usher died intestate on the First day of June Nineteen hundred and ninety; FURTHER CONSIDERING THAT under the laws of intestate succession the said the late Sir Robert Edward Usher was beneficially entitled to *inter alia* the subjects hereinafter disponed and was therefore entitled to have *inter alia* the subjects hereinafter disponed conveyed to him; FURTHER CONSIDERING THAT the said the late Sir Robert Edward Usher died intestate on the Twenty-sixth day of September Nineteen hundred and ninety-four without the subjects hereinafter disponed having been conveyed to him; FURTHER CONSIDERING that MRS JACQUELINE WOLFE MURRAY, formerly of Chesters, Ancrum, by Jedburgh, Roxburghshire now of Stonerend, Froxfield, Petersfield, Hampshire and Sir William John Tevenar Usher, Bt., late of Kayalami, PO Cramond, Natal, South Africa, confirmed to the Estate of the said the late Sir Robert Edward Usher as Executors Dative *qua* cousins of the full blood conform to Confirmation in their favour issued by the Sheriff of Lothian and Borders at Jedburgh on the Twenty-first day of March Nineteen hundred and ninety-five; FURTHER CONSIDERING THAT the said Sir William John Tevenar Usher, Bt. died on the Twenty-fifth day of July Nineteen hundred and ninety-eight; FURTHER CONSIDERING THAT for the better administration of the Estate of the said the late Sir Robert Edward Usher it is right and proper that the said Mrs Jacqueline Wolfe Murray as Executrix Dative foresaid should take title to the subjects hereinafter disponed; FURTHER CONSIDERING THAT *per incuriam* a Notice of Title in favour of the said Mrs Jacqueline Wolfe Murray as Executrix Dative foresaid recorded in the Division of the General Register of Sasines applicable to the County of Midlothian on the Twenty-eighth day of September Nineteen hundred and Ninety-eight purported to complete the title of the said Mrs Jacqueline Wolfe Murray as Executrix Dative foresaid to the subjects hereinafter disponed AND THAT the effect of the said Notice of Title has been called into question; FURTHER CONSIDERING THAT in fortification of the title of the said Mrs Jacqueline Wolfe Murray as Executrix Dative foresaid it has been agreed that these presents should be granted THEREFORE I, the said David Henry Houldsworth, as Executor Dative foresaid DO HEREBY DISPONE to the said Mrs Jacqueline Wolfe Murray as Executrix Dative foresaid and to her executors and assignees whomsoever heritably and irredeemably ALL and WHOLE (IN THE FIRST PLACE) ALL and WHOLE the Lands and Estate of Norton lying in the Parishes of

REGISTERS OF SCOTLAND 60
GENERAL REGISTER OF SASINES
COUNTY OF MIDLOTHIAN
FICHE 1039 FRAME 9

c:\nrportbl\man_docs\dhr\885925_1.doc

9

It might be asked why the above and following document is so crucial to this whole story. In this final page or so I will do my best to explain why. In late 2006 I acquired a Document from the General Register of Sasines in Edinburgh in connection with the County of Midlothian only in Scotland. The first two pages only of the fifteen pages have been illustrated here.

Ratho and Kirkliston and County of Edinburgh, now Midlothian, being the subjects described in and disponed by Disposition granted by the Trustees acting under the Trust Disposition and Settlement of the late Sir John Usher of Norton and Wells, Baronet, in favour of Sir Robert Usher, dated Fourteenth October and subsequent dates and recorded in the said Division of the General Register of Sasines for the County of Edinburgh, now Midlothian, and in the Books of Council and Session on Third November all in the year Nineteen hundred and five; (IN THE SECOND PLACE) ALL and WHOLE that house and garden at Gogarstone in the County of Midlothian described in and disponed by Disposition granted by Sir John Usher in favour of Sir Robert Usher dated Twenty-ninth January and recorded in the said Division of the General Register of Sasines on Fifth February both months in the year Eighteen hundred and eighty-seven; (IN THE THIRD PLACE) ALL and WHOLE that piece of ground near Ratho Station in the County of Midlothian described in and disponed by Disposition granted by the London and North Eastern Railway Company in favour of the said Sir Robert Usher dated Twenty-fourth September and recorded in the said Division of the General Register of Sasines on First October both months in the year Nineteen hundred and twenty-five; (IN THE FOURTH PLACE) ALL and WHOLE the subjects lying on the south side of the public road leading from Edinburgh to Uphall and Bathgate in the County of Midlothian described in and disponed by Disposition granted by the Trustees of the deceased Robert Stewart of Kinlochmoidart in favour of Sir Robert Usher dated Thirteenth October and subsequent dates and recorded in the said Division of the General Register of Sasines on Eleventh November all in the year Nineteen hundred and nine; (IN THE FIFTH PLACE) ALL and WHOLE the lands of Rathobyres in the County of Midlothian, described in and disponed by Disposition and granted by Daniel Wilkie in favour of the said Sir Robert Usher dated Fourth September and recorded in the said Division of the General Register of Sasines and in the Books of Council and Session on Eleventh November both months in the year Nineteen hundred and one; BUT EXCEPTING AND RESERVING always from the whole lands and others hereinbefore described: (One) (IN THE FIRST PLACE) ALL and WHOLE that strip of ground in the County of Midlothian extending to Three hundred and twenty-five decimal or one-thousandth parts of an acre or thereby more particularly described in, disponed by and delineated and shown coloured red on the plan marked "No. 1" annexed and signed as relative to the First aftermentioned Disposition and (IN THE SECOND PLACE) ALL and WHOLE that strip of ground in the County of Midlothian extending to Ninety-six decimal or one-hundredth parts of an acre or thereby more particularly described in, disponed by and delineated and shown coloured pink on the Plan marked "No. 2" annexed and signed as relative to Disposition by the said Sir Robert Usher in favour of the County Council of the County of Midlothian dated Twenty-first and recorded in the said Division of the General Register of Sasines on Twenty-seventh both days of July in the year Nineteen hundred and

Houldsworth of Brodies registered this Deed with the Sasines in September 2004, without informing myself nor any of the other Ultimate Beneficiaries with just the possible exception of Mrs Wolfe-Murray, Brodies' *Pretence Executor*.

The reader should run their eye down to thirteenth line up from the bottom of the previous page and then read down to the bottom of the page. The language used is (deliberately) confusing to those untrained in the law, so I shall, having battled for more then twenty years with their legal mumbo-jumbo, try to make clear what this really means in a couple of pages:

1. In 1998 Brodies conveyed to Mrs Wolfe-Murray the Title to all the remaining assets of the Usher Baronetcy Trust. So before that Mrs Wolfe-Murray and her Co-Executor my Brother, Sir John Usher of Norton and Wells, until his death in 1998, therefore never *had* had Title to sell anything belonging to the Usher Baronetcy Trust. My Brother and Mrs Wolfe-Murray had no idea that they were not the De-jure Executors of the late Sir Robert Usher, Mentally Incapacitated and Intestate, for the simple reason that Brodies had never informed them of that, for very obvious reasons.

2. However this 1998 Conveyance was called into question sometime in or before 2004. In response to their 1998 Conveyance being called into question Brodies produced another Deed of Conveyance by which they now did convey the Title to Mrs Wolfe-Murray in 2004. In this 2004 Conveyance Brodies stated that their 1998 Deed of Conveyance only purported to convey the Title to her. To fix this they used the Latin phrase, Per Incurium which approximates to 'By Cure' in English. Of course this 'Cure' could never overcome the fact that other properties on the Norton Estate had already been sold by Mrs Wolfe-Murray in the belief that she was the Executor with the right to do so. This 2004 Deed clearly demonstrated that, De Facto, she had never been the Executor with that right. The De Facto Executor was none other than Houldsworth of Brodies and it was he who had unlawfully carried out these sales. Of course Brodies again had never told us Beneficiaries of this most recent 2004 Conveyance.

What then were the consequences of this most recent 2004 Conveyance, inter-alia. They were, as follows:

CONSEQUENCE No ONE: This meant that the Wells and Pitheavlis Estates were sold by Brodies in 1995 under False Pretences.

CONSEQUENCE No TWO: This 2004 Conveyance meant that the sale of the Wells Estate, as just one example, in 1995, was an Act of Fraud by Brodies. This in turn meant that all those who had purchased properties on the Wells Estate in good faith had no Title to the various farms, houses and land which they had purchased. It follows therefore that all these properties, houses and land are presently occupied by persons, companies and entities which have no De-Jure (ie Lawful right) to be there. It follows therefore, as Day follows Night, that the De Jure owners of all these properties still remains the Usher family of Norton and Wells.

FURTHER QUESTIONS AND ANALYSIS.

Question One: Why did Brodies not tell the Ultimate Beneficiaries about the 1998 Deed of Conveyance to Mrs Wolfe-Murray?

The very short answer to that is: My Existence. By 1998 Brodies were fully aware that I, alone of all the Ultimate Beneficiaries, was well aware of many of their past Frauds. They also knew that I was very determined to expose them come hell or high water. In these circumstances Brodies just kept the dead quiet of the wrongdoer about this Deed of Conveyance.

Question Two: Why did Brodies not tell the Ultimate Beneficiaries about the 2004 Deed of Conveyance to Mrs Wolfe-Murray?

The answer to that is: The same as the answer to Question One above but with the added difference that 1) By 2004 Brodies regarded me as a much greater danger to them than I had ever been in 1998 because of all the Media reports and ultimately the Channel Four Documentary on my campaigns to expose them as the Fraudsters they truly were. Brodies were well aware that if I ever discovered those Deeds of Conveyance, which they probably thought unlikely, I would use them to discredit them to the hilt. But discover them I eventually did in late 2006.

Those Deeds of Conveyance also demonstrated that the Brodies invitation to all the ultimate Beneficiaries to meet Brodies at their office in 1994 was for the express purpose of gulling them all into thinking that whoever they elected to be the Executors to the Estate of the late Sir Robert Usher, (Down's Syndrome and Mentally Incapacitated) would be just that; that the Executors they had elected were the only Executors. In the event only Mrs Mactaggart and I attended that Meeting, as already recorded in the book, and we both agreed that my Brother, Johnny, and Mrs Wolfe-Murray be the two Executors, as also already recorded. And that both Johnny, Mrs Wolfe-Murray and all the other Beneficiaries, including myself, had no idea whatever that they were not the De-Facto Executors at all but that they were the De-Jure Executors. The single hidden De-Facto Executor was Houldsworth of Brodies. But here was the rub for Brodies; only a De-jure Executor or Executors has/have the right to sell Properties of which they are the Executors. Houldsworth of Brodies had never been the De-Jure Executor at any time since the election of Johnny and Mrs Wolfe-Murray to be the De-Jure Executors in 1994. Put another way only the De-jure (ie Lawful) Executors to a deceased person have the right to sell, inter many other alias, the assets of that deceased person.

I remained unaware that it was Houldsworth of Brodies who had sold all these properties, unlawfully, and not the elected Executors, until I discovered those Deeds of Conveyance.

Published by
Exposé Publishing
Kelso

Printed by
The Bedrule Press
Hawick